The C Toolbox

The C Toolbox

second edition

*Ready-to-Run Programs in Turbo C®,
Microsoft® C, and QuickC®*

WILLIAM JAMES HUNT

▲ **Addison-Wesley Publishing Company, Inc.**
Reading, Massachusetts   Menlo Park, California   New York
Don Mills, Ontario   Wokingham, England   Amsterdam   Bonn
Sydney   Singapore   Tokyo   Madrid   San Juan

Many of the designations used by manufacturers and sellers to distinguish their products are claimed as trademarks. Where those designations appear in this book and Addison-Wesley was aware of a trademark claim, the designations have been printed in initial capital letters or all caps.

Library of Congress Cataloging in Publication Data
Hunt, William James.
    The C toolbox : ready-to-run programs in Turbo C, Microsoft C, and Quick C / William James Hunt. — 2nd ed.
        p.   cm.
        ISBN 0-201-51815-5
        1. C (Computer program language) 2. Turbo C (Computer program) 3. Microsoft C (Computer program) 4. Microsoft QuickC (Computer program) 5. Computer programs I. Title II. Title: C toolbox.
QA76.73.C15H85   1989   89-17752
005.265—dc20   CIP

Cover design by Doliber Skeffington
Text design by Total Concepts Associates
Set in 10-point Palatino using PageMaker 3.01 on a Macintosh SE.
Linotronic film output by Advanced Computer Graphics.

ABCDEFGHIJ-AL-89
First printing, November 1989

Acknowledgments

Several years ago I read *Software Tools* by Kernighan and Plauger. It helped me to understand my years of programming experience. This book is inspired by *Software Tools* and uses a similar approach to systems programming on personal computers.

In the 16 years that I have been a professional programmer, I have learned from many co-workers. Reading programs that they had written was the essential part of my education.

My wife, Lesley, has been invaluable in many ways. Her support encouraged me to start writing a book (and to finish it). Her work in serving as editor and guinea pig for the roughest of drafts was vital too. Finally, she volunteered to learn C to be a better guinea pig. Greater love hath no spouse than to learn another programming language.

My editor, Julie Stillman, and Perry McIntosh, who supervised copyediting and layout, helped turn my manuscript into a finished book. They taught me about the computer book business and my role as an author in that business. Their patience was tested when I was too slow to deliver and too quick to anger.

Readers who commented on the first edition encouraged me and helped me to produce a better second edition.

Contents

Preface

Several years have passed since I wrote the first edition of *The C Toolbox*. New PC hardware such as display adapters have broadened the IBM PC standard. C compilers have improved greatly. The ANSI standard for C has standardized C and made it a better tool for software development. My experiences in writing a newsletter for C programmers and articles for other magazines have suggested new topics and improvements to existing topics. Finally, expectations are higher now about how much PC programs should do and how well they should operate. Almost all of the first edition of *The C Toolbox* was still relevant, but it needed to be brought up to date. Every chapter has been revised to improve the functions and to describe them more effectively. Here are the major changes and additions.

Function Prototypes and Header Files

The function prototypes defined in the ANSI standard are a major improvement to C. They allow a C compiler to check function calls for the correct number and type of arguments. They also specify the data type returned by functions. When we create a function, we also create a function prototype for that function. Function prototypes are placed in header files along with definitions of the data types and constants needed to use the function.

Compilers provide header files for their library functions. Whenever we use a library function, we include the corresponding header file.

Memory Models

Most IBM PCs now come with 640 Kbytes of RAM memory, and C compilers support multiple memory models to allow full use of that memory. In the first edition, low-level tools were provided for the small memory model only. For the second edition, all programs and tools can be used with any memory model.

Making effective use of RAM memory is now central to producing fast and flexible programs. The chapters on sorting and the B-Tree algorithm use dynamic memory allocation to make full use of available memory.

PC-Specific Library Functions

When the first edition was written, MS-DOS C compilers provided few library functions to access the capabilities of MS-DOS or of the PC hardware. The first edition emphasized developing your own low-level functions. Now C compilers come with an extensive library of functions for accessing PC capabilities from a C program. The second edition focuses on effective use of library functions.

Source Level Debuggers

Programs for debugging C programs at the level of C statements and C variables are common now. The Turbo C and QuickC environments provide limited but useful source-level debugging. Separate debuggers such as Microsoft's Codeview and Borland's Turbo Debugger provide extensive features for debugging C and assembly language programs. These tools speed up testing and debugging and reduce the need for `printf` statements and special debugging code. The second edition relates testing with modern tools to traditional methods.

Windows Display Module

A new chapter develops a set of functions for displaying multiple windows on the PC screen. This chapter also applies this module in an interactive program to produce a modern user interface.

Exercises and Enhancements

More suggested enhancements have been added in each chapter. The source code disk for the second edition provides sample implementations for many of these enhancements.

Error Handling

The discussion on handling errors in the last chapter has been expanded greatly.

Instructions for Using the Programs

Appendix A provides detailed instructions for compiling, linking and executing the programs in the second edition. Appendix B explains use of Turbo C project files and Turbo C and Microsoft C MAKE files. Any special requirements for stack size and config.sys parameters are listed for all programs.

Instructions are also provided for building .lib library files containing the tools functions presented in the second edition.

Ready-to-Run Programs for Microsoft C, QuickC, and Borland Turbo C

The source files in the second edition are fully compatible with Microsoft C, QuickC, and Borland's Turbo C compilers — the most widely used. They make realistic use of special language features and PC-specific library functions that these compilers offer. The source files and accompanying discussions are immediately applicable to C programming with these compilers.

Compiler-specific material is carefully isolated to a few source files; these source files can easily be reimplemented for other C compilers. However, the second edition does not provide support or special versions for other C compilers.

Introduction

Anyone who has used a personal computer (PC) with really good software such as Lotus 1-2-3, WordPerfect, or Microsoft's Flight Simulator knows that PCs have great potential. However, the best efforts of casual programmers are often disappointing. There is a wide gap between what average programmers can achieve and what they see professional programmers achieve. Most books on C explain the elements of C, but they fail to show how to employ those elements to build quality programs. This book helps bridge that gap.

Most professional programmers learned their trade by reading programs written by other programmers. This book presents examples of complete, useful programs and discusses how they were developed. These programs illustrate programming techniques and algorithms that are often mysterious to the casual programmer. The programs also provide a concrete basis for discussing program design, coding, and testing.

Standard C library functions are used whenever they are adequate, but MS-DOS- and IBM PC-specific capabilities are used where they are needed for good performance and features. The book discusses why PC-specific functions are used and shows practical techniques for employing such functions.

The book is also intended to be a showcase for the C language. If your experience is limited to BASIC, learning C (or another good high-level language like Pascal) is a good first step for producing high-quality programs.

Audience

I assume that readers are familiar with the basic concepts of programming and have some experience with a programming language. In addition, you should be at home using a personal computer, especially using a text editor and DOS commands such as DIR and COPY.

Previous experience with C is not necessary. Chapters 1 and 2 provide a quick tour through the basic elements of C. You should be able to relate the elements of C to those of the language you already know. Although the book contains some advanced material, it should be useful to C beginners as well as to intermediate and advanced C programmers.

Programs

To really learn about programming (and C), you need to write programs. This book provides a good starting point. Each program has been simplified so that its basic structure is obvious and the program is accompanied by a full description of what it does and how it does it. At the same time, the programs are designed to be easy to enhance for better performance and more features. Possible enhancements are discussed for each program, with many modifications that require only 10–50 lines of C code to produce useful improvements. This is much more rewarding than writing programs from scratch.

To make programs easier to understand and modify, the book uses a subset of C's features. C programs are often written in a cryptic style that makes heavy use of features unique to C. Using these features usually produces only a modest improvement in performance but a heavy penalty in program clarity. This view may be heresy to some C programmers but will prove eminently practical to many others, especially those coming to C from another language. Optimization by using C's special features is discussed in Chapter 10.

Compatibility

All the programs presented should run on any fully IBM PC-compatible computer under the MS-DOS operating system. They have been tested on PC/XT and PC/AT models. The low-level functions in Chapter 7 require full PC compatibility; changes would be required for some older MS-DOS computers such as the Hewlett-Packard touch screen computer or the Tandy 2000 computer.

Most useful PC programs require some code that is specific to the MS-DOS and PC hardware environment. That system-specific code is confined to a few source files (mostly in Chapter 7). Moving programs to a different environment such as OS/2 or UNIX requires changing only these system-specific source files. This isolation of system-specific code also makes it easier to adapt the programs to new PC hardware or to new C compilers.

The C Toolbox illustrates programs that have a realistic balance between portability and performance and effectiveness. The emphasis is on techniques for reducing the cost of that realistic balance.

What You Need

This book does not explain the use of C elements; it illustrates their use in a realistic setting. If you are new to C, you should get a primer on the C language and use it for reference as you go through this book. Appendix D lists some C primers.

You will need free access to an IBM PC or some other computer running the MS-DOS or PC-DOS operating system (version 2.0 or later). You will neither find programming enjoyable nor the advice in this book useful if you have limited and infrequent access to a personal computer.

Your C compiler manual should specify RAM memory requirements for compiling and linking C programs. Executing the programs in this book requires at least 256 Kbytes of RAM memory. Your PC should also have either two floppy disk drives or a hard disk for file storage.

Microsoft C, QuickC, and Turbo C all provide a full screen editor and a linker program. They also provide documentation of the language features and library functions they support. If you find these manuals to be insufficient, reference books for each compiler are available in bookstores.

A few functions in the book are written in assembly language. Either Microsoft's MASM assembler or Borland's TASM can be used to assemble these files.

Available Source Disk

All the programs in the book are available on a source disk package from the author, ready for editing and compilation. Since typing several hundred lines of code is tedious and can result in errors, this disk provides a convenient, safe way to work with these programs. Just copy files from the source disks to your hard disk and you are ready to revise one of the programs.

Sample solutions for many of the enhancements discussed in the book are included on the source disks. Those enhancements are marked by the disk symbol ( ) in the left margin.

The source disks also contain preassembled object files for the assembly language source files. Versions for Microsoft C, QuickC, and Turbo C are provided. This eliminates the need for an assembler program unless you wish to modify these source files.

Updated directions for using the programs with the latest releases of these C compilers are also included on the source disks. Notes on any errors discovered in the programs and corrections are also provided.

To acquire the source disks, send a check or money order for $30.00 (US orders) to William James Hunt, Toolbox Disk, 2nd Edition, P.O. Box 271965, Concord, CA 94527. The last page of this book has an order form.

Outline of the Book

Chapters 1 and 2 get you started reading and writing C. Although they provide a brief introduction in comparison to a primer, they illustrate some features and concepts that will be important in the rest of the book. Chapter 1 gives examples of short C programs and the steps needed to create and compile them. It shows those parts of C that will be relatively familiar to you. This gives you confidence that C will be easy to understand.

Programming languages are never perfect; Chapter 2 discusses the way we use C to minimize bugs and portability problems. File I/O and bit operations in C are also covered in this chapter. Sample programs illustrate storage classes and dynamic memory allocation. The accompanying text explains the purpose and use of these features.

Chapter 3 presents the VIEW program. It allows us to browse through text files composed of ASCII characters. VIEW is useful for looking at C source files as well as text files produced by word processors such as WordStar. Techniques for simple file input and for interactive keyboard and display usage are demonstrated here. Since Chapter 3 is the first chapter describing a sizable program, it goes through the program development process in detail. The following chapters do not repeat these basic points. Testing the program on a module-by-module basis is emphasized here.

Chapter 4 develops another tool for examining data files. This file dump program displays a file's contents in hexadecimal and ASCII formats much like the dump format of the MS-DOS DEBUG program. This provides a way to determine the format of any file without any prior knowledge of its content. Since this program is closely related to the VIEW program of Chapter 3, Chapter 4 shows how to make use of an existing program in developing a new but related program. This chapter discusses more aspects of the program development process.

Chapter 5 builds several tools based on sorting algorithms. Two well-known algorithms — the insertion sort and quicksort — are shown and then made into library functions usable on any kind of data. These library functions are then used in a simple program to sort lines of ASCII text. The technique of merging is introduced as a way to handle files too large to fit into RAM memory. A sort/merge library module is developed to sort data files with record types and sort keys defined by the calling program. Finally, the chapter presents a standalone sort program that allows for a number of sort keys in each record.

Chapter 6 builds a B-Tree module for indexed access to data files. This module is rather long, but it provides features such as multiple indices to a data file, duplicate keys, and variable length keys. A sample application maintains an index of correspondence documents by name of addressee, date sent, and subject.

Chapter 7 presents a toolkit of low-level functions used in the preceding chapters. These functions are based on compiler library functions where appropriate. This chapter shows practical techniques for full access to PC capabilities. Differences between library functions provided with different compilers are addressed as are bugs and poor implementations of library functions. Single key input, fast screen output, timing functions, and printer output are among the modules included in this chapter.

Chapter 8 develops a set of functions for displaying text output in multiple screen windows. These functions are used to provide a modern user interface for an interactive program (the VIEW program from Chapter 3).

Chapter 9 presents a terminal emulator program which illustrates data communications programming. The special characteristics of a real-time program are discussed, for example, unpredictable input from several sources with data being lost if the program does not keep up with all input. The techniques for handling such problems — polling input status, buffering data to relax timing requirements, and using interrupt-driven input handling — are all demonstrated.

Chapter 10 covers a few loose ends, for example, using C's unique features to optimize execution speed and handling critical errors. It also summarizes the design philosophy of the previous chapters.

Appendix A provides detailed instructions for compiling and executing the programs in Chapters 1 through 10. Appendix B discusses specific problems in using Microsoft C, QuickC, and Turbo C. Appendix C explains the RAM memory architecture of the Intel 8088/80286/80386 processor family and how C memory models use this architecture. A short bibliography in Appendix D provides a starting point for further reading.

Themes

The material presented in the book is substantial. If you do not understand a program fully at first reading, that is quite natural. Read first for general understanding, and then focus on details as you need them. Use the description of what each source file does to understand how each C statement contributes to that overall result.

Several themes occur throughout the book. They are both lessons to be learned and an aid in understanding the book. They are listed here to help you understand the book's message.

Create Order Out of Chaos

The book presents finished, working programs that I hope, do not contain bugs. It often looks as though such programs sprang forth from my brain in a complete and correct form. That is almost never the case. The process usually involves some dead ends, some back-tracking, lots of bugs, and inelegant first tries.

Each chapter presents a topic in an orderly way to make it easy to understand. Do not conclude that program development is a perfectly orderly process with uniform progress through each stage, however. Every program in this book was revised several times to make it simpler and more effective.

Despite these limitations, you should always set goals at each step. Never start writing a program until you define its function. After you complete the program, you may revise the functional specification and rewrite the program. The cardinal sin is to write a program and then figure out what function it really performs.

Keep Up Your Morale

Writing computer programs can be very hard on your ego and your morale. You will make errors in design, get the syntax of C statements wrong, and produce lots of very puzzling bugs in your programs. These problems give abundant and painful testimony to your lack of perfection before you finally get a working program. Some programmers claim to produce working programs without any such problems, but most just have memory lapses.

You can make the programming process much more pleasant if you break the problem into bite-sized pieces. Any large project can seem impossible if you don't break it into manageable steps. Write and test programs in small modules so that you get some measure of success at frequent intervals. Simplify the design of a large program and do a smaller prototype first.

Use an Experimental Approach

Reading reference manuals and computer documentation is hard, frustrating work. The information they contain is often ambiguous and incomplete. This is a fact of life for beginners and old-timers alike. The way to cope with bad documentation is to perform an experiment. Writing a short C program to see how a feature actually works is more productive and less frustrating than guessing what a cryptic description in a manual really means.

Tackle such problems one at a time. It is much easier to understand how a feature of C or the operating system works if you try it out in a controlled environment. Writing a sizable program filled with unverified assumptions about such features makes testing unnecessarily difficult.

Learn by Doing

Don't waste too much time at first studying C. Learn a little and plunge in. Start by reading a C program for general understanding of what it does. Then think of a small improvement that you would like to make. You should be able to find enhancements that require adding fewer than ten lines to the program. Concentrate on understanding how your change will affect the program — what has to be changed and how you can accomplish the change using C.

Learn C as you need it. Develop a small working vocabulary of C features and expand it as needed. You can treat much of C as material to be looked up and then forgotten, just as you would unfamiliar words.

Copy Techniques From Existing Programs

When you want to do something new, look through this book for examples that do something similar to what you want. After you copy a technique several times, you learn it without effort.

The C Toolbox

1

A Quick Tour
Through C

This chapter shows you what C programs look like. The short programs shown do not perform useful functions, but they illustrate C's basic features. This book is not a tutorial on C, but this chapter provides a foundation for later chapters. Vocabulary and concepts needed in the rest of the book are discussed here. More advanced features of C are discussed in later chapters.

There are many similarities among high-level computer languages. If you are familiar with BASIC, COBOL, PL/1, Pascal, or FORTRAN, you should be able to recognize the purpose of the features introduced and to relate them to the corresponding features in the programming language you already know. You may need to refer to a C primer for more information on each feature. If you are familiar with C, this chapter can serve as a review. You may also be familiar with the terms and concepts introduced, but the chapter explains how the book will use them.

1.1 HELLO Program: The Structure of C

The first program is very simple; it just displays

```
hello, world
```

on the screen. (This is not an original composition. I took it from *The C Programming Language , Second Edition* by Brian W. Kernighan and Dennis M. Ritchie [Englewood Cliffs, N.J.: Prentice-Hall, 1988], hereafter referred to as K&R.) It serves to illustrate the basic structure of a C program and how to convert it into an executable program.

Figure 1.1 lists the program. Line 1 tells the compiler to use the contents of a file named `stdio.h` as additional input to the compilation. The `stdio.h` file is provided with your compiler. We will explain its purpose a little later.

1

FIGURE 1.1   hello.c

```
1      #include "stdio.h"
2
3      main()
4       {
5         printf("hello,") ;
6         printf(" world") ;
7       }
```

Lines 3 to 7 define a function named `main`. Line 3 establishes the function's name, and lines 4 to 7 describe what it does. This general format is followed for all C functions:

name(...)
...
{
    what it does
}

As the ellipsis marks indicate, there may be more text that we have not yet illustrated or described. C programs are composed of function definitions. Each definition describes what happens when we *call* that function. When we execute the HELLO program, we call the `main` function. In turn it may call other functions.

The what-it-does part of a function consists of one or more *statements* (if it doesn't do anything, there would be no statements). Lines 5 and 6 in the HELLO program are such statements. Line 5 calls a function named `printf`. `printf` displays the message on the screen. When it finishes, it *returns* to the point where it was called. When we call `printf`, we specify what it is to display. In Line 6 we call `printf` again with a different message. What `printf` does depends on the information we provide it. This information is called *parameters* or *arguments*.

The `printf` function is supplied in the standard C library; we do not have to write it. The use of `printf` should be documented in your C compiler manual. With this documentation, we can use `printf` without seeing how it is implemented.

The statements illustrated in Figure 1.1 had the form

function-name(...) ;

Later programs will show other forms of statements and relate the statements shown here to a more general form.

The arguments we use in lines 5 and 6 are *character string constants*. Later we will discuss the way that C stores character strings. For now we can note that the format of such a character string constant is

"printable characters"

Although the `printf` function is supplied in the compiler's library, the compiler does not know anything about its use. The header file `stdio.h` defines the way in which the `printf` function should be used: what arguments we must pass to `printf` and what kind of data it returns. A number of header files are provided with your compiler to define usage of library functions. Your compiler manual specifies the header file to include for each library function.

Compiling and Executing the HELLO Program

Figure 1.2 illustrates the process of preparing the HELLO program on an IBM PC using the Microsoft C compiler. Although the details will depend on the compiler product that you use, similar steps for editing, compiling, linking and executing the programs are followed.

FIGURE 1.2   Preparing the HELLO program

```
1
2      C>Remark - Editing the source file
3
4      C>edlin hello.c
5      New file
6      *i
7           1:*#include "stdio.h"
8           2:*
9           3:*main()
10          4:* {
11          5:*    printf("hello,") ;
12          6:*    printf(" world") ;
13          7:* }
14          8:*^C
15     *e
16
17     C>
18
19     C>Remark - Compiling the Program
20
21     C>cl /c hello.c
22     Microsoft (R) C Optimizing Compiler Version 5.10
23     Copyright (C) Microsoft Corp 1984-1988. All rights reserved.
24
25     hello.c
26
27     C>Remark - Linking the program
28
29     C>link hello.obj, hello.exe, , ,
30
31     Microsoft (R) Overlay Linker Version 3.65
32     Copyright (C) Microsoft Corp 1983-1988.  All rights reserved.
33
34
35     C>Remark - Executing the program
36
```

Figure 1.2   continues

Figure 1.2 continued

```
37    C>hello
38    hello, world
39    C>
```

First we type in the C program using a text editor (or a word processor). When we finish typing the program, we store the entered text in a file. Lines 4 to 16 of Figure 1.2 show the editing process using the EDLIN editor provided with PC-DOS. Any text editor that produces files of ASCII characters without any special formatting information can be used. (Microsoft C, Quick, and Turbo C all provide full-screen editors that are much more pleasant to use than EDLIN.) We will refer to the file created as a *source file* since it is the source for the compilation step.

The compiler reads the source file and translates the C program into a file of instructions and data that the IBM PC can execute. Lines 21 to 26 of Figure 1.2 show the compile process for the Microsoft C compiler. By convention, C source files are normally named with a file extension of .c. Some compilers require this naming scheme. The file produced by the compiler is called an *object file*. Unless we specify a different name, the object file will be given the same file name as the source file with the .obj extension replacing the .c extension. For example, compiling hello.c produces the hello.obj object file.

The compile step has translated the source file into executable form, but we have another step before the program can be executed. The program that we wrote is not complete in itself — it uses the printf library function. The *linking* step combines our object file with any necessary functions to produce a complete program that is ready to execute. The completed program is stored in a *run file* named hello.exe.

Lines 29 to 34 of Figure 1.2 show the linking step. We specify that the hello.obj file is the input to the linking process and that the resulting program be named hello.exe. The linker searches one or more *library files* for the printf function (and for any library functions that printf uses). The linker also searches for a special object file, which sets up the environment expected by C functions. The final program includes all the object files we specified as input and any library functions that are used by our object files. The names of the library files to be searched were listed in the object files themselves. For other C compilers such as Turbo C, you must specify the names of the libraries and the name of the special startup object file.

Now we are ready to execute the program. Lines 37 to 38 of Figure 1.2 show the execution of the HELLO program. We type the name of the program's run file to execute it. Note that we need not type the complete file name— the .exe extension is assumed. When we execute hello.exe, we are calling the main function. C expects to find a function named main in every program; when we named our function main, we were saying to the C compiler, "When you execute the program, begin here."

This example is specific to the Microsoft C compiler, but a similar sequence would be followed for QuickC or Turbo C. In Figure 1.2, each step required us to type a DOS command. All three compilers provide a command-line version of the compiler that works in this way. QuickC and Turbo C also provide an integrated environment in which editing, compiling, and linking are all accomplished without returning to the MS-DOS command line prompt. For example, in the Turbo C environment, we would issue the following series of commands:

```
TC  hello.c                  (enters the environment)
#include "stdio.h"           (type in the program)
...
}
Press F2                     (saves the source file)

Press Alt-C                  (selects the Compile Menu)
Press c                      (selects the Compile option)
                             (compiles the file)

Press Alt-C                  (selects the Compile Menu)
Press l                      (selects the Link option)
                             (links the program)

Press Alt-R                  (selects the Run menu)
Press r                      (selects the Run option)
                             (runs the program)
```

Both command-line and integrated environments allow you to perform several steps with a single command. Keep in mind that the same edit-compile-link-run cycle is present even if the compiler combines several steps.

1.2 Sum of Squares Program: Variables, Arithmetic, and Loops

The C program shown in Figure 1.3 displays a table of the sum of squares for the numbers from 1 through 11. It illustrates comments, variables, arithmetic, and some C statement types. Figure 1.4 lists a sample output from this program.

FIGURE 1.3   sumsq.c

```
 1      /* sumsq.c - print sum of squares table */
 2      #include <stdio.h>
 3
 4      main()
 5      {
 6          int i ;
 7          int sum ;
 8
 9          sum = 0 ;
10          i = 0 ;
11          while( i < 11 )
12            { i = i + 1 ;
13              sum = sum + i*i ;
14              printf(" %d   %d \n",i,sum) ;
15            }
16      }
```

FIGURE 1.4   Output from SUMSQ

```
 1    C>sumsq
 2       1   1
 3       2   5
 4       3   14
 5       4   30
 6       5   55
 7       6   91
 8       7   140
 9       8   204
10       9   285
11      10   385
12      11   506
13
14    C>
```

Line 1 in Figure 1.3 is a comment, which the compiler ignores. In C, comments begin with the characters /* and end with the */ characters. We place such a comment at the beginning of each file with the name of the file and a few words about its purpose. When the source file is listed, the comment identifies what we are listing.

As in the HELLO program, line 2 brings the stdio.h file into the compilation to define the proper use of the printf function. Although printf is a commonly used function and most C programmers quickly learn how to use it, it is good practice to let the compiler check for errors. The #include statement in line 2 surrounds the file name with the angle bracket characters (< and >) rather than the double quote characters (") used in Figure 1.1. When the bracket characters are used, the compiler looks for the header file in a standard file directory (normally where the other compiler files are stored). When the double quote characters are used, the compiler may search for the header file in different file directories in addition to the standard locations. For header files supplied with the compiler, either syntax may be used. For header files we create, the double quote characters should be used.

Lines 6 and 7 declare *variables* named i and sum. Such *declarations* serve two purposes:

1. They define the variable names and associate them with a data type (here integer).
2. They allocate space to store the variable's value.

Unlike BASIC and FORTRAN, C expects explicit declarations for data variables. Variable declarations have the following format:

data-type variable-name ;

Lines 9 to 10 assign the value zero to i and sum. Note that each *assignment statement* ends with a semicolon. The format of an assignment statement is

where-to-put-it = a-value-to-store ;

The value to store is an *expression*. Expressions can be single variables or constants or they can involve several operators as in line 12. In our examples we put the expression into a variable. But the where-to-put-it part of the statement could also be an expression with several operators. All that C requires is that the left side define an address at which we can store the value.

Line 13 has another assignment statement in which the *arithmetic operators* + and * are used. In addition to the addition (+) and multiplication (*) operators, C supports subtraction (–) and division (/) operators. All these operators are *binary operators*. They use two operands, one in front of the operator and one after it:

operand binary-operator operand

C also has *unary operators* that use a single operand. The unary minus (–) is one operator that is common to many other languages. The unary minus gives the negative of its operand. The following examples show the general format and a use of the unary minus:

unary-operator operand
–i (a unary minus)

Since the same operator is used for subtracting and the unary minus, C has a rule for distinguishing these uses. If the – operator has an expression on either side, it is the binary subtraction operator. If not, it is the unary minus.

Lines 11 to 15 are a while statement. In English it means

"keep executing lines 12-15 as long the value of the
variable i is less than 11."

As this explanation suggests, the < operator compares what is on its left to what is on its right. The result — true or false — will be used to control program execution. C provides the usual set of comparison operators:

Operator	Meaning
a < b	true if a is less than b
a <= b	true if a is less than or equal to b
a > b	true if a is greater than b
a >= b	true if a is greater than or equal to b
a == b	true if a is equal to b
a != b	true if a is not equal to b

The format of a while statement is

```
while( condition to be tested )
    statement to be repeated
```

The condition is tested before the statement is executed.

Since we wanted the three statements on lines 12 to 14 to be repeated, we enclosed them in brackets to make a *compound statement*. The entire compound statement is repeated for as long as the condition is true.

Line 14 calls the printf function used in the HELLO program. This time we pass three arguments:

1. A control string of characters. The % characters tell printf that a format for data to be printed follows. The d character specifies that an integer value is to be printed in decimal notation. The number is converted into a series of characters and printf goes back to scanning the character string. Having found the second %d specification, printf looks for a third argument. This argument is converted into a series of characters, and scanning of the character string continues. Since no more % characters are found, the rest of the string is printed and printf returns to the hello function that called it.
2. The value of variable i.
3. The value of the variable sum.

We used one argument in the HELLO program and three here. How did printf understand our intentions? The two %d specifications in the string told printf to look for and output two extra arguments. Because the number of arguments passed to printf depends on what is in the control string, the compiler cannot detect some errors in the use of printf.

Line 14 illustrates another format for a statement:

```
function-name(...) ;
```

In fact we can make a C statement with any expression:

```
expression ;
```

The assignments on lines 9 and 10 and the function call on line 14 are examples of C expressions. Although C allows assignments and function calls inside more complicated expressions, we will keep our uses simple for readability.

The character string in line 14 includes something else new: \n. Some characters we need to output have a special meaning to the C compiler and cannot be used in the string directly. The newline character is one such *control character*. C recognizes a special notation for that character. The backslash character \ signals that the next character, n, will identify a control character. When we send the newline character out, it causes the subsequent output to start on a new line.

1.3   WEATHER Program: Console Input, for Statements, Variable Addresses, and Symbolic Constants

The next program (Figure 1.5) accepts a week's worth of daily temperatures and calculates the average temperature for the week. It also counts the number of days when the temperature was below freezing. A sample run is shown in Figure 1.6.

FIGURE 1.6   Output from WEATHER

```
1      /* weather.c - calculate average temp. and # cold days */
2      #include "stdio.h"
3
4      #define FREEZE      32     /* freezing temperature  */
5
6      main()
7      {
8          int i , temp , ncold ;
9          float sum ;
10
11         printf(" enter temperatures for the week \n");
12         ncold = 0 ;
13         sum = 0 ;
14         for(i=0 ; i < 7 ; i=i+1 )
15           { scanf("%d",&temp) ;
16             sum = sum + temp ;
17             if( temp < FREEZE )
18                 ncold = ncold + 1 ;
19           }
20
21         printf(" average temperature was %3.1f \n", sum / 7.0 ) ;
22         printf(" %d days below freezing \n", ncold);
23      }
```

FIGURE 1.5   weather.c

```
1    C>weather
2     enter temperatures for the week
3    15 20 32 40 65 72 55
4     average temperature was 42.7
5     2 days below freezing
6
7    C>
```

The WEATHER program uses several new features of C: the scanf function is used to collect keyboard input; a for statement is used to provide a program loop; the address of a variable is passed as an argument; and a *symbolic name* is defined for a numeric constant.

Line 4 defines the word FREEZE as the number 32. The rest of the program will refer to FREEZE instead of using the number 32. If we wanted to convert the program to the use of centigrade temperatures, we would change line 4, leaving the rest of the program unchanged. Although this is not important for our small example, defining names for numeric constants is a good practice for real programs. It eliminates the possibility of changing a numeric constant in some places but not in other places. Note that there is no semicolon in line 4. The #define statement is not an assignment statement; it means "from now on replace the word FREEZE by what is on the rest of this line (32) before compiling the line."

Line 9 declares sum as a floating-point variable. C relies on explicit declarations to identify the type of data to be stored in a variable. In contrast, BASIC expects integer variable names to end in %, whereas string variable names have $ as the last character.

Lines 14 to 19 show a for statement. Its format is

```
for( do-first ; test-condition ; do-every-time )
    repeat-this-statement
```

It is a shorthand equivalent of the following sequence, which uses the while statement:

```
do-first ;
while( test-condition )
    { repeat-this-statement
      do-every-time ;
    }
```

In this case the for statement repeats lines 15 to 19 with i equal to $0, 1, 2 \ldots 6$. Although C allows any expressions in the for statement, the programs in this book have a simple form:

```
for( variable=starting value ; variable < final value ; variable = variable + 1 )
    statement
```

(We will use other comparison operators and add or subtract values other than 1.) This use of C's for statement is much like the for statement in BASIC or Pascal.

Line 15 accepts a temperature value from the keyboard. The scanf function works much like printf. The first argument tells scanf how to interpret characters typed at the keyboard. Subsequent arguments tell scanf where to put the data it has collected from the keyboard. When we pass arguments to a called function, we are passing values, not the location where a variable is stored. We use the & operator to give the *address* of the variable temp. We pass this address to scanf so that scanf can store a value there.

Like printf, scanf is a library function provided with the C compiler. The stdio.h header file also defines its use. Like printf, scanf allows for a variable number of arguments, and the C compiler cannot fully check for errors in its use. It is up to you to remember that printf requires data values as arguments, whereas scanf needs addresses.

printf and scanf are console I/O functions. They are intended for communicating with the PC keyboard and screen. They perform the same kinds of functions that INPUT and PRINT do in BASIC.

Lines 17 to 18 contain an if statement. Line 17 tests the temperature value just entered to see if it is below freezing. Line 18 is executed only if the condition is true.

Line 16 shows arithmetic with mixed data types: integer and floating point. C has fixed rules for handling arithmetic on mixed data types. You can force conversions of data in cases where the default action that C would take is not what you require.

Line 14 uses the integer constant 7 as the limit on the execution of the for loop. In line 21 the floating-point constant 7.0 is used to compute the average temperature. Although we could have used an integer constant 7 in line 21 and relied on C's automatic conversion rules, using the appropriate data type ourselves makes the program more understandable.

Line 21 shows another format for numeric output. The %3.1f description says that a floating-point number is being supplied as an argument and that it is to be displayed with a decimal point. Three digits are to be printed, followed by the decimal point and one fraction digit. The number is rounded to one decimal place before being displayed.

1.4 SORTNUM Program: Arrays, Function Return Values, and Pointers

The next program, shown in Figure 1.7, accepts a list of numbers from the keyboard, sorts them in ascending order, and displays them in this sorted order. The program can sort up to 100 numbers. We signal the end of the input by typing a nonnumeric character instead of a number. The program shows several new features: arrays, function return values, and pointers to variables. Figure 1.8 gives an example of running the program.

FIGURE 1.7 sortnum.c

```
1      /* sortnum.c - sort input numbers */
2      #include "stdio.h"
3                             /* function prototypes */
4      void sortn( int [], int ) ;
5      void swap( int * , int * ) ;
6
7      main()
8       {
9         int i , n , t ;
10        int a[100] ;
11
12        printf(" enter numbers - (type q to stop)");
13        n=0 ;
14        while( scanf("%d",&t) != 0 )
```

Figure 1.7   continues

Figure 1.7   continued

```
15              { a[n] = t ;
16                n = n + 1 ;
17              }
18
19         sortn(a,n) ;
20
21         for(i=0 ; i < n ; i=i+1 )
22            { printf(" %d",a[i] ) ; }
23      }
24
25
26
27    void sortn(x,nx)              /* sort an array of integers */
28     int x[] ;                    /* the array of integers */
29     int nx ;                     /* number of items to sort */
30     {
31        int i , j , pick ;
32
33        for(i=0 ; i < (nx-1) ; i=i+1 )
34           {                      /* find smallest remaining number */
35             pick = i ;
36             for(j=i+1 ; j < nx ; j=j+1 )
37                { if( x[j] < x[pick] )
38                     pick = j ;   /* x[pick] is smallest so far */
39                }
40             swap( & x[pick], & x[i] ); /* put smallest first */
41           }
42     }
43
44
45
46    void swap(p1,p2)              /* swap two numbers */
47     int *p1 ;                    /* points to first number */
48     int *p2 ;                    /* points to second number */
49     {
50        int temp ;
51
52        temp = *p1 ;
53        *p1 = *p2 ;
54        *p2 = temp ;
55     }
```

FIGURE 1.8   Output from SORTNUM

```
1    C>sortnum
2     enter numbers - (type q to stop) 4 6 5 3 2 1 q
3     1 2 3 4 5 6
4    C>
```

Line 10 in Figure 1.7 declares an array of integers. It allocates space for 100 integers with indices from 0 to 99. It is up to us to be sure that we do not refer to any index outside this range. C does not provide any checking for us. Lines 15 and 22 demonstrate how we refer to an element of the array.

Lines 12 to 17 accept input from the keyboard. When the scanf function is called, it *returns* a value: the number of items that were successfully received. The program accepts input until scanf fails to find a number. (scanf is looking for a number; it stops looking when a q or other nonnumeric character is found.)

Line 19 calls a function named sortn. We supply the array and the count of numbers read into the array as arguments. Lines 27 to 42 define the sortn function. Lines 28 and 29 define the type of arguments that sortn will expect. These declarations are similar to the variable declarations on lines 9 and 10. The array declaration differs in that we need not describe the size of the array passed to sortn — any size array of integers can be used successfully. C treats array arguments differently from ordinary variables. It actually passes the location of the array — not the value of all its elements. The void data type indicates that sortn does not return a value.

The numbers are sorted by selection. First the smallest number is found and placed first. Then the next smallest is selected from what remains and placed second. This process is repeated until only one element of the array remains unselected. Lines 33 to 41 implement this algorithm. Two for loops are used — one nested inside the other. There is nothing special here — the inner for statement is just one of the statements inside the braces marking the body of the outer for statement.

At each step when the smallest remaining number has been selected, the swap function is called to exchange it with the first number in the unsorted area. We pass the addresses of the array elements to be swapped. As in the WEATHER program, we use the address operator & to get these addresses.

In the swap function, lines 47 and 48 define the arguments representing the locations of the numbers to be swapped. The asterisk describes p1 and p2 as pointing to integers rather than being integers themselves. When we refer to the locations of the variables, we also use an asterisk before the pointer argument. We will often choose names beginning with p for pointers to remind us what they are. Here is an English translation of line 53:

> "Take the value of the location pointed to by p2 and store it at the location pointed to by p1."

We will see other uses of pointers later, but the basic lesson is that C allows us to work with addresses of variables as easily as with their values.

When we use a library function supplied with our compiler, we need not worry about the usage checking information in the accompanying header files. When we create functions and call them, we must supply the usage information, called *function prototypes*. Lines 4 and 5 of Figure 1.7 provide the function prototypes for the sortn and swap functions. Function prototypes have a form similar to regular declarations of functions. Data types are supplied for arguments, but names are not required. The body of the function is not present; a semicolon follows the closing parentheses. We will return to function prototypes in Section 1.6.

1.5   SENTENCE Program: File I/O, Characters, and I/O Redirection

Figure 1.9 shows a program that counts the sentences in a file. It simply counts the number of times that a period, question mark, or an exclamation point occurs. Although this may be too simple to be really useful, it provides a first look at file I/O and character constants.

FIGURE 1.9   sentence.c

```
1     /* sentence.c - count sentences */
2     #include "stdio.h"
3
4     void check_end( int ) ;        /* function prototype */
5     int ns ;
6
7     main()
8       {
9         int c ;
10
11        ns = 0 ;
12                                    /* get each character and check it */
13        c = getchar() ;
14        while( c != EOF )
15          { check_end(c) ;
16            c = getchar() ;
17          }
18
19        printf(" %d sentences",ns) ;
20      }
21
22
23
24    void check_end(ch)             /* check for end-of-sentence char. */
25     int ch ;                      /* char to check */
26     {
27       if(    (ch == '.')
28          || (ch == '?')
29          || (ch == '!') )
30            ns = ns + 1 ;
31     }
```

The program relies on I/O redirection to provide input from a disk file rather than from the keyboard. We will examine how it is executed after looking at the program itself. The overall logic of the program is quite simple. The program gets the first character from the file and checks it to see if it is an end-of-sentence character. If so, it adds one to the count. These two steps are repeated until no more characters remain in the file.

We use the `getchar` library function to fetch characters from a file one by one. Like `printf` and `scanf`, `getchar` is provided in the standard C library. It returns the next character in the file each time it is called. `getchar` needs no arguments passed to it, so the function call has the parentheses with no arguments inside.

When no more characters remain, `getchar` returns a special value to signal the end of the file. This value is defined by the symbolic constant EOF in the `stdio.h` file provided with the compiler. Whenever we use the EOF constant in a source file, we should include the `stdio.h` header file. When `getchar` returns a character, the value returned will range from 0 through 255. (This maximum value depends on the amount of storage the compiler uses for a character. For the IBM PC and most other modern computers, characters are stored in 8 bits, allowing for a range from 0 through 255.) The end-of-file value EOF is guaranteed to be different from any of these values. (It is often −1.) Although the size of an integer variable varies for different C compilers, it is always large enough to make EOF distinct from all characters returned by `getchar`.

Because `getchar` returns an integer value, we declare the variable c as an integer not a character. Had we declared it as a character, the EOF value could not be kept distinct from all possible character values. C allows us to look at characters as numeric values and provides automatic conversion of characters to integer values.

Lines 24 to 31 define the function `check_end`. This function checks the character just read to see if it is an end-of-sentence character. If so, it adds one to the count of sentences found. The `if` statement used makes several comparisons. The || operator means *or*. The statement on line 28 is executed if the character is a period, a question mark, or an exclamation point. C also provides an operator meaning *and*: the && operator. Note that we used parentheses around each comparison in lines 27 to 29. C has rules to specify the order of evaluation of several operators in a single expression, but we can control the order of evaluation by enclosing parts of the whole expression in parentheses.

The count of sentences ns is declared outside any function. This allows it to be used in both `main` and `check_end` without passing it as a parameter.

The comparisons in lines 27 to 29 use *character constants* for the period, question mark, and exclamation characters. Character constants are written with a single quote before and after the character. We use character constants for single characters and string constants where we need a series of one or more characters. Section 1.6 discusses the way C represents each kind of constant.

Running SENTENCE: I/O Redirection

The `getchar` function is a console I/O function like `printf` and `scanf`. MS-DOS provides a way to substitute a file for keyboard input. When we execute the SENTENCE program, we follow the program's name with the < character and the name of a file to be used as input. Figure 1.10 illustrates this feature.

FIGURE 1.10   Output from SENTENCE

```
1    C>type test
2    I write short sentences.   I like them.   Do you?
3    I hope you agree!
4
5    C>sentence <test
6      4 sentences
7    C>
```

C provides another library function called putchar to output a single character. Its output normally is displayed on the screen, but it can be redirected to a file. The following program fragment outputs letters of the alphabet. If we execute it with >afile following the program name, the output is placed in a file named afile.

```
...
main()
{
    int c ;
    for(c= 'a' ; c <= 'z' ; c=c+1)
        { putchar(c) ; }
}
```

1.6 REVERSE Program: Character Arrays and Strings, Separate Compilation

The program shown in Figure 1.11 tests a phrase to see if it is a palindrome (the same read forward and backward). If the phrase is a palindrome, the program says so, and if not, it prints the reverse of the phrase. REVERSE accepts an entire line of input as the phrase to be tested. Two sample runs are shown in Figure 1.12.

FIGURE 1.11   reverse.c

```
1    /* reverse.c - checks a phrase to see if it is a palindrome */
2    #include "stdio.h"
3    #include "string.h"
4    #include "getstr.h"
5                                    /* function prototype */
6    void do_reverse( char [] , char [] ) ;
7
8    main()
9      {
10        char phrase[81] ;
11        char rev_phrase[81] ;
```

Figure 1.11   continues

Figure 1.11 continued

```
12
13            printf("type a phrase : \n");/* prompt for a phrase */
14            getstr(phrase,80) ;              /* and get it from the keyboard */
15
16            do_reverse(phrase,rev_phrase) ; /* build reverse of phrase */
17            if( strcmp(phrase,rev_phrase) == 0 ) /* compare to original */
18                  printf(" ** palindrome ** ");
19            else printf(" reverse = %s",rev_phrase) ;
20        }
21
22
23
24      void do_reverse(s1,s2)         /* reverse a string */
25        char s1[] ;                  /* the string to be reversed */
26        char s2[] ;                  /* place its reverse here */
27        {
28          int i , j ;
29                                       /* copy chars starting at end of s1 */
30          i= 0 ;
31          j = strlen(s1) - 1 ;        /* find index of last char in s1 */
32          while( j >= 0 )
33            { s2[i] = s1[j] ;
34              i = i + 1 ;
35              j = j - 1 ;
36            }
37          s2[i] = 0 ;                  /* mark end of string */
38        }
```

FIGURE 1.12   Output from REVERSE

```
1
2     C>reverse
3     type a phrase :
4     ana
5      ** palindrome **
6     C>
7
8     C>reverse
9     type a phrase :
10    anvil
11     reverse = livna
12    C>
```

The program demonstrates character arrays and the conventions that C uses for strings. Several library functions for string handling are used. The program is composed of two source files and provides an example of *separate compilation*.

Lines 10 and 11 of Figure 1.11 declare two arrays of characters. They store the phrase to be tested and its reverse. The declarations are like the array declaration in the sortnum program, but here the data type is char instead of int.

Line 13 prompts for a phrase, and line 14 calls the function getstr to collect the phrase from the keyboard. getstr is not defined in the reverse.c file nor is it in the C standard library — it will be defined in a separate source file. There are several reasons for placing the `getstr` function in a separate source file:

1. `getstr` can be used in other programs. Collecting a line of keyboard input and storing it in character string form is a general function that may be useful in many programs. If it is placed in a separate source file, it can be used as easily as standard library functions.
2. It is easier to edit and compile small source files. Packaging programs in several small 50- to 100-line source files keeps editing and compilation times down to a few seconds.
3. Testing small single-purpose modules is much easier and more effective than testing whole programs. Modifying programs is also easier when they are composed of small single-purpose modules.

The phrase that `getstr` accepts from the keyboard is stored in the character array `phrase` in the string format that C supports. The characters in the word are stored consecutively in `phrase` with a character with the value zero at the end. We have been using string constants (`"hello,"` for example) in previous programs. The C compiler allocates space for them and stores them in this same format. For example, the `"hello,"` string would be stored as

```
position      0    1    2    3    4    5    6
char value    h    e    l    l    o    ,    \0
```

The notation `\0` represents a zero (or null) value just as `\n` represented a newline control character.

The `do_reverse` function on lines 24 to 38 of Figure 1.11 reverses the phrase, placing the result into the array provided. It uses the library function `strlen` to find the end of the string. `strlen` returns the number of characters in the string, not counting the null character at the end. Since C arrays are indexed starting at zero, a string having n characters has its last character at index $n-1$.

When all the characters in the string have been copied, the value zero is stored to mark the end of the string. The character constant `'\0'` represents a character with the value zero.

When the reverse of the string has been constructed, line 17 uses the library function `strcmp` to compare the word and its reverse. C does not support assignments or comparisons on strings, but the library does provide functions to perform several string operations. Line 3 includes the header file `string.h`, which defines the proper use of `strcmp` and `strlen`.

Figure 1.13 shows the source file containing the `getstr` function. It expects two arguments: a character array to hold the word entered and a maximum length to allow. `getstr` accepts characters from the keyboard using `getchar` until it receives a newline character or until the array is filled.

FIGURE 1.13   getstr.c

```
1    /* getstr.c - get a line of input from keyboard */
2    /* like fgets() but does not place the '\n' in the string */
3    #include "stdio.h"
4
5    int getstr(s,maxs)          /* get a line of input */
6     char s[] ;            /* place the input here in string form */
7     int maxs ;            /* limit on characters allowed */
8     {             /* returns string length */
9       int i , c ;
10
11      i=0 ;
12      c = getchar() ;          /* get first character */
13              /* repeat until full, EOF or end-of-line */
14      while( (i < maxs) && (c != '\n') && ( c != EOF) )
15        { s[i] = c ;          /* place char in string */
16          i = i + 1 ;          /* advance char count   */
17          c = getchar() ;        /* and get another character */
18        }
19      s[i] = '\0' ;
20      return( i ) ;        /* return count of characters */
21
```

Figure 1.14 is a header file with a function prototype for the getstr function. Any source file that uses getstr should include its header file. There need not be a separate header file for every source file, but header files should be organized to match source file organization. The following rules should help you use function prototypes:

- A function prototype must be located before the call to the function.
- Data types must be defined before they appear in a function prototype.
- The source code that defines a function (lines 24 to 38 for do_reverse) does not provide error-checking information to the compiler unless the arguments are fully declared within the parentheses following the function name.

In the following chapters, we will use function prototypes, which are separate from the function definition. When a function is to be used in other source files, a prototype is created for the function and placed in a header file. That header file is included in all source files that use the function.

FIGURE 1.14   getstr.h

```
1    /* getstr.h - header file for getstr function */
2    int getstr( char [] , int ) ;
```

Separate Compilation

Figure 1.15 shows how we build the REVERSE program from two source files. First each source file is compiled. Then we run the linker program with both object files as inputs. This produces a single executable file. Although it is not necessary in our example, most useful programs should be split into several source files.

FIGURE 1.15   Building the REVERSE program

```
1    C>cl /c reverse.c
2    Microsoft (R) C Optimizing Compiler Version 5.10
3    Copyright (c) Microsoft Corp 1984-1988.  All rights reserved.
3
4    reverse.c
5
6    C>cl /c getstr.c
7    Microsoft (R) C Optimizing Compiler Version 5.10
8    Copyright (c) Microsoft Corp 1984-1988.  All rights reserved.
9
10   getstr.c
11
12   C>link reverse.obj+getstr.obj,  reverse.exe, , ,
13
14   Microsoft (R) Overlay Linker  Version 3.65
15   Copyright (C) Microsoft Corp 1983-1988.  All rights reserved.
15
16   C>
```

In Figure 1.15 we used separate commands for each step of the process so the steps would be clear. We could compile and link the REVERSE program using a single command (`cl reverse.c getstr.c`). Both QuickC and Turbo C provide similar commands in the command-line versions of the compilers.

QuickC and Turbo C also provide a more convenient mechanism for defining the source files to be used in creating a program in the integrated environment. In the Turbo C environment, you create a project file — a text file listing the source files to be compiled. For the REVERSE program, that file lists `reverse.c` and `getstr.c`. Then you specify this file as the project file. When you link or rebuild the REVERSE program, the compiler and linker use this project file to define what source files are to used. In the QuickC environment, you build a program list of source files. Both QuickC and Turbo C automate compiling and linking so that it requires you to type only one or two keystrokes.

1.7 CURVE Program: Defining Data Types, Using Structures

The program in Figure 1.16 grades student work on the curve. It assigns a passing grade to the top 70% of the class and fails the bottom 30%. It accepts a list of students' names and numerical grades from the keyboard. It prints out the students' names and a pass/fail grade. The names are ordered by numerical grade — highest first. Figure 1.17 lists a sample run.

FIGURE 1.16   curve.c

```
1     /* curve.c - assigns pass/fail grades on a curve system */
2     #include "stdio.h"
3     #include "string.h"
4
5     typedef struct      /* definition of student data type*/
6       { char name[30] ;
7         int grade ;
8       } STUDENT ;
9
10    STUDENT class[40] ;   /* student data for entire class */
11
12                            /* function prototypes */
13    void sortclass( STUDENT [] , int ) ;
14    void swap( STUDENT * , STUDENT * ) ;
15
16
17    main()
18      {
19        int ns ;                    /* count of students in the class */
20        int i , cutoff ;
21
22                               /* get list of students and grades */
23        printf(" number of students: \n");
24        scanf("%d",&ns) ;
25        printf("enter name and grade for each student \n");
26        for( i=0 ; i < ns ; i=i+1 )
27          { scanf("%s %d", class[i].name, & class[i].grade ); }
28                              /* now sort them */
29        sortclass(class,ns) ;
30        cutoff = (ns * 7) / 10  - 1 ;
31        printf("\n");
32        for( i=0 ; i < ns ; i=i+1 )
33          { printf("%-6s %3d", class[i].name, class[i].grade) ;
34            if( i <= cutoff )
35                  printf(" pass \n");
36            else printf(" fail \n");
37          }
38      }
39
40
41
42    void sortclass(st,nst)        /* sort by numeric grade */
43      STUDENT st[] ;              /* array of student data structures */
```

Figure 1.16   continues

Figure 1.16   continued

```
44      int     nst  ;              /* number of students */
45      {
46        int i , j , pick ;
47
48        for(i=0 ; i < (nst-1) ; i=i+1 )
49          { pick = i ;
50             for(j=i+1 ; j < nst ; j=j+1 )
51               { if( st[j].grade > st[pick].grade )
52                    pick = j ;
53               }
54             swap(& st[i] , & st[pick] ) ;
55          }
56      }
57
58      void swap(ps1,ps2)          /* swap data for two students */
59       STUDENT *ps1 ;             /* location of one student's data */
60       STUDENT *ps2 ;             /* location of other student's data */
61       {
62         STUDENT temp ;
63
64         strcpy(temp.name, ps1->name ) ;
65         temp.grade = ps1->grade ;
66
67         strcpy(ps1->name,ps2->name) ;
68         ps1->grade = ps2->grade ;
69
70         strcpy(ps2->name,temp.name) ;
71         ps2->grade = temp.grade ;
72       }
```

FIGURE 1.17   Output from CURVE

```
1
2      C>curve
3        number of students:
4      5
5       enter name and grade for each student
6       Fred 35
7       Mary 76
8       Joe   0
9       Bill 98
10      Sam   40
11
12      Bill     98 pass
13      Mary     76 pass
14      Sam      40 pass
15      Fred     35 fail
16      Joe       0 fail
17
18      C>
```

The program is similar to the SORTNUM program. First the names and numeri-cal grades are accepted. Then the names and grades are sorted. The algorithm used is the same one used in the SORTNUM program. Then the sorted list is printed. The word "pass" or the word "fail" is printed after each name. We will use a sorting function much like that in the SORTNUM program; instead of sorting numbers, it sorts a list of names and grades. The program illustrates two new ideas about C:

1. We can define new data types.
2. We can declare structures composed of several members of different types.

Lines 5 to 8 in Figure 1.16 define a new data type called STUDENT. It is like the int or char data type, but we defined it. This data type has two members: an array of characters for the student's name and an integer variable to hold the number grade. This is an example of a *structure*. Like an array, it may contain more than one member; unlike an array, the members may be of different data types and each member has a separate name.

Line 10 declares an array named class to hold data for up to 40 students. Each element of the array is a STUDENT data structure. Line 19 declares an integer, ns, which is the number of students in the class.

In line 27 we call scanf with the addresses of the members of the STUDENT structure. Since name is an array, its address is passed without a & operator.

Line 33 shows how the members of the student data structure are referenced. The class variable is an array; when we refer to one student's data, we use an index:

```
class[i]
```

The sortclass function in lines 42 to 56 is quite similar to the sort function in the SORTNUM program. The syntax for referencing structures differs from that for integers, but most of the function is unchanged. (Chapter 6 discusses sort functions that work for all kinds of data.) Line 54 passes the addresses of the two array elements that are to be swapped. Note that we pass the address of the whole student data structure; we want to exchange both the student name and the number grade.

The swap function works just like the one in the SORTNUM program. The pointers ps1 and ps2 are declared to point to data of the STUDENT type instead of to int data. The temporary variable is declared to be of type STUDENT also. swap exchanges each member individually. The string copy library function strcpy is used to exchange the student name strings. The header file string.h defines the use of strcpy. Lines 64 to 71 show the C notation for using pointers to structure members:

```
pointer->member  name
```

In contrast, the notation

```
variable.member  name
```

is used when the variable is declared to be of the structured type. Modern C compilers allow entire structures to be assigned with a single statement so that lines 64 to 71 could be replaced by the following C statements:

```
temp = *ps1 ;          /* move 1st student's data to temp */
*ps1 = *ps2 ;          /* move 2nd student's data to 1st */
*ps2 = temp ;          /* move 1st student's data to 2nd */
```

Line 30 calculates a pass/fail cutoff point: 70% of the students pass. Division of integers truncates the result so that the cutoff point is actually below 70% unless the class size is evenly divisible by 10.

1.8 NOTABS Program: Switch, Break Statements, and More Loops

The NOTABS program in Figure 1.18 converts tab characters into strings of space characters. All other input characters are simply output using the putchar library function discussed in Section 1.5. NOTABS keeps track of the column position where the current character would be displayed or printed. Normal characters move this position to the right by one column, and carriage return and line feed characters move the position to column one. When tab characters are encountered, NOTABS outputs enough space characters to move the position to the next tab stop.

FIGURE 1.18   notabs.c

```
1    /* notabs.c - turn tabs into blanks */
2    #include "stdio.h"
3
4    void do_it( int ) ;          /* function prototype */
5
6    #define TS 8                  /* tab stop interval */
7    int col ;                     /* current column position */
8
9
10   main()
11    {
12       int c ;
13
14       col = 1 ;
15       while( 1 == 1 )      /* get chars from input */
16         { c = getchar() ;
17           if( c == EOF )        /* until EOF is reached */
18               break ;
19           do_it(c) ;
20         }
21    }
22
23
24   void do_it(ch)          /* handle one char */
25    int ch ;               /* the character */
26     {
```

Figure 1.18   continues

Figure 1.18 continued

```
27          switch( ch )        /* classify ch */
28            {
29            case '\t' :       /* tab char */
30              do
31                  { putchar(' ') ; /*      put out blanks */
32                    col = col + 1 ;
33                    } while( (col % TS) !=1);/* until we reach a tab stop */
34              break ;
35            case '\r' :       /* carriage return */
36            case '\n' :       /* or line feed (newline) */
37              putchar( ch) ;        /*      output it */
38              col = 1 ;       /*      back to column 1 */
39              break ;
40            default :              /* any other char - assume printable */
41              putchar( ch) ;        /*      output it */
42              col = col + 1 ;       /*      advance to next column */
43              break ;
44            }
45      }
```

NOTABS illustrates several new features: the *remainder* operator (%), the break and switch statements, and the do {} while loop.

The main function collects input, one character at a time, using the getchar function discussed earlier. The while loop in lines 15 to 20 stops when getchar returns an EOF value, but it is different from while loops in previous programs. The test in line 15 (1 == 1) is always true; it never terminates the execution of lines 16 to 20. The if statement in lines 17 and 18 checks for EOF, and when it is found, the break statement in line 18 terminates the loop.

The do_it function in lines 24 to 45 handles each input character. The switch statement in lines 27 to 44 classifies the character and performs the appropriate action. if statements evaluate an expression as true or false and select from two outcomes; the switch statement allows us to specify more than two outcomes. The format of the switch statement is

```
switch( expression )
    {
    case value-1:    /* start here if exp == this value */
        some statements
        break ;
    case value-2:    /* start here if exp == this value */
        some-more-statements
        break ;
    case value-3:    /* start here if exp == this value */
    case value-4:    /*                        or this value */
        more-statements
        break ;
    ...
    default:      /* start here if no case fits */
```

```
    more-statements
    break ;
}
```

The value specified in each case must be an expression that the compiler can evaluate fully; expressions with constants and multiple operators may appear, but variables may not appear. The cases specify where to start executing C statements; execution continues until the end of the `switch` statement or until a `break` statement is encountered. We use the `switch` statement in a rigid way: several case labels may share the same starting point (as value-3 and value-4 do), but each case must end with a `break` statement.

For carriage return or line feed characters (lines 35 to 39), the character is output and the current position set to column one. For any other characters except tab characters, lines 41 to 43 output the character and advance the current position.

Lines 30 to 34 handle the case of tab characters. The program outputs space characters and advances the column position until a tab stop is reached. At least one space character is always output. The `do {} while` loop statement in lines 30 to 33 repeats lines 31 and 32 until the test in line 33 fails. Unlike the `while` loop already discussed, this loop executes the body once before checking the test condition. The `%` operator in line 33 divides `col` by the constant `TS`, producing the remainder. Tab stops lie at columns 1, 9, 17, ..., (n*8+1), so this test checks to see if we have reached a tab stop.

The format of the `do {} while` statement is

```
do
    { statements to be repeated
    } while( condition-to-be-tested ) ;
```

The remainder operator, `%`, is a binary operator like the regular division operator. For integers, the division operator produces the quotient truncating any fractional part; the `%` operator provides the remainder. In other languages, the mod operator or function performs the same function as `%` does in C. The following examples should make its operation clear:

```
1 % 8 is 1
7 % 4 is 3
6 % 3 is 0
```

The NOTABS program shows two uses of the `break` statement, but `break` can also be used to exit from a `for` statement or a `do {} while` statement. The `break` statement always refers to the immediately enclosing `while`, `switch`, `for`, or `do {} while` statement.

Figure 1.19 shows a sample run with input redirected to the `testtabs` file and output redirected to the `testo` file. The output file looks the same when listed but is longer because tabs have been replaced by multiple space characters.

FIGURE 1.19   Output from NOTABS

```
 1    C>type testtabs
 2    abc
 3             def
 4     12345678901234567890123456 7890
 5     123        9012345 7
 6     1                        7
 7     12         9
 8
 9    C>notabs <testtabs >testo
10
11    C>type testo
12    abc
13             def
14     12345678901234567890123456 7890
15     123        9012345 7
16     1                        7
17     12         9
18
19    C>dir test*
20
21     Volume in drive C is HARD1
22     Directory of   c:\CTOOLBOX\CHAP1
23
24     TESTTABS         71    2-24-89    5:58p
25     TESTO            99    2-24-89    6:03p
26             2 File(s)  24782848 bytes free
```

1.9   Summary of Definitions and Concepts

The preceding sections have introduced some definitions and concepts needed in the rest of the book. Here is a summary of those terms:

Program Preparation

C programs are created in a three-step process. First they are typed into the computer using a text editor. The *source file* produced is given a file name with a .c extension. The *compiler* reads this source file and produces an *object file*, a translation into instructions understood by the computer being used. The *linker* reads this object file (and perhaps others) along with a *library* of standard C functions and produces an executable program. The user executes this program from DOS by typing the name of the executable file.

Separate Compilation

A C program can be composed of several source files. Each is compiled separately, and the linker combines the produced object files into an executable program.

Source Files and Text Editors

C source files must contain standard ASCII characters, no special formatting characters such as those used by several word processing programs are allowed. Any text editor or word processor program that produces such files can be used to enter and edit C source files.

Functions

C programs are composed of *functions*. Function definitions specify what data variables will be created and used and what *statements* will be executed. A single source file may contain more than one of these functions. Functions are *called* to execute them. Executing a C program causes the function named `main` to be executed.

Libraries

A library of standard functions is provided with almost all C compilers. C programs that you write can use these functions and the linker will incorporate those needed into your executable program.

Function Prototypes and Header Files

Function prototypes define proper use of C functions so that the compiler can check for errors. Header files furnished with the compiler provide function prototypes for standard library functions. When we write a function to be called by our C programs, we write a matching function prototype and place it in a header file that we create.

Variables and Data Types

C provides several types of data: characters, integers and floating point for example. Variables must be declared explicitly to tell the compiler their type. Declaring variables allocates space to hold the variable's value and makes its name and data type known to the compiler.

Parameters or Arguments

Functions may expect to be *passed* values when they are called. These *parameters* or *arguments* are used by the called function much as variables defined within the function would be.

Arrays and Subscripts or Indices

We can define *arrays* of variables as well as single variables. We refer to one element of the array by number using a *subscript* or *index*.

Structures and Member Names

Structures allow several *members* of different data types to be combined into a single data type. The structure may be assigned or passed as an argument and individual members may be referenced by name.

Addresses or Pointers

We can find the location of a variable when necessary. This *address* or *pointer* can be passed to a function. Variables which contain such addresses can be defined as well.

Console I/O

The C library provides some library functions for input from the *console* (the keyboard and display screen.) These functions are a special case of file I/O functions. Using I/O redirection, we were able to perform file input using these console I/O functions.

2

Adapting C
to Our Use

This chapter introduces more features of C and presents some useful tools. It also shows how to improve the readability and portability of C programs. Concrete examples are the basis for discussing C's features. We illustrate our points with a C program and then discuss the new features in general.

2.1 File I/O: Three Programs to Copy Files

The programs in Chapter 1 performed some kind of input or output. Most performed only console I/O, but in the SENTENCE program we used redirection to read a file. What if a program must accept input from the keyboard and from a file? The C standard library provides more functions for file I/O. In this section we use these functions to copy the contents of a file. Our program (COPYA) expects the names of input and output files to be typed on the command line when the program is executed. For example, to copy the `test.in` file to a new file named `test.out`, we would type

```
copya test.in test.out
```

in response to the DOS prompt (`C>`). If the input file does not exist or if the output file cannot be created, the program displays a message and exits.

Our C compiler's library gives us more than one way to accomplish the job, so we show three programs (Figures 2.1, 2.2, and 2.3). The COPYA program in Figure 2.1 uses the *buffered file I/O* or *stream I/O* library functions `getc` and `putc` for input and output. They are similar to the `getchar` and `putchar` functions used in Chapter 1.

31

FIGURE 2.1   copya.c

```
1       /* copya.c - copy a file with getc/putc    */
2       #include <stdio.h>
3
4
5       main(argc,argv)
6        int argc ;
7        char *argv[] ;
8        {
9           FILE   *in ,              /* file pointer for input file */
10                  *out ;            /* file pointer for output file */
11          int c ;
12          long n ;
13
14          if( argc < 3 )            /* check for file names */
15             { printf(" USAGE - copya input-file output-file \n");
16               exit(1);
17             }
18
19          in  = fopen(argv[1],"r"); /* open input file for reading */
20          out = fopen(argv[2],"w"); /* open output file for writing */
21                    /* files opened successfully? */
22          if( (in == NULL) || (out ==NULL) )
23             { printf("can't open a file");
24               exit(0) ;
25             }
26
27          n = 0L ;
28          c = getc(in) ;            /* get first character */
29          while( c != EOF )         /* stop at end of file */
30             { n = n + 1 ;
31               putc(c,out);         /* output the character */
32               c = getc(in) ;       /* get next character */
33             }
34          fclose(in);              /* close both files */
35          fclose(out);
36          printf(" %ld characters copied",n) ;
37        }
```

Using getc and putc is somewhat more complicated than using getchar and putchar. Before we can perform any input or output, we must *open* the files. Then, after we finish doing input and output, we must *close* the files.

Our first job in the program is to get the file names typed on the command line following the program name. C compilers provide access to the characters typed on the command line in a standard way. The line is scanned and divided into words separated by spaces or tab characters. Each word is stored in string format. The main function receives two parameters: a count of words found (argc) and an array of pointers to those words (argv[]). The first pointer, argv[0], points to the name of the program; when older versions of MS-DOS (prior to version 3.0) are being used, the program name is not available and a dummy name ("c") is substituted.

Lines 6 and 7 show how we declare these arguments. The input and output file names should be pointed to by argv[1] and argv[2]. Lines 19 and 20 pass the addresses of these names to the `fopen` function. The `fopen` function returns a value that identifies the file just opened. Subsequent file I/O function calls present this value as one of the arguments to identify the file to which they apply. These values are pointers to a data type called `FILE`. Lines 9 and 10 declare two variables to hold these pointer values. The `FILE` data type is defined in the `stdio.h` file. We do not have to worry about what that definition is; we just declare *file pointers* as shown.

If the `fopen` function cannot open the file successfully, it returns a special value — `NULL`. Like `FILE` and `EOF`, `NULL` is defined in `stdio.h`. We can use `NULL` as a symbolic constant without being concerned about its definition.

Lines 28 to 33 perform the actual input and output. We use `getc` and `putc` in almost the same way that we used `getchar` and `putchar` in Chapter 1. The difference is that we supply the file pointer as an argument to `getc` and `putc`.

After we finish input and output, we *close* the file using the `fclose` function. This tells the library functions and DOS that we have finished with these files. The library functions and DOS then perform any internal housekeeping needed to complete our I/O operations. (Files opened with `fopen` are automatically closed when a C program finishes execution, but it is good programming practice to close all files explicitly.)

We count the number of characters copied with a *long* variable (n). It is declared in line 13 and used in lines 28, 31, and 37. Long variables are like integers but may be capable of storing numbers of larger magnitude. Line 28 shows a long constant — a number followed by the letter `L` (or lowercase `l`). In line 31 we add an integer constant (1) to n. Since long numbers are potentially larger in magnitude than integers, the integer constant is first converted to the long data type and then added. Lines 28 and 31 are both correct; we used one to show the form of a long constant and the other to discuss integer to long data conversions.

In line 37 we use `printf` to display the count of characters. The format specification (`%ld`) tells `printf` to expect a long data item rather than an integer. The `long` data type is normally represented in memory differently than is the integer data type. When we pass data to functions, we must ensure that the data type we pass is what the functions expect.

Copying a File with fscanf and fprintf Functions

Just as `getchar` and `putchar` had more general analogs for file I/O, the `scanf` and `printf` functions have more general forms. The `fscanf` and `fprintf` functions work like `scanf` and `printf`, except that the first argument to each is a file pointer. For example, to read an integer we would use

```
scanf("%d",&i) ;      or           fscanf(in,"%d",&i) ;
```

Figure 2.2 shows a file copy program, COPYB, written using these functions. Since we just want to read and write single characters, we use the `%c` format specification rather than %d as in previous programs. This format tells `fscanf` to collect one character from the file (or `fprintf` to output one character). We detect the end of the input file when `fscanf` returns a zero value. The rest of the program is just like the COPYA program using `getc` and `putc`.

FIGURE 2.2 copyb.c

```
1    /* copyb.c - copy a file with fscanf/fprintf   */
2    #include <stdio.h>
3
4
5    main(argc,argv)
6     int argc ;
7     char *argv[] ;
8     {
9        FILE   *in ,             /* file pointer for input file */
10              *out ;            /* file pointer for output file */
11       char c ;
12       int nr ;
13       long n ;
14
15       if( argc < 3 )          /* check for file names */
16         { printf(" USAGE - copyb input-file output-file \n");
17           exit(1);
18         }
19
20       in  = fopen(argv[1],"r"); /* open input file for reading */
21       out = fopen(argv[2],"w"); /* open output file for writing */
22               /* files opened successfully? */
23       if( (in == NULL) || (out ==NULL) )
24         { printf("can't open a file");
25           exit(0) ;
26         }
27
28       n = 0L ;
29       nr = fscanf(in,"%c",&c) ; /* get first character */
30       while( nr > 0 )           /* stop when no character found */
31         { n = n + 1 ;
32           fprintf(out,"%c",c);  /* output the character */
33           nr = fscanf(in,"%c",&c) ; /* get next character */
34         }
35       fclose(in);               /* close both files */
36       fclose(out);
37       printf(" %ld characters copied",n) ;
38     }
```

Like `scanf` and `printf`, `fscanf` and `fprintf` are very versatile. In practice, their use would be more appropriate in more complicated formatting tasks where they can interpret and transform the data.

The file I/O functions we used in Chapter 1 — `getchar`, `putchar`, `scanf` and `printf` — are special cases of the file I/O functions just introduced. Since we use console I/O in almost all programs, the C library provides several shortcuts. The console I/O functions actually use file pointers just like those used in COPYA and COPYB. These file pointers — stdin for keyboard input and stdout for screen output — are defined for us. We do not have to open them before use or close them when we are finished. As a further convenience, the console functions do not require that the file pointer be passed as an argument. getchar and scanf always refer to stdin, whereas putchar and printf refer to stdout.

Copying a File Using read and write Functions

C compiler libraries provide another kind of file I/O functions: *unbuffered file I/O* functions. These functions read and write blocks of data directly, based on the MS-DOS file I/O services. Although unbuffered I/O functions are not part of the ANSI C standard, they are available in Microsoft C, QuickC, and Turbo C.

Unbuffered I/O requires the sequence of operations as for buffered I/O: first files must be opened, then input and output can be performed, and finally the files are closed. Open files are identified by an integer value called a *file handle*. The functions used for unbuffered I/O are different from those used in Figures 2.1 and 2.2, but they are parallel. The following table shows how the functions relate:

Purpose	Buffered I/O Function	Unbuffered I/O Function
Open a file	fopen	open
Input data	getc or fscanf	read
Output data	putc or fprintf	write
Close a file	fclose	close

The COPYC program in Figure 2.3 uses unbuffered functions to copy a file. The open function accepts a mode argument that defines whether the file will be read, written, or both. This argument also specifies whether the file already exists or will be created. The read and write functions can transfer more than one byte; they are normally used to transfer hundreds or thousands of bytes. In the program we transfer 1,024 bytes at a time. (MS-DOS stores data on disks in *sectors* of 512 bytes. Our operations will be somewhat faster if we transfer data in multiples of 512 bytes when it is convenient.) We detect the end of input data when the read function fails to read any data at all.

The read and write functions are simple in purpose; they just transfer data between a file and a data area we specify. We provide a file handle that identifies the file, the address of a data area, and a maximum number of bytes to transfer as arguments. The data area we provided here was an array; its address is just the name of the array. If we used a single variable or a structure as a data area, we would use the address of operator (&) before the name of the variable (&c , for example).

FIGURE 2.3   copyc.c

```
 1      /* copyc.c - copy a file using read/write */
 2      /* for Microsoft C or Turbo C */
 3      /* changes for other compilers indicated */
 4      #include <stdio.h>
 5      #include <sys\types.h>      /* compiler dependent */
 6      #include <sys\stat.h>       /* compiler dependent */
 7      #include <io.h>             /* compiler dependent */
 8      #include <fcntl.h>          /* compiler dependent */
 9      #define READ_SIZE   1024    /* number of bytes to read */
10
11
12      main(argc,argv)
13       int argc ;
14       char *argv[] ;
15       {
16          int    in ,              /* file handle for input */
17                 out ;             /* file handle for output */
18          long n ;
19          char buffer[ READ_SIZE ] ;
20          int nr ;
21
22          if( argc < 3 )           /* check for file names */
23            { printf("USAGE - copyc input-file output-file \n");
24              exit(1);
25            }
26
27          in = open(argv[1],O_RDONLY); /* open input file */
28                                   /* create output file */
29          out = open(argv[2], O_WRONLY | O_CREAT , S_IREAD | S_IWRITE);
30          if( (in < 0) || (out < 0) )   /* files opened successfully? */
31            { printf("can't open a file");
32              exit(2) ;
33            }
34
35          n = 0L ;
36          nr = read(in,buffer,READ_SIZE) ; /* read first block */
37          while( nr > 0 )                  /* stop when no chars found */
38            { n = n + nr ;
39              write(out,buffer,nr);
40              nr = read(in,buffer,READ_SIZE) ; /* read next block */
41            }
42          close(in);                       /* close both files */
43          close(out);
44          printf(" %ld characters copied",n) ;
45       }
```

2.2 File I/O Performance

Comparing Copy Programs

Figure 2.4 shows elapsed times required to copy a single 30,000-byte file with the three copy programs. These times were measured on an 8-MHz IBM AT with a fast hard disk, but similar results would be found for other PC systems. The `read/write`-based copy program is the fastest, with the `getc/putc` version being a bit slower. The `fscanf/fprintf` version is much slower — over four times as long for this test.

FIGURE 2.4   COPY Program's Execution Speeds

Program	Time To Copy 30,000 Bytes (seconds)
COPYA (getc/putc)	4.8
COPYB (fscanf/fprintf)	13.3
COPYC (read/write)	3.1

If the `read/write` version is fastest, what is the point of the other versions? Each set of file I/O functions has a different role to play:

- The `read/write` version transferred 1,024 bytes of data in each operation. It is the fastest way to move such large blocks of data. If we change the program to transfer one byte of data at a time, it takes 122 seconds. `read` and `write` are not intended to transfer single characters efficiently.
- The `getc/putc` functions are nearly as fast as `read` and `write`, but they give us convenient access to characters one at a time. For programs such as the SENTENCE program in Chapter 1 where we need to look at each character individually, these functions offer a practical compromise between execution speed and ease of writing the program.
- The `fscanf` and `fprintf` functions are too slow for simple input and output of characters, but they are very appropriate when we need to interpret a character stream as a number or a character string. Such tasks often involve a small volume of data, and the effort of writing the formatting functions ourselves is too great for the resulting improvement in speed.

We can think of these three levels of file I/O functions in terms of the grocery business:

1. `read` and `write` are like buying groceries wholesale. If you need a thousand loaves and fishes, buy them wholesale and save lots of money. For a single fish, buying wholesale is not practical. `read` and `write` deliver data by the freezerful.
2. `getc` and `putc` are like buying at a supermarket. You pay more per fish, but it is a better way to get the food for tonight's dinner. `getc` and `putc` give you data in meal-sized portions.
3. `fscanf` and `fprintf` are like eating at a seafood restaurant. It is too expensive to do every night, but when you are hungry right now and do not want to cook, the restaurant is convenient. `fscanf` and `fprintf` serve up data in cooked form.

Improving File I/O Performance

The wholesale versus retail analogy provides a clue to improving file I/O performance. At 10 to 30 milliseconds each, file I/O operations are slow compared to executing computer instructions, which take a few microseconds each. However, file I/O operations take almost as much time to transfer a few bytes as to transfer a few thousand bytes. We can often speed up file I/O by making fewer I/O operations with more bytes moved in each operation. For the COPYC program, we can change the READ_SIZE constant to make larger transfers. The COPYA program uses buffered I/O; we need to change the size of the buffer the library functions use for actual file I/O. The `copyd.c` source file in Figure 2.5 uses the standard library function `setvbuf` to assign a file buffer whose size we specify. Lines 34 and 35 assign our buffers to the input and output files after the files are opened and before any I/O operations have been executed. A separate buffer must be supplied for each file; buffers for different files may be different in size. The constant _IOFBF, which specifies full buffering, is defined in the `stdio.h` file as is the function prototype for `setvbuf`.

The arrays `inbuf` and `outbuf` are used as the file buffers. The variable `bsize` holds the buffer size to be used. It is initialized in line 4 to be 1,024 bytes, but lines 23 and 24 get a new buffer-size value from the command line. The `sscanf` library function performs input conversion parallel to that in the `scanf` function, but `sscanf` gets its input from a character string specified as its first argument.

Figure 2.6 lists results copying a 30,000-byte file with COPYC and COPYD for different transfer sizes. Note that the COPYD program has another new element: Lines 26 and 27 open input and output files in *binary mode*. The difference between binary mode and the default text mode is the subject of the next section.

FIGURE 2.5   copyd.c

```
1     /* copyd.c - copy a file with getc/putc - binary mode  */
2     #include <stdio.h>
3
4     int bsize = 1024 ;           /* size for file buffers */
5     char inbuf[ 8192 ] ;         /* buffer for input file */
6     char outbuf[ 8192 ] ;        /* buffer for output file */
7
8
9     main(argc,argv)
10     int argc ;
11     char *argv[] ;
12     {
13         FILE   *in ,             /* file pointer for input file */
14                *out ;            /* file pointer for output file */
15        int c ;
16        long n ;
17
18        if( argc < 3 )            /* check for file names */
19          { printf(" USAGE - copyd input-file output-file \n");
20            exit(1);
21          }
22
23        if( argc > 3 )            /* get buffer size */
24            sscanf(argv[3],"%d",& bsize) ;
25
26         in  = fopen(argv[1],"rb"); /* open input file for reading */
27         out = fopen(argv[2],"wb"); /* open output file for writing */
28                                  /* files opened successfully? */
29        if( (in == NULL) || (out ==NULL) )
30          { printf("can't open a file");
31            exit(10) ;
32          }
33                                  /* assign large buffers for files */
34        if(   (setvbuf(in,  inbuf,  _IOFBF , bsize ) != 0 )
35          && (setvbuf(out, outbuf, _IOFBF , bsize ) != 0 ) )
36            { printf("can't assign file buffer \n") ;
37              exit(20) ;
38            }
39
40        n = 0L ;
41        c = getc(in) ;            /* get first character */
42        while( c != EOF )         /* stop at end of file */
43          { n = n + 1 ;
44            putc(c,out);          /* output the character */
45            c = getc(in) ;        /* get next character */
46          }
47        fclose(in);               /* close both files */
48        fclose(out);
49        printf(" %ld characters copied",n) ;
50     }
51
```

FIGURE 2.6   File I/O Speed and Buffer Size

	Time To Copy 30,000 Bytes (seconds)	
Transfer Size (bytes)	COPYC(read/write)	COPYD(getc/putc)
512	5.3	5.6
1024	3.7	4.0
2048	3.0	3.0
4096	2.6	2.7
8192	2.4	2.4

2.3   Text and Binary Files

As is often the case with computers, there are a few messy details that defy logic but nevertheless must be understood. The C library evolved on the UNIX system, and its functions were defined to fit well with the file I/O services provided by the UNIX operating system. These services (and the conventions used by application programs in the UNIX environment) are somewhat different from those provided by MS-DOS. The means by which MS-DOS C compiler libraries resolve these differences is the subject of this section. We must start by identifying how UNIX and MS-DOS file-handling services differ.

UNIX keeps track of file sizes to the byte. UNIX application software and utilities let the operating system tell them when the end of data is reached. Although MS-DOS can also record file sizes to the byte, some application software writes data in fixed-size blocks with a control character (value 26 decimal, called *control-Z*) marking the actual end of data. The marker and any data following it are not treated as part of the file's contents. This convention, inherited from the CP/M operating system, is used only for files composed of character text. These files are often called *ASCII* or *text* files. Files that contain nontext data may contain the control-Z value as part of the data; in such *binary* files the control-Z value is not interpreted as the end of the file's contents.

Thus our first problem is that in the MS-DOS environment, files may be interpreted in two different ways. The choice of these interpretations depends purely on the file's content — neither MS-DOS nor the C library can make the choice automatically. It is up to us to supply explicit choices when we write C programs for the MS-DOS environment.

In the UNIX environment, application programs and utilities expect lines of text to be ended by a single control character (the ASCII line feed character) called *newline* in UNIX and C documentation. In the MS-DOS environment, a two-character sequence (carriage return followed by line feed) marks the end of each line in text files.

To make it easy to use existing C programs, MS-DOS C compilers provide automatic conversion between the end-of-line sequences expected by existing C programs and those normal in the MS-DOS environment. Such conversions make sense only for files composed of lines of text. As with the end-of-file convention, the programmer must make an explicit choice.

For buffered I/O functions, we can specify text or binary mode when the file is opened with `fopen`. To specify binary mode, we append the letter b to the file mode string passed to `fopen` (`"rb"` for example). Text mode is the default mode. This method of specifying the file mode is standardized and supported by recent versions of C compilers.

Unbuffered I/O functions are not included in the ANSI C standard; most C compilers provide these functions, but the names of symbolic constants used as function arguments may differ and the names of header files that define them may be different. Fortunately, recent versions of Microsoft C and Turbo C provide similar names for constants and header files. The following code fragment shows how Lines 27 and 29 in Figure 2.5 would be changed to specify binary mode.

```
in = open(argv[1], O_RDONLY | O_BINARY ) ;
...
out = open(argv[2], O_WRONLY | O_CREAT | O_BINARY ,
              S_IREAD | S_IWRITE ) ;
```

Text mode is useful for console I/O and for running C programs from C primers. However, the conversions required for text mode slow down file I/O and may give invalid results for anything but text files. Binary mode is the better choice for most serious C programs.

2.4   Bit Operations: Cleaning Up Word Processor Files

Many word processing programs store documents in a format similar to that of normal ASCII text files. However, the differences in format often make DOS utilities such as the TYPE and PRINT commands useless on these document files. The CLEAN program shown in Figure 2.7 reads a document file and writes a cleaned-up version acceptable as an ASCII text file. CLEAN fixes the major problems with document files created with the WordStar program. The manual page in Figure 2.8 documents use of CLEAN. We will use this *manual page* documentation for both programs and for functions that are reusable tools.

FIGURE 2.7   clean.c

```
 1     /* clean.c - strip high-order bits and control chars from file */
 2     #include "stdio.h"
 3
 4
 5     main(argc,argv)
 6      int argc ;                    /* number of command-line words */
 7      char *argv[] ;                /* pointers to each word */
 8      {
 9        int c ;
10        FILE *in ;                  /* use this file for input */
11        FILE *out ;                 /* use this file for output */
12        long nin , nout ;           /* counts of chars in and out */
13
14        if( argc < 3 )        /* has command line enough words? */
15           { printf(" USAGE - clean input-file output-file \n");
16             exit(1) ;
17           }
18
19        in = fopen(argv[1],"r") ; /* open input file */
20        if( in == NULL )
21           { printf(" can't open input file - %s \n",argv[1]);
22             exit(2) ;
23           }
24
25        out = fopen(argv[2],"w") ; /* open output file */
26        if( out == NULL )
27           { printf(" can't open output file - %s \n",argv[2]);
28             exit(3) ;
29           }
30
31        nin = 0 ;
32        nout = 0 ;
33        c = getc(in) ;
34        while( c != EOF )         /* get chars until end reached */
35           { nin = nin + 1 ;
36             c = c & 127 ;        /* strip high-order bit */
37             /* now see if it is a non-control char */
38             /* or Carriage Return , Line Feed, Tab or Form Feed */
39             if(   ( (c >= ' ') && (c <= '~') )  || (c == '\n')
40                || (c == '\r') || (c == '\t') || (c == '\f') )
41                { nout = nout + 1 ;  /* good char - output it */
42                  putc(c,out) ;
43                }
44             c = getc(in) ;
45           }
46        fclose(in) ;
47        fclose(out) ;
48        printf(" %10ld characters read \n",nin) ;
49        printf(" %10ld characters written \n",nout) ;
50      }
```

FIGURE 2.8   **CLEAN Program Description**

Name
CLEAN   make text file from WordStar document file

Usage
From DOS, type CLEAN and the names of input and output files.

```
C>CLEAN input-file-name   output-file-name
```

Function
CLEAN reads the input file specified on the command line and transforms it into an ASCII text file. As the input file is read, the high-order bit in each character is set to zero, ensuring that all characters have values from 0 through 127.

Printable ASCII characters are copied without change to the output file as are the control characters, carriage return, line feed, tab, and form feed. Other control characters are discarded.

Notes
CLEAN uses a simple-minded approach not based on detailed understanding of the structure of word processor formatting information in the input file. CLEAN provides a quick and dirty way to get a printable text file from a word processor document file.

CLEAN fixes two problems. First, normal ASCII characters are represented by values from 0 through 127. This requires 7 bits in an 8-bit byte. The eighth bit is set equal to 0 for normal ASCII text. WordStar sets this bit to 1 in some characters to mark formatting information. For example, the last character in each word has this bit set equal to 1. When a DOS utility such as TYPE processes such characters, they appear as special graphic symbols. Here is a table of normal ASCII values versus these special character values:

	Bit Number							
	7	6	5	4	3	2	1	0
Normal ASCII	0	x	x	x	x	x	x	x
Special Characters	1	x	x	x	x	x	x	x

An x denotes a bit value that depends on the character stored. Our program must replace the 1 in bit 7 with a 0 to make such characters acceptable to DOS utilities. Bit

7 is the most significant bit in the character. We refer to it as the *high-order bit*. Since it corresponds to the parity bit used in asynchronous transmission, it is sometimes called the *parity bit*.

Second, the document file may contain ASCII control characters that convey special formatting information. For example, WordStar uses a Control-B character (value 2) to mark the beginning and end of boldface emphasis. CLEAN removes all control characters except carriage return, line feed, tab, and form feed characters.

The overall structure of the CLEAN program in Figure 2.7 is similar to that of the COPYA program in Figure 2.1. We use the same library functions, getc, putc, and fclose, for file I/O. As each character is read with getc, we perform two operations on it. In line 36 of Figure 2.7 we set the high-order bit to 0. Then we check the character to see if it should be written out. We compare it to the acceptable control characters and check it against the lowest and highest noncontrol characters. Characters that pass this check are written with putc. At the end of the program, we display counts of characters read and written. These counts may not be vital information, but displaying them gives some confirmation that the program ran and processed about the right number of characters.

Line 36 contains new ideas and deserves a full explanation. We have already explained what we want to do, but how does this statement accomplish it? The & operator combines its left and right operands bit by bit to form a result. The value of bit 0 in the result depends only on the values of bit 0 in the two operands, not on the values of bits 1–7. The rule that the & operator uses is simple: If a bit is 1 in both operands, it is 1 in the result. Otherwise, the bit is 0 in the result. Here is an example:

	Bit Number							
	7	*6*	*5*	*4*	*3*	*2*	*1*	*0*
Left Operand	0	0	1	1	1	1	0	0
Right Operand	0	1	0	1	0	1	0	1
Result	0	0	0	1	0	1	0	0

In line 36, the right operand for & is the constant 127. The individual bits in the number 127 are as follows:

	Bit Number							
Value	*7*	*6*	*5*	*4*	*3*	*2*	*1*	*0*
127	0	1	1	1	1	1	1	1

When we combine the character c just read with 127, the result is as follows:

| | Bit Number | | | | | | | |
	7	6	5	4	3	2	1	0
Character c	x	x	x	x	x	x	x	x
Constant 127	0	1	1	1	1	1	1	1
Result	0	x	x	x	x	x	x	x

Since bit 7 in the constant 127 is 0, bit 7 in the result must be 0 no matter what the value of bit 7 is in c. Bits 0 through 6 of 127 are 1, so those bits in the result depend on the corresponding bits in c. The values of bits 0 through 6 in the result will reproduce those bits in c. We store the result back in c. So the effect of this statement is to set bit 7 to 0, leaving the other bits unchanged.

The comparisons in lines 39 and 40 use the escape notation for the control character constants. We have already seen the newline (\n), tab (\t), and carriage return (\r) characters. The form feed character (\f) causes a printer to start a new page.

2.5   Hexadecimal Notation

The number 127 that we used in the CLEAN program produces the right results, but it looks mysterious at first glance. *Hexadecimal* notation (hex) often makes more sense in bit-level operations. Each hexadecimal digit represents a value between 0 and 15; to display these values we use the letters A through F for values 10 through 15. The advantage of hexadecimal is that each hexadecimal digit corresponds to four bits.

C interprets numbers as hexadecimal constants when they begin with 0x (or 0X). Either uppercase or lowercase letters may be used for the digits A through F. The constant 127 has the value 0x7f in hexadecimal notation. The relation between hex digits and bits is shown in the following diagram:

| | Bit Number | | | | | | | |
	7	6	5	4	3	2	1	0
127	0	1	1	1	1	1	1	1
Hex Digit			7				f	

As an example of the usefulness of hexadecimal, the following table shows the result of line 36 in the CLEAN program for different character values:

Character Value In				Character Value Out		
Decimal		Hexadecimal		Decimal		Hexadecimal
13	or	0D	gives	13	or	0D
141		8D		13		0D
10		0A		10		0A
138		8A		10		0A
32		20		32		20
160		A0		32		20
97		61		97		61
225		E1		97		61

Each pair of rows shows the result for characters with bit 7 equal to 0 and equal to 1. In hexadecimal notation, the numbers show that the lower four bits are unchanged. A more careful examination would be needed to see that only bit 7 was affected. But in decimal notation, there is no obvious relationship at all.

2.6   More Bit Operations and Macros

In addition to the *bitwise AND* operator (&) used in the CLEAN program, C has several other bit-level operators. The ones that we will be using are the *bitwise OR* operator (|), the *bitwise Exclusive OR* or XOR operator (^), and the *not* Operator (~). Like the bitwise AND operator, the | and ^ operators require two operands. The NOT operator (~) (called the one's complement operator in K&R) requires only one operand. Here are word and tabular definitions of what these operators do:

Bitwise OR: Operates in a bit-by-bit manner. If either or both operands have a 1 value for a bit, the corresponding bit is set to 1 in the result. A bit in the result is 0 only if the corresponding bits in both operands are 0.

Bitwise Exclusive OR: Operates in a bit-by-bit manner. Result bits are 0 when both operand bits are 0 or both bits are 1. Result bits are 1 when one operand has a 1 bit and the other has a 0 bit.

Cases	Left Operand	Right Operand	OR Result	AND Result	XOR Result
Both zero	0	0	0	0	0
Zero / One	0	1	1	0	1
One / Zero	1	0	1	0	1
One / One	1	1	1	1	0

Bitwise Not: Operates in a bit-by-bit manner on a single operand. A result bit is 0 when the operand bit is 1 and is 1 when the operand bit is 0.

Cases	Operand	Result
Zero	0	1
One	1	0

C also provides operators to shift bits right and left within a value. These operators are sometimes useful when several data values are packed within one byte or integer value. We will discuss them later when they are used.

Practical Uses of Bit Operations

Bit operations are often difficult to understand even for fairly experienced programmers. They do have practical uses and understanding these uses may help you to accept bit operations. This section illustrates a few uses and shows how to hide the messy details.

The CLEAN program showed one common use of bit operations: forcing the high-order bit of a character to be 0. This task and the related one of testing to see if the high-order bit is 0 are needed in many character-handling programs. We can use the #define statement to define a *macro* for this operation:

```
#define toascii(a)   ( (a) & 0x7f )
```

We follow the macro's name toascii by parentheses with parameters inside. When we use this macro, the parameter a in the definition will be replaced by whatever we place inside the parentheses. These examples should show how the macro works:

```
toascii(c)              means       ( (c) & 0x7f )

toascii( buf[i+1] )     means       ( (buf[i+1]) & 0x7f )
```

In the same way, we can define the macro isascii to test whether the high-order bit of a character is 0:

```
#define isascii(a)    ( ((a) & 0x80) == 0 )
```

In both these macros we used parentheses liberally. This ensures that the macro will work as intended when the parameter is a complicated expression or when the macro is embedded in a complicated expression. Since we will not be looking at the *expansion* of the macro, the extra parentheses do not have any real disadvantages.

C does not specify whether character values are to be treated as signed or unsigned values when they are converted to integers. Some compilers treat characters as values from −127 through +127, whereas others view characters as numbers from 0 through 255. When we use a character value as a numeric value in a program, this difference in representation can introduce subtle bugs. It is often convenient to force a character value to have a positive value. For example, when we use a character value as a subscript, it must be a positive value.

When a character value appears in a C expression, it is converted to an integer value before use. It is that conversion which we must understand and control. On the IBM PC positive and negative integers are represented in memory as follows:

	Bit Number															
	15	14	13	12	11	10	9	8	7	6	5	4	3	2	1	0
Positive	0	x	x	x	x	x	x	x	x	x	x	x	x	x	x	x
Negative	1	x	x	x	x	x	x	x	x	x	x	x	x	x	x	x

where x indicates that the value of the bit depends on the particular number represented. Characters are stored in single 8-bit bytes. The following table shows how characters are converted to integers for both positive values:

	Bit Number															
	15	14	13	12	11	10	9	8	7	6	5	4	3	2	1	0
Character as signed value																
Positive	0	0	0	0	0	0	0	0	0	x	x	x	x	x	x	x
Negative	1	1	1	1	1	1	1	1	1	x	x	x	x	x	x	x
Character as unsigned value																
	0	0	0	0	0	0	0	0	x	x	x	x	x	x	x	x

If we want a character value to yield a positive number, we must defeat the effect of sign extension. We want to leave the low-order 8 bits unchanged and force higher bits to be zero. A bitwise AND operation with the constant 0xff as one operand and the character value as the other operand accomplishes this result. For example, using the character variable s[i]

```
s[i] & 0xff
```

Since the constant 0xff has 1 as the value for its lowest eight bits and 0s for all higher bits, the result will have bits 0 through 7 unchanged from the variable s[i]. But all higher bits (including the sign bit) will be zero. We can define a macro for this operation:

```
#define tochar(a)    ( (a) & 0xff )
```

This macro works whether our compiler interprets the character type `char` as signed or unsigned. However, if the `char` type is unsigned, we can make the macro more efficient:

```
#define tochar(a)      (a)
```

Sometimes individual bits in a variable are used to store separate yes/no values. Such *flag bits* are often used by operating systems, and if we use operating system services directly, we need to manipulate such flag bits. These operations must check or change the value of a single bit in a variable independent of the other bits in a word.

Hexadecimal notation is useful for defining constants with single bits equal to 1. The following table gives some examples:

Bit Equal to 1	Constant Value
0	0x01
1	0x02
2	0x04
3	0x08
4	0x10
5	0x20
6	0x40
7	0x80

The symbolic constants O_RDONLY, O_WRONLY, and O_CREATE used in Figure 2.3 to specify read or write access in opening a file were flag bits. We used the bitwise OR operator to set several flag bits in one value. These symbolic constants are defined by the `fcntl.h` header file. We need not know which bits specify which option.

Setting a bit (to 1), clearing a bit (setting it to 0), and testing the value of a bit are operations we need. Here are some examples:

```
Setting bit 7      c = c | 0x80 ;
Clearing bit 0     c = c ^ 0x01 ;
Testing bit 6      if( (c & 0x40) == 0 ) ...
```

2.7   Controlling the Order of Evaluation: Operator Precedence

What happens when several operators appear in a single C statement? What rules does C use to specify the order in which the operations are carried out? First, operators are assigned a precedence level so that high-precedence operators are evaluated before lower level operators. Several operators may share the same precedence level; as a tie-breaking rule, a fixed order of evaluation is defined for groups of operators at the same level. (This order is left to right for some operators and right to left for other operators.)

In all, there are fifteen precedence levels. Twelve of these levels group left to right, and three group right to left. Most books on C discuss the operator precedence table and the grouping rules adequately. However, since we think the rules are too complicated to remember reliably, we provide a simpler approach. The following six-level table shows our precedence rules (highest precedence first):

Type of Operator	Operators at This Level	Purpose of operators
1. Primary expression	`a[1]`	Subscript
	`sortn()`	Function call
	`st.grade`	Structure member
	`p->grade`	Pointer reference to structure member
2. Unary operators	`+  -`	Unary plus, minus
	`!  ~`	Negation, one's complement
	`*  &`	Indirection, address of
	`sizeof`	Size of data type
	`++  --`	Increment, decrement
3. Binary operators (multiplicative)	`*  /  %`	Multiplication and division
4. Binary operators (other than multiplicative)	`+  -  <<  >>`	Add, subtract, shift
	`<  <=  >  >=`	Comparison
	`==  !=`	Equality
	`&  ^  |`	Bitwise
	`&&  ||`	Logical
	`?  :`	Conditional operator
5. Assignment Operators	`=  +=  -=` ,etc.	Assignment
6. Comma Operator	`,`	

We have listed all of C's operators in the table for completeness. Some operators not mentioned so far are discussed when they are used; others are discussed in Chapter 10 in connection with optimization. A few are not used in this book (the comma operator, for example).

We need some additional rules to make our simplified precedence table work correctly:

- Use parentheses whenever the simplified precedence table does not define the result completely.
- Primary expressions group left to right: thus, `s[i].name[j]` is equivalent to `(s[i]).name[j]`. For other precedence levels we do not rely on grouping rules.

- Avoid side effects that depend on the order of evaluation. Do not use the value of a variable in the same statement where its value is changed.
- Use parentheses whenever the simplified precedence table does not define the result completely.
- Test everything before using it. Rely on your knowledge of C when you write programs but not when you test them.

We cannot change the way C works, but we can simplify the way we use its features.

2.8 Using C Data Types

The programs presented so far have used `char`, `integer`, `long`, and `float` data types. C provides other data types as well. Using C data types in a clear and safe manner is an essential part of writing good programs. This section presents some rules for using data types.

Declare the Right Data Type

Function prototypes tell the compiler the data types of the function input arguments and of the function's return value. Without that information, the compiler may assume that the wrong data type is used. Such an error can be very difficult to find. It may not show up until a different set of compilation options or a different compiler is used. For example, a common error is to fail to declare the prototype for a function that returns a pointer value. The compiler would assume that the function returned an integer value. The program would work correctly for a memory model for which integers and pointers are the same size. However, the program would work incorrectly when compiled with a memory model for which integers and pointers are different in size.

We can make similar mistakes when we declare and use variables. In the past, C programmers declared variables as integers even when they held unsigned data and were always interpreted in that way. Whenever possible, declare functions and variables with data types that reflect their actual use.

Control Type Conversions

When we mix data types in an expression, C provides automatic conversion. The rules for these conversions are good ones, but it is up to us to ensure that the result is what we want. We must be aware of the conversions that are implied in our programs. When those automatic conversions are not satisfactory, we can specify an explicit conversion with the *cast* operator:

(new-type) value-to-be converted

Whenever possible, conversions preserve the value of the expression. For example, when an integer type is converted to a long type, its value is unchanged. But, in some cases, a value cannot be preserved. When an integer value is converted to char type (as when it is assigned to a character variable), the value is truncated to the low-order 8 bits. When an integer type is converted to the unsigned type, the bit pattern is unchanged. Positive integers are unchanged, but negative integers will be interpreted as positive unsigned values with the same bit pattern.

Localize Data Type Choices

The C language does not specify how data types will be represented in memory or the range of values they can accommodate. Each C compiler can implement data types to be efficient for that computer architecture. C does specify ranges of values that each data type must represent as a minimum requirement. The following table shows those ranges:

Data Type	Minimum Range of Values
char	−128 through 127 or 0 through 255
signed char	−128 through 127
unsigned char	0 through 255
int	−32767 through 32767
(also short)	
unsigned	0 through 65535
(also short unsigned)	
long	−2,147,483,647 through 2,147,483,647
unsigned long	0 through 4,294,967,295
float	1E−38 through 1E+38
(also double and long double)	

We can use integers for routine purposes where very large numbers are not expected and longs where we expect large numbers. However, we sometimes need to be able to select data types that will be efficient in use of memory and in execution speed. We do not want to make our programs specific to one compiler. For example, in one environment, an integer variable might be large enough to represent the values we need. In another environment, a long variable might be needed. We cannot solve this problem completely, but we can make it manageable. We can define our own data types with the typedef statement and refer to those data types throughout the rest of our program. The following fragment illustrates the use of typedef statements:

```
typedef   int   line_counter ;
...
line_counter lc ;
```

Sometimes it is important that we control the way in which a variable is represented. For example, when we use operating system services, we must use 16-bit values where the operating system expects them. We can use the `typedef` statement to define data types `INT16`, `INT32`, `WORD16`, and `WORD32` for use when the exact size of a variable is important. For the Microsoft and Turbo C compilers in the MS-DOS environment, the following definitions are appropriate:

```
typedef int INT16 ;
typedef long INT32 ;
typedef unsigned WORD16 ;
typedef unsigned long WORD32 ;
```

Use the void Data Type

The `void` data type does not specify an actual data type, but it is useful for writing safe C programs. It has special meanings in function declarations, function prototypes, and in pointer definitions:

```
void  fun1() ;          /* fun1 does not return a value */
int   fun2(void) ;      /* fun2 does not expect input arguments */
void *fun3() ;          /* fun3 returns a generic pointer */
void *p ;               /* p is a generic pointer */
```

A generic pointer value does not point to any data type. However, we can convert back and forth between a generic pointer and another pointer type without changing the pointer's value. Generic pointers are useful for storing the address of a memory area whose data type is not known.

Use Pointers Carefully

Pointers have data types, too. A pointer to an integer is a different type from a pointer to a character. C does not specify whether pointers to different data types have the same representation in memory. The cast operator should be used to convert the pointer type when a pointer is used to reference data of a different type.

C allows arithmetic on pointer values, but that arithmetic has a special meaning. Adding 1 to a pointer produces a pointer to the next object of the same data type. The following examples show the effect of adding 1 for pointers to character, integer, and long data:

```
char *pc ;          /* suppose pc is 1000 */
int  *pi ;          /* suppose pi is 2000 */
long *pl ;          /* suppose pl is 3000 */
pc+1    is   1001
pi+1    is   2002
pl+1    is   3004
```

These examples assume that integers require 2 bytes of memory and long values require 4 bytes, as is the case for Microsoft C and Turbo C in the IBM PC MS-DOS environment.

2.9 Types of Storage: Scope and Duration

C allows us to select the data type of each variable to be appropriate to its use. We can also specify how widely a variable may be used in a program (its *scope*) and for how long the variable endures (its *duration*). We have ignored those characteristics in explaining previous examples, but we will explain them now.

The NOTABS program in Figure 1.18 illustrates C rules for scope. The variable c was defined within the main function. It was only defined for use inside that function. If we referred to c in the do_it function the compiler would describe c as an undefined variable. Variables defined within a function are visible to the compiler only within that function. Variables defined outside a function are visible from the point of definition to the end of the source file. In Figure 1.18, the variable col was declared outside any function so that it may be used in both main and do_it to keep track of the current column number.

The revised NOTABS program in Figures 2.9 and 2.10 shows how a variable can be used in more than one source file. Line 6 of Figure 2.9 defines the variable ts outside any function. Line 4 of Figure 2.10 declares ts in a second source file. The keyword extern informs the compiler that ts is defined elsewhere. We will refer to variables like ts, which are visible in more than one source file, as *public* or *global* variables. Public variables should be defined in a single source file without the extern keyword. Declarations in all other source files should include the extern keyword.

Line 5 of Figure 2.10 defines the variable col and gives it a starting value of 1. It need not be used in the other source file. The keyword static specifies that col will not be visible in other source files. Variables declared with the static keyword (and automatic variables) are private to a single source file. If the same name is used to declare private variables in several source files, a separate variable is created for each declaration. In a large program, conflicts between names used in different source files is a serious problem. Variables should not be made public unless it is necessary to the logic of the program.

Figures 1.18 and 2.10 also illustrate the concept of duration for variables. An automatic variable is created when the function that defines it is entered. The variable ceases to exist when the function returns to its caller. Variables declared

FIGURE 2.9   notabs2.c

```
1     /* notabs2.c - turn tabs into blanks */
2     #include "stdio.h"
3
4     void do_it( int ) ;           /* function prototype */
5
6     int ts = 8 ;                  /* tab stop interval */
7
8
9     main(argc,argv)
10     int argc ;
11     char *argv[] ;
12     {
13        int c ;
14
15        if( argc > 1 )            /* tab interval on command line? */
16            sscanf(argv[1],"%d",& ts) ;
17
18        while( 1 == 1 )           /* get chars from input */
19          { c = getchar() ;
20            if( c == EOF )        /* until EOF is reached */
21                break ;
22            do_it(c) ;
23          }
24     }
```

FIGURE 2.10   do_it.c

```
1     /* do_it.c - process one char - turn tabs into blanks */
2     #include <stdio.h>
3
4     extern int ts ;               /* tab stop interval */
5     static int col = 1 ;          /* current column position */
6
7
8     void do_it(ch)                /* handle one char */
9      int ch ;                     /* the character */
10     {
11        switch( ch )              /* classify ch */
12          {
13          case '\t' :             /* tab char */
14            do
15              { putchar(' ') ; /*    put out blanks */
16                col = col + 1 ;
17              } while( (col % ts) !=1);/* until we reach a tab stop*/
18            break ;
19          case '\r' :             /* carriage return */
20          case '\n' :             /* or line feed (newline) */
21            putchar( ch) ;        /*    output it */
22            col = 1 ;             /*    back to column 1 */
23            break ;
24          default :               /* any other char - assume printable*/
25            putchar( ch) ;        /*    output it */
26            col = col + 1 ;       /*    advance to next column */
27            break ;
28          }
29     }
```

outside a function are created before the `main` function is entered, and they endure until execution ceases. Variables declared with the `static` or `extern` keyword have this same duration even if they are declared within a function. The variable `col` must retain the current column number between calls to the `do_it` function. In Figure 1.18, `col` was declared outside any function. In Figure 2.10, it is declared with the `static` keyword as well.

Figure 2.11 documents use of the NOTABS2 program.

FIGURE 2.11   NOTABS2 Program Description

Name
NOTABS2   expand tabs in a text file

Usage
From DOS, type NOTABS2, the input file name, and the names of input and output files. Use the DOS input redirection symbol (<) before the input file name and the output redirection symbol (>) before the output file name. The interval between tab stops may also be specified on the command line.

```
C>NOTABS2  <input-file-name   >output-file-name  tab-interval
```

Function
NOTABS2 copies console input to console output, replacing tab characters by a series of one or more blanks. Other characters are copied without change. The default tab stop interval is 8, placing tab stops at columns 1, 9, 17, ... The command line may specify a different tab interval.

Notes
NOTABS2 uses text mode and is intended for use with files made up of ASCII text files.

2.10 Dynamic Allocation: Printing the Last Lines in a File

The storage classes just discussed provide some control over the allocation and release of memory. The C library provides functions for explicit allocation and deallocation of memory by a C program — *dynamic allocation*. The program shown in Figure 2.12 uses these dynamic allocation functions to print the last *n* lines of a file. TAIL reads the input file from `stdin` and writes the last *n* lines to `stdout`. TAIL is normally used with redirected input from a file. Output from TAIL appears on the PC screen unless it is redirected to a file.

Our algorithm for the TAIL program is simple: We provide character arrays for *n* lines of input. The first *n* lines of the file are placed in these arrays; line 1 goes in

FIGURE 2.12   tail.c

```
1      /* tail.c - output last N lines of a file */
2      #include <stdio.h>
3      #include <stdlib.h>
4      #include <string.h>
5      #define MAXL  201            /* allow 200 chars max per line */
6      typedef char * PCHAR ;       /* pointer to char data type */
7      int ntail = 10 ;             /* number of lines to output */
8
9      main(argc,argv)
10      int argc ;
11      char *argv[] ;
12      {
13        long l , nl ;            /* line number and line count */
14        PCHAR pline ;            /* points to a line space */
15        PCHAR *lines ;           /* start of line pointer array */
16
17        if( argc > 1 )           /* get no. tail lines  */
18             sscanf(argv[1],"%d",& ntail) ; /* from command line */
19
20                                 /* allocate line pointer array */
21        lines = (PCHAR *) calloc(ntail, sizeof(PCHAR) ) ;
22        if( lines == NULL )
23          { fprintf(stderr,"can't allocate line array\n");
24            exit(10) ;
25          }
26        for(l=0; l<ntail ; l=l+1) /* allocate space for ntail lines */
27          { lines[l] = (char *) malloc(MAXL) ;
28            if( lines[l] == NULL )
29               { fprintf(stderr,"can't allocate line space\n");
30                 exit(20) ;
31               }
32          }
33
34        nl = 0 ;
35        while( 1 == 1 )           /* read input file and store lines */
36          { pline = lines[ nl % ntail ];/* point to next line space */
37            if( fgets(pline,MAXL-1,stdin) == NULL ) /* get line and */
38               break ;            /*  check for end of file */
39            nl = nl + 1 ;
40          }
41
42        if( nl >= ntail )         /* find start of tail area */
43             l = nl - ntail ;
44        else l = 0 ;
45
46        while( l < nl )           /* output tail lines in order */
47          { pline = lines[ l % ntail ] ;
48            fputs(pline,stdout) ;
49            l = l + 1 ;
50          }
51
52        for(l=0; l<ntail; l=l+1)/* free space for ntail lines */
53          { free( lines[l] ) ; }
54        free(lines) ;            /* free line pointer array */
55      }
```

array 0 and line *n* goes in array *n*−1. With input line *n*+1, we start over using array 0. When we finish reading the input file, the last *n* lines will remain in the *n* arrays.

Line 7 of Figure 2.12 declares the `ntail` variable that will contain the number of lines to be printed and sets the default value of 10 lines. Variables can be initialized when they are declared, but the initializing value must be a constant. Lines 17 and 18 collect the specification of the number of lines to be printed from the command line if it is present.

When we use dynamic allocation, we define pointers to refer to the allocated areas. Declaration of these pointers and their data types can become complicated. Defining data types with `typedef` can reduce this compilation. Line 6 defines the data type `PCHAR` as a pointer to a character. Using the `PCHAR` data type simplifies subsequent pointer declarations. Line 14 defines a variable `pline` of this `PCHAR` type, and line 15 defines a pointer to the `PCHAR` type. Without the `PCHAR` type, these lines and lines 21 and 27 would be more complicated:

```
char *pline ;                                      /* line 14 */
char **lines ;                                     /* line 15 */
lines=(char **) calloc(ntail, sizeof(char *) ) ;   /* line 21 */
pline=(char *) malloc(MAXL) ;                       /* line 27 */
```

The TAIL program works for any value of `ntail` that does not require more memory than is available. We do not want to guess a maximum value when we write the program. If we run the program on different PCs, that maximum value may be different for each PC. Instead we allocate the exact amount of space needed when TAIL is executed. Line 21 allocates space for an array of pointers to the individual character arrays. This shows a common reason for using dynamic allocation: We do not know the size of an array until the program is being executed. Lines 26 to 32 allocate a character array for each line. In this case we know the size of the array when the program is written, but we do not know how many arrays will be needed.

We supply two arguments for the `calloc` function: the number of items required and the size of each. The size of the pointer to characters data type depends on the compiler we use and the memory model we specify. The `sizeof` operator in line 21 provides the size of the specified data type; the `tail.c` source file will be correct for any C compiler and memory model. The `malloc` function in line 27 expects only one argument, the number of bytes to be allocated. The `calloc` and `malloc` functions can be used to allocate objects of any data type. They return a pointer to `char` type; we must convert this return value to the data type we need. The *cast* operators in lines 26 and 33 perform these conversions.

Lines 22 to 25 and 28 to 31 check each allocation request for successful completion. The `malloc` and `calloc` functions indicate allocation failure by returning the `NULL` pointer value. Our programs must check for that value explicitly. We must ensure that subsequent operations do not attempt to store values using a `NULL` pointer.

Lines 35 to 40 read the input file and store each line. The `fgets` function reads each line; it returns a `NULL` value when the end-of-file marker is reached. The `nl` variable counts lines and the expression `nl % ntail` determines the array in which each line is stored. Note that we used an array subscript with the pointer `lines` in line 36. C allows subscripts to be used with pointers; `lines[1]` is equivalent to `lines+1`. Both forms point to the second object of type PCHAR past the one to which `lines` points.

When the entire input file has been read, lines 42 to 44 determine the line number of the first line to be printed. Lines 46 to 50 print the last lines in order using the expression, `l % ntail`, similar to the one in line 36.

Lines 52 to 54 free the character arrays and the array of pointers to those lines. In this short program, this step in not needed since the program is finished. In a larger program, freeing allocated space allows it to be reused for a different purpose.

The TAIL program illustrates the use of dynamic allocation functions and their purpose. They allow the size of an array to be determined when the program is executed. They are also useful when a number of data structures must be allocated and that number cannot be determined until the program is executed. With dynamic allocation, a program can be written to operate successfully in a PC with limited memory but also to make efficient use of all available memory in a PC with more memory. Figure 2.13 documents the use of the TAIL program.

FIGURE 2.13   TAIL program description

Name
TAIL   copy the last lines of a text file

Usage
From DOS, type TAIL, the input file name, and the names of input and output files. Use the DOS input redirection symbol (<) before the input file name and the output redirection symbol (>) before the output file name. The number of lines to be copied may also be specified on the command line.

```
C>TAIL <input-file-name   >output-file-name tab-interval
```

Function
TAIL copies the last lines of the console input to console output. The default is to copy the last 10 lines of the input. A different number of lines may be specified on the command line.

If TAIL cannot allocate enough space for the number of lines specified, an error message is written to the standard error stream and execution ends without copying the input.

Figure 2.13   continues

Figure 2.13   continued

TAIL provides space for a maximum of 200 characters per line. Longer lines will be split and treated as multiple lines.

Notes
TAIL uses text mode file I/O and is intended for use with files made up of ASCII text files only.

2.11 Using Header Files

The `cminor.h` header file in Figure 2.14 contains the data types and macros defined in this chapter. We could copy those definitions in any program where they are needed. Placing them in a header file is more convenient and avoids the risk of typing them incorrectly. As we develop more programs in later chapters, we will define more header files. Systematic use of header files is part of good C programming as is the use of multiple source files and separate compilation.

FIGURE 2.14   cminor.h

```
1    /* cminor.h - enhancements to C syntax */
2
3
4    /* use the following when the compiler treats char as signed */
5    #define tochar(c)   ( (c) & 0xff )
6
7    /* use the following  when char is treated as unsigned   */
8    /* #define tochar(c)   c      */
9
10
11   /* toascii - strip parity bit from a char value */
12   #define toascii(c)  ( (c) & 0x7f )
13
14   /* test a char to see whether the high order bit is zero */
15   #define isascii(c)  ( ((c) & 0x80) == 0 )
16
17   /* test a char to see if it is printable (ASCII graphic) */
18   #define isgraphic(c)   ( ((c) >= ' ') && ((c) <= '~') )
19
20
21   /* fixed size portable data types */
22   /* define with both upper and lower case */
23   typedef int          int16 ;   /* signed 16 bit integer */
24   typedef int          INT16 ;   /* signed 16 bit integer */
25   typedef long         int32 ;   /* signed 32 bit integer */
26   typedef long         INT32 ;   /* signed 32 bit integer */
27   typedef unsigned     word16 ;  /* unsigned 16 bit number */
28   typedef unsigned     WORD16 ;  /* unsigned 16 bit number */
29   typedef unsigned long word32 ; /* unsigned 32 bit number */
30   typedef unsigned long WORD32 ; /* unsigned 32 bit number */
31
```

2.12 Summary

Chapter 2 discussed more advanced features of C than those in Chapter 1: file I/O, bit operations, storage classes, and dynamic allocation. It also tailored C to make it easier to use and more portable. We have been laying a foundation for reading, understanding, and modifying real C programs. The rest of the book is devoted to presenting such programs. Each program will be accompanied by an explanation of what the program does. You should use this description to understand how individual C statements do their job. If you find parts of these programs hard to understand, refer back to Chapters 1 and 2 for easier examples. You should also use a C primer for more detailed explanations of C features.

3
Viewing ASCII Files

This chapter follows the development of a single program from its specification through completion. The program is larger than those in Chapters 1 and 2, and it is the first program intended to perform a useful function rather than just be an appropriate example. Since this is the first real application to be presented, this chapter discusses the development process from beginning through end. Defining the functional specifications for the program, writing pseudo-code, testing the individual parts of the program, and measuring its performance are topics discussed in this chapter.

The program we develop in this chapter, VIEW, is a tool for browsing through text files. It displays a screenful of text at a time and then waits for an input command. Keyboard commands let us navigate about in the file at will. VIEW gives us a way to look at long text files without waiting for a printed listing or wasting paper.

3.1 Specifying the VIEW Program

Before we can design the VIEW program, we need a thorough description of its function. Sometimes we do not know everything about the program's function at this point. For example, we may not know the best form for input commands or output formats. It is still worthwhile to specify what we can and to outline the parts that cannot be specified. It is always easier to produce programs to meet a specification than to develop the specifications as we write the program.

We will start with an informal discussion of what VIEW should do. When we have a good description of its functions, we can write a formal manual page to document its specifications.

VIEW should display one screenful of text and stop automatically. It should then wait for a command describing what it should do next. It should never write so much data that part of it scrolls off the screen.

VIEW should provide commands for movement in the file in big and little steps: by lines of text, whole screenfuls, or all the way to the beginning or end of the file. We would like to use VIEW as a window into the file — a window that we can move through the file at will. Moving backward should be as easy and as well supported as moving forward.

We want to use familiar commands in VIEW. Since many other programs on the IBM PC use cursor control keys for movement in a file, we would like to use them here. In addition, we want to specify commands by pressing a single key. Pressing return after each command should not be necessary.

We may not use VIEW very often. We would like to reduce the effort of remembering how to use it by displaying a list of commands (and the keys to press) on the screen.

We should be able to use VIEW to examine not only text files but also files made by word processors. VIEW will use the same techniques that we developed for the CLEAN program; it will ignore the setting of the high-order bit in a character. Most control characters other than tab and newline will be ignored.

Figure 3.1 documents these requirements in a manual page description. As the manual page shows, cursor movement and other commands are consistent with usage in popular application programs. The display format follows the guidelines just discussed; it should describe where you are and what you can do next.

FIGURE 3.1   VIEW Program Description

Name
VIEW   displays a text file a screenful at a time

Usage
From DOS, type VIEW and the name of file to be viewed:

```
C>VIEW  file-name
```

If you do not specify a file name, VIEW will prompt for a file name.

Function
VIEW displays a text file on the screen. On entry VIEW displays the first screenful in the file and waits for a command. Single key commands provide movement in the file by single lines or pages. Commands for movement to the beginning and end of the file are also supported.

The high-order bit of characters in the text file is ignored. Control characters other than line feed and tab are ignored when the file is displayed. A control-Z character in the last 128-byte block of the file is interpreted as the effective end of data.

Commands
Inside the VIEW program the following list of single key commands (you don't need to press the return key) are recognized:

Figure 3.1   continues

Figure 3.1   continued

```
HOME            - displays the first page in the file.
END             - displays the last page in the file.
PgUp            - moves backward in the file almost one page.
PgDn            - moves forward in the file almost one page.
Down Arrow   - moves forward in the file by one line.
Up Arrow     - moves backward in the file by one line.
Space Bar    - moves to a position you specify.
Escape       - ends the program and returns to DOS.
```

The program displays three areas on the screen: a heading, the text itself (16 lines), and a prompt describing the input commands.

```
FILE - sample.txt    POSITION - 0    FILE SIZE - 750
------------------------------------------------------------
first line of the page.
  .
  .
  .
16-th line of the page.
------------------------------------------------------------
Type one of these Input Commands
HOME = First Page    ↑  = Prev. Line    PG UP = Prev. Page
END  = Last  Page    ↓  = Next Line     PG DN = Next  Page
Esc  = Exit Pgm    Space = Move to Position
```

Limitations
VIEW handles long lines poorly.

3.2   Pseudo-Code for VIEW

We have specified what the program as a whole is to do. Now we need to elaborate, describing how the program will work in increasing levels of detail. We use a pseudo-code language to describe the operation of the VIEW program. We delay writing any C statements until we have broken the problem into many small parts and described the functions of each. We do not consider exception conditions or fine points yet but just focus on the normal function of the program.

Overall Structure

The program must perform this sequence of steps:

Find out the name of the file to be used.
Display the first page of the file.
Get an input command.
Execute that command.

Get another input command (not an exit program command).
Execute it.

.

.

.

Get another input command (exit program command).
Exit to the operating system.

The program is controlled by input from the keyboard. Our pseudo-code will make that control explicit in its structure. The program repeats the steps "get an input command" and "execute that command" indefinitely. Our pseudo-code will contain a loop control structure to reflect the function required. The pseudo-code representing the overall program is as follows:

```
view program—overall function
      get file name
      display the first page of the file
      repeat until an exit command is received
            display a prompt describing input commands
            get the next input command
            execute the command
      close the file
end
```

Some of the individual steps are still vague, so we will describe them in more detail. The order in which the steps are described is somewhat different from their order of appearance in the overall pseudo-code. Some of the steps can be written down without further explanation:

```
get_the_file_name
      get a file name from the command line
      if( a file name not specified on the command line )
            prompt for the file name
            get a file name from the keyboard
end

get_next_input_command
      get the command from keyboard input
      classify it
end
```

Executing the Input Command

Executing the input command requires a more detailed description. Seven commands are defined; we describe the process by a large `switch` statement with a separate case for each input command. Although there may be some steps in common, this will keep the pseudo-code understandable.

```
execute_input_command
    switch( input command )
        {
        case Next Page :
            move forward almost a full page
            display the page
        case Previous Page :
            move backward almost a full page
            display the page
        case First Page :
            move to beginning of file
            display the page
        case Last Page :
            move to end of the file
            move backward a full page
            display the page
        case Move To Position :
            move to specified position in file
            move backward to beginning of line
            display the page
        case Previous Line :
            move backward one line
            display the page
        case Next Line :
            move forward one line
            display the page
        case Exit Program :
            no action needed
        } /* end of switch statement */

end
```

The move_forward and move_backward functions need more detail as does the display_page function.

Moving Forward/Backward

The move_forward function moves forward in the file, reading characters until it has found the beginning of the nth line after the current line. The new position is at the beginning of this line.

```
move_forward(n lines)
     start at the top of the current page
     get the next char from the file
     repeat until the nth end-of-line is found
          get the next char from the file
     position after the last end-of-line found
end
```

The move_backward function is similar, but it must skip over the end-of-line marker at the beginning of the current line. The final position is at the beginning of the nth preceding line.

```
move_backward(n lines)
     start at the top of the current page
     find the beginning of the current line
     get the previous char from the file
     repeat until the nth end-of-line is found )
          get the previous char from the file
     position after the last end-of-line found
end
```

The following diagrams may clarify these functions.

move_forward 2 lines

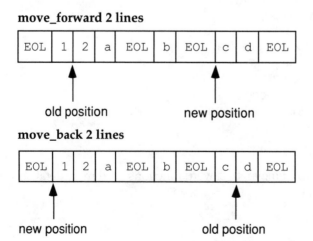

Displaying a Page of Text

Our design displays the entire page of text no matter what the input command is. For the previous line and next line commands, only part of the screen need be updated. We do not use shortcuts for these commands because we have to display an entire new page for some commands. If we use the same function for all commands, we save the effort of writing functions for the special cases. Our approach is very flexible; new commands can be added without writing special display functions for them.

Our version of VIEW is a starting point. It is better strategy to implement it in a quick and simple way. Then our experience with it can guide enhancements. The pseudo-code itself is straightforward at this level of detail:

```
display_page
     write heading — file name, position in file, file size
     start at the top of the display page
     repeat until a page has been displayed
          get next char from the file
          display a char
end


display_a_char
     if( char is a graphic ASCII char )
          display it
     else if( char is an end of line marker )
          display a newline char
     else if( char is tab char )
          display a space char
          repeat until we reach a tab stop
               display a space char
     else ignore other control character
end
```

Important Constants and Data

The most important data used by VIEW is the text file itself. In addition, however, VIEW needs the file's name, the location of the display page in the file, and the size of the file. We also need to store the type of input command requested and to define constants for the valid input commands. Other information may be needed in the implementation of VIEW, but we can see the need for this data from the pseudo-code alone.

In this case, it seemed natural to outline the program's logic and let the data required be defined by the logic. In other programs, the data required may be a better starting point.

Exception Conditions

We ignored exceptions and error conditions in the pseudo-code, which allowed us to concentrate on the basic structure of the VIEW program. Now we have a framework for identifying some exceptions that VIEW must accommodate.

First, we may reach the end of the file while we are moving forward in the file or while displaying a page of text . The move_forward function must stop on reaching the end of the file even if the requested number of lines has not been skipped. The display_page function must fill out the page with blank lines if the end of the file is reached before a full page is displayed.

Second, we may reach the start of the file while moving backward in the file. The move_backward function must handle this exception by stopping early.

Third, the file may contain lines of text that are too long to fit on one line of the display screen. We will handle long lines by wrapping them around onto another screen line. The display_page function must allow for such long lines in sensing when a full page has been written. In our first version of the VIEW program, we will allow the move_forward and move_backward functions to count lines of text, not lines on the screen. This may produce larger movements than we would like on files with many long lines.

Fourth, keyboard input — a file name, input commands, or a new file position — may be invalid. All input must be fully checked. After invalid input, a warning message should be displayed and new input accepted.

Finally, we may not be able to read the file because of a faulty diskette or a hardware problem. We rely on the default critical error handling provided by DOS for now.

We will leave the pseudo-code simple and uncluttered, but we must remember these exceptions and ensure that the VIEW program does handle them. We have used the pseudo-code as a design tool. For that purpose we glossed over details that must be addressed in the actual program. Pseudo-code is also useful in the implementation stage. There we include much more detail in the pseudo-code. It is important to keep these stages separated; until the big picture is understood, the details can be confusing.

3.3 Implementing VIEW

The next job is to translate the pseudo-code into a C program that can be executed. Much of this work is now straightforward and can be done immediately. However, we may not know how to implement some functions in C. Thus we need a combination of research and experiment. The research into the facilities provided by C and our operating system will supply ideas. A short experimental program helps to verify that we understand the facility we want to use.

It may seem inefficient to detour from our objective to write an experimental program, but it often shortens the time to get a working program. It is frequently difficult and time consuming to understand what a new facility does when it is in the middle of a program that you are trying to test.

Reading a File

Before we can write the VIEW program, we need to find out how to read the file and to discover the typical structure of a file. We have these requirements:

- We want to get a single character at a time.
- We want to read characters from the file moving backward as well as moving forward (the normal case.)
- We must be able to change position within the file. We do not want to be restricted to reading the file sequentially.
- We want to get characters from the file without any translation by the operating system or by the file I/O functions we use.

The buffered I/O functions discussed in Chapter 2 meet most of these requirements. The fopen function provides a portable way to open the file, and fclose closes the file when we are finished. The getc function reads the next character from the file. Reading a character with getc advances our position in the file so that the next call to getc will read the following character. The fseek function, not discussed in Chapter 2, allows us to change our position in the file. The new position can be specified relative to the beginning of the file, the end of the file, or the current position in the file. Another function, ftell, gives us the current position in the file.

At first glance, text mode appears to fit our requirements. We need to recognize a control-Z as the effective end of the file, and text mode provides this. But the translation of end-of-line markers also provided makes the use of fseek unpredictable. The safe course is to use binary mode and recognize control-Z ourselves.

A short data file was prepared with the EDLIN editor supplied with DOS. It consists of two lines, abc and 123. Figure 3.2 shows its creation. The program shown in Figure 3.3 reads this file using the I/O functions just discussed. Figure 3.4 shows the output produced by this program.

FIGURE 3.2   Making a Text File

```
 1
 2    A>edlin test.dat
 3    New file
 4    *i
 5          1:*abc
 6          2:*123
 7          3:*^C
 8    *e
 9
10    A>dir test.dat
11    TEST       DAT          11    2-01-89    1:14p
12          1 File(s)
13    A>
```

FIGURE 3.3   expread.c

```
1      /* expread.c - try reading a file */
2      #include <stdio.h>
3
4      FILE * fp ;                 /* file pointer */
5      int get_and_print(void) ;   /* function prototype */
6
7
8      main()
9       {
10                                  /* open the file   */
11          fp = fopen("test.dat","rb") ;
12          printf("\n fopen returns - %d \n",fp) ;
13
14          printf("\n position     char    char      position");
15          printf("\n  before      read    value      after\n");
16
17          printf("\n                                          ");
18          printf("   read from beginning");
19
20          /* read the file one character at a time */
21          /* stop when we get to the end of the file */
22
23          while( get_and_print() != EOF )
24            { ; }
25                                  /* now move around and read chars */
26          printf("\n");
27          printf("\n                                          ");
28          printf("   move to position %2d ",5) ;
29          printf("\n                                          ");
30          printf("   and read next char ") ;
31          fseek(fp,5L,SEEK_SET);
32          get_and_print();
33
34
35          printf("\n");
36          printf("\n                                          ");
37          printf("   move to position %2d,",5) ;
38          fseek(fp,5L,SEEK_SET);
39          printf("\n                                          ");
40          printf("   back up 1 char and read");
41          fseek(fp,-1L,SEEK_CUR);
42          get_and_print();
43
44          fclose(fp);
45       }
46
47
48      int get_and_print()  /* get next char and print it */   •
49       {
50        int c ;
51
52        printf("\n     %2ld ",ftell(fp));
53        c = getc(fp);
54        printf("        ");
55        if( (c >= ' ') && (c <= '~') )
56            printf("    %c",c);
```

Figure 3.3   continues

Figure 3.3   continued

```
57          else if( c == '\n' )
58              printf("    LF");
59          else if( c == '\r' )
60              printf("    CR");
61          else if( c == EOF )
62              printf("    EOF");
63          else if( c == 26 )
64              printf("ctl-Z");
65          else printf("    ");
66
67          printf("    %3d",c);
68          printf("          %2ld ",ftell(fp)); /* position */
69          return(c);
70      }
```

FIGURE 3.4   Output from expread

```
 1      C>expread
 2        fopen returns - 1106
 3
 4        position       char    char    position
 5         before        read    value    after
 6
 7                                                    read from beginning
 8            0             a      97        1
 9            1             b      98        2
10            2             c      99        3
11            3            CR      13        4
12            4            LF      10        5
13            5             1      49        6
14            6             2      50        7
15            7             3      51        8
16            8            CR      13        9
17            9            LF      10       10
18           10          ctl-Z     26       11
19           11           EOF      -1       11
20
21                                                    move to position  5
22                                                    and read next char
23            5             1      49        6
24
25                                                    move to position  5,
26                                                    back up 1 char and read
27            4            LF      10        5
28      C>
```

The file position before and after each character is read is displayed so that we can understand fully how getc works. The first line in the file (abc) is present and is followed by both an ASCII carriage return character (13 Decimal) and an ASCII line feed (10 Decimal) character. The second line (123) is followed by the same 13 and 10 characters with a single control-Z character (26) after that. As described in Section 2.2, this character marks the effective end of the file.

Each line of the file is marked by two characters: a carriage return character (13) followed by a line feed character (10). VIEW can treat the line feed (LF) character as the end-of-line marker and ignore the carriage return (CR) character. This strategy works for files with CR-LF pairs or for files with only the LF character. It does not work for files with only a CR as an end-of-line marker. Fortunately the CR-LF marker is the standard for text files in the DOS environment.

Reading a File Backward

The previous section gave an example of reading a file forward one character at a time. Neither the C standard I/O library nor DOS supplies a function to read a file backward. We have to synthesize a function from the available facilities.

We will define a new function, get_previous_char, which is a mirror image of getc. get_previous_char reads one character from the file. It returns the character preceding the file position and moves the file position backward. Successive get_previous_char operations get data from the file in sequence moving backward.

For implementing get_previous_char, the raw materials are the file operations getc, fseek, and ftell that the C standard I/O library provides. The following three-step sequence appears to meet our needs. We will use the test.dat file from the preceding section to illustrate the steps. We will start with the file position equal to 5 as it would be after the statement

```
fseek(fp,5L,SEEK_SET)
```

This diagram shows the starting position of after fseek(fp,5L,SEEK_SET). Similar diagrams are used to show the situation after each step is executed.

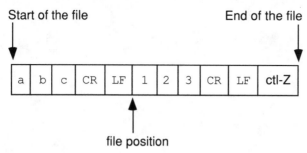

Step 1. Position the file in front of the character we want to read (LF). We do this with

```
fseek(fp,-1L,SEEK_CUR)
```

This positions the file as shown:

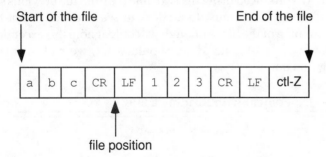

Step 2. Read the character with `c = getc(fp)`. The line feed character (LF) is returned and the file position is advanced:

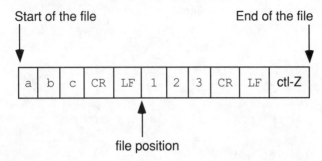

Step 3. Use `fseek(fp,-1,CURR_REL)` to position the file in front of the character just read. This leaves the file position less by one character than it was before Step 1.

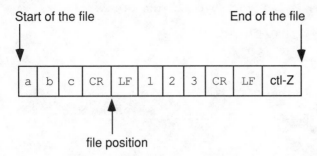

To continue reading the file backward, we would repeat these three steps: move backward one position (in front of CR), call `getc` (returns CR), and then move backward one position (in front of CR).

Our use of the `fseek` function relies on opening the file in binary mode. In text mode, the automatic conversion of carriage return/line feed sequences to single newline characters makes calculation of file positions uncertain.

The experimental program in Figure 3.5 checks out our plan. The accompanying output in Figure 3.6 was produced using the two-line file from the previous section. Note that `get_previous_char` must first check to see whether or not the file position is at the beginning of the file. Although we could ignore this exception case in working out how `get_previous_char` should work, we had to cover it to produce a working function.

FIGURE 3.5   expback.c — Experiment with Reading a File

```
1     /* expback.c - try reading a file backward */
2     #include <stdio.h>
3
4     #define BOF   (-2)              /* beginning of file return value */
5
6     FILE * fp ;                     /* file pointer */
7
8     int get_and_print(void) ;   /* function prototypes */
9     int get_previous_char(void) ;
10
11    main()
12     {
13         fp = fopen("test.dat","rb") ; /* open the file  */
14         printf("\n fopen returns - %d \n",fp) ;
15
16         printf("\n position     char    char      position");
17         printf("\n  before      read    value      after\n");
18
19         printf("\n                                          ");
20         printf("    start at end of file") ;
21         printf("\n                                          ");
22         printf("    and read backward");
23         fseek(fp,0L,SEEK_END);
24
25         /* read the file one character at a time */
26         /* stop when we get to the beginning of the file */
27
28         while( get_and_print() != BOF )
29           { ; }
30
31         printf("\n");
32         printf("\n                                          ");
33         printf("    move to position %2d", 5) ;
34         printf("\n                                          ");
35         printf("    and read next char") ;
36         fseek(fp,5L,SEEK_SET);
37         get_and_print();
38
39         printf("\n");
40         printf("\n                                          ");
41         printf("    move to position %2d,", 5) ;
42         fseek(fp,5L,SEEK_SET);
43         printf("\n                                          ");
44         printf("    back up 1 char and read");
45         fseek(fp,-1L,SEEK_CUR);
46         get_and_print();
```

Figure 3.5   continues

Figure 3.5   continued

```
47
48          fclose(fp);
49      }
50
51    int get_and_print()
52      {
53        int c ;
54
55        printf("\n     %2ld ",ftell(fp));
56        c = get_previous_char();
57        printf("        ");
58        if( (c >= ' ') && (c <= '~') )
59            printf("    %c",c);
60        else if( c == '\n' )
61            printf("   LF");
62        else if( c == '\r' )
63            printf("   CR");
64        else if( c == EOF )
65            printf("   EOF");
66        else if( c == BOF )
67            printf("   BOF");
68        else if( c == 26 )
69            printf("ctl-Z");
70        else printf("    ");
71
72        printf("     %3d",c);
73        printf("             %2ld ",ftell(fp)); /* position */
74        return(c);
75      }
76
77    int get_previous_char()    /* get character before current */
78      {                        /* file position */
79        int c ;
80
81        if( ftell(fp) > 0 )
82          { fseek(fp,-1L,SEEK_CUR); /* back up 1 char */
83            c = getc(fp);
84            fseek(fp,-1L,SEEK_CUR); /* back up again */
85            return( c ) ;
86          }
87        else return( BOF ) ;
88      }
```

These experiments have demonstrated what a file looks like and how we can build up a new facility for reading a file backward. The examples chosen illustrate a method of solving problems. Reading language reference manuals and operating system manuals is a valuable skill, but a little empirical testing often clears up the obscure explanations you may find in those manuals.

FIGURE 3.6   Output from expback

```
 1    C>expback
 2     fopen returns - 1172
 3
 4     position      char    char      position
 5      before       read    value      after
 6
 7                                                start at end of file
 8                                                and read backward
 9        11        ctl-Z      26          10
10        10          LF       10           9
11         9          CR       13           8
12         8           3       51           7
13         7           2       50           6
14         6           1       49           5
15         5          LF       10           4
16         4          CR       13           3
17         3           c       99           2
18         2           b       98           1
19         1           a       97           0
20         0         BOF       -2           0
21
22                                                move to position  5
23                                                and read next char
24         5          LF       10           4
25
26                                                move to position  5,
27                                                back up 1 char and read
28         4          CR       13           3
29    C>
```

3.4   The VIEW Program Listing

The VIEW program is composed of a number of functions grouped into seven source files, each having a single purpose:

Source File	Functions	Purpose
view.c	main	Overall flow.
viewget.c	get_cmd	Input a command.
viewexec.c	exec_cmd	Execute a command.
viewgetf.c	get_filename	Input file name.
	get_pos, flush_line	Input file position.
viewfind.c	move_forward ,	Move display page.
	move_backward,	
	set_top_page	
viewdisp.c	display_page	Display a page.
	disp_char	
	disp_prompt	Display prompt.

Source File	Functions	Purpose
`viewio.c`	`open_file , close_file,` `set_filesize , move_to,` `where_now, get_next_char,` `get_previous_char` `check_ctrl_z`	Handle file I/O.

The following *hierarchy diagram* shows the calling relationship of these functions. The functions called by `main` are indented below it. Below each of these functions are listed the functions it calls, indented another level. This indented list of called functions is repeated to more levels until no further functions calls occur. If a function occurs more than once, the functions it calls are shown only once.

```
main
     get_filename
          open_file
     get_filesize
     get_cmd
          getkey
          prompt
     exec_cmd
          get_pos
               flush_line
          move_to
          set_top_page
               where_now
          move_forward
               get_next_char
               move_to
               set_top_page
          move_backward
               get_previous_char
               move_to
               set_top_page
          display_page
               move_to
               get_next_char
               disp_char
     disp_prompt
     close_file
```

Two include files, `viewcmds.h` (Figure 3.7) and `viewparm.h` (Figure 3.8), define constants needed in more than one file. `viewcmds.h` contains the definitions of allowed input commands, and `viewparm.h` has parameters such as the

FIGURE 3.7   viewcmds.h

```
 1      /* viewcmds.h - definition of codes for input commands */
 2
 3      #define   NEXTPAGE          0
 4      #define   PREVPAGE          1
 5      #define   FIRSTPAGE         2
 6      #define   LASTPAGE          3
 7      #define   MOVETOPOS         4
 8      #define   EXITPGM           5
 9      #define   NEXTLINE          6
10      #define   PREVLINE          7
11      #define   INVALIDCMD        99
```

FIGURE 3.8   viewparm.h

```
 1      /* viewparm.h - parameters for view program */
 2
 3      /* number of lines in a display page */
 4      #define  PAGE_SIZE      16
 5
 6      /* number of lines of overlap between display pages */
 7      #define  LINES_OVERLAP    2
 8
 9      /* return values for get_next_char and get_previous_char */
10      /* indicating beginning or end of the file has been reached */
11      #define  EOF_MARK       -1
12      #define  BOF_MARK       -2
13
14      /* definition of control char marking the end of a line */
15      #define  END_LINE        10
16
17      /* define success/failure for return codes */
18      #define SUCCESS   1
19      #define FAILURE   0
20
21                                  /* function prototypes */
22      int get_cmd(void) ;         /* get a command */
23      void exec_cmd(int) ;        /* execute a command */
24      void move_forward(int) ;    /* move forward in file */
25      void move_backward(int) ;   /* move backward in file */
26      void set_top_page(void) ;   /* set top of page variable */
27      void display_page(void) ;   /* display a page of text */
28      void disp_char(int) ;       /* display one char */
29      void disp_prompt(void) ;    /* display the prompt */
30      long get_pos(long) ;        /* get file position input */
31      void get_filename(char *) ;/* get file name input */
32      int open_file(char *) ;     /* open the file */
33      void set_filesize(void) ;   /* find file size */
34      void check_ctrl_z(void) ;   /* adjust file size for control Z */
35      void move_to(long) ;        /* change file position */
36      long where_now(void) ;      /* return file position */
37      int get_next_char(void) ;   /* get a character - forward */
38      int get_previous_char(void) ;  /* get a character - backward */
39      void close_file(void) ;     /* close the file */
```

number of lines to be displayed at a time. Function prototypes for the functions in the VIEW program are also defined in `viewparm.h`.

The following sections discuss interesting points in each module of the program. Complete source file listings are included for VIEW and for the programs presented in later chapters. Most of VIEW's modules correspond closely to one or more pseudo-code functions, but the I/O module groups all functions that do any operations on the text file. The order of discussion is somewhat different from that of Section 3.2.

view.c

`view.c` shown in Figure 3.9, corresponds to the overall pseudo-code in Section 3.2. The individual lines of pseudo-code have been translated into calls to C functions. The `main` function does not collect input or produce output; it controls the actions of the functions that accomplish individual activities.

FIGURE 3.9   view.c

```
 1      /* view.c -  VIEW program - main function */
 2      #include <stdio.h>
 3      #include <string.h>
 4      #include "viewcmds.h"
 5      #include "viewparm.h"
 6
 7      char filename[65] = "" ;
 8
 9      main(argc,argv)
10       int argc ;
11       char *argv[] ;
12       {
13          int cmd ;                   /* holds current cmd      */
14
15          if( argc >= 2 )             /* get file name from command line */
16             strcpy(filename,argv[1]) ;   /* (if present) */
17
18          get_filename(filename);/* get file name and open file */
19          set_filesize();         /* set up file size variable */
20          check_ctrl_z() ;        /* adjust file size for control Z */
21          cmd = FIRSTPAGE ;       /* force display of 1st page */
22
23          while( cmd != EXITPGM )/* repeat until told to exit */
24             { exec_cmd(cmd);     /* execute the current command */
25                disp_prompt() ;   /* display command prompt */
26                cmd = get_cmd();  /* get the next command */
27             }
28
29          close_file() ;
30       }
```

The declaration of the `filename` array on line 7 initializes it to a null string. Lines 15 and 16 copy a command line argument into the file name if there is anything present.

The call to the `set_filesize` function does not correspond to anything in the pseudo-code. It was added because the file I/O functions in `viewio.c` need to know the location of the effective end of the data in the file being read. After the file size is set, a call to `check_ctrl_z` modifies the file size if a control-Z character is present.

The pseudo-code specified that the program should display the first page of the file before accepting an input command. Since there is a command to display the first page in the file, the program executes that command immediately, before it accepts an input command. This solution makes the loop on lines 23 to 27 compact and avoids the need for a special function to display the first page of text.

Long, descriptive names are used for variables and functions to make the program more understandable. In some environments, the compiler and linker may use only a few characters to distinguish names. It is a good practice to make names unique in their first 6 to 8 characters to avoid trouble. (Recent versions of Microsoft C and Turbo C treat up to 31 characters as significant. The ANSI C standard specifies that a minimum of 6 characters may be significant in names. Keeping only 8 characters in variable and function names is common in older computer environments, including early versions of the Microsoft MS-DOS linker.)

viewget.c

The `get_cmd` function accepts a single keystroke input and translates it into an input command value. It must act on each keystroke as typed; it cannot wait for a carriage return. In addition, the key pressed must not be echoed on the screen. For most C compilers, the standard console input function `getchar` fails one or both of these conditions. What can we do?

The `getkey` function described in Figure 3.10 fits our needs. (`getkey`'s implementation will be discussed in Chapter 7.) Here we can use `getkey` just as we would use a C library function. A header file `keyio.h` (Figure 3.11) defines symbolic constants for special keys. With the manual page description and the header file, we should be able to use `getkey` without knowing how it is implemented. When we compile and link VIEW, we compile and link the `keyio.c` file with the other source files. Or we include the `toolkit.lib` object library when we link VIEW as described in Appendix A.

The `viewget.c` file is shown in Figure 3.12. The `getkey` function waits for a key to be pressed. A `switch` statement (lines 17 to 28) classifies the key in terms of input commands. Since the key pressed may not correspond to a valid command, the process will be repeated until a valid command is received.

FIGURE 3.10 KEYIO description

Name

```
getkey      get one keystroke from the keyboard.
keypress    check for waiting keystroke.
keyflush    discard any waiting keystroke input.
waitcr      discard keyboard input until CR pressed.
```

Usage

```
int getkey() ;
int c , input_waiting ;
c = getkey();
input_waiting = keypress() ;
keyflush() ;
waitcr() ;
```

Function

`getkey` waits for the next keystroke from the keyboard. It returns an ASCII code(0–127) for keys corresponding to ASCII chars and values from 256 up for special keys such as function keys or cursor control keys. These special keystrokes are returned as (256 + extended code) using the extended code described in the *IBM PC Technical Reference Manual*.

The include file `keyio.h` defines symbolic constants for the values returned for many special keys.

`keypress` returns a zero value if no keyboard input is waiting and a nonzero value if some input is waiting. `keyflush` checks for keyboard input using `keypress` and discards it using `getkey` until no more input is waiting. `waitcr` uses `keypress` and `getkey` to discard input until the return key is pressed.

Keyboard input is not echoed by any of these functions. Input is available as soon as a single key is pressed; it is not queued until an entire line has been typed.

Examples

```
if( getkey() == UPARROW )
   { /* start scrolling up */
     keyflush() ;
     printf(" press a key to stop scrolling\n");
     while( keypress() == 0 )
        { scroll_up() ; }
   }
...
printf(" press return to continue\n");
waitcr() ;
```

FIGURE 3.11   keyio.h

```
 1      /* keyio.h  - definitions of values returned by getkey() */
 2
 3     /* keypress return values */
 4     #define NO_INPUT    0
 5     /* non-zero return means there is input waiting */
 6
 7                                     /* ASCII control characters */
 8     #define   ASCNUL      (256+3)
 9     #define   ASCBEL         7
10     #define   ASCBS          8
11     #define   ASCTAB         9
12     #define   ASCLF        0xA
13     #define   ASCFF        0xC
14     #define   ASCCR        0xD
15     #define   ASCESC       0x1B
16     #define   ASCDEL       0x7F
17     #define   ASCSPACE     0x20
18
19                                     /* special keys for IBM PC */
20     #define   HOMEKEY     (256+71)
21     #define   BACKTAB     (256+15)
22     #define   UPARROW     (256+72)
23     #define   LEFTARROW   (256+75)
24     #define   RIGHTARROW  (256+77)
25     #define   ENDKEY      (256+79)
26     #define   DOWNARROW   (256+80)
27     #define   PGUPKEY     (256+73)
28     #define   PGDNKEY     (256+81)
29     #define   INSERTKEY   (256+82)
30     #define   DELETEKEY   (256+83)
31     #define   CTLPRTSC    (256+114)
32     #define   CTLLARROW   (256+115)
33     #define   CTLRARROW   (256+116)
34     #define   CTLEND      (256+117)
35     #define   CTLPGDN     (256+118)
36     #define   CTLHOME     (256+119)
37     #define   CTLPGUP     (256+132)
38
39                                     /* function key codes */
40     #define   F1KEY       (256+59)
41     #define   F11KEY      (256+84)
42     #define   F21KEY      (256+94)
43     #define   F31KEY      (256+104)
44
45                                     /* alt-key + number key (top row) */
46     #define   ALT1KEY     (256+120)
47
48
49                                     /* function prototypes */
50     int getkey(void) ;
51     int keypress(void) ;
52     void keyflush(void) ;
53     void waitcr(void) ;
```

FIGURE 3.12   viewget.c

```
 1    /* viewget.c - get_cmd function - get an input command  */
 2    #include <stdio.h>
 3    #include "viewcmds.h"
 4    #include "viewparm.h"
 5    #include "keyio.h"
 6
 7
 8    int get_cmd()              /* get next input command from keyboard */
 9     {                              /* returns the command type entered */
10        int key ;                  /* the keyboard input value */
11                                   /* ( see keyio.h ) for values */
12        int cmd ;                  /* the command type value */
13
14        cmd = INVALIDCMD;      /* get next keyboard input */
15        while( cmd == INVALIDCMD )
16          { key = getkey() ;/* get next keyboard input */
17            switch( key )    /* classify the key pressed */
18              {
19                case PGDNKEY : cmd = NEXTPAGE       ;break;
20                case PGUPKEY : cmd = PREVPAGE       ;break;
21                case ASCESC  : cmd = EXITPGM        ;break;
22                case ' '     : cmd = MOVETOPOS      ;break;
23                case HOMEKEY : cmd = FIRSTPAGE      ;break;
24                case ENDKEY  : cmd = LASTPAGE       ;break;
25                case UPARROW : cmd = PREVLINE       ;break;
26                case DOWNARROW : cmd = NEXTLINE     ;break;
27                default      : cmd = INVALIDCMD     ;
28              } /* end of switch stmt */
29          }
30        return(cmd) ;
31     }
```

viewexec.c

This file, shown in Figure 3.13, is a direct translation of the execute_input_command pseudo-code. Each input command is handled by a separate case in a switch statement. It would be possible to shorten the function by combining cases in a clever way, but the savings in program size would be trivial and the cost in clarity significant. As it is written, the exec_cmd function has no secrets; a single reading shows exactly what it does for each command.

The filesize variable is used to move to the end of the file. It is defined and allocated storage in the viewio.c source file. Here we declare it with the extern storage class. This tells the compiler that it is defined in some other file and allocated storage there. Note that we still must describe the variable's data type.

The MOVETOPOS command accepts a new file position from the keyboard. After exec_cmd moves to this new file position, it adjusts the position so that the display page starts at the beginning of a line. This is treated as a special case (zero lines) by move_backward.

FIGURE 3.13   viewexec.c

```
1      /* viewexec.c file - executes one input command   */
2      #include <stdio.h>
3      #include "viewcmds.h"
4      #include "viewparm.h"
5      extern long filesize ;        /* position of effective eof */
6
7      void exec_cmd(cmd)            /* execute input command */
8       int cmd ;                    /* command to execute */
9       {
10          long new_pos ;
11
12          switch( cmd )   {
13            case PREVPAGE   :      /* move backward to last page */
14                  move_backward(PAGE_SIZE - LINES_OVERLAP) ;
15                  display_page() ;
16                  break;
17            case NEXTPAGE   :      /* move forward to next page */
18                  move_forward(PAGE_SIZE - LINES_OVERLAP);
19                  display_page() ;
20                  break;
21            case EXITPGM :
22                  break;
23            case MOVETOPOS :
24                  new_pos = get_pos(filesize) ; /* get file position */
25                  move_to(new_pos) ;  /* move to specified position */
26                  set_top_page() ;    /* make it top_of_page for now */
27                  move_backward(0);   /* move to start of this line */
28                  display_page() ;
29                  break;
30            case FIRSTPAGE  :
31                  move_to(0L);        /* move to beginning of file */
32                  set_top_page() ;    /* make it the top of the page */
33                  display_page() ;
34                  break;
35            case LASTPAGE   :
36                  move_to(filesize) ; /* move to end of file */
37                  set_top_page() ;    /* make it the top of the page */
38                  move_backward(PAGE_SIZE);/* back up to put end of */
39                  display_page() ;     /* file at bottom of screen */
40                  break;
41          case   PREVLINE :
42                  move_backward(1) ;  /* move back one line */
43                  display_page() ;
44                  break;
45          case   NEXTLINE :
46                  move_forward(1);    /* move forward one line */
47                  display_page() ;
48                  break;
49          }
50      }
```

exec_cmd uses other functions to do all the work. This keeps the viewexec.c file manageable in size and makes it easier to use the same C statements for several input commands.

viewgetf.c

Figure 3.14 shows the viewgetf.c file. The get_filename function validates the file name by calling open_file to open the file. The while loop on lines 15 to 19 repeats the process until a valid file name is received and the file successfully opened.

The get_pos function accepts a new file position from the keyboard. In this case, we can use a standard library function — scanf — for getting the position. We want each digit to be echoed as typed, and we want to wait until a full line of input is typed. The basic function of get_pos is simple and would require only two C statements:

```
printf("\n new file position:");
scanf("%ld",&pos);
```

As Figure 3.14 shows, making get_pos usable and bulletproof requires a lot more effort. It must check that scanf found a number (line 31), that the number is positive or zero (line 35), and that it is not greater than the size of the file (line 39). If the new position passes these tests, get_pos returns it (line 46). If any test fails, a warning message is displayed and the prompt displayed again. The while loop from line 29 to line 48 repeats the process until get_pos can return a successful

FIGURE 3.14   **viewgetf.c**

```
1       /* viewgetf.c -  get file name and position input */
2      #include <stdio.h>
3      #include <string.h>
4      #include "viewparm.h"
5      void flush_line(void) ;      /* function prototype */
6
7      void get_filename(fn)         /* get name of file and open it */
8       char *fn ;                   /* file name string */
9       {                            /* (filled out by caller) */
10         if( strlen(fn) == 0 )
11           { printf("file name:") ;
12             scanf("%s",fn) ;
13           }
14                                    /* open the file (verify name) */
15         while( open_file(fn) == FAILURE )
16           { printf("\n file - %s can not be opened\n",fn);
17             printf("file name:") ;      /* try again */
18             scanf("%s",fn) ;
19           }
20       }
21
22      long get_pos(filesize)        /* get file position input */
23       long filesize ;              /* use to validate new position */
24       {                            /* return the new position */
25          long pos ;
26
27          /* get a new position from the keyboard and validate it */
```

Figure 3.14   continues

Figure 3.14   continued

```
28              /* if it is not valid, repeat the process */
29              while( 1 == 1 )
30                 { printf("\n new file position: ");
31                   if( scanf("%ld",&pos) == 0 )
32                      { printf("\n file position must be numeric") ;
33                        flush_line() ;
34                      }
35                   else if( pos < 0L )/* got a number - check its range */
36                      { printf("\n file position must be >= zero");
37                        flush_line() ;
38                      }
39                   else if( pos > filesize )
40                      { printf("\n file position must be <= ");
41                        printf(" %ld",filesize) ;
42                        flush_line() ;
43                      }
44                   else                    /* valid file position */
45                      { flush_line() ; /* get rid of rest of this line */
46                        return( pos ) ;   /* return this new position */
47                      }
48                 }
49           }
50
51     void flush_line()            /* get rest of input line */
52        {
53          while( getchar() != '\n' )
54             { ; }
55        }
```

value. Note that the condition tested by the while loop (1 == 1) is always true; line 46 exits from the loop and from get_pos when a valid position is found.

scanf stops processing characters as soon as the end of the number is found. Calls to flush_line ensure that the next call to scanf will start with a new line of input. This is done for valid input as well as invalid input.

viewfind.c

The viewfind.c file, shown in Figure 3.15, contains the move_forward and move_backward functions. These functions use the get_next_char and get_previous_char functions to do the actual file reading operations. This keeps the movement functions small and simple and allows us to implement the file reading operations as we choose to implement them without affecting these functions.

Special return values tell us when we reach the beginning or end of the file. When these values are found, the position is marked as the top of the page, and the function returns to the caller. Although testing for these exception conditions could have been built into the while loop, using a separate test and an immediate return statement seems a simpler solution. The details of detecting the beginning or end of the file are hidden in get_next_char and get_previous_char.

The set_top_page function is called by move_forward, move_backward, and exec_cmd to make the current position in the file the new top of the display page. The corresponding variable `top_of_page` is declared in `viewfind.c`. It is defined outside `set_top_page` so that its value will be retained after `set_top_page` returns to its caller. The value of `top_of_page` is also used by `exec_cmd` and `display_page`. There it is declared as

```
extern long top_of_page ;
```

FIGURE 3.15   viewfind.c

```
1     /* viewfind.c file - moves to new positions in the file */
2     #include <stdio.h>
3     #include "viewparm.h"
4     long top_of_page ;          /* file position - top of display page */
5
6
7     void move_forward(nlines)   /* move forward n lines */
8      int nlines ;               /* number of lines to move */
9      {
10        int c ;                  /* hold chars read here */
11
12        move_to(top_of_page) ;    /* start at top of page */
13        while( nlines > 0 )
14          { c = get_next_char() ;
15            if( c  == END_LINE )  /* check for end of line */
16                nlines = nlines - 1 ;
17            if( c == EOF_MARK )   /* check for end of file */
18              { set_top_page() ;  /* yes - mark as top of the page */
19                return ;          /*         and exit */
20              }
21          }
22        set_top_page() ;          /* mark this as top of the page */
23      }
24
25
26    void move_backward(nlines)  /* move backward n lines */
27     int nlines ;               /* number of lines to move */
28     {                          /* (zero means start of this line) */
29        int c ;                  /* hold char here */
30
31        move_to(top_of_page) ;    /* start at top of page */
32        nlines = nlines + 1 ;     /* add one for current line */
33        while( nlines > 0 )
34          { c = get_previous_char();
35            if(  c  == END_LINE )
36                nlines = nlines - 1 ;
37            if( c == BOF_MARK )   /* check for BOF */
38              { set_top_page() ;  /* yes - mark as top of page */
39                return ;          /* and exit */
40              }
41          }
42                                  /* we're before an end_line */
43        get_next_char() ;         /* move past it */
44        set_top_page() ;          /* mark as top of page */
45      }
46
47
48    void set_top_page()
49      {
50        top_of_page = where_now() ;
51      }
```

viewdisp.c

Figure 3.16 shows the `display_page`, `disp_char`, and `disp_prompt` functions. The page is displayed using regular `printf` and `putc` functions. Since the C library functions do not provide us with a way to find out how many lines of text have been displayed, we keep track ourselves. The row and column variables are updated when a character is displayed. `disp_char` also uses the column variable to display the correct number of spaces when a tab character is encountered.

FIGURE 3.16   viewdisp.c

```
1     /* viewdisp.c file - display current page of file */
2     #include <stdio.h>
3     #include "viewparm.h"
4
5     #define TAB_WIDTH     8
6     #define PAGE_WIDTH    80
7     extern char    filename[] ;
8     extern long    filesize ;     /* size of file in bytes */
9     extern long    top_of_page;   /* file position of top of page */
10    int   row ;                   /* current line of page */
11    int   col ;                   /* current column of page */
12
13
14    void display_page()           /* display a page on screen */
15    {
16        int c ;                   /* hold the character here */
17        int i ;                   /* counter for loop */
18
19        move_to(top_of_page);     /* start at top of the page */
20                                  /* write a header line */
21        printf("\n FILE - %s    POSITION - %ld    FILE SIZE - %ld \n"
22            ,filename,top_of_page,filesize);
23
24                                  /* write a border line of dashes */
25        for( i=1 ; i <= 80 ; i = i + 1 )
26            { putchar('-'); }
27
28        /* get chars from file until we've written (PAGE_SIZE) */
29        /* lines or we have reached the end of the file */
30        row = 1 ;                 /* starting row & column values */
31        col = 1 ;
32        c = get_next_char() ;
33        while( c != EOF_MARK ) /* quit at end of file */
34            { disp_char(c) ;      /* display current character */
35              if(row > PAGE_SIZE)/* quit at end of page */
36                break ;
37              c = get_next_char();/* get next char */
38            }
39
40        while( row <= PAGE_SIZE )  /* pad out page if eof reached */
41            { putchar('\n'); row = row + 1 ; }
42
43                                  /* write a border line of dashes */
44        for( i=1 ; i <= 80 ; i = i + 1 )
45            { putchar('-'); }
```

Figure 3.16   continues

Figure 3.16   continued

```
46      }
47
48
49
50      void disp_char(c)              /* display one char */
51                                     /* and update row and column */
52      int c ;                        /* char to write */
53      {
54          /* classify the character and handle accordingly */
55
56          if( (c >= ' ') && (c <= '~') )
57              { putchar(c);          /* ASCII graphic char - display it */
58                col = col + 1 ;      /* advance column number */
59                if( col > PAGE_WIDTH ) /* check for wrap-around */
60                    { row = row + 1 ;/*      yes - advance row no and */
61                      col = 1 ;        /*            set to first column */
62                    }
63              }
64          else if( c == END_LINE )
65              { putchar('\n') ;      /* end_line char - force a new line */
66                row = row + 1 ;      /* advance row no. */
67                col = 1 ;            /* set column back to first col */
68              }
69          else if( c == '\t' )
70              {
71                do                      /* tab - expand it */
72                  { putchar(' ');       /* print spaces      */
73                    col = col + 1 ;     /* and advance column no. */
74                    if( col > PAGE_WIDTH )   /* check for wrap-around */
75                        { row = row + 1 ;
76                          col = 1 ;
77                        }
78                  } while( ( col % TAB_WIDTH ) != 1);/* until tab stop */
79              }
80      }
81
82
83      #define  UP_A  24               /* displays up arrow */
84      #define  DN_A  25               /* displays down arrow */
85
86      void disp_prompt()              /* display prompts for commands */
87      {
88          printf(  "\n          Type one of these Input Commands");
89          printf(  "\n HOME  = First Page         ");
90          printf(    "  %c   = Previous Line      ",UP_A);
91          printf(     "PG UP = Previous Page ");
92          printf(  "\n END   = Last  Page         ");
93          printf(    "  %c   = Next Line          ",DN_A);
94          printf(     "PG DN = Next Page ");
95          printf(  "\n ESC   = Exit Pgm           ");
96          printf(     "SPACE = Move to position \n");
97      }
```

`display_page` displays the file's name, the position in the file of the top of the page, and the file's size. All these variables are defined in other source files so they are declared in lines 7 to 9 to be `extern`.

`display_page` may find the end of the file before it displays a full page. Handling this exception is easy: The loop on lines 33 to 38 ends when a full page is displayed or when the end of the file is reached. (Line 33 performs the test for the end-of-file marker, and line 35 tests for the end of the display page.) Lines 40 and 41 then pad out the displayed page if fewer than `PAGE_SIZE` lines have been written.

Tab stops are fixed at every eighth column starting at column 1. The division remainder operator, `%`, is used in line 78 to check for a tab stop. The `do { } while` loop in lines 71 to 78 executes the body of the loop before testing, ensuring that at least one space character is displayed.

The `disp_prompt` function in lines 86 to 97 displays a menu of commands and corresponding keys. The characters that display up and down arrows are not defined in the ASCII character set, so we specify numbers for them in lines 83 and 84.

viewio.c

The `viewio.c` file in Figure 3.17 groups all operations on the data file. It uses standard I/O library functions for actual I/O, but it keeps these details private to this source file. We can change the way we read the data file without affecting other parts of the program. This lets us fix bugs or make enhancements without causing problems in the rest of the program.

FIGURE 3.17   viewio.c

```
 1    /* viewio.c file - I/O module for VIEW program */
 2    #include <stdio.h>
 3    #include "cminor.h"
 4    #include "viewparm.h"
 5
 6    #define   CTL_Z       26     /* marks EOF in some text files */
 7    #define   BSIZE     8192     /* buffer size */
 8    char buf[ BSIZE ] ;          /* file buffer */
 9
10    FILE *fp ;                   /* file pointer for text file */
11    long filesize ;              /* size of the file in bytes */
12
13
14    int open_file(fn)            /* open a file */
15      char fn[] ;                /* file name string */
16      {                          /* return success or failure */
17          fp = fopen(fn,"rb") ;
18          if(fp != NULL)
19             { setvbuf(fp,buf, _IOFBF, BSIZE ) ;
20               return(SUCCESS) ;
21             }
22          else return( FAILURE ) ;
23      }
```

Figure 3.17 continues

Figure 3.17   continued

```
24
25
26     void set_filesize()             /* set up file size */
27      {
28          fseek(fp,0L,SEEK_END) ;   /* get size of file */
29          filesize = ftell(fp) ;
30      }
31
32     void check_ctrl_z()
33      {
34          long back ;
35          int c ;
36
37          /* check last 128 byte block for a CTL-Z */
38          back = filesize % 128 ;/* how far back to start of block? */
39          if( (back == 0) && (filesize > 0))/* if at start of block */
40              back = 128 ;         /*          last block is full */
41          fseek(fp, filesize - back ,SEEK_SET);
42          c = getc(fp);
43          while( c != EOF )
44            { if( c == CTL_Z )    /* look for control-Z */
45                 { filesize = ftell(fp) - 1 ;
46                   return ;      /* found - adjust file size and exit */
47                 }
48              c = getc(fp);
49            }
50      }
51
52
53     void move_to(new_pos)        /* move to specified position */
54      long new_pos ;
55      {
56          fseek(fp,new_pos,SEEK_SET);
57      }
58
59
60     long where_now()             /* return current position */
61      {
62          return( ftell(fp) ) ;
63      }
64
65
66     int get_next_char()          /* get char at file position */
67      {
68          char c ;
69
70          if( ftell(fp) == filesize ) /* are we at end of file ? */
71              return( EOF_MARK ) ;    /* yes - return end file mark */
72          else                        /* no -                      */
73            { c = getc(fp);           /*        get a char and */
74              return( toascii(c) ) ;  /*        force to be ascii */
75            }                         /*        return it */
76      }
77
78
79     int get_previous_char()            /* read the char in front of */
80      {                                 /* current file position */
81          char c ;
```

Figure 3.17   continues

Figure 3.17   continued

```
82
83              if( ftell(fp) != 0L )        /* check for beginning of file */
84                { fseek(fp,-1L,SEEK_CUR); /* back up one char */
85                  c = getc(fp);             /* read a char*/
86                  fseek(fp,-1L,SEEK_CUR) ;/* back up again */
87                  return( toascii(c) ) ;   /* force to be ascii */
88                }                           /* and return the char */
89              else return(BOF_MARK) ;       /* at beginning of file */
90          }
91
92
93      void close_file()            /* close the file */
94          {
95          fclose(fp) ;
96          }
```

The open_file function, lines 14 to 23, just hides the details of opening a file. Since it returns an integer success/failure value, the caller does not need to know whether a buffered file pointer or a file handle for unbuffered I/O is used. The success or failure of open_file is used by its caller to validate the file name. Opening the file is necessary before the file can be read and doing it in get_filename serves the need for validating the file name. Note that the file is opened in binary mode, as discussed in Section 3.3.

The set_filesize function (lines 26 to 30) finds out how big the operating system thinks the file to be. The check_ctrl_z function in lines 32 to 50 checks for the presence of a control-Z character (26) in the last 128-byte block of the file. The file size used will correspond to the position of this character if one is present. This allows movement in the file to behave sensibly when the control-Z end-of-file convention is used. We have confined the details of end-of-file conventions to this single function. The rest of the I/O module will use the filesize variable to specify the end of the file.

The move_to and where_now functions hide the details of using fseek and ftell from other parts of the VIEW program. move_to and where_now let us get or set the current file position, but we rely on the library functions to keep track of this file position.

The get_next_char and get_previous_char functions use fseek and ftell to change or to determine the current position in the file. get_previous_char is implemented just as in the experimental program in Section 3.3.

3.5   Testing VIEW

The real purpose of testing is to raise our level of confidence that the program is correct. That means that we must explicitly test the program for each case in which we expect its behavior to be different.

We will take a methodical approach. We will test each function separately and verify its operation before we put the program together. This requires extra work before the testing can begin, but it has several advantages:

- We can test each function thoroughly. When we finish testing a function, we have confidence that it works.
- Each test is well controlled. When a function fails a test, we can usually fix the problem immediately. In the usual approach to testing, the hardest job is often to understand what the program is doing when it does not appear to work correctly.
- Test data are easier to construct. We can test display functions without placing the test data into files. Constructing test data is often a difficult job in the usual way of testing. The result is often that testing is not comprehensive.

The following sections discuss the testing of each function: what we test and how we test. We group the tests by source files; the functions in a single source file cannot be separated, so we test them together.

Testing view.c

The `main` function consists mostly of calls to other functions: `get_filename`, `set_filesize`, `get_cmd`, `exec_cmd`, and `close_file`. We will verify that these are called in the right sequence and with the right arguments. We expect `main` to keep calling `get_cmd` and `exec_cmd` until `get_cmd` returns an `EXITPGM` command.

It is important that we understand what we are trying to prove before we begin testing. The specification we made for the program, the pseudo-code, and the source listing are all useful in deciding what to test and what to expect.

We test `main` using special versions of the functions it calls. These contain `printf` statements to tell us when they are called. Parameters received are displayed, and any values to be returned are accepted from the keyboard. Such dummy versions of functions are often called *stubs*. Figure 3.18 shows the stubs we will use to test `main`.

FIGURE 3.18   testmain.c

```
1      /* testmain.c - test view.c (main function) */
2      #include <stdio.h>
3      #include "cminor.h"
4      #include "viewparm.h"
5
6      void get_filename(fn)
7      char fn[] ;
8      {
9          printf("\n get_filename called - fn = <%s>",fn);
10     }
11
```

Figure 3.18   continues

Figure 3.18   continued

```
12      void set_filesize()
13      {
14          printf("\n set_filesize called ");
15      }
16
17      void check_ctrl_z()
18      {
19          printf("\n check_ctrl_z called \n");
20      }
21
22      int get_cmd()
23      {
24          int cmd ;
25          printf("\n get_cmd called");
26          printf("   -- cmd:");
27          scanf("%d",&cmd);
28          return(cmd);
29      }
30
31      void exec_cmd(cmd)
32      int cmd ;
33      {
34          printf("\n execcmd called ");
35          printf("-- cmd= %d  \n",cmd);
36      }
37
38      void disp_prompt()
39      {
40          printf("\n disp_prompt called ");
41      }
42
43      void close_file()
44      {
45          printf("\n close_file called ");
46      }
```

We compile and link view.c and testmain.c together to produce a special test program. When we execute this test program, we expect the following results:

    get_filename called
    set_filesize called
    check_ctrl_z called
    exec_cmd called (with a FIRSTPAGE cmd)
    disp_prompt called
    get_cmd called (we specify a command)
    disp_prompt called
    exec_cmd called (with the cmd we specified to get_cmd)
    ...
    get_cmd called (we specify an EXITPGM command)
    close_file called
    program terminates

FIGURE 3.19   Testing view.c

```
 1    C>testmain abcdef
 2     get_filename called - fn = <abcdef>
 3     set_filesize called
 4     check_ctrl_z called
 5
 6     execcmd called -- cmd= 2
 7
 8     disp_prompt called
 9     get_cmd called   -- cmd:0
10     execcmd called -- cmd= 0
11
12     disp_prompt called
13     get_cmd called   -- cmd:1
14     execcmd called -- cmd= 1
15
16     disp_prompt called
17     get_cmd called   -- cmd:2
18     execcmd called -- cmd= 2
19
20     disp_prompt called
21     get_cmd called   -- cmd:3
22     execcmd called -- cmd= 3
23
24     disp_prompt called
25     get_cmd called   -- cmd:4
26     execcmd called -- cmd= 4
27
28     disp_prompt called
29     get_cmd called   -- cmd:6
30     execcmd called -- cmd= 6
31
32     disp_prompt called
33     get_cmd called   -- cmd:7
34     execcmd called -- cmd= 7
35
36     disp_prompt called
37     get_cmd called   -- cmd:5
38     close_file called
39    C>
```

We can run this test without adding any special testing statements to main itself. Figure 3.19 shows the test run.

Our approach relied on printf statements to track program execution and scanf statements to supply return values for stub functions. Microsoft C, Turbo C, and QuickC all provide source code debuggers that simplify the job of testing. We still have to write stub functions, but we can use the debugger's features to track program execution, to examine variables and function arguments, and to set return values. Although Microsoft's CodeView and the Borland Turbo Debugger provide many commands, even the Turbo C and QuickC integrated debuggers provide the basic features we need:

Breakpoints: We can set breakpoints at each stub function. When program execution reaches a breakpoint, execution is suspended and the line at which execution was suspended is highlighted. This is a substitute for a `printf` statement announcing that the function was called.

Watch expressions: We can define watch expressions for function arguments or other variables that we want to observe.

Setting variables: The Turbo C command *Evaluate expression* and the QuickC command *Modify value* allow us to examine and set values of variables. This provides control over function return values.

Trace and step commands: The Trace command executes the next C statement and stops. If the statement calls another function, execution stops in the called function. The Step command is similar, but if a function call is made, execution does not stop in the called function. These commands allow us to follow execution one statement at a time, observing the effect of each statement.

None of the `printf` or `scanf` statements in Figure 3.18 would be needed if we relied on a source code debugger. But those `printf` statements provide a compact, printed record of testing `view.c`. That printed record is useful when we revise `view.c` and must test it again. The printed record is also useful in describing the testing process, so in the rest of this chapter, we present test programs with `printf` statements and the output they produce.

Testing viewget.c

To test the `viewget.c` file, we revise the stub file, removing the dummy `get_cmd` function (see Figure 3.20). Since the `main` function now works, we can use it in testing `get_cmd`. `main` calls `get_cmd` and then `exec_cmd`. The dummy `exec_cmd` function in the stub file displays the command it receives. This serves to tell us what value `get_cmd` returned to `main`.

Should we use the real `getkey` function or a stub function? In this case we chose to use the real function. Had using the real `getkey` function made the test more difficult, we might have chosen to run the test first with a stub `getkey` function.

We compile and link this revised test program, as the following command for Microsoft C shows:

```
cl view.c viewget.c testget.c keyio.c
```

What must we test? We should type all valid commands to `getkey` and try the invalid keys as well. What do we expect to see? The output should show a sequence of events like that in the previous test. Instead of the line `get_cmd called` and a prompt for a return value, we should see the cursor stop as `getkey` waits for a valid command. Since `getkey` does not echo the characters typed, there will be no direct evidence of the command we typed. When keys that do not correspond to valid commands are pressed, the program should just wait for further input. Figure 3.21 shows the results from a test run.

FIGURE 3.20   testget.c

```
1       /* testget.c - test viewget.c (get_cmd function) */
2       #include <stdio.h>
3       #include "cminor.h"
4       #include "viewparm.h"
5
6       void get_filename(fn)
7        char fn[] ;
8        {
9            printf("\n get_filename called - fn = <%s>",fn);
10       }
11
12      void set_filesize()
13       {
14           printf("\n set_filesize called ");
15       }
16
17      void check_ctrl_z()
18       {
19           printf("\n check_ctrl_z called \n");
20       }
21
22      void exec_cmd(cmd)
23       int cmd ;
24       {
25           printf("\n execcmd called ");
26           printf("-- cmd= %d   \n",cmd);
27       }
28
29      void disp_prompt()
30       {
31           printf("\n disp_prompt called ");
32       }
33
34      void close_file()
35       {
36           printf("\n close_file called ");
37       }
```

FIGURE 3.21   testget Output

```
1       C>testget
2        get_filename called - fn = <>
3        set_filesize called
4        check_ctrl_z called
5
6        execcmd called -- cmd= 2
7
8        disp_prompt called   [ PgDn key pressed ]
9        execcmd called -- cmd= 0
10
11       disp_prompt called   [ PgUp key pressed ]
12       execcmd called -- cmd= 1
13
14       disp_prompt called   [ Home key pressed ]
15       execcmd called -- cmd= 2
16
```

Figure 3.21   continues

Figure 3.21   continued

```
17      disp_prompt called   [ End key pressed ]
18      execcmd called -- cmd= 3
19
20      disp_prompt called   [ Space Bar key pressed ]
21      execcmd called -- cmd= 4
22
23      disp_prompt called   [ Down Arrow key pressed ]
24      execcmd called -- cmd= 6
25
26      disp_prompt called   [ Up Arrow key pressed ]
27      execcmd called -- cmd= 7
28
29      disp_prompt called   [ Esc key pressed ]
30      close_file called
31    C>
```

Testing viewexec.c

The procedure we used to test get_cmd is useful for testing the exec_cmd function, too. We edit the stub file again, removing the dummy exec_cmd function. The real exec_cmd function calls a number of new functions (move_backward, move_forward, display_page, set_top_page, move_to, and get_pos), so we add stub versions to this file. The new test file is shown in Figure 3.22.

This technique of starting with the main function and successively replacing stubs by the actual functions is called *top-down testing*. If we continue using it until all of the program is tested, we wind up with the entire program working together. This may not always be practical, but this method of testing is often useful.

FIGURE 3.22   testexec.c

```
1     /* testexec.c - test viewexec.c (exec_cmd function) */
2     #include <stdio.h>
3     #include "cminor.h"
4     #include "viewparm.h"
5
6     long filesize ;
7
8
9     void get_filename(fn)
10    char fn[] ;
11    {
12        printf("\n get_filename called - fn = <%s>",fn);
13    }
14
15    void set_filesize()
16    {
17        printf("\n set_filesize called ");
18        printf("\n filesize:") ;
19        scanf("%ld",& filesize) ;
20    }
21
```

Figure 3.22   continues

Figure 3.22   continued

```
22    void check_ctrl_z()
23    {
24        printf("\n check_ctrl_z called \n");
25    }
26
27    void disp_prompt()
28    {
29        printf("\n disp_prompt called ");
30    }
31
32    void close_file()
33    {
34        printf("\n close_file called ");
35    }
36
37
38    void move_backward(nlines)
39     int nlines ;
40    {
41        printf("\n move_backward called nlines= %d ",nlines);
42    }
43
44    void move_forward(nlines)
45     int nlines ;
46    {
47        printf("\n move_forward called nlines= %d ",nlines);
48    }
49
50    void display_page()
51    {
52        printf("\n display_page called ");
53    }
54
55
56    void set_top_page()
57    {
58        printf("\n set_top_page called ");
59    }
60
61
62    void move_to(pos)
63     long pos ;
64    {
65        printf("\n move_to called  - pos= %ld ",pos);
66    }
67
68
69    long get_pos(fs)
70     long fs ;
71    {
72        long pos ;
73
74        printf(" \n get_pos(%ld) called ",fs);
75        printf("\n filesize = %ld ",filesize ) ;
76        printf("\n new position:");
77        scanf("%ld",&pos) ;
78        return( pos) ;
79    }
```

The exec_cmd function does not do anything but make a series of function calls. We want to verify that exec_cmd makes the right series of function calls for each input command. The messages from the stub functions should allow us to demonstrate this. Figure 3.23 lists output from a test run. To keep it brief, we suppressed even more of the prompting messages from get_cmd.

Testing viewgetf.c

We could test the viewgetf.c file with the same top-down testing method we have been discussing. We need only delete stub functions for the get_filename

FIGURE 3.23   testexec Output

```
 1    C>testexec
 2      get_filename called - fn = <>
 3      set_filesize called
 4      filesize:80000
 5      check_ctrl_z called
 6
 7      move_to called   - pos= 0
 8      set_top_page called
 9      display_page called
10      disp_prompt called              [ PgDn key pressed ]
11      move_forward called nlines= 14
12      display_page called
13      disp_prompt called              [ PgUp key pressed ]
14      move_backward called nlines= 14
15      display_page called
16      disp_prompt called              [ Home key pressed ]
17      move_to called   - pos= 0
18      set_top_page called
19      display_page called
20      disp_prompt called              [ End key pressed ]
21      move_to called   - pos= 80000
22      set_top_page called
23      move_backward called nlines= 16
24      display_page called
25      disp_prompt called              [ Space Bar key pressed ]
26      get_pos(80000) called
27      filesize = 80000
28      new position: 40000
29      move_to called   - pos= 40000
30      set_top_page called
31      move_backward called nlines= 0
32      display_page called
33      disp_prompt called              [ Down Arrow key pressed ]
34      move_forward called nlines= 1
35      display_page called
36      disp_prompt called              [ Up Arrow key pressed ]
37      move_backward called nlines= 1
38      display_page called
39      disp_prompt called              [ Esc key pressed ]
40      close_file called
41    C>
```

and `get_pos` functions and add `viewgetf.c` to the files being compiled and linked. However, it would be hard to interpret the resulting test because of all the messages from stub functions. This difficulty illustrates a problem with top-down testing: As more real functions replace stubs, it becomes more difficult to design tests that are both thorough and concise. Figure 3.24 shows an alternative for testing `viewgetf.c`. This program stands alone; we do not need any of the functions already tested. We just compile and link `testgetf.c` with `viewgetf.c`.

The stub function `open_file` in Figure 3.24 lets us test `get_filename` for both valid and invalid file names. Testing for invalid input is sometimes difficult, but it is an essential part of the development process. The `testgetf.c` file also tests the

FIGURE 3.24   testgetf.c

```
1        /* testgetf.c - test get_filename and get_pos */
2       #include <stdio.h>
3       #include "cminor.h"
4       #include "viewparm.h"
5
6       static long filesize ;
7       static char filename[200] ;
8
9       main()
10        {
11          long pos ;
12
13           printf("\n\n testing get_filename\n");
14           printf("file name:");
15           gets(filename) ;
16           get_filename(filename) ;
17
18           printf("\n\n testing get_pos\n");
19           printf("file size:");
20           scanf("%ld",& filesize) ;
21           pos = get_pos(filesize) ;
22           while( pos != 999 )
23             { printf(" get_pos = %ld \n",pos) ;
24               pos = get_pos(filesize) ;
25             }
26        }
27
28
29
30       int open_file(fn)
31        char fn[] ;
32        {
33           int ret ;
34           printf("\n open_file called - fn= <%s>\n",fn);
35           printf("return code:");
36           scanf("%d",&ret);
37           return(ret);
38        }
```

get_pos function. Although the basic function of get_pos is simple, there are lots of exceptions to test:

1. The keyboard input may be nonnumeric.
2. The input value may be negative.
3. The input value may be larger than the file size.
4. A second value may be typed on the same line. get_pos must ensure that these characters are discarded.

We must check that get_pos recognizes all these exceptions and recovers properly. It is also wise to try both small and large values for the file size and file position to ensure that the long number variables are handled correctly. Finally, the boundary values zero and the file size should be tried as file positions. Figure 3.25 shows the result of a test run with testgetf.c.

FIGURE 3.25   Testing viewgetf.c

```
 1    C>testgetf
 2      testing get_filename
 3    file name:
 4      open_file called - fn= <abc>
 5    return code:0
 6      file - abc
 7      can not be opened
 8    file name:def
 9      open_file called - fn= <def>
10    return code:1
11
12      testing get_pos
13    file size:80000
14     new file position:x
15      file position must be numeric
16     new file position:-1
17      file position must be >= zero
18     new file position:0
19     get_pos = 0
20
21     new file position:10000
22     get_pos = 10000
23
24     new file position:40000
25     get_pos = 40000
26
27     new file position:80000
28     get_pos = 80000
29
30     new file position:80001
31      file position must be <=   80000
32     new file position:999
33
34    C>
```

Testing viewfind.c

Next we test the functions in the viewfind.c source file: move_forward, move_backward, and set_top_page. The top-down method is not very convenient for this test: thus, we will use the standalone test program shown in Figure 3.26. We supply a main program, which calls the functions to be tested as well as stubs for any functions the functions in viewfind.c call.

The set_top_page function is used by move_forward and move_backward, so we test it first. Its role is to set the variable top_of_page. Before we call set_top_page, we place a recognizable value in top_of_page. We must ensure

FIGURE 3.26   testfind.c

```
1    /* testfind.c - test viewfind.c */
2    #include <stdio.h>
3    extern long top_of_page ;
4    long pos ;
5
6    main()
7      {
8        int c ;
9        int n ;
10       char s[81];
11
12        printf(" testing set_top_page \n");
13        top_of_page = -999L ;
14        pos = 7 ;
15        printf(" before call - top_of_page = %ld \n",top_of_page);
16        set_top_page() ;
17        printf(" after call - top_of_page = %ld \n",top_of_page);
18
19        printf("\n test move forward \n");
20        while( 1 == 1 )
21          { printf("\n nlines:"); scanf("%d",&n);
22           if( n < 0 )
23               break ;
24           move_forward(n) ;
25            printf(" top_of_page = %ld \n",top_of_page);
26          }
27
28        printf("\n test move_backward \n");
29        while( 1 == 1 )
30          { printf("\n nlines:"); scanf("%d",&n);
31           if( n < 0 )
32               break ;
33           move_backward(n) ;
34            printf(" top_of_page = %ld \n",top_of_page);
35          }
36      }
37
38
39    int get_next_char()
40      {
41        int c ;
42
43        printf(" get next char called");
```

Figure 3.26   continues

Figure 3.26   continued

```
44              printf("  - return(decimal):");
45              scanf("%d", & c);
46              if( c != -1 )
47                 pos = pos + 1 ;
48              return(c) ;
49          }
50
51      int get_previous_char()
52          {
53              int c ;
54
55              printf(" get previous char called");
56              printf("  - return(decimal):");
57              scanf("%d", & c);
58              if( c != -2 )
59                 pos = pos - 1 ;
60              return(c);
61          }
62
63      void move_to(p)
64        long p ;
65          {
66              pos = p ;
67              printf(" move to called -  position = %ld \n",pos);
68          }
69
70      long where_now()
71          {
72              printf(" where now called \n") ;
73              return( pos ) ;
74          }
```

that a call to set_top_page really changes the variable, not just that the value looks right after a call is made.

The key to testing move_forward and move_backward is the stub functions for get_next_char and get_previous_char. These functions accept return values from the keyboard, not from a data file. This gives us the flexibility to test thoroughly. Constructing one or more data files to test move_forward and move_backward completely would take a lot of effort.

There are several special cases to be tested for move_forward: end-of-file, one line, and more than one line, lines with only the end-of-line character, end-of-line as the first character found. Testing move_backward is similar, but zero lines is an additional case to be tested. A sample test run is shown in Figure 3.27.

Testing viewdisp.c

Figure 3.28 shows another standalone test program. It tests first disp_char, then display_page, and finally disp_prompt. display_page depends on disp_char for updating row and column variables. It is wise to make sure that disp_char works correctly before tackling display_page. This illustrates a weakness with

FIGURE 3.27   Testing viewfind.c

```
 1    C>testfind
 2    testing set_top_page
 3    before call - top_of_page = -999
 4    where now called
 5    after call - top_of_page = 7
 6
 7    test move forward
 8    nlines: 0
 9    move to called -   position = 7
10    top_of_page = 7
11
12    nlines: 1
13    move to called -   position = 7
14    get next char called  - return(decimal): 2
15    get next char called  - return(decimal): 3
16    get next char called  - return(decimal): 10
17    where now called
18    top_of_page = 10
19
20    nlines: 2
21    move to called -   position = 10
22    get next char called  - return(decimal): 1
23    get next char called  - return(decimal): 10
24    get next char called  - return(decimal): 2
25    get next char called  - return(decimal): 10
26    top_of_page = 14
27
28    nlines: 1
29    move to called -   position = 14
30    get next char called  - return(decimal): 2
31    get next char called  - return(decimal): -1
32    where now called
33    top_of_page = 15
34
35    nlines: -1
36    test move_backward
37    nlines: 0
38    move to called -   position = 15
39    get previous char called  - return(decimal): 10
40    get next char called  - return(decimal): 10
41    where now called
42    top_of_page = 15
43
44    nlines: 0
45    move to called -   position = 15
46    get previous char called  - return(decimal): 1
47    get previous char called  - return(decimal): 10
48    get next char called  - return(decimal): 10
49    where now called
50    top_of_page = 14
51
52    nlines: 1
53    move to called -   position = 14
54    get previous char called  - return(decimal): 1
55    get previous char called  - return(decimal): 10
56    get previous char called  - return(decimal): 2
57    get previous char called  - return(decimal): 3
```

Figure 3.27   continues

Figure 3.27   continued

```
58      get previous char called  - return(decimal): 10
59      get next char called  - return(decimal): 10
60      top_of_page = 10
61
62      nlines: 1
63      move to called -  position = 10
64      get previous char called  - return(decimal): -2
65      where now called
66      top_of_page = 10
67
68      nlines: -1
69
70   C>
```

FIGURE 3.28   testdisp.c

```
1      /* testdisp.c - test viewdisp.c */
2      #include <stdio.h>
3      #include "cminor.h"
4      #include "viewparm.h"
5
6      char filename[81] ;
7      char s[256] ;
8      extern int row,col ;
9      long filesize ;
10     long top_of_page ;
11     int ix ;                    /* index into char string */
12     int silent ;                /* flag for get_next_char */
13
14
15     main()
16      {
17        int c ;
18        char a ;
19        int i ;
20
21        printf("\n testing disp_char");
22        while( 1 == 1 )
23          {
24            printf("\n char (decimal):");
25            scanf("%d",&c);
26            if( c == -1 ) break ;
27            printf("\n col:");
28            scanf("%d",&col);
29            printf("\n row:");
30            scanf("%d",&row);
31            printf("\n12345678901234567890\n");
32
33            for( i=1 ; i < col ; i= i + 1 )
34              {
35                printf(">");
36              }
37            disp_char(c) ;
38            printf("<  row= %d  col= %d \n",row,col);
39          }
40
```

Figure 3.28   continues

Figure 3.28   continued

```
41          printf("\n\n testing display_page \n");
42
43          strcpy(filename,"< file name >") ;
44          top_of_page = 333000000 ;
45          filesize = 444000000 ;
46
47       silent = 0 ;
48        printf("\n   show get_next_char calls\n");
49        display_page() ;
50
51
52        printf("\n test with get_next_char silent\n");
53        silent = 1 ;
54        printf("\n test with full page \n");
55        strcpy(s,"1234567890");
56        ix = 0 ;
57        display_page() ;
58        scanf("%c%c",&a,&a) ;    /* pause before next test */
59        printf("   eof in 3rd line-no output from get_next_char \n");
60        strcpy(s,"1\n2\n\f");
61        ix = 0 ;
62        display_page() ;
63        scanf("%c%c",&a,&a) ;    /* pause before next test */
64
65        printf("\n\n testing disp_prompt ---\n");
66        disp_prompt() ;
67        printf(">\n-------------------- \n\n") ;
68
69        printf("\n test with full page and prompts\n");
70        printf("************** \n");
71        strcpy(s,"1234567890");
72        ix = 0 ;
73        display_page() ;
74        disp_prompt() ;
75        getkey() ; getkey() ;    /* pause before next test */
76        ix = 0 ;
77        display_page() ;
78        disp_prompt() ;
79        getkey() ; getkey() ;    /* pause before next test */
80        ix = 0 ;
81        display_page() ;
82        disp_prompt() ;
83        getkey() ; getkey() ;    /* pause before next test */
84        printf("************** \n");
85
86    }
87
88
89    int get_next_char()
90    {
91        int c ;
92
93        if( silent == 0 )
94          { printf("\n get_next_char called\n") ;
95            printf("\n row= %d   col= %d \n",row,col);
96            printf("value to return:");
97            scanf("%d",&c);
98            return(c);
```

Figure 3.28   continues

Figure 3.28   continued

```
 99              }
100          else if( s[ix] == '\0' )   /* end of string- NL ,start over */
101             { ix = 0 ;
102               return( '\n' ) ;
103             }
104          else                        /* not end of string return char */
105             { c = tochar( s[ix] ) ;
106               ix = ix + 1 ;
107               if( c == '\f' ) c = EOF_MARK ;
108               return( c ) ;
109             }
110       }
111
112    void move_to(pos)
113      long pos ;
114      {
115          printf("\n move to called - position = %ld \n",pos) ;
116      }
```

top-down testing: Functions like disp_char are tested after the functions that call them. Our approach of testing the lower functions before those that call them is called *bottom-up testing*.

Figure 3.29 shows part of a test run. The part shown checks disp_char. As with viewfind.c, we supply characters interactively. We also specify the row and column values before each character is processed. For each test we are concerned with two results: what is displayed on the screen and how the row and column variables are changed. We must try a variety of cases for disp_char: normal and control characters, and tab characters at tab stops and off them. We also test the behavior when column 80 is reached for normal characters, end-of-line characters, and tab characters.

Once the disp_char function works correctly, we are ready to test the display_page function. (These test results are not shown in Figure 3.29. How-

FIGURE 3.29   testdisp Output

```
 1    C>testdisp
 2
 3     testing disp_char
 4     char (decimal):32
 5     col:1
 6     row:1
 7    12345678901234567890
 8     <   row= 1   col= 2
 9
10     char (decimal):48
11     col:79
12     row:2
13    12345678901234567890
14     >>>>>>>>>>>>>>>>>>>>>>>>>>>>>>>>>>>>>>>>>>>>>>>>>>>>>>>>>>>>>>>>>>>>>>>>>>>>>>>0<
15      row= 1   col= 80
16
17     char (decimal):97
18     col:80
```

Figure 3.29   continues

Figure 3.29   continued

```
19    row:3
20    12345678901234567890
21    >>>>>>>>>>>>>>>>>>>>>>>>>>>>>>>>>>>>>>>>>>>>>>>>>>>>>>>>>>>>>>>>a
22    <  row= 3   col= 1
23
24    char (decimal):1
25    col:2
26    row:2
27    12345678901234567890
28    ><  row= 2   col= 2
29
30    char (decimal):10
31    col:3
32    row:3
33    12345678901234567890
34    >>
35    <  row= 4   col= 1
36
37    char (decimal):13
38    col:4
39    row:4
40    12345678901234567890
41    >>>< row= 4   col= 4
42
43    char (decimal):127
44    col:5
45    row:5
46    12345678901234567890
47    >>>>< row= 5   col= 5
48
49    char (decimal):9
50    col:1
51    row:1
52    12345678901234567890
53          <  row= 1   col= 9
54
55    char (decimal):9
56    col:8
57    row:2
58    12345678901234567890
59    >>>>>>> <  row= 2   col= 9
60
61    char (decimal):9
62    col:79
63    row:3
64    12345678901234567890
65    >>>>>>>>>>>>>>>>>>>>>>>>>>>>>>>>>>>>>>>>>>>>>>>>>>>>>>>>>>>>>>>
66    <  row= 4   col= 1
67
68    char (decimal):9
69    col:80
70    row:5
71    12345678901234567890
72    >>>>>>>>>>>>>>>>>>>>>>>>>>>>>>>>>>>>>>>>>>>>>>>>>>>>>>>>>>>>>>>>>
73    <  row= 5   col= 1
74
75    char (decimal):-1
76    ...
77    C>
```

ever, you should be able to follow the test program itself.) We are interested in two cases: when a full page is displayed without reaching the end of file and when the end of the file is reached before a full page is displayed. The expected outcome is that exactly 16 lines are displayed on the screen in each case.

Since `display_page` writes to the screen itself, our testing output interferes with normal output. The solution is to run one test to see that the loops in `display_page` work correctly. For this, use `get_next_char` to display the current row and column values and to accept the character value from the keyboard. Then test `display_page` with no test output to check the layout on the screen.

The last part of Figure 3.28 tests the `disp_prompt` function. A series of calls to `display_page` and `disp_prompt` verifies that the full screen layout is what we expect.

Testing viewio.c

We packaged all the file access functions into the `viewio.c` source file. This allowed us to test the rest of the VIEW program without creating any special data files for testing. But in testing `viewio.c` we cannot avoid actual file I/O.

Building suitable files is a new element in the testing process. Most of the testing can be done with a small file such as the one created in Section 3.3. However, we should also test with a large file of 40,000 or more characters to ensure that the long values for the file's size and the file position are handled correctly.

Figure 3.30 shows our test program, and Figure 3.31 shows test results using the `test.dat` file from Section 3.3. As in the previous sections, we use a standalone program. We call the functions in `viewio.c` directly and display the results after the calls to get clear test results.

FIGURE 3.30   testio.c

```
1      /* testio.c - test viewio.c */
2      #include <stdio.h>
3      #include "cminor.h"
4      #include "viewparm.h"
5
6      extern FILE *fp ;
7      extern long filesize ;
8
9      main()
10       {
11         long pos ;
12         int c , i ;
13         char fn[65] ;
14
15         printf("\n testing I/O module\n");
16
17         printf("\n file name:");
18         scanf("%s",fn) ;
19         printf(" open_file = %d ",open_file(fn) ) ;
20         printf("\n fp = %x ",fp);
```

Figure 3.30   continues

Figure 3.30   continued

```
21
22              printf("\n calling set_filesize");
23              filesize = -1L ;
24              set_filesize();
25              printf("\n filesize= %ld  \n",filesize);
26              printf("\n calling check_ctrl_z");
27              check_ctrl_z();
28              printf("\n filesize= %ld  \n",filesize);
29
30          pos = 3  ;
31          printf("\n move_to %ld",pos);
32          move_to(pos) ;
33          c = get_next_char() ;
34          printf("\n next char is %d  where_ now = %ld  ftell=%ld",
35             c, where_now() , ftell(fp) );
36          c = get_next_char() ;
37          printf("\n next char is %d  where_ now = %ld  ftell=%ld",
38             c, where_now() , ftell(fp) );
39          pos = 1  ;
40          move_to(pos) ;
41          printf("\n move_to %ld",pos);
42          c = get_next_char() ;
43          printf("\n next char is %d  where_ now = %ld  ftell=%ld",
44             c, where_now() , ftell(fp) );
45
46          scanf("%c%c",&c,&c);   /* pause here */
47
48          /* test  get next char */
49          move_to(0L) ; /* start at beginning of file */
50          printf("\n test get next char - sequential reads \n ") ;
51          c = get_next_char() ;
52          i = 0;
53          while( c != EOF_MARK )
54            { printf("  c=%d",c);
55              c = get_next_char() ;
56              i = i + 1 ;
57              if( i > 100 )
58                  break ;
59            }
60        printf("\n eof reached - c=%d \n",c);
61        scanf("%c%c",&c,&c);   /* pause here */
62
63
64          move_to(filesize) ;    /* start at end of file */
65          printf(" test get next char - at eof \n ") ;
66          for(i=0 ; i < 10 ; i=i+1)
67            { printf("  c=%d",get_next_char() ) ; }
68          printf("\n thru  \n");
69        scanf("%c%c",&c,&c);   /* pause here */
70
71
72          /* test  get previous char */
73          printf(" test get previous char \n ") ;
74          i = 0 ;
75          c = get_previous_char() ;
76          while( c != BOF_MARK )
77            { printf("  c=%d",c);
78              c = get_previous_char() ;
```

Figure 3.30   continues

Figure 3.30 continued

```
79                 i = i + 1 ;
80                 if( i > 100 )
81                      break ;
82            }
83        printf("\n bof reached - c=%d \n",c);
84        scanf("%c%c",&c,&c);   /* pause here */
85
86        move_to(0L) ;
87        printf(" test get previous char - at BOF \n ") ;
88        for(i=0 ; i < 10 ; i=i+1)
89             { printf("   c=%d",get_previous_char() ) ; }
90        printf("\n thru ");
91
92        close_file() ;
93    }
```

FIGURE 3.31   testio Output

```
1      C>testio
2       testing I/O module
3
4       file name: test.dat
5       open_file = 1
6       fp = 590
7       calling set_filesize
8       filesize= 11
9
10      calling check_ctrl_z
11      filesize= 10
12
13      move_to 3
14      next char is 13   where_ now = 4   ftell=4
15      next char is 10   where_ now = 5   ftell=5
16      move_to 1
17      next char is 98   where_ now = 2   ftell=2
18
19      test get next char - sequential reads
20        c=97  c=98  c=99  c=13  c=10  c=49  c=50  c=51  c=13  c=10
21      eof reached - c=-1
22
23
24      test get next char - at eof
25        c=-1  c=-1  c=-1  c=-1  c=-1  c=-1  c=-1  c=-1  c=-1  c=-1
26      thru
27
28
29      test get previous char
30        c=10  c=13  c=51  c=50  c=49  c=10  c=13  c=99  c=98  c=97
31      bof reached - c=-2
32
33
34      test get previous char - at BOF
35        c=-2  c=-2  c=-2  c=-2  c=-2  c=-2  c=-2  c=-2  c=-2  c=-2
36      thru
37
38    C>
```

The tests are fairly simple. All the functions except `open_file` require that the data file be opened and that a file pointer identify the open file. So we start with `open_file`. Since the other functions also require that the `filesize` variable be set properly, `set_filesize` is tested next. As each function is tested, it can be used to aid in testing the other functions. The `move_to` and `where_now` functions are useful in this way.

Testing Summary

We have covered testing the individual functions in VIEW. The next chapter discusses more topics: testing the program as a whole, building test data files, and tracking down the bugs exposed by testing.

The test programs that we wrote have lasting value; we should not throw them away as soon as the VIEW program works. Bugs often turn up later, and these testing tools will help find them. Successful programs evolve with enhancements added as practical use suggests them. These enhancements need testing to ensure that they do what was intended and do not interfere with the rest of the program. Without available test programs, there is an irresistible temptation to bypass thorough testing of enhancements. With test programs already written, it is easy and relatively painless to modify them and run new tests.

The VIEW program went through several revisions to make it simpler and more clear in structure. The test programs evolved along with VIEW and made the revision process much easier.

We have presented a very methodical approach of testing programs. Each step is small and fairly quick. It produces steady progress and gives positive feedback at short intervals. The problem is that we set out to write one program and wound up writing several more. You may feel that even if it is the best way to do the job, it is too much work to be practical. The following paragraphs give reasons why it is actually the quicker and easier way to produce useful programs.

The usual method of testing is to add a few `printf` statements at key points in the program and run the whole program. Each time the program does something wrong, you must figure out what it is actually doing and then try to pinpoint the cause of the problem. This usually requires adding some new `printf` statements and running the program again.

Since the `printf` statements intrude on the normal operation of the program, they are usually removed when the bug is found. When the next bug is found, some new `printf` statements are inserted, and the detective work begins again. After the program is believed to work, the `printf` statements are removed. When enhancements are made, some fresh `printf` statements are inserted, and the testing process starts from scratch.

None of the test programs we presented requires a source code debugger such as Codeview or the debuggers built into Turbo C or QuickC. Such tools make the job of testing quicker, but they do not change the nature of testing. We may need fewer printf statements and fewer uses of scanf to set return values, but we still need to define the cases to be tested and to devise efficient tests.

Our methodical approach to testing does require some support from the computer and its software. It requires that editing, compiling, and linking a 50- to 100-line program be quick and easy (no more than 1 to 2 minutes). Access to a computer for at least an hour a day is also necessary. The language used must allow separate compilation and must support modular programs composed of many small functions. Fortunately, using C on a PC meets these requirements.

3.6   Measuring the Performance of VIEW

Now that the VIEW program works correctly, we can see how well it performs. Since VIEW is an interactive program, we want to know how long it takes to respond to an input command. We can use a stopwatch to time the interval from pressing a key for an input command until the updating of the screen has been completed. The following table shows our results using Microsoft C and Turbo C:

| | Time (in seconds) | |
Operation	Microsoft C	Turbo C
View file-name	2	2
Next page	2	2
Previous page	2	40
First page	2	2
Last page	3	5
Move to position 20,000	2	2
Next line	2	2
Previous line	2	2
Exit to DOS	0.5	0.5

These results were measured for a file of about 60K bytes on an IBM AT with a fast hard disk. Times are equivalent for Microsoft C and Turbo C are equivalent except for the Previous Page command.

The next step is to find out how different parts of the program are contributing to the overall response time. We can collect this information by modifying the programs we used earlier for testing. For example, Figure 3.32 shows a program to measure the performance of the display_page and disp_prompt functions. As we did in the testing of VIEW, we replace some real functions by stub functions. This allows us to measure the speed of display_page independent of the real get_next_char function.

Some parts of VIEW need no measurements; they are used only on entry or exit. Others are executed once and perform only a few statements. The table on page 118 shows timings for functions that might be contributing to response time.

FIGURE 3.32 perfdisp.c

```
1     /* perfdisp.c - measure the performance of disp_page */
2     #include <stdio.h>
3     #include <string.h>
4     #include "viewparm.h"
5     char filename[81] ;
6     char s[2500] ;
7     extern int row,col ;
8     long filesize ;
9     long top_of_page ;
10    int ix ;
11
12    main()
13     {
14       int  j  , ll ;
15       char c;
16
17       /* initialize filename , top_of_page and filesize */
18       strcpy(filename,"< file name >");
19       top_of_page = 3000 ;     filesize = 123456789 ;
20
21       /* build list of chars to be displayed */
22       printf("\n line length:");
23       scanf("%d",&ll);
24       for( j=0 ; j < ll ; j = j + 1 )
25          { s[j] = ' '+ j  ;  }
26       s[ll] = '\0' ;
27
28       printf("\n press enter to start"); /* standing start */
29       scanf("%c%c",&c,&c);
30
31       for( j=1; j <= 10 ; j = j + 1) /* display the page 10 times */
32          {  display_page() ;
33              disp_prompt() ;
34          }
35       printf("\n ** thru **");
36     }
37
38    int get_next_char()
39     {
40       if( s[ix] == '\0' )
41          { ix = 0 ;
42              return('\n') ;
43          }
44       else
45          { ix = ix + 1 ;
46              return( s[ix-1] ) ;
47          }
48     }
49
50    void move_to(pos)
51     long pos ;
52     {
53        ix = 0 ;
54     }
```

| | Time (in seconds) | |
Operation	Microsoft C	Turbo C
display_page		
10 char lines	1.0	1.0
20 char lines	1.1	1.2
40 char lines	1.3	1.4
80 char lines	1.3	1.4
move_forward(16 lines)		
40 char lines	0.016	0.012
80 char lines	0.033	0.027
move_backward(16 lines)		
40 char lines	0.018	0.012
80 char lines	0.033	0.028
get_next_char(16 lines)		
40 char lines	0.22	0.22
80 char lines	0.45	0.45
get_previous_char(16 lines)		
40 char lines	0.85	19
80 char lines	1.5	42

These figures give us a roadmap to follow if we want to improve the performance of the VIEW program. For example, we can see that making the `move_forward` function faster would have little effect on overall performance. The `display_page` and `get_previous_char` functions are both candidates for improvement. For Turbo C, the `get_previous_char` function is very slow; it makes the VIEW program unusable as it stands. Although experienced programmers can often guess at the location of performance bottlenecks., surprises like this one are always possible. Measurement is a much better guide for enhancements than is guesswork because it allows us to concentrate our efforts where they will be fruitful.

Conclusions about performance bottlenecks may be different for your compiler and environment. You should run similar tests for your system to guide your enhancements to VIEW.

3.7   Enhancing VIEW

The VIEW program meets the functional specification that we defined for it. That specification was kept simple to allow the program to be small and to have a clear structure. There is room for improvement, however. The more useful a program is, the more enhancements come to mind. Some possibilities are listed in this section.

For the enhancements marked with the disk symbol, sample solutions are provided on the source code disk.

Faster Screen Output

Although VIEW is fast enough to be useful, it is not fast enough to be pleasant to use. Displaying a page of text on the screen is one area for improvement. Further performance measurements suggest that the limitation is mostly due to the speed of output through the operating system's standard output services. The direct screen output functions from Chapter 7 are much faster and reduce the display bottleneck. Chapter 4 enhances the similar file dump program to use direct screen updating.

Eliminating Scrolling

When a new command is entered and the screen updated, the screen is scrolled upward as each new line is written. This is distracting, especially when a single line movement is involved. Reducing the amount of extraneous motion would make VIEW more pleasant to use. Erasing the screen and positioning the cursor at the top of the screen is one way to accomplish this.

In addition, we need rewrite only part of the screen. The command prompts and the dashed lines above and below the text area do not change. We can position the cursor to update file position and then position the cursor to update the text display area.

A Modern User Interface

VIEW provides a simple user interface. The menu of commands is always visible on the screen. This approach uses up 6 lines on the screen that we could have used to display more text. If more commands were supported, the approach would not be feasible at all. A better user interface would leave more space for text but still provide clues about entering commands. We should also provide a Help key that invokes a pop-up menu of available commands. A directory listing of file names would make it easier to specify the file name we want to view.

Chapter 8 revises VIEW to use multiple windows with a pop-up Help screen.

Movement by Line Number

The MOVETOPOS command specifies a new file position in terms of characters from the beginning of the file. It would be more useful to specify a number of lines from the beginning. To implement this feature, we need to know where lines begin in the file. We could scan the file looking for end-of-line markers when VIEW starts executing. Or we could scan the file when the MOVETOPOS command is first executed.

The VIEW program as presented does not store the file in memory. It requires no more memory to handle very large files. Keeping track of line numbers would seem to require an array locating the beginning of each line. How can we implement the line number feature without limiting VIEW to small files?

Keeping track of line numbers also makes it easy to move backward in a file and solves performance problems with the get_previous_char function.

Different End-of-Line Conventions

Some text files may contain a single carriage return character (13) to mark the end of a line of text. A way to accommodate such files would make VIEW more useful.

We could define an option on the command line to select a end-of-line marker character other than the line feed character. A better approach would be to modify viewfind.c and viewdisp.c to recognize a carriage return, a line feed, or both as an end-of-line marker. This would add some complication, but it might make VIEW applicable to more text files.

Tab Size on the Command Line

VIEW always expands tab characters based on an interval of 8 columns between tab stops. Some files are designed to be printed with other tab intervals. Allowing the tab interval to be specified by a command-line argument would make VIEW more useful.

Long Lines of Text

VIEW handles files with an occasional line a little longer than 80 columns in an acceptable way. But it would not be satisfactory for files with many long lines or lines that were much longer than 80 columns. Moving forward and backward in the file in terms of lines on the screen would work more smoothly.

Moving forward in the file would require VIEW to keep track of the current row and column as we moved forward in the file. This would be similar to the logic of the disp_char function.

Moving backward would require an extra step. We would have to find the beginning of the previous line and then move forward in that line, keeping track of the current row and column. The search for the beginning of the line would be limited to some maximum number of characters to prevent looking through an entire file when no end-of-line character is present.

💾   **Printed Output**

VIEW is designed for interactive use. We can quickly move around in a file, examining its structure without waiting for a bulky printed file dump. But sometimes we want to produce a printed listing of an interesting part of a file. VIEW needs a command to print all or part of a file. We might specify beginning and ending file positions of the area to be printed. Commands for marking the beginning and ending of a file would be easier to use.

💾   **Search Commands**

Additional commands to search forward or backward in the file for a string of characters would make VIEW more useful on large files. This would require changes in several places. New constants would be added to `viewparm.h` and new cases added to `get_cmd` to recognize these commands. `exec_cmd` would also need cases for these commands. Finally, functions to perform the search operations would be needed. The following pseudo-code provides a guide for implementing the search functions:

```
exec_cmd case for forward search
    get string from keyboard
    search forward
    move backward half a page
    (puts string in middle of page)
    display the new page
end



search_forward for a string(s)
    start at top of page
    repeat until first char matched
        get next char from file
        compare to 1st char of string
    remember this position
    repeat until no match or end of string
        get next char from file
        compare to next char in string
    restore remembered position
    if entire string matched
        make top_of_page
        return to caller
    (if matching failed, we will try again)
end
```

3.8   Fixing the get_previous_char Function

VIEW is not a usable program if we compile it with Turbo C. Our job is not finished yet. Performance tests showed that the `get_previous_char` function is the problem — the `fseek` function is not designed to be called for each character read.

Figure 3.33 shows our replacement: the `get_p_char` function. `get_p_char` returns the preceding character from the `buf` array on each call. When we reach the beginning of this array, the `fill_array` function reads n characters before the current position. We keep track of our position in the file with the `pos` variable and in the array with the `bix` variable. The `start_back` function must be called before calls to `get_p_char`; it sets the current file position, `pos`, and the buffer index, `bix`. The `end_back` function is called when the final position has been reached. `end_back` calls the `move_to` function to set the real file position to our position in the buffer.

FIGURE 3.33   viewback.c

```
1    /* viewback.c - replacement for get_previous_char */
2    #include "viewparm.h"
3
4    #define ARRAY_SIZE   ( (PAGE_SIZE + 1) * 80 )
5    static char buf[ ARRAY_SIZE ] ; /* buffer for preceding chars */
6                                    /* exact size not important */
7    static int bix ;                /* position in buf */
8    static long pos ;               /* our position in the file */
9                                    /* corresponding to our position */
10                                   /* in the buffer (bix) */
11
12   void fill_array(void) ;
13
14   start_back()                    /* initialize buffer */
15   {
16       pos = where_now() ;         /* get our file position   */
17       bix = 0 ;                   /* start with empty buffer */
18   }
19
20
21   int get_p_char()                /* get previous char */
22   {
23       bix = bix - 1 ;             /* reduce buffer index */
24       if( bix < 0 )               /* at end of buffer ? */
25         { if( pos == 0 )          /*    yes - check for file begining */
26              return( BOF_MARK);/*        yes - return BOF */
27           fill_array() ;          /*        no - fill buffer */
28         }
29       pos = pos - 1 ;
30       return( buf[ bix ] ) ; /* return corresponding char */
31   }
32
33
34   void end_back()                 /* set real file position to ours */
35   {
36       move_to( pos ) ;
37   }
38
```

Figure 3.33   continues

Figure 3.33   continued

```
39
40    void fill_array()              /* refill buf with n preceding chars*/
41      {
42        int n ;                    /* number chars to read */
43
44        n = ARRAY_SIZE ;
45        if( n > pos )              /* check for file beginning */
46            n = pos ;
47        move_to( pos - n ) ;       /* set position */
48        for( bix=0 ; bix < n ; bix = bix + 1 )  /* read n chars */
49            { buf[ bix ] = get_next_char() ; }
50        bix = n - 1 ;              /* decrement bix for get_p_char */
51      }
```

FIGURE 3.34   viewfin2.c

```
 1    /* viewfin2.c file - move_backward enhancement for Turbo C */
 2    #include <stdio.h>
 3    #include "viewparm.h"
 4    long top_of_page ;           /* file position - top of display page */
 5
 6    void start_back( void ) ;
 7    int get_p_char( void ) ;
 8    void end_back( void ) ;
 9
10    void move_forward(nlines)    /* move forward n lines */
11     int nlines ;               /* number of lines to move */
12      {
13        int c ;                  /* hold chars read here */
14
15        move_to(top_of_page) ;     /* start at top of page */
16        while( nlines > 0 )
17          { c = get_next_char() ;
18            if( c  == END_LINE )  /* check for end of line */
19                nlines = nlines - 1 ;
20            if( c == EOF_MARK )   /* check for end of file */
21              { set_top_page() ;  /* yes - mark as top of the page */
22                return ;          /*        and exit */
23              }
24          }
25        set_top_page() ;         /* mark this as top of the page */
26      }
27
28
29    void move_backward(nlines)   /* move backward n lines */
30     int nlines ;               /* number of lines to move */
31      {                          /* (zero means start of this line) */
32        int c ;                  /* hold char here */
33
34        move_to(top_of_page) ;     /* start at top of page */
35        start_back() ;             /* set up for backing up */
36        nlines = nlines + 1 ;      /* add one for current line */
37        while( nlines > 0 )
38          { c = get_p_char();
39            if(  c  == END_LINE )
40                nlines = nlines - 1 ;
```

Figure 3.34   continues

Figure 3.34 continued

```
41                 if( c == BOF_MARK )    /* check for BOF */
42                    { end_back() ;       /* finished backing up */
43                       set_top_page() ;  /* yes - mark as top of page */
44                       return ;          /* and exit */
45                    }
46                 }
47                                         /* we're before an end_line */
48             end_back() ;                /* finished backing up */
49             get_next_char() ;           /* move past it */
50             set_top_page() ;            /* mark as top of page */
51          }
52
53
54       void set_top_page()
55       {
56          top_of_page = where_now() ;
57       }
```

A few changes must also be made to the move_backward function as shown in Figure 3.34. Calls to start_back and end_back are added and get_p_char is used instead of get_previous_char.

3.9 Summary

In this chapter we followed the development of the VIEW program from its initial design through implementation and testing. We concluded with a discussion of possible enhancements to the VIEW program and implemented one enhancement. The C language provided a tool for implementation, but the success or failure of the VIEW program is mostly determined by the work we do in design, implementation, and testing. Without explicit, detailed specifications, our programs will not perform useful functions. Without careful testing, we cannot trust our programs. Without orderly, modular implementation, our programs will not be an efficient starting point for enhancements. There is much more to good programming than learning the elements of C. This chapter is a first look at using C to write serious, useful programs.

4
Dumping Files in
Hexadecimal Notation

The VIEW program presented in Chapter 3 interprets a file as a sequence of ASCII characters. It is a useful tool for looking at text files of ASCII characters. Sometimes we need a tool for looking at a file on a lower level. For example, if we need to read a file created by a program such as WordStar, dBase III, or Lotus 1-2-3, we need to find out exactly how the file is formatted. Such products rarely provide adequate documentation of file formats; it is usually up to us to figure out how the file is formatted. Once we understand the structure of a file, writing a C program to read it is usually feasible. We need a tool that shows every byte in a file, and whether it represents a control character, a printable ASCII character, or any other possible 8-bit pattern (such as part of a integer).

The file dump program (FD) developed in this chapter serves this purpose. It displays the contents of a file in two formats: hexadecimal and a modified ASCII format. This kind of dump program is common on larger systems. Software products with this function are also available for the IBM PC. FD is traditional in the kind of dump format it displays; there is no need for a unique approach.

4.1 Specifying the FD Program

We already have one program, VIEW, to display a file interactively. Much of the design (and the C source files themselves) are applicable to the FD program. This can save time in implementing FD, and it makes good use of our experience with VIEW. We will use the same input commands and the same keys to invoke them as in VIEW.

The only part of the specification that must be changed from that for VIEW is the display format. Since we can copy the display format from existing utilities (such as the MS-DOS debugger), we can specify FD without much creative effort. Figure 4.1

FIGURE 4.1   Description of File Dump Program (FD)

Name
FD   displays a file in Hex form a screenful at a time.

Usage
From DOS, type FD and the name of file to be viewed.

```
C>FD file-name
```

If you do not specify a file name, FD will prompt for a name.

Function
FD displays the contents of a data file on the screen. Data is displayed byte-by-byte in hexadecimal form and as ASCII characters. On entry FD displays the first screenful in the file and waits for a command. Single key commands provide movement in the file by single lines or pages. Commands for movement to the beginning and end of the file are also provided.

Bytes are displayed as two hexadecimal digits and as ASCII characters. Bytes that correspond to ASCII graphic characters are displayed. Carriage return, line feed, and control-Z are displayed as special symbols (paragraph sign, down arrow, and a left arrowhead). Other byte values are displayed as a block graphic symbol.

Commands
Inside FD, the following list of single key commands (you do not need to press the return key) are recognized:

```
HOME                    displays the first page in the file.
END                     displays the last page in the file.
PgUp                    moves backward in the file almost one page.
PgDn                    moves forward in the file almost one page.
Down Arrow              moves forward in the file by one line.
Up Arrow                moves backward in the file by one line.
Space Bar               moves to a positionyou specify.
Escape                  ends the program and returns to DOS.
```

The program displays three areas on the screen: a heading, the data itself (16 lines with 16 bytes per line), and a prompt describing the input commands.

```
FILE - sample.txt    POSITION - 0    FILE SIZE - 750
------------------------------------------------------------
0000 | 41 32 48 97 0D 0A 1A 8D ...      | A 0a    ...
0016 ...
  .
  .
  .
------------------------------------------------------------
Type one of these Input Commands
HOME = First Page    ↑  = Prev. Line    PG UP = Prev. Page
END  = Last  Page    ↓  = Next Line     PG DN = Next  Page
Esc  = Exit Pgm    Space= Move to Position
```

describes FD. There is only one creative element: We display interesting control characters such as carriage return, line feed and control-Z as special IBM PC graphic symbols. This will help us see the line structure in text files.

There are a few minor choices to made made. Instead of the two-line overlap between pages in VIEW, FD has no overlap between pages. FD displays a fixed number of bytes on each line; 16 bytes fit comfortably in 80 columns.

Our choice of hexadecimal notation for displaying byte values follows many other dump programs, but it has clear justifications over using decimal notation:

1. Hexadecimal requires 2 digits per byte against 3 for decimal.
2. A 2-byte integer value can be read easily. You just put the hex digits for each byte together. For example, the byte values `0x12` followed by `0x34` are the integer `0x3412`. (On the Intel 8086 family of computers, the least significant byte is stored first.) In contrast, the decimal byte values `12` followed by `34` correspond to the integer value `34*256+12` or `8716`.
3. The relation between ASCII characters and hexadecimal values is useful in deciphering bytes. Values from `00` through `1F` are ASCII control characters, whereas values from `20` through `7E` are graphic (printable) characters. Values from `80` through `FF` have the high-order bit set. For example, the value `0D` is a carriage return, whereas `8D` is a carriage return with the high-order bit set.

So you can accept our choice of hexadecimal notation on faith or believe our reasons. You can even modify the program to display byte values as you wish.

4.2 Pseudo-Code for FD

In designing FD, we have a different job than we did in designing VIEW. We have decided to make FD similar to the VIEW program. We can go through the pseudo-code for VIEW and identify differences:

- Overall structure: No difference.
- Getting a file name: No difference.
- Getting an input command: No difference.
- Executing an input command: Movement in the file can still be described in lines and pages but they are fixed in length in FD.
- Moving forward/back: Fixed size lines.
- Displaying a page: Each byte is displayed twice, once in hexadecimal and once in ASCII form.

We will ignore the differences between VIEW and FD in all but the moving forward/back function and the display page function. The revised pseudo-code for moving forward and backward is made simpler by the fixed line size in FD as follows:

```
move_forward(n lines)
        move the file position forward (n*line_size) characters
end

move_backward(n lines)
        move the file position backward (n*line_size) characters
end
```

The display_page function differs more from that in VIEW. For every line of data, there are several separate activities, for example, displaying the corresponding file position and displaying bytes in hexadecimal and in ASCII. So display_page is organized around lines of 16 bytes rather than single characters. The following pseudo-code shows this organization:

```
display_page
        write heading - file name, position in file and file size
        for each of page_size lines
                read a line of data
                display the line of data
end


display_line
        display starting position of line
        for each of 16 bytes of data
                display in Hex format
        for each of 16 bytes of data
                display in ASCII form
end


display_in_ASCII_form
        if( char is a graphic ASCII char )
                display it
        else if( char is Carriage Return char )
                display as CR graphic
        else if( char is Line Feed )
                display as LF graphic
        else if( char is CTL-Z char )
                display as CTL-Z graphic
        else display as non-printable graphic
end
```

FD requires the same constants and data as VIEW. Many of the same exceptions apply — reaching the beginning or end of the file, for example.

4.3   The FD Program Listing

FD is structured just as VIEW was. The following hierarchy of function calls is very similar to that for VIEW. Since `display_page` performs a different function in FD, it calls different functions.

```
main
      get_filename
      set_filesize
      get_cmd
            getkey
      exec_cmd
            move_forward
                  move_to
                  set_top_page
                        where_now
            move_backward
                  move_to
                  set_top_page
            move_to
            get_pos
      disp_prompt
      display_page
            read_line
            prtline
                  disp_char
```

The functions are grouped in source files in much the same way, too. The new source files are named `fdxxxx.c` in this case, but the groupings are the same:

Source File	Functions	Purpose
`fd.c`	`main`	Overall flow.
`viewget.c`	`get_cmd`	Input a command.
`fdexec.c`	`exec_cmd`	Execute a command.
`viewgetf.c`	`get_pos`	Input file name.
	`get_filename`	Input file position.
`fdfind.c`	`move_forward`	Move display page.
	`move_backward`	
	`set_top_page`	
`fddisp.c`	`display_page`	Display a page.
	`prtline`	
	`disp_char`	
	`disp_prompt`	Display prompt.
`fdio.c`	`open_file, close_file`	
	`set_filesize`	Handle file I/O.
	`move_to, where_now`	
	`read_line`	

Two header files, `viewcmds.h` and `fdparm.h`, are used in FD. Since FD uses the same commands that VIEW used, the `viewcmds.h` file can be used with changes. The `fdparm.h` file shown in Figure 4.2 is based on `viewparm.h`. The constant specifying the number of lines of overlap between old and new pages is changed to 0. In addition, a new parameter, LINE_SIZE, specifies the number of bytes displayed on each line. Function prototypes are declared for the functions used in FD.

The `fd.c` file in Figure 4.3 is based on `view.c`. There are two changes: `fdparm.h` is included instead of `viewparm.h` and `check_ctrl_z` is not called. In FD we do

FIGURE 4.2   fdparm.h

```
 1      /* fdparm.h - parameters for FD program */
 2
 3      /* number of lines in a display page */
 4      #define  PAGE_SIZE      16
 5
 6      /* number of bytes per line */
 7      #define  LINE_SIZE      16
 8
 9      /* number of lines of overlap between display pages */
10      #define  LINES_OVERLAP   0
11
12      /* return values from get_next_char and get_previous_char  to */
13      /* indicate that beginning or end of the file has been reached */
14      #define  EOF_MARK        -1
15      #define  BOF_MARK        -2
16
17      /* definition of control char marking the end of a line */
18      #define  END_LINE        10
19
20      /* define success/failure for return codes */
21      #define SUCCESS   1
22      #define FAILURE   0
23
24                                  /* function prototypes */
25      int get_cmd(void) ;         /* get a command */
26      void exec_cmd(int) ;        /* execute a command */
27      void move_forward(int) ;    /* move forward in file */
28      void move_backward(int) ;   /* move backward in file */
29      void set_top_page(void) ;   /* set top of page variable */
30      void display_page(void) ;   /* display a page of text */
31      void disp_char(int) ;       /* display one char */
32      void disp_prompt(void) ;    /* display the prompt */
33      long get_pos(long) ;        /* get file position input */
34      void get_filename(char *) ; /* get file name input */
35      int open_file(char *) ;     /* open the file */
36      void set_filesize(void) ;   /* find file size */
37      void check_ctrl_z(void) ;   /* adjust file size for control Z */
38      void move_to(long) ;        /* change file position */
39      long where_now(void) ;      /* return file position */
40      int get_next_char(void) ;   /* get a character - forward */
41      int get_previous_char(void) ;   /* get a character - backward */
42      void close_file(void) ;     /* close the file */
43      void prtline(char *,int) ;  /* print one line - hex and ASCII */
44      int read_line(char *,int);  /* read N characters */
```

FIGURE 4.3 fd.c

```
1      /* fd.c -  FD program - main function */
2      #include <stdio.h>
3      #include <string.h>
4      #include "viewcmds.h"
5      #include "fdparm.h"
6
7      char filename[65] = "" ;
8
9      main(argc,argv)
10      int argc ;
11      char *argv[] ;
12      {
13         int cmd ;                  /* holds current cmd      */
14
15         if( argc >= 2 )           /* get file name from command line */
16            strcpy(filename,argv[1]) ;   /* (if present) */
17
18         get_filename(filename);/* get file name and open file */
19         set_filesize();          /* set up file size variable */
20
21         cmd = FIRSTPAGE ;          /* force display of 1st page */
22
23         while( cmd != EXITPGM )/* repeat until told to exit */
24            { exec_cmd(cmd);       /* execute the current command */
25              disp_prompt() ;      /* display command prompt */
26              cmd = get_cmd();     /* get the next command */
27            }
28
29         close_file() ;
30      }
```

not interpret control-Z in a special way; it should not adjust the file size based on the presence of a control-Z in the file.

The fdexec.c file is not shown. The only change to viewexec.c (Figure 3.13) is to include fdparm.h instead of viewparm.h.

Since FD uses the same input commands and the same way of accepting a new file position, the viewget.c and viewgetf.c files need not be changed. In fact, they need not be recompiled. We can link the object files viewget.obj and viewgetf.obj with the new object files.

fdfind.c

The functions in fdfind.c (Figure 4.4) are different from those in viewfind.c. In FD, the definition of a line is very simple: 16 bytes. The move_forward and move_backward functions do not have to look at the contents of the file. Handling the beginning and the end of file exception cases is also simple; we test the new file position to see that it is between 0 and the file size.

FIGURE 4.4   fdfind.c

```
1    /* fdfind.c file - move to new positions in the file */
2    #include <stdio.h>
3    #include "fdparm.h"
4
5    long top_of_page ;          /* file position of display page */
6    extern long filesize ;      /* length of file in bytes */
7
8
9    void move_forward(nlines)
10    int nlines ;               /* number of lines to move */
11    {
12        long new_pos ;
13
14        new_pos = top_of_page + (nlines*LINE_SIZE) ;
15        if( new_pos > filesize)
16            new_pos = filesize ;
17        move_to(new_pos) ;      /* start at top of page */
18        set_top_page() ;        /* make new top of display page */
19    }
20
21
22    void move_backward(nlines)
23    int nlines ;               /* number of lines to move */
24    {                          /* 0 = start of current line */
25        long new_pos ;
26
27        new_pos = top_of_page - (nlines*LINE_SIZE) ;
28        if( new_pos < 0L )
29            new_pos = 0L ;
30        move_to(new_pos) ;      /* start at top of page */
31        set_top_page() ;        /* make new top of display page */
32    }
33
34
35    void set_top_page()
36    {
37        top_of_page = where_now() ;
38    }
```

fddisp.c

The display_page function in Figure 4.5 has a structure similar to that of its namesake in the VIEW program. It displays a heading, uses prtline to display each line of data, and pads out the page if the end of the file is reached before a full page is displayed. A line of dashes separates the heading line from the lines displaying data. Another line of dashes precedes the list of input command prompts to be written by the disp_prompt function. Once again we use the structure established for VIEW, keeping the changes to a few lower level functions.

The display_page function reads one line of data at a time. Since each byte of data will be used twice—once for the hexadecimal format display and once for the ASCII format display—it is convenient to read the whole line first. Near the end of the file, the read_line function may read less than a full line of data.

FIGURE 4.5   fddisp.c

```
1     /* fddisp.c file - display current page of file */
2     #include "stdio.h"
3     #include "cminor.h"
4     #include "fdparm.h"
5
6     extern char    filename[] ;
7     extern long    filesize ;    /* size of file in bytes */
8     extern long    top_of_page; /* file position of top of page */
9
10    /*  special symbols for CR, LF, CTL-Z, and other ctl chars */
11    #define PRT_CR    20
12    #define PRT_LF    25
13    #define PRT_CTLZ 17
14    #define PRT_OTHER 22
15    #define ASC_CTLZ  26
16
17    int  row ;                    /* current line of page */
18    long start ;
19
20    void display_page()          /* displays current page */
21    {
22        char block[ LINE_SIZE ] ;
23        int  nbytes ;
24        int i ;                   /* index for loops  */
25
26        move_to(top_of_page);    /* start at top of the page */
27                                 /* write a header line */
28        printf("\n FILE - %s    POSITION - %ld    FILE SIZE - %ld \n"
29            ,filename,top_of_page,filesize);
30
31                                 /* write a border line of dashes */
32        for( i=1 ; i <= 80 ; i = i + 1 )
33            { putchar('-'); }
34
35        /* get chars until we've written (PAGE_SIZE) lines */
36        /* or we've reached the end of the file */
37        row = 1 ;                 /* starting row values */
38        start = top_of_page ;
39        while( row <= PAGE_SIZE  )
40            { nbytes = read_line(block,LINE_SIZE) ;
41              if( nbytes <= 0 )
42                  break ;
43              prtline(block,nbytes) ;
44              start = start + nbytes ;
45              row = row + 1 ;
46            }
47
48        while( row <= PAGE_SIZE )   /* pad out page if eof reached */
49          { putchar('\n'); row = row + 1 ; }
50
51                                 /* write a border line of dashes */
52        for( i=1 ; i <= 80 ; i = i + 1 )
53            { putchar('-'); }
54    }
55
56
```

Figure 4.5   continues

Figure 4.5   continued

```
57      void prtline(block,nbytes) /* prints one line */
58       char block[] ;
59       int  nbytes ;
60       {
61           int i ;
62
63           printf("%8ld  | ",start) ;     /* print file pos. */
64           for(i=0 ; i < LINE_SIZE ; i=i+1) /* print bytes in Hex. */
65             { if ( i < nbytes )
66                     printf("%02x ",( tochar(block[i]) ) ) ;
67               else printf("   ") ;        /* out of data - fill in */
68             }
69
70           printf("| ") ;
71
72           for(i=0; i < nbytes ; i = i+1 ) /* display in ASCII form */
73               { disp_char( tochar(block[i]) ) ; }
74           putchar('\n');
75       }
76
77
78      void disp_char(c)               /* display one char in ASCII form */
79       int c ;                        /* value of char to display */
80       {
81           /* classify the character and handle accordingly */
82
83           if( (c >= ' ') && (c <= '~') )
84               ;                      /* ASCII graphic - just display it */
85           else if( c == '\n' )
86               c = PRT_LF ;           /* newline (LF) - display symbol */
87           else if( c == '\r' )
88               c = PRT_CR ;           /* Carr. Return - display symbol */
89           else if ( c == ASC_CTLZ )
90               c = PRT_CTLZ ;         /* CTL-Z - display symbol */
91           else c = PRT_OTHER ;       /* other char - display symbol */
92
93           putchar(c) ;
94       }
95
96
97      #define  UP_A  24              /* displays up arrow */
98      #define  DN_A  25              /* displays down arrow */
99
100     void disp_prompt()             /* display prompts for commands */
101     {
102         printf( "\n          Type one of these Input Commands");
103         printf( "\n HOME  = First Page       ");
104         printf( "   %c   = Previous Line    ",UP_A);
105         printf( "  PG UP = Previous Page ");
106         printf( "\n END   = Last  Page       ");
107         printf( "   %c   = Next Line        ",DN_A);
108         printf( "  PG DN = Next Page ");
109         printf( "\n ESC   = Exit Pgm         ");
110         printf( "   SPACE = Move to position \n");
111     }
```

The prtline function displays one line of data. If less than a full line of data is present, prtline fills the space with blanks instead of displayed data. This preserves the column alignment of the ASCII format display regardless of the number of bytes of data present.

The disp_char function displays a single character in a modified ASCII form. Non-ASCII graphic characters are displayed using special symbols available on the IBM PC display. The carriage return, line feed, and control-Z characters are displayed with the symbols ¶, ↓, ◁, whereas other nongraphic characters are displayed as the symbol ■.

fdio.c

The fdio.c file in Figure 4.6 is similar to the viewio.c file. Only the read_line function has been added. read_line reads the number of bytes requested (using the getc library function) unless the end of the file is reached first. In either case, it returns the number of bytes actually read.

FIGURE 4.6 fdio.c

```
1    /* fdio.c file - I/O module for FD program */
2    #include <stdio.h>
3    #include "cminor.h"
4    #include "fdparm.h"
5
6    #define   CTL_Z       26      /* marks EOF in some text files */
7    #define   BSIZE     8192      /* buffer size */
8    char buf[ BSIZE ] ;           /* file buffer */
9
10   FILE *fp ;                    /* file pointer for text file */
11   long filesize ;               /* size of the file in bytes */
12
13
14   int open_file(fn)             /* open a file */
15    char fn[] ;                  /* file name string */
16    {                            /* return success or failure */
17        fp = fopen(fn,"rb") ;
18        if(fp != NULL)
19           { setvbuf(fp,buf, _IOFBF, BSIZE ) ;
20             return(SUCCESS) ;
21           }
22        else return( FAILURE ) ;
23    }
24
25
26   void set_filesize()           /* set up file size */
27    {
28        fseek(fp,0L,SEEK_END) ;   /* get size of file */
29        filesize = ftell(fp) ;
30    }
31
32   void check_ctl_z()
33    {
34        long back ;
35        int c ;
```

Figure 4.6   continues

Figure 4.6   continued

```
36
37              /* check last 128 byte block for a CTL-Z */
38              back = filesize % 128 ;    /* find start of last block? */
39              if( (back == 0) && (filesize > 0) ) /* at start of block? */
40                 back = 128 ;            /*    yes - use previous block */
41              fseek(fp, filesize - back ,SEEK_SET);
42              c = getc(fp);
43              while( c != EOF )
44                { if( c == CTL_Z )     /* control-Z? */
45                    { filesize = ftell(fp) - 1 ;
46                      return ;           /*   yes - adjust file size and exit */
47                    }
48                  c = getc(fp);
49                }
50          }
51
52
53      void move_to(new_pos)           /* move to specified position */
54        long new_pos ;
55        {
56            fseek(fp,new_pos,SEEK_SET);
57        }
58
59
60      long where_now()                /* return current position */
61        {
62          return( ftell(fp) ) ;
63        }
64
65
66      int get_next_char()             /* get char at file position */
67        {
68          char c ;
69
70          if( ftell(fp) == filesize ) /* are we at end of file ? */
71              return( EOF_MARK ) ;    /*   yes - return end-of-file */
72          else                        /*   no  -                      */
73            { c = getc(fp);           /*        get a char and */
74              return( toascii(c) ) ;  /*        force to be ascii */
75            }                         /*        return it */
76        }
77
78
79      int get_previous_char()             /* read the char in front of */
80        {                                 /* current file position */
81          char c ;
82
83          if( ftell(fp) != 0L )         /* check for beginning of file */
84            { fseek(fp,-1L,SEEK_CUR); /* back up one char */
85              c = getc(fp);             /* read a char*/
86              fseek(fp,-1L,SEEK_CUR) ;/* back up again */
87              return( toascii(c) ) ;  /* force to be ascii */
88            }                           /* and return the char */
89          else return(BOF_MARK) ;     /* at beginning of file */
90        }
91
92
93      void close_file()             /* close the file */
```

Figure 4.6   continues

Figure 4.6   continued

```
94        {
95            fclose(fp) ;
96        }
97
98
99
100    int read_line(buf,nread)            /* read a line of characters */
101      char buf[] ;                        /* put the data here */
102      int nread ;                         /* number of bytes to read */
103      {
104          int i , c ;
105
106          i = 0 ;
107          for( i=0 ; i < nread ; i=i+1 )
108              {
109                  c = getc(fp) ;
110                  if( c == EOF )
111                      break ;
112                  buf[i] = c ;
113              }
114          return( i ) ;                   /* return number of chars read */
115      }
```

In the VIEW program, bytes were interpreted as ASCII characters. Both `get_next_char` and `get_previous_char` forced the high-order bit of each character returned to be 0. FD displays byte values as they exist in the file. So `read_line` returns characters without altering the high-order bit.

Although the `get_next_char` and `get_previous_char` functions are not used in FD, we left them in `fdio.c`. These functions do not add much to the size of the program and they might be useful for enhancements to FD.

4.4   Testing FD

Testing the individual source files of FD is much the same as it was for the VIEW program. FD has a few new functions for which we need additional tests, but the process is the same. However, there are some aspects of testing that were not covered in the preceding chapter. Although we covered testing individual modules in detail, we did not discuss integrating the modules and testing the entire program. That is the subject of this section.

What do we test after the modules operate correctly? There may be mistakes in naming functions and global variables. Linking all the object files makes such mistakes appear as unresolved references or as duplicate names. If the cause of the problem is not obvious, the linker can produce a .MAP file, which lists public names and the module where they appeared. Careful reading of this listing and of the source files is usually adequate to locate the problem.

Different modules may have conflicts in the use of function arguments or return values. Thorough use of function prototypes puts the compiler to work finding conflicts; fewer errors in argument use get through compilation to be located later by our testing. Where we have tested groups of functions together in a top-down way, these problems have already been checked. For functions where the calling function and the called function have not been tested together, we need to verify that they work together. Sometimes we can do this by observing the behavior of the program without adding any special testing functions. In other cases, we need to insert statements for testing in the source files. To test the interface between the `fdfind.c` and `fdio.c` modules, we might add testing statements like the following to display arguments passed to `move_to` and values returned by `where_now`:

```
. . .
/* ??? */       printf(" calling move_to %ld \n",new_pos);
move_to(new_pos)  ;
. . .
top_of_page = where_now()  ;
/* ??? */       printf(" where_now returns %ld \n",top_of_page);
```

In the `fdio.c` source file, corresponding statements would show the arguments received and the values to be returned. When FD is compiled and executed with these versions of `fdfind.c` and `fdio.c`, we can verify that these function calls work correctly. With a source code debugger, we can set a breakpoint at the call to `where_now` and trace execution through the `where_now` function.

These testing statements present a messy problem. We want them present for testing but not when we use the program. As is often the case with problems, there are several partially satisfactory answers. In the example shown, the testing statements are marked by a comment, `/* ??? */`, on the same line. This makes it easy to find and delete them when we finish testing. Of course, we will need the testing statements again when enhancements are made. Instead of deleting these statements after testing, we could enclose them in comments, as in this example:

```
/*    printf(" calling move_to %ld \n",new_pos); */
```

We can also use the C preprocessor to skip the testing statements as the following code fragment shows:

```
#ifdef TEST_SWITCH
printf(" calling move_to %ld \n",new_pos);
#endif
```

To get a version of the module with the testing statements present, we would define the identifier `TEST_SWITCH` at the beginning of the source file:

```
#define TEST_SWITCH 1
```

If `TEST_SWITCH` is not defined, the testing statements would not be part of the compiled module. However, the presence of testing statements in source files makes them hard to read and understand. Reading source files is an important part of the testing process and understandable source files are vital when programs are enhanced. Clear, understandable listings are also important in this book; we will omit such testing statements from the source files.

If we rely on a source debugger and breakpoints, we have a different problem. We have no testing statements to clutter up source files. However, we have no record of what we tested and what the correct results should be.

After we link the entire program and verify the function call interfaces, bugs may still exist. Assumptions made in one part of the program may be inconsistent with those made in another part of the program. To find such bugs, we must run the program with a variety of files. By this time the program usually works fairly well, and our confidence in it rises rapidly. It is important to remain suspicious and alert in using the program at first. The program's output probably looks plausible, but we must make the effort to verify that it really is correct.

Getting good test data is a one part of the problem. Small files such as the `test.dat` file created in Section 3.4 are convenient for module testing. We also need to test our programs with large files. Good test data files should meet three criteria:

1. They should cover all cases.
2. We must understand exactly what they contain.
3. They must help us decipher the test results easily.

Existing files are easy to use, but they do not meet these criteria very well. Writing a short program to generate test data is often the best solution. Figure 4.7 shows a program to generate test data for FD. We specify the size of the file we want. It generates all 256 possible byte values. Since the value of a byte is related to its position (position modulo 256), we can check movement in the file quite easily. In addition, the regular pattern of the data makes it easier to spot bugs.

FIGURE 4.7   gendata.c

```
1      /* gendata.c - generate test data for FD program */
2      #include <stdio.h>
3
4
5      main(argc,argv)
6       int argc ;
7       char *argv[] ;
8       {
9          long nc , i ;
10         char b ;
11         FILE *fp ;
12
13         if( argc < 2 )
14             exit(1) ;
15         fp = fopen(argv[1],"wb") ;
16         if( fp == NULL )
17             exit(2) ;
18
```

Figure 4. 7   continues

Figure 4.7   continued

```
19          printf("number of characters:");
20          scanf("%ld",&nc) ;
21
22          for(i=0 ; i<nc ; i=i+1)
23            { b = i ;
24               putc(b,fp) ;
25            }
26          fclose(fp) ;
27        }
```

Chapter 3 did not discuss testing VIEW as a whole. But the methods we have just discussed apply there, too. Figure 4.8 shows a program to generate a text file for testing VIEW. The line numbers identify position in the file, and the fixed line size helps in translating a line number into a byte position.

When we test a program, we often need a second opinion — an independent way of doing the same thing. For example, the DOS TYPE command provides another way to display a text file. We can use it as an independent check on VIEW. The DOS DEBUG command can provide a similar check on the operation of FD. Once FD is operating correctly, it can be used to check other programs that read files.

FIGURE 4.8   gendata2.c

```
 1      /* gendata2.c - generate test data for VIEW program */
 2      #include <stdio.h>
 3
 4
 5      main(argc,argv)
 6       int argc ;
 7       char *argv[] ;
 8       {
 9          long nc , i , nl ;
10          char s[100] ;
11          FILE *fp ;
12
13          if( argc < 2 )
14              exit(1) ;
15          fp = fopen(argv[1],"wb") ;
16          if( fp == NULL )
17              exit(2) ;
18
19          printf("number of chars /line:");
20          scanf("%ld",&nl) ;
21          nl = nl - 8 ;     /* allow for line no. and CR/LF */
22          for(i=0 ; i< nl ; i=i+1)   /* set up string for line */
23            { s[i] = ' ' + i ; }
24          s[i] = '\0' ;
25
26          printf("number of lines:");
27          scanf("%ld",&nc) ;
28
29          for(i=0 ; i<nc ; i=i+1)
30            { fprintf(fp,"%5ld %s\r\n",i,s) ; }
31          fclose(fp) ;
32        }
```

4.5   Measuring FD's Performance

As for the VIEW program, response times for input commands are the important quantities to measure. The results are a bit different from those for VIEW; all the commands (except the exit command) take about 2 seconds to execute. Another look at the FD source files gives the reason — in FD the `move_forward` and `move_backward` functions do a little arithmetic rather than scanning the file as in VIEW. The measurements on individual functions in the following table show that displaying the page of data and writing the prompt message are responsible for the overall response times. Most of the time for displaying a page is spent in `prtline`. (The time for `display_page` includes `prtline`, but a dummy function is used in place of `read_line`.)

Function	Speed (seconds)
disp_prompt	0.3
display_page	1.7
prtline	1.4
read_line	0.1

These times were measured on a PC AT with a fast hard disk. For a PC XT with a slow hard disk, times would be two to three times as long. Results are similar to those for VIEW. Since the page to be displayed is only 256 bytes rather than up to 1,280 bytes as for VIEW, the time to read a page from the file is less. However, the time required to display the page is somewhat longer. To improve performance, we must concentrate on the display module.

4.6   Enhancements for FD

FD is a useful tool as it stands. I have used it daily to help debug other programs and to discover the format of a file produced by a commercial program. Successful use has suggested many ideas for enhancement. Some parallel enhancements to VIEW and some are new.

💾 Faster Screen Output

FD responds to commands in about 2 seconds. That sounds fast, but when you are looking at the screen, 2 seconds seems to take forever. When interactive programs use single keystroke commands, response times longer than 0.1 to 0.2 seconds are noticeable. So there is still room to improve FD's performance. Section 4.7 investigates the bottlenecks in the `fddisp.c` module and makes enhancements.

💾   **Eliminating Scrolling**

As in the VIEW program, scrolling is a distraction. Section 4.7 enhances FD to clear the screen and set the cursor to the start of each area to be updated.

💾   **A Modern User Interface**

FD displays 256 bytes of data at a time. That is adequate for some uses, but it is inconvenient when we look at records longer than 256 bytes. A pull-down menu user interface would allow us to display several more lines of data.

💾   **Printed Output**

FD is designed for interactive use. We can move around in a file, examining its structure without waiting for a bulky printed file dump. If we want to produce a printed listing of an interesting part of a file, FD needs a command to print all or part of a file. We canspecify beginning and ending file positions of the area to be printed. Commands for marking the beginning and end of a file would be easier to use.

💾   **Search Commands**

When we examine a file with FD, we are often looking for the occurrence of a character string or a sequence of byte values. FD should provide search commands with the search string specified as an ASCII string or as a series of byte values in hexadecimal notation.

Combining VIEW and FD

The VIEW program tries to interpret the input file as a text file — to make it readable as ASCII text. FD provides exact information about the contents of a file at the expense of an less readable format. For files that combine ASCII text with some non-ASCII formatting information, a single program combining VIEW and FD would be useful. This program would provide a command to switch display modes. We could start in VIEW mode to locate an interesting line or record and then switch to FD mode to examine the exact contents of the area.

Movement by Records

When we examine a file composed of records, we often want to move to the next or previous record. FD should allow us to specify a record length and provide commands to move to the next or previous record.

Hexadecimal Input for a File Position

Sometimes it is more convenient to specify a file position using hexadecimal notation. We could modify the `get_pos` function to accept a file position in hexadecimal or decimal notation. The convention for hexadecimal notation used in C source files — `0x` preceding hexadecimal digits — could be used to distinguish it from decimal input.

We might also want the file position, the file size, and the starting position for each line to be displayed in hexadecimal. This suggests another alternative — a command to select decimal or hexadecimal for both input and output.

4.7 Improving FD's Performance

FD takes about 2 seconds to respond to an input command. We would like to reduce that time to less than 1 second. Although we may be disappointed that our first version of FD is a bit slow, we have a working program — all we have to worry about now is making it faster. The performance measurements in Section 4.5 point us to the display module and to `prtline` in particular. We start there and try to find out what in the display module is causing the slow response.

Levels of I/O Functions

Instead of making further measurements on the display module, we will explore how console I/O works. When we call `printf` or `putchar` to display something, several layers of software are invoked. The following table shows how `printf` and `putchar` calls use lower levels

Level	Sample Function
Formatting	`printf`
Buffered I/O	`putchar`
Unbuffered I/O	`write`
DOS console I/O	DOS function code 2
or file I/O	function code 0x40
BIOS video I/O	write_tty
Direct screen write	—

Each level makes use of the lower levels to update the screen. With so many levels of software involved, it is not surprising that the performance of `printf` or `putchar` is a bit disappointing. The IBM PC is simply not fast enough to hide this overhead.

Measuring I/O Performance

We can perform an experiment to see where the bottlenecks really are. Figure 4.9 shows a program to measure the `putchar` function. By substituting functions to access other levels of I/O functions directly, we can compare performance at each level. The following table gives the results with the equivalent to `putchar`:

Level	Function Used	Time (in seconds) for 2,000 Characters
Formatting	`printf("%c ",c)`	2
Buffered I/O	`putchar(c)`	2
Unbuffered I/O	`write(1,&c,1)`	2
DOS console I/O	fun. call 2	1.8
or DOS file I/O	fun. call 0x40	1
BIOS video I/O	`vid_tc(c)`	1
Screen write	`scn_wc(c,&sc)`	0.08

The functions `vid_tc` and `scn_wc` are from Chapter 7. DOS function call 2 was performed with the Microsoft `bdos` function and function call 0x40 was performed with the Microsoft `_dos_write` functions.

The results are surprising and encouraging. We should be able to improve the display module by writing directly to the PC screen. Further experiments give us more information: Writing a line feed character or scrolling the screen takes seven times as long as writing a normal character at the BIOS level. Another approach would be continue to use buffered I/O functions but to eliminate scrolling.

FIGURE 4.9   expio.c

```
 1      /* expio.c - test console I/O performance */
 2      #include <stdio.h>
 3
 4      main()
 5      {
 6          int it , i , c ;
 7          char b ;
 8
 9          printf("\n char value (decimal):") ;
10          scanf("%d",&c) ;
11          printf("\n no. chars to write:") ;
12          scanf("%d",&it) ;
13
14          for( i=1; i <= it ; i=i+1)
15            { putchar(c) ;  }
16          printf("\n ** thru ** \n");
17
18      }
```

Modifying FD

Now we are ready to work on FD. Chapter 7 provides the VIDEO module for access to PC BIOS functions. The `fddisp2.c` function in Figure 4.10 uses two BIOS functions: The `vid_up` function clears the screen before each page is displayed. The `vid_set_cur` function sets the position of the blinking screen cursor — where the next character will be displayed. In lines 27 and 28, the `display_page` function clears the first 19 lines of the screen and sets the cursor at the top left corner of the screen. The `disp_prompt` function clears the rest of the screen and locates the cursor on line 19.

FIGURE 4.10   fddisp2.c

```
1     /* fddisp2.c file - display current page of file - no scroll*/
2     #include <stdio.h>
3     #include "cminor.h"
4     #include "fdparm.h"
5     #include "video.h"
6
7     extern char    filename[] ;
8     extern long    filesize ;    /* size of file in bytes */
9     extern long    top_of_page; /* file position of top of page */
10
11    /*  special symbols for CR, LF, CTL-Z, and other ctl chars */
12    #define PRT_CR   20
13    #define PRT_LF   25
14    #define PRT_CTLZ 17
15    #define PRT_OTHER 22
16    #define ASC_CTLZ  26
17
18    int  row ;                   /* current line of page */
19    long start ;
20
21    void display_page()          /* displays current page */
22      {
23        char block[ LINE_SIZE ] ;
24        int  nbytes  ;
25        int i ;                  /* index for loops  */
26
27        vid_clr_scn(0,0,18,79,NORMAL_DISPLAY);/* clr header & text */
28        vid_set_cur(0,0) ;       /* cursor at top of screen */
29        move_to(top_of_page);    /* start at top of the page */
30                                 /* write a header line */
31        printf(" FILE - %s     POSITION - %ld    FILE SIZE - %ld \n",
32            filename,top_of_page,filesize);
33
34                                 /* write a border line of dashes */
35        for( i=1 ; i <= 80 ; i = i + 1 )
36           { putchar('-'); }
37
38        /* get chars until we've written (PAGE_SIZE) lines */
39        /* or we've reached the end of the file */
40        row = 1 ;                /* starting row values */
41        start = top_of_page ;
42        while( row <= PAGE_SIZE   )
43           { nbytes = read_line(block,LINE_SIZE) ;
```

Figure 4.10   continues

Figure 4.10   continued

```
44                  if( nbytes <= 0 )
45                      break ;
46                  prtline(block,nbytes) ;
47                  start = start + nbytes ;
48                  row = row + 1 ;
49              }
50
51          while( row <= PAGE_SIZE )    /* pad out page if eof reached */
52              { putchar('\n'); row = row + 1 ; }
53
54                                  /* write a border line of dashes */
55          for( i=1 ; i <= 80 ; i = i + 1 )
56              { putchar('-'); }
57      }
58
59
60      void prtline(block,nbytes) /* prints one line */
61      char block[] ;
62      int  nbytes ;
63      {
64          int i ;
65
66          printf("%8ld  | ",start) ;     /* print file pos. */
67          for(i=0 ; i < LINE_SIZE ; i=i+1) /* print bytes in Hex. */
68            { if ( i < nbytes )
69                      printf("%02x ",( tochar(block[i]) ) ) ;
70              else printf("   ") ;        /* out of data - fill in */
71            }
72
73          printf("| ") ;
74
75          for(i=0; i < nbytes ; i = i+1 ) /* display in ASCII form */
76              { disp_char( tochar(block[i]) ) ; }
77          putchar('\n');
78      }
79
80
81      void disp_char(c)              /* display one char in ASCII form */
82      int c ;                        /* value of char to display */
83      {
84          /* classify the character and handle accordingly */
85
86          if( (c >= ' ') && (c <= '~') )
87              ;                       /* ASCII graphic - just display it */
88          else if( c == '\n' )
89              c = PRT_LF ;            /* newline (LF) - display symbol */
90          else if( c == '\r' )
91              c = PRT_CR ;            /* Carr. Return - display symbol */
92          else if ( c == ASC_CTLZ )
93              c = PRT_CTLZ ;          /* CTL-Z - display symbol */
94          else c = PRT_OTHER ;        /* other char - display symbol */
95
96          putchar(c) ;
97      }
98
99
100     #define  UP_A  24              /* displays up arrow */
```

Figure 4.10   continues

Figure 4.10   continued

```
101     #define  DN_A  25              /* displays down arrow */
102
103     void disp_prompt()            /* display prompts for commands */
104     {                             /* clear part of screen */
105         vid_clr_scn(19,0,24,79,NORMAL_DISPLAY) ;
106         vid_set_cur(19,0) ;       /* cursor at top of screen */
107
108        printf(  "\n          Type one of these Input Commands");
109        printf(  "\n HOME  = First Page      ");
110        printf(    "  %c   = Previous Line   ",UP_A);
111        printf(      "PG UP = Previous Page ");
112        printf(  "\n END   = Last  Page      ");
113        printf(    "  %c   = Next Line       ",DN_A);
114        printf(      "PG DN = Next Page ");
115        printf(  "\n ESC   = Exit Pgm        ");
116        printf(      "SPACE = Move to position \n");
117     }
```

This modified version of FD only requires about 1.5 seconds to respond to a command and, without scrolling, it is more pleasant to use. But the printf and putchar functions are still a bottleneck. The SCN module from Chapter 7 is the basis for the next improvement. Our approach is simple—we replace calls to putchar by calls to scn_wc and calls to printf by calls to scn_ws. The examples show sample replacements:

```
putchar(c);           to           scn_wc(c, &sc) ;

printf("| ");         to           scn_ws("| ", &sc) ;
```

As the examples suggest, the screen writing functions expect as second argument the address of a structure. This structure is defined by the data type SCN_DATA in the header file scn.h (also from Chapter 7). We need to include this header file and to declare a variable (sc) of type SCN_DATA. Before we use scn_wc or scn_ws, we must call scn_init to initialize the data in sc. The structure, sc, contains the location on the screen where characters will be written. Calls to scn_pos set the row and column to be written next. The SCN module does not use the position of the blinking cursor but maintains a separate screen position pointer.

The screen-writing functions are limited in the services they provide. They do not recognize control characters such as carriage return or newline, and they do not perform scrolling. Instead of outputing '\n' characters in putchar or printf statements, we have to call scn_pos to move to a new line.

Figure 4.11 shows the modified source file fdedisp3.c. Screen-writing functions replace printf statements here as well as in display_page, prtline, and disp_char. Before the page is displayed, line 30 uses another function from Chapter 7, vid_clr_scn, to erase the screen.

Line 30 in display_page clears the first 19 lines of the screen and sets the screen position at the top left corner. Line 31 positions the blinking cursor on line 24; the get_pos function still uses printf and scanf functions, so we ensure that those

FIGURE 4.11 fddisp3.c

```
1    /* fddisp3.c file - FD display module - fast screen output */
2    #include "stdio.h"
3    #include "cminor.h"
4    #include "fdparm3.h"
5    #include "video.h"
6    #include "scn.h"
7
8    extern char    filename[] ;
9    extern long    filesize ;     /* size of file in bytes */
10   extern long    top_of_page;  /* file position of top of page */
11   static SCN_DATA sc ;          /* screen data structure */
12
13   /*   special symbols for CR, LF, CTL-Z, and other ctl chars */
14   #define PRT_CR   20
15   #define PRT_LF   25
16   #define PRT_CTLZ 17
17   #define PRT_OTHER 22
18   #define ASC_CTLZ  26
19
20   int  row ;                   /* current line of page */
21   long start ;
22
23   void display_page()          /* displays current page */
24    {
25        char block[ LINE_SIZE ] ;
26        int  nbytes ;
27        int  i ;                 /* index for loops  */
28        char s[81] ;
29
30        vid_clr_scn(0,0,18,79,NORMAL_DISPLAY);/* clr header & text */
31        vid_set_cur(24,0) ;      /* cursor at bottom of screen */
32        scn_pos(& sc,0,0) ;      /* set writing position */
33        move_to(top_of_page);    /* start at top of the page */
34
35                                 /* write a header line */
36        sprintf(s,
37         " FILE - %s     POSITION - %ld     FILE SIZE - %ld ",
38          filename,top_of_page,filesize);
39        scn_ws(& sc, s ) ;
40
41        scn_pos(& sc,1,0) ;      /* position on next line */
42                                 /* write a border line of dashes */
43        for( i=1 ; i <= 80 ; i = i + 1 )
44          { scn_wc(& sc , '-'); }
45
46        /* get chars until we've written (PAGE_SIZE) lines */
47        /* or we've reached the end of the file */
48        row = 1 ;                /* starting row values */
49        start = top_of_page ;
50        while( row <= PAGE_SIZE  )
51          { nbytes = read_line(block,LINE_SIZE) ;
52            if( nbytes <= 0 )
53                break ;
54            scn_pos(& sc, row+1 , 0 ) ;
55            prtline(block,nbytes) ;
56            start = start + nbytes ;
57            row = row + 1 ;
```

Figure 4.11   continues

Figure 4.11   continued

```
58              }
59
60          /* no need to pad out page */
61
62                                      /* write a border line of dashes */
63          scn_pos( & sc, PAGE_SIZE+2 , 0 ) ;
64          for( i=1 ; i <= 80 ; i = i + 1 )
65              { scn_wc(& sc , '-'); }
66      }
67
68      char hex[] = "0123456789ABCDEF" ; /* hex digits */
69
70      void prtline(block,nbytes) /* prints one line */
71       char block[] ;
72       int   nbytes ;
73      {
74          int i ;
75          unsigned t ;
76          char s[81] ;
77
78          sprintf(s,"%8ld  | ",start) ;     /* print file pos. */
79          scn_ws(& sc, s) ;
80          for(i=0 ; i < LINE_SIZE ; i=i+1) /* print bytes in Hex. */
81              { if ( i < nbytes )
82                  { t = ( block[i] >> 4) & 0xf ;
83                    scn_wc( & sc , hex[t] ) ;
84                    t = block[i] & 0xf ;
85                    scn_wc( & sc , hex[ t ] ) ;
86                    scn_wc( & sc , ' ' ) ;
87                  }
88              else scn_ws( & sc, "   " ) ; /* out of data - fill in */
89              }
90
91          scn_ws( & sc, "| " ) ;
92
93          for(i=0; i < nbytes ; i = i+1 ) /* display in ASCII form */
94              { disp_char( tochar(block[i]) ) ; }
95      }
96
97
98      void disp_char(c)              /* display one char in ASCII form */
99       int c ;                       /* value of char to display */
100     {
101         /* classify the character and handle accordingly */
102
103         if( (c >= ' ') && (c <= '~') )
104             ;                      /* ASCII graphic - just display it */
105         else if( c == '\n' )
106             c = PRT_LF ;           /* newline (LF) - display symbol */
107         else if( c == '\r' )
108             c = PRT_CR ;           /* Carr. Return - display symbol */
109         else if ( c == ASC_CTLZ )
110             c = PRT_CTLZ ;         /* CTL-Z - display symbol */
111         else c = PRT_OTHER ;       /* other char - display symbol */
112
113         scn_wc( & sc, c ) ;
114     }
```

Figure 4.11   continues

Figure 4.11   continued

```
115
116
117
118    void disp_prompt()            /* display prompts for commands */
119    {
120        int r ;                    /* row number */
121
122        r = PAGE_SIZE + 3 ;
123        vid_clr_scn(r,0,24,79,NORMAL_DISPLAY);/* clear prompt area */
124        r = r + 1 ;
125        scn_pos(& sc, r,0) ;  /* position under display area */
126
127        scn_ws(& sc, "            Type one of these Input Commands");
128        r = r + 1 ;
129        scn_pos(& sc, r,0) ;
130        scn_ws(& sc, " HOME  = First Page        ");
131                              /* 0x18 displays up arrow */
132        scn_ws(& sc, "  \x18   = Previous Line   ");
133        scn_ws(& sc, "PG UP = Previous Page ");
134        r = r + 1 ;
135        scn_pos(& sc, r, 0 ) ;
136        scn_ws(& sc, " END   = Last  Page        ");
137                              /* 0x19 displays down arrow */
138        scn_ws(& sc,   "  \x19   = Next Line        ");
139        scn_ws(& sc,    "PG DN = Next Page ");
140        r = r + 1 ;
141        scn_pos(& sc, r, 0 ) ;
142        scn_ws(& sc, " ESC   = Exit Pgm         ");
143        scn_ws(& sc,     "SPACE = Move to position ");
144    }
145
146
147    void init_disp()
148    {
149        scn_init( & sc) ;
150    }
```

functions will display characters on the blank line at the bottom of the screen. Line 36 uses sprintf to format a string with the file name, file position, and file size. The sprintf library function performs the same formatting as does printf, but it places its output in a string. Line 39 writes this string to the screen. The disp_prompt function clears lines 18 through 24 of the screen and sets the screen position to line 20. Lines 132 and 139 use escape notation to represent the special up and down arrow characters in the string to be displayed.

The prtline function has also been modified to display hexadecimal digits more efficiently. Line 68 defines an array, hex, containing the characters to be displayed for each hexadecimal digit. Line 82 extracts the high-order hexadecimal digit from the next byte. Line 83 uses this value to select the corresponding character from the hex array. Lines 84 and 85 extract the low-order digit and display the corresponding character.

The init_disp function on lines 147 to 150 initializes the screen data structure. A call to this function is added to the main function as shown in Figure 4.12.

FIGURE 4.12   fd3.c

```
1      /* fd3.c -  FD - main function - fast screen output */
2      #include <stdio.h>
3      #include <string.h>
4      #include "viewcmds.h"
5      #include "fdparm3.h"
6
7      char filename[65] = "" ;
8
9      main(argc,argv)
10      int argc ;
11      char *argv[] ;
12      {
13         int cmd ;                  /* holds current cmd     */
14
15         if( argc >= 2 )            /* get file name from command line */
16            strcpy(filename,argv[1]) ;  /* (if present) */
17
18         get_filename(filename);/* get file name and open file */
19         set_filesize();           /* set up file size variable */
20         init_disp() ;             /* initialize display */
21         cmd = FIRSTPAGE ;         /* force display of 1st page */
22
23         while( cmd != EXITPGM )/* repeat until told to exit */
24           { exec_cmd(cmd);        /* execute the current command */
25             disp_prompt() ;       /* display command prompt */
26             cmd = get_cmd();      /* get the next command */
27           }
28
29         close_file() ;
30      }
```

Figure 4.13 shows the modified header file, fdparm3.h, with a function prototype added for the init_disp function.

The final version using fast screen output responds to commands in less than half
a second. Although the original FD program was usable, the enhanced version is
fun to use.

These enhancements apply to VIEW as well. Bypassing layers of I/O functions
and writing directly to the screen is often necessary for really fast response.
Although it makes the program less portable, it also makes the program more
pleasant to use.

FIGURE 4.13   fdparm3.h

```
1      /* fdparm3.h - parameters for FD program */
2
3      /* number of lines in a display page */
4      #define  PAGE_SIZE       16
5
6      /* number of bytes per line */
7      #define  LINE_SIZE       16
8
9      /* number of lines of overlap between display pages */
```

Figure 4.13   continues

Figure 4.13   continued

```
10      #define  LINES_OVERLAP    0
11
12      /* return values from get_next_char and get_previous_char to */
13      /* indicate that beginning or end of the file has been reached */
14      #define  EOF_MARK        -1
15      #define  BOF_MARK        -2
16
17      /* definition of control char marking the end of a line */
18      #define  END_LINE        10
19
20      /* define success/failure for return codes */
21      #define SUCCESS   1
22      #define FAILURE   0
23
24                                  /* function prototypes */
25      int get_cmd(void) ;         /* get a command */
26      void exec_cmd(int) ;        /* execute a command */
27      void move_forward(int) ;    /* move forward in file */
28      void move_backward(int) ;   /* move backward in file */
29      void set_top_page(void) ;   /* set top of page variable */
30      void display_page(void) ;   /* display a page of text */
31      void disp_char(int) ;       /* display one char */
32      void disp_prompt(void) ;    /* display the prompt */
33      long get_pos(long) ;        /* get file position input */
34      void get_filename(char *) ;/* get file name input */
35      int open_file(char *) ;     /* open the file */
36      void set_filesize(void) ;   /* find file size */
37      void check_ctrl_z(void) ;   /* adjust file size for control Z */
38      void move_to(long) ;        /* change file position */
39      long where_now(void) ;      /* return file position */
40      int get_next_char(void) ;   /* get a character - forward */
41      int get_previous_char(void) ;  /* get a character - backward */
42      void close_file(void) ;     /* close the file */
43      void prtline(char *,int) ;  /* print one line - hex and ASCII */
44      int read_line(char *,int);  /* read N characters */
45      void init_disp(void) ;      /* initialize display */
```

4.8 Summary

From VIEW, we developed another interactive program, FD, for examining files. Enhancing FD for better performance gave us insight into the workings of console I/O and an example of direct screen output. This knowledge can be applied to other interactive programs.

The enhanced program performs a useful function and does it well enough to be usable. Snooping around in data files made by commercial software such as WordStar, dBase III or Lotus 1-2-3 is fun and educational, too. FD is also a practical tool to help in debugging and testing file-oriented programs.

5
Tools for Sorting

This chapter builds several general-purpose tools based on sorting algorithms. Although two complete programs are presented, the point of the chapter is to develop general-purpose sort modules for use in your programs. Sorting data is a common requirement in many applications, yet many programmers do not have the training or confidence to write sort functions. The modules we present allow you to concentrate on your application. Even if enhancements to the sort modules are necessary, starting with correct, working functions is much easier than starting from scratch.

Sorting algorithms have been a favorite topic for computer science research since computers were first developed. The subject allowed virtuoso feats of mathematical analysis, and the extensive use of sorting programs meant that there were practical benefits. This combination of practical applications and elegant mathematics attracted lots of work and gave us many very useful algorithms. Our job is to put some of these algorithms to good use. We start with programs to sort arrays of integers to illustrate sorting algorithms. Then we discuss using the library function `qsort`, which is based on one of those algorithms. Next we develop a special quicksort function adapted to sorting arrays of pointers.

There are two kinds of sorting problems: those where all the data fits into RAM memory at once, and those where it doesn't. The chapter begins with algorithms for the first case, *internal sorting*, and then the second part of the chapter adds the algorithms needed for the second case, *external sorting*. A program to sort a file consisting of lines of text provides a concrete basis for developing the external sorting algorithms. Next we construct a set of library functions for sorting a file containing any data type. Finally, we build a complete sort/merge program that works for different types of files using these library functions.

5.1   Internal Sorting Algorithms: Insertion and Quicksort

Insertion Sorting—A Simple Algorithm

There are many different algorithms for sorting data. To start, we will look at a simple one, insertion sorting. This technique is based on the way a bridge player sorts his or her cards. The player picks up one card at a time and inserts it at the proper position in the set of cards already picked up. Our algorithm sorts an array of integers using the same method. The following diagrams show insertion sorting on an array of four integers (ascending order is chosen for the example, but the algorithm is applicable to descending order, too). When we begin the process, the sorted area consists of only the first element. When we finish, it includes all elements of the array.

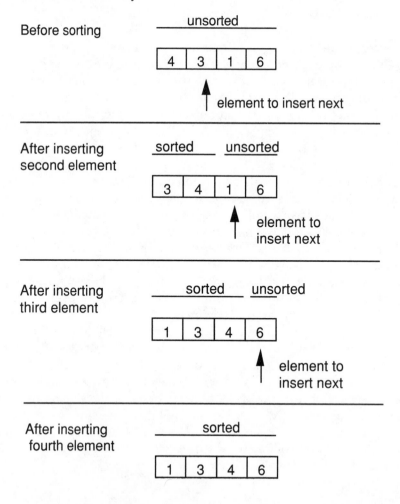

Pseudo-code

The pseudo-code to describe the insertion sort is simple and compact:

```
insert
    repeat for each element from the second through the last
        compare to sorted elements to find where to insert it.
        move sorted elements to make room for this one.
        insert it in order.
end
```

The `inserti` function is shown in Figure 5.1. It is written as a function to be called with any size array of integers. The array elements are indexed as 0 through na-1. The loop on lines 10 to 19 starts with element 1 — the second in the array. Note that the inner loop on lines 14 to 17 combines two functions. It compares elements to the one being inserted to find where it belongs and moves elements upward to make room for this element. Line 18 inserts the new element when its proper place has been found.

Some details affect the performance of `inserti`. The function as written requires little extra memory — two loop indices and a temporary variable for the element being inserted. The inner loop begins comparing elements just below the element being inserted; this ensures that the loop will end immediately if the array is already in order. If we had started the inner loop at element 0, the loop would terminate only when all the sorted elements had been compared.

Simply examining the insert algorithm can supply some information about its performance. For example, we can see that the best case occurs when the array is already in order. In that case, inserting each element requires a single comparison

FIGURE 5.1   inserti.c

```
 1     /* inserti.c - insertion sort for an array of integers */
 2
 3     void inserti(a,na)
 4      int a[] ;                   /* array of integers to be sorted */
 5      int na  ;                   /* number of integers to be sorted */
 6      {
 7        int i , j ;               /* indices for loops */
 8        int temp ;                /* temporary space for one element */
 9
10        for( i=1 ; i < na ; i = i + 1 )
11          {                       /* insert the i-th element */
12            temp = a[i] ;         /* into the sorted array */
13            j = i - 1 ;           /* find where new element goes */
14            while( (j >= 0) && (temp < a[j]) )
15              { a[j+1] = a[j] ;/*   not here - move this one up */
16                j = j - 1 ;
17              }
18            a[j+1] = temp ;
19          }
20      }
```

and no movement of elements already sorted. So an array of n elements would require $(n-1)$ comparisons. An array with elements in reverse order would require comparisons to every element already sorted. The total number of comparisons would be about $(n*n/2)$. For randomly ordered data, each element would be compared to about half the elements already sorted. This total is about $(n*n/4)$ comparisons.

Questions

1. The inner loop contains two tests that must be performed for each iteration. How could the test for the beginning of the array be eliminated? (*Hint*: What if `a[0]` were reserved for a dummy element?)
2. The algorithm works best for an array that is already sorted. How could it be rewritten to perform best on an array that is in reverse order?

Quicksort: A Faster Algorithm

The insertion sort function is simple but not very fast for sorting large arrays. We need a better sorting algorithm. The quicksort algorithm invented by C. A. R. Hoare (1962) is a little more complicated to describe and to program but is very fast for sorting large arrays.

Quicksort is based on the idea of partitioning the array so that all elements in one subarray have values that are less than or equal to all the elements in the second subarray. This practice reduces the size of the sorting problem because we only need to sort the two partitions individually. We apply the same partitioning process to each subarray separately. As each subarray is partitioned, we partition its parts. One large sorting problem is replaced by a series of smaller problems.

In practice, we pick a test value and rearrange the array so that all the elements in left subarray are less than or equal to the test value, and so that those in the right subarray are greater than or equal to the test value. The overall pseudo-code is as follows:

```
quicksort
    select a test value
    partition the array using the test value
    sort the left subarray with quicksort
    sort the right subarray with quicksort
end
```

We use the middle element of the array as the test value. (We will discuss this choice later.)

The partitioning is simple. We compare each element to a test value to decide in which partition it belongs. We start at the left and right ends of the array and scan toward the middle. On the left, we stop the scan when we find an element that belongs in the right partition. We stop the right scan when we find an element that belongs in the left partition. Then we exchange the two elements and continue the scans just past the exchanged elements. The process ends when the two scans meet. We show the pseudo-code first as a series of steps and then with a loop:

```
partition an array with a test value
      start with left scan index at array[0]
            and right index at array[n]
      scan from left for element >= test value
      scan from right for element <= test value
      exchange elements
      move left index to the right one element
      move right index to the left one element
      scan from left for element >= test value
      scan from right for element <= test value
      exchange elements
      ...
      scan from left for element >= test value
      scan from right for element <= test value
      ( scans meet and the process ends )
end


partition an array with a test value  (with loop)
      start with left scan index at array[0]
            and right index at array[n]
      repeat until scans meet
            scan from left for element >= test value
            scan from right for element <= test value
            exchange elements
            move left index right one element
            move right index left one element
end
```

We will demonstrate the partitioning process on the six-element array starting on the next page. We use the third element (whose value is 4) as the test value so that the left partition contains values less than or equal to 4 and the right partition contains values greater than or equal to 4.

Figure 5.2 lists a quicksort function `qsorti` for sorting an array of integers. It performs the function described by the pseudo-code, but the scanning loops in lines 20 and 23 have been rearranged for faster execution. The do while loop advances the array subscripts `i` and `j` before the array element is compared to the pivot. Line 17 initializes `i` and `j` so that they refer to the first and last array elements when the first

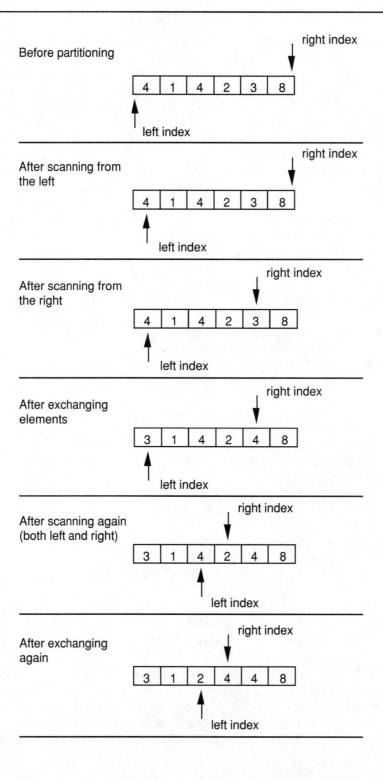

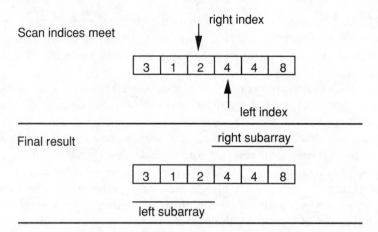

comparison is made. The loop in line 20 stops when a[i] is greater than or equal to the test value part. The loop in line 23 stops when a[j] is less than or equal to the test value.

FIGURE 5.2   qsorti.c

```
1    /* qsorti.c - performs a quicksort on an array of integers */
2
3    void qsorti(a,na)
4     int a[] ;                    /* array of integers to be sorted */
5     int na  ;                    /* number of elements to be sorted */
6     {
7       int i , j ;                /* indices for loops */
8       int temp ;                 /* temporary storage for an element */
9       int nr ;                   /* number in right partition */
10      int part ;                 /* element used as partition value */
11
12      if( na < 2  )
13          return ;
14
15      part = a[na/2] ;           /* use middle element for partition */
16
17      i = -1 ; j = na ;
18      while( 1 == 1 )
19         {                       /* find first element to move right */
20           do { i = i + 1 ; } while( a[i] < part ) ;
21
22                                 /* find first element to move left */
23           do { j = j - 1 ; } while( a[j] > part ) ;
24
25           if( i >= j )          /* have the boundaries met ? */
26               break ;           /*     yes - through partitioning */
27                                 /*     no  - swap i and j elements */
28           temp = a[i] ;   a[i] = a[j] ; a[j] = temp ;
29         }
30
31      nr = na - i ;
32                                 /* now sort each partition */
33      qsorti( a , i ) ;          /* sort left side  */
34      qsorti( &(a[i]),nr);       /* sort right side */
35    }
```

Lines 33 and 34 use `qsorti` itself to sort the partitioned subarrays. `qsorti` expects the address of an array as its first parameter. For the left subarray, this is just the address of the array. For the right subarray, it is the address of the first element in the subarray, `& a[i]`.

The `qsorti` function is *recursive* ; that is, it calls itself to sort the two subarrays it produces. The test in line 12 stops this recursion when a subarray of one element is produced. Each call to `qsorti` produces a different *activation* with its own arguments and local variables. Recursion may seem to be a complicated concept, but it allows us to write a program that corresponds closely to our pseudo-code.

Several subtle details in the `qsorti` function deserve more attention. For example, selecting the middle element as the test value rather than the first element makes `qsorti` work better for data that is already in order. A check to see whether the scans have met is placed in the middle of the loop to avoid duplicating statements. The initialization of left and right indices in line 17 and the `do { }` `while` loops in lines 20 and 23 remove the need for extra statements to advance the indices after an exchange.

Quicksort works best when it partitions the array evenly at each step. An array of n elements would yield partitions of $n/2, n/4, \ldots$ down to 1 element in approximately $\text{Log}(n)$ Base 2 steps. About n comparisons are required in each step. (Although partitions get smaller at each step, they get more numerous. There are p partitions of n/p elements each.) The total number of comparisons would be proportional to $(n*\text{Log}(n))$.

The quicksort algorithm performs worst when it partitions the array unevenly at each step. When one partition always contains a single element, $(n-1)$ steps are required. In this case, the total number of comparisons is proportional to $(n*n)$. Fortunately the worst case is quite rare. For large arrays, almost all arrangements of elements are sorted quite efficiently.

Special cases such as an array that is already in order or an array that is in reverse order are important. An array with all elements equal is another important case. For all of these situations, `qsorti` produces best case results — a result of choosing the middle element as the test value.

Questions

1. The scanning loops in lines 20 and 23 use the sentinel idea. They do not check for the end of the array. Do the loops as written always stop? (The first time each scan must stop when the element chosen as a test value is reached if not before. What happens on the next scan?) Would `qsorti` still work if the tests in lines 20 and 23 were changed to `a[i] <= part` and `a[j] >= part`?

2. In our example of partitioning a six-element array, the result was subarrays with three elements each. What will happen when the three element subarray `{3 4 6}` is partitioned?

3. Work through the special cases to see how quicksort works. What if we used the first or last element of each partition instead of the middle one?

5.2   Generalizing the Internal Sort Functions: qsort

Both the insertion and quicksort algorithms can be applied to any kind of data. However, the actual C functions we presented are very specific; they work only for arrays of integers. We need general-purpose functions that will sort any kind of data — even character strings of varying length. We could use Figures 5.1 and 5.2 as models for writing sort functions for other types of data, but what we really want is general functions that we can compile once and use in our programs without further attention. Fortunately C has the features we need to make general-purpose sort functions that accept any data type.

For the quicksort algorithm, such a function has already been written and is included in the compiler's standard library. The manual page in Figure 5.3 describes the use of `qsort`. As in our `qsorti` function, the array address and the number of elements to be sorted are input arguments. Since `qsort` does not know the array's data type, it does not know the size of an array element or how to compare two elements. We specify the size of an array element as an argument. We also supply the address of a function to be called to compare two array elements.

FIGURE 5.3   qsort Function Description

Name

`qsort`   sorts data in RAM memory using quicksort algorithm

Usage

```
qsort(base,nelem,width,  compare)  ;
void *base ;            /* start of array to sort */
size_t nelem ;          /* number of elements in the array */
size_t width ;          /* element size in bytes */
                        /* comparison function */
int (*compare) (void *, void *) ;
```

Function

`qsort` sorts data in RAM memory using the quicksort algorithm. `qsort` can be used for any kind of data. The argument `base` is a pointer to the start of an array of `nelem` elements, each of `width` bytes. The array will be sorted in increasing order.

The argument `compare` is a pointer to a user-supplied function that compares two array elements. `qsort` calls the compare function passing pointers to the two elements to be compared. The compare function should return the following values:

less than 0	if element 1 is less than element 2
0	if element 1 is equivalent to element 2
greater than 0	if element 1 is greater than element 2

The argument `base` should be converted to the data type `void *`. In the `compare` function, the two arguments should be declared as `void *`.

Figure 5.3   continues

Figure 5.3   continued

Example

```
int   na = 10 ;
int a[10] ;
...
int intcomp(void *, void *) ;
     memsort(pa, na, sizeof(int), intcomp) ;
...


int intcomp(p1,p2)              /* sort function */
void *p1 ;                      /* points to first element */
void *p2 ;                      /* points to second element */
 {
   return( ( * (int *)p1) - ( * (int *) p2 ) ) ;
 }
```

Notes

The qsort function is defined in the ANSI C standard and is included in the compiler library.

The quicksort algorithm is very fast ($n*\log n$ time dependence) for almost all cases. But a worst case arrangement of data can produce slow sorting ($n*n$ dependence).

We need not write the qsort function, but we need to understand how to employ it. Figure 5.4 shows *compare* functions for several data types. Figure 5.5 defines function prototypes for these functions. The following code fragments illustrate the use of each compare function:

```
#include  "cmpfuns.h"
int a[10] ;
char sa [ 3 ] [10] ;      /* array of strings of up to 9 chars */
char *ps[ 20 ] ;          /* 20 pointers to strings */
char *pca[ 10 ] ;         /* 10 pointers to char arrays */
                          /* each array is 4 chars long */
...
qsort(a, 10, sizeof(int) , icmp) ;   /* ascending integer sort */
qsort(a, 10, sizeof(int) , icmpd) ; /* descending integer sort */
qsort(sa, 3, sizeof(sa[0]) , scmp); /* sort array of strings */
qsort(ps,20, sizeof(char *),pscmp); /* sort pointers to strings */
qsort(ps,20, sizeof(char *),pscmpi);/* sort disregarding case */
ca_length = 4 ;
qsort(pca,10, sizeof(char *),cacmp);/* sort char arrays */
```

These examples show some of the flexibility of qsort. By defining an appropriate compare function, we can produce ascending or descending order or disregard upper-/lowercase differences. Note the differences in the compare function scmp for sorting an array of character strings and the function pscmp for sorting an array of pointers to strings. The cacmp function compares fixed length char arrays rather than strings ended by the \0 character. The examples use the sizeof operator to

FIGURE 5.4   cmpfuns.c

```
1      /* cmpfuns.c - compare functions for use with qsort */
2      #include <string.h>
3
4      int ca_length ;            /* length for char arrays */
5
6
7      int icmp(p1,p2)            /* compare integers - ascending order */
8       void *p1 ;
9       void *p2 ;
10      {
11         return( ( * (int *) p1) - ( * (int *) p2) ) ;
12      }
13
14
15      int icmpd(p1,p2)           /* compare integers - descending order*/
16       void *p1 ;
17       void *p2 ;
18      {
19         return( ( * (int *) p2) - ( * (int *) p1) ) ;
20      }
21
22
23      int scmp(p1,p2)            /* compare strings */
24       void *p1 ;
25       void *p2 ;
26      {
27         return( strcmp( (char *) p1, (char *) p2)  ) ;
28      }
29
30
31      int pscmp(p1,p2)           /* compare strings - using pointers */
32       void *p1 ;
33       void *p2 ;
34      {
35         return( strcmp( * (char **) p1, * (char **) p2)  ) ;
36      }
37
38
39      int pscmpi(p1,p2)          /* compare string ptrs-disregard case */
40       void *p1 ;
41       void *p2 ;
42      {
43         return( stricmp( * (char **) p1, * (char **) p2)  ) ;
44      }
45
46
47      int cacmp(p1,p2)           /* compare char arrays */
48       void *p1 ;
49       void *p2 ;
50      {
51         return( memcmp( * (void **) p1, * (void **) p2, ca_length) ) ;
52      }
```

FIGURE 5.5   cmpfuns.h

```
 1    /* cmpfuns.h - function prototypes for compare functions */
 2
 3    extern int ca_length ;      /* length of char array key */
 4
 5    int icmp(void * , void *) ;
 6    int icmpd(void * , void *) ;
 7    int scmp(void * , void *) ;
 8    int pscmp(void * , void *) ;
 9    int pscmpi(void * , void *) ;
10    int cacmp(void * , void *) ;
```

specify element size; this avoids mistakes and makes the source code usable with any memory model.

In calling qsort, we must pass a pointer to the compare function instead of invoking that function. Referring to a function without following parentheses produces a pointer to a function. In order for the C compiler to know that the name refers to a function, we must precede the reference by a function prototype declaration or the definition of the function itself.

Questions

1. How would you use qsort to sort the student data array in Figure 1.16? What value would you specify for the width argument? Write a suitable compare function and modify the program to use qsort.
2. qsort does not return a success or failure indication; are there any conditions under which it does not operate correctly? (What about space for variables storing information about subarrays? See Appendix B for a discussion of setting stack size and Appendix C for a discussion of PC architecture.)

5.3   Performance Analysis of Sort Functions

Figure 5.6 shows some results using inserti and qsorti to sort arrays of integers. The results in the figure refer to a single execution of the sort function; enough iterations were run to permit accurate timing. Tests were run on a PC AT with programs compiled under Microsoft C (small memory model). Three kinds of data were sorted: arrays already in order, arrays in reverse order, and arrays of disordered data with many duplications. The following function was used to generate the disordered data:

```
long nxt = 13 ;
disorder(a,n)
 int a[] ;
 int n ;
```

```
{
  int i ;
  for(i=0 ; i < n ; i=i+1)
    { nxt = nxt * 1220703125L ;
      a[i] = nxt % 13 ;
    }
}
```

FIGURE 5.6   Performance of Internal Sorts (Times in Seconds)

Array Size	10	100	1000	2000	5000
Ordered Data					
inserti	0.00038	0.0037	0.036	0.072	0.18
qsorti	0.0011	0.013	0.16	0.33	0.89
qsort (Microsoft)	0.00040	0.0036	0.034	0.072	0.18
qsort (Turbo C)	0.0015	0.022	0.28	0.61	1.7
Reversed Data					
inserti	0.00080	0.056	5.33	21.3	133.2
qsorti	0.0012	0.014	0.17	0.35	0.93
qsort (Microsoft)	0.0023	0.14	12.7	50.6	315.2
qsort (Turbo C)	0.0016	0.023	0.29	0.63	1.8
Data All the Same					
inserti	0.00038	0.0037	0.036	0.072	0.18
qsorti	0.0013	0.019	0.24	0.51	1.4
qsort (Microsoft)	0.00040	0.0036	0.035	0.072	0.18
qsort (Turbo C)	0.0019	0.120	11.1	44.1	--
Disordered Data					
inserti	0.00052	0.027	2.51	10.2	64.4
qsorti	0.0013	0.018	0.23	0.50	1.37
qsort (Microsoft)	0.0016	0.033	0.83	2.52	12.2
qsort (Turbo C)	0.0014	0.028	0.72	2.34	12.8

The figure's results match our analysis of insertion and quicksort algorithms. The insertion sort function inserti is adequate for small arrays but terrible for large arrays. However, insertion is very fast for arrays that are already in order. The quicksort function qsorti is fast for all sizes and all kinds of data. Although qsorti was not intended for actual use, it does show that the quicksort algorithm is very effective.

Figure 5.6 also shows results for qsort functions from the Microsoft and Turbo C libraries. Both functions are effective for some cases, but each function has a serious problem. The Microsoft qsort function performs poorly for arrays in reverse order. The Turbo qsort function is very slow for arrays whose elements are all the same. In addition, the Turbo qsort function causes a stack overflow error when sorting an array of 5,000 elements. Neither function is really satisfactory for serious use.

5.4 Enhancements and Projects for qsort

Measuring Your Compiler's qsort Function

The qsort results in Figure 5.6 were measured for Version 5.1 of Microsoft C and Version 2.0 of Turbo C. Results may be different for the compiler version you are using. Before using the qsort function from your compiler's library, you should measure its performance. Be sure to try important special cases:

1. The array is already in order.
2. The array is in reverse order.
3. All array elements have equivalent values.

You should also be sure that qsort has enough space for automatic variables on the stack. (See Appendix B for information on setting stack size.)

Improving on qsort

The quicksort algorithm has been analyzed thoroughly and many refinements identified. Sometimes compiler library functions can be beaten by replacements based on improved algorithms. (References in Appendix D describe refinements to quicksort.) For example, the quicksort algorithm is not especially fast for sorting small subarrays. Switching to a simple method such as insertion sorting for small subarrays can save up to 20% over the straight quicksort method. Try developing your own replacement for qsort. (Do not name your function qsort. It is dangerous to give any function that you write the same name as that of an existing library function.)

Another Fast Sort Algorithm

Although qsort is very fast for almost all arrangements of array elements, there is some worst case arrangement for which qsort will be little faster than insertion sorting. When even a slight chance of worst case performance cannot be tolerated, a different sorting algorithm is needed. The *heapsort* algorithm is a good choice; both the average and worst case performances are proportional to n*log n base 2. (Appendix D lists some references for heapsort.) Like quicksort, the heapsort algorithm can be described best as a recursive function. However, a recursive heapsort function is not very efficient. The source code disk provides both recursive and iterative versions of heapsort.

5.5   A Specialized Sort Function: memsort

Although the Microsoft and Turbo C qsort functions are not entirely satisfactory, we do not want to duplicate that work here. Instead, we develop a more specialized quicksort function. This function, memsort, sorts an array of pointers. However, we employ a separate compare function so that memsort can sort pointers to any kind of data.

Figure 5.7 lists the memsort function. As in qsorti, the pointer array and its size are the first and second arguments. The third argument is a pointer to a compare function. This compare function should work as specified for the qsort function. The syntax for declaring pointers to functions looks a bit strange. You will not need it often, so copying from a working example is a practical way to deal with function pointers.

FIGURE 5.7   memsort.c

```
1      /* memsort.c - quicksort array of pointers with compare fun. */
2      #include <stdio.h>
3      #include <stdlib.h>
4      #include "memsort.h"
5
6      #define LIMIT 8              /* use insert if fewer elements */
7
8
9      void memsort(pa,na,pcomp)
10      void *pa[] ;               /* array of pointers to be sorted */
11      size_t na  ;               /* number to be sorted */
12      int (*pcomp) (void *,void *) ; /* pointer to compare function */
13     {
14         int i,j ;               /* indices for loops */
15         void  *ptemp ;          /* temporary storage for 1 pointer */
16         int    nr ;             /* number in right partition */
17         void  *ppart ;          /* pointer to partition value */
18
19         while( 1 == 1 )
20           { if( na < LIMIT  )    /* use insert sort for small arrays */
21               { insert(pa,na,pcomp) ;
22                 return ;
23               }
24
25             ppart = pa[na/2] ;  /* pick middle element as pivot */
26             i = -1 ; j = na ;
27             while( 1 == 1 )
28               { do                  /* find first element to move right */
29                   { i = i + 1 ;
30                   } while( (*pcomp)(& pa[i],& ppart) < 0 ) ;
31
32                 do                  /* find first element to move left */
33                   { j = j - 1 ;
34                   } while( (*pcomp)(& pa[j], & ppart) > 0 ) ;
35
36                 if( i >= j )     /* have the boundaries met ? */
37                     break ;      /*    yes - through partitioning */
38
```

Figure 5.7   continues

Figure 5.7   continued

```
39                                          /* swap i and j elements */
40              ptemp = pa[i] ;   pa[i] = pa[j] ; pa[j] = ptemp ;
41            }
42
43          nr = na - i ;
44          if( i < (na/2) )      /* now sort each partition */
45            { memsort( pa , i , pcomp) ;   /* sort left side   */
46              pa = & pa[i] ;   /* sort right side here */
47              na = nr ;        /* memsort(&(pa[i]),nr,pcomp); */
48            }
49          else
50            { memsort(&(pa[i]),nr,pcomp);/* sort right side */
51                                /* sort left side here */
52              na = i ;          /* memsort( pa , i , pcomp) ; */
53            }
54        }
55    }
```

The memsort function is similar to qsorti in Figure 5.2. The loops in lines 28 to 30 and 32 to 34 employ the pcomp function pointer to compare elements. Note that we pass the addresses of the two elements rather than the elements themselves. The syntax for calling a function through a pointer is parallel to the syntax of the pointer declaration. The ANSI C standard allows a function pointer to be used in a simpler way: pcomp(& pa[i] , & ppart).

As we suggested in Section 5.4, quicksort is not efficient for small array sizes. Lines 20 to 23 use insertion sorting for arrays of fewer than 8 elements. Figure 5.8 lists the insert function, which is based on the inserti function from Figure 5.1.

FIGURE 5.8   insert.c

```
1     /* insert.c - insertion sort function */
2     /* uses pointers to the data elements and a compare function */
3     #include "stdlib.h"
4     #include "memsort.h"
5
6
7     void insert(pa,na,pcomp)      /* insertion sort for pointers */
8      void *pa[] ;                 /* array of pointers */
9      size_t na ;                  /* number of elements */
10     int (*pcomp) (void * , void *) ; /* compare function */
11     {
12        int i ;                    /* index for element being inserted */
13        int j ;                    /* index for inner loop */
14        void *ptemp;               /* scratch space for one pointer */
15
16        for( i=1 ; i < na ; i = i + 1 )
17           { /* insert the i-th element into the sorted array */
18             ptemp = pa[i] ;
19             j = i - 1;             /* find where it goes */
20             while( (j >= 0) && ( (*pcomp)(& ptemp,& pa[j]) < 0 ) )
21                { pa[j+1] = pa[j] ;
22                  j = j - 1 ;
23                }
24             pa[j+1] = ptemp ;
25           }
26     }
```

The `memsort` function has also been modified to improve performance in the worst case. Each recursive call consumes some memory for local variables, arguments, and housekeeping information. If the partitioning process works unevenly, up to (*n*–1) recursive calls might be needed to sort an array of *n* elements. For large arrays (1,000 to 5,000 elements), this might exhaust available memory. `memsort` avoids this problem by sorting the smaller partition first. Then, rather than calling itself to sort the remaining partition, it changes the values of `pa` and `na`. The `while` loop starting at line 19 and ending at line 54 repeats the sorting process until the remaining partition is small enough to be sorted by insertion. The `return` statement on line 22 is the mechanism for escaping from the loop. Each partitioning step produces two subarrays; we use recursion to sort the smaller one and iteration to sort the larger one. This limits the number of recursive calls to about log(*n*) base 2.

The `memsort.h` file in Figure 5.9 provides function prototypes for both functions and Figure 5.10 documents use of `memsort`.

FIGURE 5.9   memsort.h

```
1    /* memsort.h - function prototypes for memsort, insert */
2
3    void memsort( void *[] , size_t ,
4        int (*) (void *,void *) ) ;
5    void insert( void *[] , size_t ,
6        int (*) (void *,void *) ) ;
```

FIGURE 5.10   memsort Function Description

Name
memsort   sorts pointer array in RAM memory using quicksort algorithm

Usage
```
memsort(pa,nelem, compare) ;
void *pa[] ;            /* array of pointers to sort */
size_t nelem ;          /* number of elements in the array */
                        /* comparison function */
int (*compare) (void *, void *) ;
```

Function
memsort sorts an array of pointers in RAM memory using the quicksort and insertion algorithms. memsort can be used for any kind of data. The argument pa is an array of nelem elements. The pointer array will be sorted in increasing order.

The argument compare is a pointer to a user-supplied function that compares two array elements. memsort calls the compare function passing pointers to the two array elements (themselves pointers) to be compared. The compare function should return the following values:

less than 0	if element1 is less than element 2
0	if element1 is equivalent to element 2
greater than 0	if element1 is greater than element 2

Figure 5.10   continues

Figure 5.10   continued

The argument `pa` should be converted to the data type `void *[]`. In the compare function, the two arguments should be declared as `void *`. Compare functions prepared for `qsort` can be used with `memsort`. (The compare functions must be for comparing elements that are pointers.)

Example
```
int   na = 10 ;
int a[10] ;
int pa[10] ;        /* assume that pa[i] points to a[i] ; */
...
int pintcomp(void *, void *) ;
    memsort(pa, na, pintcomp) ;
...

int pintcomp(p1,p2)                /* sort function */
void *p1 ;                         /* points to first element */
void *p2 ;                         /* points to second element */
  {
    return( ( ** (int **)p1) - ( ** (int **) p2 ) ) ;
  }
```

Notes
The quicksort algorithm is very fast (n*log n time dependence) for almost all cases. But a worst case arrangement of data can produce slow sorting (n*n dependence). The `memsort` requires less than 500 bytes of stack space in the worst case.

For small files, `memsort` is faster than `qsorti` or the library `qsort` function. For larger files, `memsort` takes up to 60% more time than `qsorti` requires. However, `memsort` is usually faster than the library `qsort` function. And `memsort` produces consistent results for all the special cases discussed in Section 5.3.

5.6   An Application: Sorting Lines of Text

Now we that we have tools for sorting data, we can put them to use in an application: sorting lines in a text file. Such a program would be useful for sorting a list of names, but it gives us an opportunity to illustrate a real program using `memsort`. In addition, it provides an introduction to sorting `records` in data files. By records we mean the units of data to be compared and rearranged. In this case the records are lines of ASCII text. But the same logic applies to other types of data files as well.

The SORTTEXT program reads a text file into a storage area, sorts the individual lines of text, and writes the sorted lines of text to an output file. A manual page description is shown in Figure 5.11.

FIGURE 5.11   SORTTEXT Program Description

> **Name**
> SORTTEXT   sorts a text file (lines of ASCII characters)
>
> **Usage**
> ```
> C>sorttext input-file   output-file
> ```
>
> **Description**
> SORTTEXT reads a file of ASCII text and sorts it. The entire line is used as the sorting key with the normal ASCII collation sequence. Control-Z is recognized as the effective end of the file.
>
> **Limitations**
> Lines longer than 500 characters are split into two or more lines. SORTTEXT is limited to files of 200 lines maximum. In addition, file size is limited by available RAM memory. The entire file is loaded into RAM memory.

Pseudo-Code

The pseudo-code for this program is as follows:

```
sort text  file
     read lines of text into memory
     sort lines of text in memory
     write sorted lines to output file
end


read lines of text into memory
     get 1st line
     repeat until end-of-file reached
          place line in free part of storage area
          set up a pointer to the line of text
          update info on free space in storage area
          get another line of text
end


write sorted lines to output file
     open output file
     repeat for each line of text
          get pointer to next sorted line of text
          output the line of text
end
```

Some variables that will be needed include an area for storing lines of text in RAM, an array of pointers to the lines of text, and a count of lines of text read in.

The pseudo-code ignores some problems. For example, the program may not be able to open either the input or the output file; the text file may be too large to fit into the storage area; the file may contain a line too long to be handled as a unit. Our program must allow for these problems.

SORTTEXT Source Files

The SORTTEXT program is shown in Figures 5.12 through 5.17. The `sorttext.h` file in Figure 5.12 defines constants needed in the source files: the maximum length of a text record, the maximum number of lines, and sizes for input and output file buffers. Lines 11 to 29 define symbolic names for return values (mostly error conditions).

FIGURE 5.12   sorttext.h

```
1    /* sorttext.h - constants for sorttext program */
2
3                               /* size parameters */
4    #define MAX_REC    2000    /* max number of records */
5    #define MAX_RSIZE   503    /* max. size for a record */
6    #define IN_BSIZE   8192    /* input buffer size */
7    #define OUT_BSIZE  8192    /* output buffer size */
8
9
10                              /* (error) return values */
11   #define OK            0    /* normal return - no error */
12
13                              /* from dosort */
14   #define ALLOC_FAIL       1 /* couldn't allocate ptr array */
15   #define OPEN_READ_FAIL   2 /* couldn't open input file */
16   #define CLOSE_READ_FAIL  3 /* couldn't close input file */
17   #define OPEN_WRITE_FAIL  4 /* couldn't open output file */
18   #define CLOSE_WRITE_FAIL 5 /* couldn't close output file */
19
20                              /* from readfile */
21   #define AT_EOF        0    /* end-of-file reached */
22   #define NO_SPACE      6    /* ran out of space */
23   #define NO_PTR        7    /* ran out of record pointers */
24   #define READ_ERROR    8    /* couldn't read a record */
25
26                              /* from writefile */
27   #define WRITE_ERROR   9    /* couldn't write a record */
28
29
30
31                              /* read / write mode constants */
32   #define SF_READ  0         /* open for reading */
33   #define SF_WRITE 1         /* open for writing */
34
35
```

Figure 5.12   continues

Figure 5.12 continued

```
36                                   /* function prototypes */
37    int dosort(char *, char *) ;
38    int readfile(void *[], size_t , size_t * , FILE *) ;
39    void clean_read(void *[] , size_t ) ;
40    int writefile(void *[] , size_t , int , FILE *) ;
41    FILE *do_open(char *, int, size_t) ;
42    int getl(char *, int , FILE *) ;
43    int putl(char *, int , FILE *) ;
44    int do_close(FILE *) ;
```

The sorttext.h file also defines function prototypes for the functions that make up the SORTTEXT program. Note that some arguments are defined to be of the size_t data type, which is defined in the stdlib.h header file provided with the compiler. This data type is appropriate for specifying sizes of buffers or other arrays that will be allocated with the malloc or calloc functions.

The following hierarchy diagram shows the function call structure of SORTTEXT. The functions follow the pseudo-code outlined earlier. We discuss the program one source file at a time with the file containing the main function first.

```
main
      dosort
            do_open
            readfile
                  getl
            memsort
            do_close
            writefile
                  putl
            clean_read
```

sorttext.c

The file sorttext.c (Figure 5.13) contains the main function. It checks to be sure that two file names were specified on the command line and calls dosort to sort the file. Lines 7 to 13 define error messages corresponding to the return codes in sorttext.h.

FIGURE 5.13 sorttext.c

```
1    /* sorttext.c - sort a text file (lines of ASCII characters) */
2    #include  <stdio.h>
3    #include <stdlib.h>
4    #include "sorttext.h"
5
6                                   /* error messages */
```

Figure 5.13 continues

Figure 5.13   continued

```
 7     char *err_msg[] = { "OK",
 8            "can't allocate line pointers",    /* from dosort */
 9            "can't open input file" , "can't close input file" ,
10            "can't open output file" , "can't close output file" ,
11            "ran out of space" ,                /* from readfile */
12            "too many lines" , "can't read input" ,
13            "can't write output" } ;            /* from writefile */
14
15
16     main(argc,argv)
17      int argc ;      /* number of words in command line */
18      char *argv[] ;/* pointers to each word */
19      {
20          int ret ;
21
22          if( argc < 3 )              /* file names specified? */
23             { fputs(                 /*    no - exit */
24                " USAGE: sortfile  input-file  output-file", stderr) ;
25               exit(1);
26             }
27
28          ret = dosort(argv[1],argv[2]) ; /* do the sort */
29
30          if( ret != OK )
31             { fputs( err_msg[ret] , stderr ) ;
32               exit( 10 + ret ) ;
33             }
34      }
```

dosort.c

dosort in Figure 5.14 follows the overall pseudo-code presented earlier. Line 21 allocates space for an array of pointers. This array will record the position of each line of text in RAM memory. Line 31 calls the readfile function to read the text file and set the line pointer array. memsort sorts the lines of text, and writefile writes them in sorted order. Line 50 calls the clean_read function when the space used to store text lines can be released. The do_open and do_close functions open and close files. This isolates dosort.c from file I/O. Lines of text are stored as character strings and compared using the pscmp function from Figure 5.4.

FIGURE 5.14   dosort.c

```
1     /* dosort.c - read, sort, write a text file */
2     #include <stdio.h>
3     #include <stdlib.h>
4     #include <string.h>
5     #include "sorttext.h"
6     #include "cmpfuns.h"
7     #include "memsort.h"
8
```

Figure 5.14   continues

Figure 5.14   continued

```
 9
10      int dosort(fromfile,tofile)
11       char fromfile[] ;              /* input for sort */
12       char tofile[] ;               /* put the output here */
13       {
14          size_t   nrec ;
15          int   ret ;
16          void   **p  ;              /* pointers to lines of text */
17          FILE *in ;                 /* input file */
18          FILE *out ;                /* output file pointer */
19
20                                     /* allocate pointer array */
21          p = (void **) calloc(MAX_REC, sizeof(void *) ) ;
22          if( p == NULL )
23              return( ALLOC_FAIL ) ;
24
25                                     /* open input file */
26          in = do_open(fromfile,SF_READ,IN_BSIZE) ;
27          if( in == NULL )
28              return( OPEN_READ_FAIL ) ;
29
30                                     /* read text file into RAM */
31          ret = readfile(p,MAX_REC,& nrec,in) ;
32          if( ret != AT_EOF)
33              return( ret ) ;
34
35          if( do_close(in) != 0 )/* close input file */
36              return( CLOSE_READ_FAIL ) ;
37
38          memsort(p,nrec,pscmp) ;/* sort pointers to lines */
39
40                                     /* write sorted lines out */
41                                     /* open input file */
42          out = do_open(tofile,SF_WRITE,OUT_BSIZE) ;
43          if( out == NULL )
44              return( OPEN_WRITE_FAIL ) ;
45
46           ret = writefile(p,nrec,MAX_RSIZE,out);/* write sorted lines*/
47          if( ret != OK )
48              return( ret ) ;
49
50          clean_read(p,nrec) ;    /* free space for records */
51
52          if(do_close(out) != 0) /* close file */
53              return( CLOSE_WRITE_FAIL ) ;
54          else return( OK ) ;
55      }
```

readfile.c

The readfile.c file in Figure 5.15 reads the text file line by line and stores it in the area passed as an argument. As each line is read, space is allocated for it and that address is stored in the pointer array. The process can end in one of several ways: the end of the file may be reached, the pointer array may be filled, or storage space for

FIGURE 5.15   readfile.c

```
1      /* readfile.c - read text file into RAM memory */
2      #include <stdio.h>
3      #include <stdlib.h>
4      #include <string.h>
5      #include "sorttext.h"
6
7      static int rsize ;            /* size of record found */
8      static char rec[ MAX_RSIZE ] ; /* storage for one record */
9
10
11     int readfile(p,psize,pnrec,in) /* read entire file */
12     void *p[] ;                   /* store pointers to records here */
13     size_t psize ;                /* size of p[] - (max. no. records) */
14     size_t *pnrec ;               /* store no. of records here */
15     FILE *in ;                    /* input file */
16     {
17        int nrec ;                 /* number of records found so far */
18        void *pnew ;               /* points to space just allocated */
19
20        nrec = 0 ;
21        rsize = getl(rec,MAX_RSIZE,in) ; /* get 1st record */
22
23        while( rsize > 0 )        /* stop at end-of-file */
24          { if( nrec >= psize ) /* room in pointer array? */
25              { *pnrec = nrec ; /*   no - error return */
26                 return( NO_PTR ) ;
27              }
28                                    /* allocate space for record */
29            pnew = (void *) malloc( rsize ) ;
30            if( pnew == NULL )  /* check for allocation failure */
31              { *pnrec = nrec ;
32                 return( NO_SPACE ) ;
33              }
34            memcpy( pnew, rec,rsize) ; /* copy record to its space */
35            p[nrec] = pnew ;     /* store pointer to record */
36            nrec = nrec + 1 ;    /* count it */
37
38            rsize = getl(rec,MAX_RSIZE,in) ; /* get next record */
39          }
40        *pnrec = nrec ;
41        if( rsize < 0 )           /* did we stop because of an error? */
42            return( READ_ERROR) ; /*  yes - error return */
43        else return( AT_EOF ) ; /*     no  - normal return */
44     }
45
46
47     void clean_read(p,nrec)       /* clean up after sorting */
48     void *p[] ;
49     size_t nrec ;
50     {
51        while( nrec > 0 )         /* free space for records */
52          { nrec = nrec - 1 ;
53             free( p[nrec] ) ;
54          }
55     }
```

the text lines may be exhausted. The `return` statements on lines 26, 32, and 42 reflect these conditions by returning different values.

Lines 21 and 38 read the next line of text into the `rec` array, whose size is the maximum allowed. Once the line's actual size is known, line 29 allocates the exact amount of space needed. Line 34 copies the line into the allocated space, and line 35 records the location of the line in memory.

The `clean_read` function frees the space for all lines. In SORTTEXT, this is not necessary, but in the sort module developed later in this chapter, it will be essential to free memory as soon as it is no longer needed.

writefil.c

Figure 5.16 shows the `writfil.c` source file. The `writefile` function uses the pointer array reordered by `memsort` to write the text lines in sorted order.

FIGURE 5.16   writefil.c

```
 1     /* writefil.c - write out sorted file */
 2     #include "stdio.h"
 3     #include "sorttext.h"
 4
 5     int writefile(prec,nrec,rsize,out)/* write lines, sorted order */
 6     void *prec[] ;              /* array of pointers to records */
 7     size_t nrec ;               /* number of records to be output */
 8     int rsize ;                 /* record size */
 9     FILE *out ;                 /* output file pointer */
10     {
11       int i , ret ;
12
13       for(i=0; i < nrec; i=i+1)/* write in sorted order */
14         {                        /* output one record */
15           ret = putl( prec[i], rsize, out) ;
16           if( ret != 0 )         /* and check for I/O error */
17             return( WRITE_ERROR); /*  yes - error return */
18         }
19
20       return( OK ) ;
21     }
```

sortio.c

The `sortio.c` file in Figure 5.17 contains I/O functions used by other source files. The `do_open` function uses `fopen` to open the file in binary mode and then assigns a file buffer with the `setvbuf` function. Since a NULL value is supplied as the buffer address, `setvbuf` will allocate the buffer. The `do_close` function uses the `fclose` function to close files.

FIGURE 5.17 sortio.c

```
1      /* sortio.c - I/O functions for sorttext program */
2      /* do_open , do_close , getl , putl */
3      #include <stdio.h>
4      #include <stdlib.h>
5      #include "sorttext.h"
6
7      #define CTRL_Z  26            /* control Z character value */
8
9      static char *iomodes [2] = { "rb" , "wb" } ;
10
11                                   /* open file and assign buffer */
12     FILE *do_open(fname,fmode,bsize)
13      char fname[] ;               /* file name string */
14      int fmode ;                  /* sort file mode see header file */
15      size_t bsize ;
16      {                            /* return a FILE pointer */
17         FILE *fd ;
18
19                                   /* open the file */
20         fd = fopen(fname,iomodes[fmode] ) ;
21         if( fd != NULL )          /* check for errors */
22            {                      /* assign buffer to the file */
23               if( setvbuf(fd,NULL,_IOFBF,bsize) != 0 )
24                  { fclose(fd) ;   /*   failed - close file */
25                    return( NULL );/*        error return */
26                  }
27            }
28         return( fd ) ;
29      }
30
31
32     int do_close(fd)              /* close file and check for errors */
33      FILE *fd ;                   /* file pointer */
34      {
35         return( fclose( fd ) ) ;
36      }
37
38
39     int getl(s,maxs,fd)          /* get one line from file */
40      char *s ;                    /* put it here in string form */
41      int maxs ;                   /* maximum length permitted */
42      FILE *fd ;                   /* file pointer for input file */
43      {                            /* getl returns no. chars used in s */
44                                   /* (or -1 if EOF reached) */
45         int n , c ;
46
47         n = 0 ;
48
49         while( 1 == 1 )           /* repeat until we get a line */
50            { c = getc(fd) ;       /* get next char */
51               if( c == EOF )      /* check for end-of-file */
52                  { if( ferror(fd) != 0 ) /* or error */
53                     { s[n] = '\0' ;
54                       return( -2 ) ;
55                     }
56                     if( n == 0 )     /* if we don't have a line yet */
```

Figure 5.17   continues

Figure 5.17   continued

```
58                           return( 0);/*  no - return 0 as length */
59                 }
60                 s[n] = '\r' ;    /*   yes - partial line, add CR  */
61                 s[n+1] = '\n' ; /*          and LF  */
62                 n = n + 2 ;      /*          adjust length */
63                 break ;          /* we have a line - normal return */
64             }
65         if( c == CTRL_Z )
66             { ungetc(c,fd) ;
67             if( n == 0 )      /* if we don't have a line yet */
68                 { s[0] = '\0';/*   no - return 0 as length */
69                 return( 0) ;
70                 }
71             s[n] = '\r' ;    /*      yes - partial line, add CR  */
72             s[n+1] = '\n' ; /*             and LF  */
73             n = n + 2 ;      /*             adjust length */
74             break ;
75             }
76         s[ n ] = c ;
77         n = n + 1 ;
78         if( c == '\n' )
79             break ;
80         if( n >= (maxs-3) ) /* reached maximum length? */
81             { s[n] = '\r' ;    /*   yes - add CR  */
82             s[n+1] = '\n' ; /*          and LF  */
83             n = n + 2 ;      /*          adjust length */
84             break ;          /*          and leave */
85             }
86     }
87
88     s[ n ] = '\0' ;              /* add end-of-string marker */
89     return( n+1 ) ;             /* return line length with '\0' */
90 }
91
92
93 int putl(s,rsize,fd)             /* output one line of text */
94     char *s ;                    /* line to output - string form */
95     int rsize ;                  /* record size (dummy for putl) */
96     FILE *fd ;                   /* output file pointer */
97     {
98     if( fputs(s,fd) == EOF)/* use fputs, check for error */
99         return( -1 ) ;      /*          yes - error return */
100    else return( 0 ) ;      /*          no  - normal return */
101    }
```

The get1 function gets a line of text from the file identified by the argument fd. It stops when a newline or line feed character (\n) signals the end of a line. get1 may also stop when it reaches the end of the file (or finds a control-Z character). If get1 has accumulated part of a line, it will return that line. It will return a 0 line length on the next call. get1 may also stop if the maximum line length is reached. In all cases, the line returned by get1 will be ended by an end-of-line marker. The line is in C string form, terminated by a zero character value (\0). The length returned by get1 includes this zero character.

The putl function is much simpler. It uses the fputs library function to write the line to the file specified by fd.

SORTTEXT Organization

Much of the SORTTEXT program is devoted to detecting errors and to handling them gracefully. The action needed when an error is detected is very specific to the context in which the error occurred. The structure of the program must allow errors to be detected and then allow a graceful recovery. Note that all file I/O actions and memory allocation calls are checked for errors.

Using memory effectively is crucial to the success of SORTTEXT. Memory is required for file buffers, the pointer array, and for storing lines of text. Each use benefits from more memory. Larger buffers make file I/O faster. A larger pointer array allows larger files to be sorted as does more memory for dynamic allocation. Making effective tradeoffs between these is the secret to a successful sort program.

SORTTEXT is a small program, but we have spread it over several source files. This keeps each source file simple and focused on one level of detail. It also provides a foundation for continued development. The next sections build on this version of SORTTEXT to develop programs for external sorting.

Performance measurements show that reading and writing the file take over half the total execution time. The `memsort` function consumes another 20 to 30%, and allocating and freeing space for lines of text takes about 10 to 15% of execution time.

5.7 Enhancements to SORTTEXT

💾 Case-Independent Sorting

We often want to ignore uppercase-lowercase differences in sorting text. We should provide a command line option to select a case-independent compare function.

💾 Specifying a Starting Point and Length for the Sort Key

Sometimes we want to use part of each line of text as the sort key. In addition, that key might not be located at the beginning of the line. SORTTEXT should accept a command line option specifying where the key starts and its length.

5.8 External Sorting Algorithms: Merging Records

The SORTTEXT program makes good use of the `memsort` function, but it is limited to files that fit into the available RAM memory. When all the data are in RAM memory, any element can be accessed in a few microseconds. When the data are in a disk file, this access takes many milliseconds. memsort relies on free access to every element being sorted. We need an algorithm that fits the limitations of disk file access. The merge algorithm meets our needs; it will be the basis for an *external sorting* module. The SORTTEXT program is a standalone program specific to sorting text files; our next goal here is to develop a library module that is not limited to one type of file.

The merge algorithm combines two or more sorted sequences of records to produce a single, sorted sequence of records. The process can be described as follows:

Step 1. Get the first record from each file.

Step 2. Select the record with the lowest key.

Step 3. Place it in the output file.

Step 4. Replace the record with the next from the same input file.

Step 5. Repeat steps 2–4 until all input files are exhausted.

We can illustrate the process with two arrays of integers:

Before merging

Output Array

1 4 ———— Input Array 1

2 3 7 ———— Input Array 2

After first element
selected

Output Array

1 ————

4 ———— Input Array 1

2 3 7 ———— Input Array 2

After second element
selected

Output Array

1 2 ————

4 ———— Input Array 1

3 7 ———— Input Array 2

After third element
selected

Output Array

1 2 3 ——— 4 ————— Input Array 1

7 ————— Input Array 2

After fourth and fifth
elements selected

Output Array

————— Input Array 1

1 2 3 4 7 ————— Input Array 2

The merge algorithm works well with data stored on floppy or hard disks. Only one record at a time is required from each input file, and records are retrieved sequentially. This limits the amount of RAM memory needed and allows efficient disk I/O operations. The merge algorithm is the heart of the program. We need an initial step to prepare sorted *runs*. Then we use the merge process to combine these runs into fewer but longer runs.

Pseudo-code for External Sorting: A SORTMERG Module

Now we can write pseudo-code for external sorting. The overall pseudo-code follows the explanation just given:

```
sort-merge function
    build sorted runs
    merge runs
    copy final merged result to output file
end
```

Building runs is much like the SORTTEXT program. We read records from the input file until a storage area is filled. Then we sort the records (with `memsort`) and write them to an output file. Each batch of records sorted together is one run. We repeat this process until the entire input file has been read.

```
build runs
    until all of input file read
        fill storage area with records
        sort records
        output sorted records
end
```

The merge process is carried out in passes. On each pass, the existing runs are combined into new, longer runs. The number of runs that can be combined in one step is limited by the resources such as RAM memory and the number of files that can be open. For example, if this limit is four runs at a time, twenty initial runs are combined into five runs on the first pass. Those five runs are combined into two runs on the second pass. The third pass combines these two runs into a single run, ending the merging process. The following pseudo-code performs this iteration.

```
do merges
     repeat until a single run is produced
          merge existing runs into longer runs
end
```

The next level of detail describes a single pass of the merge process. Here, the existing runs are grouped into sets of *m* runs each. Each set is merged into a single new run.

```
merge existing runs
     repeat until all existing runs are merged
          select the next (m) runs
          merge (m) runs
end
```

Merging a single set of runs into one new run requires another level of pseudo-code:

```
merge (m) runs
     get 1st record from each run
     sort these records
     repeat until all (m) runs are exhausted
          pick record with the lowest key
          place it in the output run
          get  a replacement record from same input run
end
```

Data Structures

Managing disk space is central to the merge process. We will store a set of runs in a single disk file. For example, when we build initial runs, we write each run in the same file. We record the starting position in the file and the number of records present for each run. On each merge pass, we read the input runs and create a new disk file containing the output runs. When a merge pass is finished, the file containing input runs is no longer needed and can be deleted.

Efficient file I/O is necessary for good performance. In building initial runs, we need two open files — one for input and one for output. The merge process reads records from *m* runs in an unpredictable order. To make disk I/O efficient, we open the input disk file *m* times, so that each run has a separate buffer area.

Managing RAM memory is also important. Forming runs is similar to the SORTTEXT program. We need a storage space for the records in an entire run and an array of pointers to those records. We also need large file buffers to make file I/O efficient. In the merge step, we need a file buffer and space for one record for *m* input runs. We need a single file buffer for output.

Exceptions

The same exceptions that we met in the SORTTEXT program must be handled here. Input and output file names may be missing or invalid. We may run out of room on a disk while writing a scratch file or the final output file. Long records may exceed the size of the area we reserve for storing a record.

5.9   Source Files for the SORTMERG Library Module

The SORTMERG module is a set of functions to be called by an application program. The manual page in Figure 5.18 documents its use. When we call the `sortmerge` function, we specify names for the file to be sorted and of the output file. We also specify the functions to be used for file I/O through the third argument, `psio`. The fourth argument specifies the function to be called to compare records. For fixed length records, the record size argument is the actual record size. For lines of text, the record size argument is the maximum record size expected (including end-of-line markers and a terminating null character).

FIGURE 5.18   SORTMERG Module Description

Name
sortmerge   sorts data files using the merge algorithm

Usage
```
#include  "sortmerg.h"
int  sortmerge(infile,outfile,pio,pcomp,rec_size)  ;
char *infile ;        /* name of input file */
char *outfile ;       /* name of output file */
SIO_FUNS *pio ;       /* identifies I/O functions */
                      /* comparison function */
int (*pcomp) (void *, void *) ;
int rec_size ;        /* record size */
```

Function
sortmerge reads the file specified by the C string `infile`, sorts the records, and writes the sorted records in the file specified by the C string `outfile`. The

Figure 5.18   continues

Figure 5.18   continued

functions to be used for file I/O are specified by the pointer `pio`. The `pcomp` argument specifies the function to be called to compare two records.

The global variable `lines_of_text` defines I/O functions for sorting lines of text, and the variable `fixed_records` defines functions for sorting records of fixed length.

A return value of `0` indicates that `sortmerge` was successful. A nonzero return value indicates that the sort process failed and identifies the cause of the failure. The `sortmer2.h` file defines symbolic constants for return codes.

The argument `pcomp` is the address of a function that compares two pointers to records. The two arguments passed to the function are pointers to pointers. The following examples show compare functions for two cases. The compare function should return the following values:

less than 0	if element 1 is less than element 2
0	if element 1 is equivalent to element 2
greater than 0	if element 1 is greater than element 2

The `rec_size` field specifies the actual record length for fixed length records and the maximum length for lines of text. (Lines of text are stored with carriage return and line feed present in C string form. The maximum must allow for end-of-line and null characters.)

Example

```
                              /* sorting lines of text */
                              /* 200 chars lines max */
#include  "sortmerg.h"
int *pscmp( void *, void *) ;
char *infile = "c:input" ;
char *outfile = "d:output" ;
ret = sortmerge(infile,outfile,& lines_of_text,
          pscmp, 200) ;
...
int pscmp(p1,p2)
 void *p1 , *p2 ;
 {
    return( strcmp( * (char **) p1 , * (char **) p2 ) ) ;
 }

...                           /* sort fixed length records */
                              /* 50 bytes long */
ret = sortmerge(infile,outfile,& fixed_records,prcmp, 50) ;
...
int prcmp(p1,p2)       /* integer keys at offset 0 */
 void *p1 , *p2 ;
 {
    return( *(int **) p1 - * (int **) p2  ) ;
 }
```

Figure 5.18   continues

Figure 5.18 continued

Notes

The limits of the `sortmerge` function depend on the memory model used. The following table lists those limits:

	Small or Medium Model	Large, Compact, or Huge Model
Files open	8	15
RAM memory used	50 Kbytes	150 Kbytes
File size	10 Mbytes	50 Mbytes
Number of records	400 K	400 M

Limits for RAM memory, file size, and number of records are approximate.

The following hierarchy diagram shows the pattern of function calls in the SORTMERG module:

```
sortmerge
    formruns
        (open function)
        (close function)
        (tell function)
        init_read
            (read function)
        readrun
            (read function)
        memsort
        clean_read
        writerun
            (write function)
    domerge
        dopass
            (open function)
            (close function)
            (seek function)
            (tell function)
            smerge
                (write function)
                insertm
                resortm
                    get_run
                        (read function)
```

Functions for file I/O are called via function pointers. These functions are shown in parentheses.

sortmerg.h

The `sortmerg.h` header file in Figure 5.19 supplies definitions needed in the application program that calls the `sortmerge` function. A function prototype defines the arguments expected by the `sortmerge` function. As in the SORTTEXT program, sizes of buffers and arrays are specified to be the `size_t` data type defined in `stdlib.h`.

The `SFILE` data type isolates the application and the SORTMERG module from the details of the file I/O functions used. The `SIO_FUNS` data type provides a mechanism for the application program to specify the functions to be used for reading and writing records. It holds pointers to the file I/O functions to be used. The global variable `lines_of_text` specifies appropriate functions for reading and writing lines of text. The variable `fixed_records` specifies functions for fixed-length records.

FIGURE 5.19   sortmerg.h

```
1    /* sortmerg.h - definitions for using sortmerge module */
2
3                                  /* sort file opening modes */
4    #define SF_READ   0           /* open file for reading */
5    #define SF_WRITE  1           /* open file for writing */
6
7
8                                  /* data types */
9
10   typedef void SFILE ;          /* dummy sort file type */
11
12   typedef struct
13     { SFILE *(*popen)(char *, int, size_t) ; /* open file */
14       int   (*pclose) (SFILE *) ;           /* close file */
15       int   (*pget) (void *, int , SFILE *) ; /* read record */
16       int   (*pput) (void *, int , SFILE *) ; /* write record */
17       int   (*pseek)(SFILE *, long, int ) ;  /* seek function */
18       long (*ptell)(SFILE *) ;              /* tell position */
19     } SIO_FUNS ;
20
21
22                                  /* global variables */
23
24                                  /* pre-defined sort I/O functions */
25   extern SIO_FUNS lines_of_text ; /* for lines of text */
26   extern SIO_FUNS fixed_records ; /* for fixed length records */
27
28
29                                  /* function prototype */
30   int sortmerge(char *, char *, SIO_FUNS *,
31        int (*) (void *, void*) , size_t ) ;
```

sortmer2.h

The sortmer2.h header file in Figure 5.20 provides definitions needed within the SORTMERG module. The sortmer2.h file is similar to the sorttext.h header file from Figure 5.12. More function prototypes are declared, and two new data structures are defined. The RDATA data type records data for a run — its starting position and the number of records present. The MDATA data type stores data for a run being merged: its starting point and number of records remaining, the file pointer for reading records, and a pointer to the record area.

FIGURE 5.20   sortmer2.h

```
1     /* sortmer2.h - internal definitions for sortmerg module */
2
3     #include "sortmerg.h"
4
5                               /* default values for parameters */
6
7                               /* small/medium model */
8     #define SM_MAX_REC      2000   /* max number of records */
9     #define SM_MAX_RSIZE     500   /* max. size for a record */
10    #define SM_IN_BSIZE     8192   /* input buffer size */
11    #define SM_OUT_BSIZE    8192   /* output buffer size */
12    #define SM_M_IN_BSIZE   4096   /* merge input buffer sizes */
13    #define SM_M_OUT_BSIZE  8192   /* merge output buffer size */
14    #define SM_MAX_RUNS      200   /* maximum number of runs allowed */
15    #define SM_MAX_MERGE       7   /* maximum merge order */
16
17                               /* large/compact/huge model */
18    #define LG_MAX_REC      8000   /* max number of records */
19    #define LG_MAX_RSIZE     500   /* max. size for a record */
20    #define LG_IN_BSIZE     8192   /* input buffer size */
21    #define LG_OUT_BSIZE    8192   /* output buffer size */
22    #define LG_M_IN_BSIZE   8192   /* merge input buffer sizes */
23    #define LG_M_OUT_BSIZE 16384   /* merge output buffer size */
24    #define LG_MAX_RUNS      500   /* maximum number of runs allowed */
25    #define LG_MAX_MERGE      14   /* maximum merge order */
26
27
28
29                               /* return codes */
30    #define OK                 0   /* normal return - no error */
31
32                               /* from formruns */
33    #define ALLOC_FAIL         1 /* couldn't allocate ptr array */
34    #define OPEN_READ_FAIL     2 /* couldn't open input file */
35    #define CLOSE_READ_FAIL    3 /* couldn't close input file */
36    #define OPEN_WRITE_FAIL    4 /* couldn't open output file */
37    #define CLOSE_WRITE_FAIL   5 /* couldn't close output file */
38    #define TOO_MANY_RUNS     16 /* max. number of runs reached */
39
40                               /* from readrun */
41    #define AT_EOF             0   /* end-of-file reached */
42    #define NO_SPACE           6   /* ran out of space */
43    #define NO_PTR             7   /* ran out of record pointers */
```

Figure 5.20   continues

Figure 5.20   **continued**

```
44      #define READ_ERROR    8       /* couldn't read a record */
45
46                                    /* from writerun */
47      #define WRITE_ERROR   9       /* couldn't write a record */
48
49                                    /* from dopass */
50      #define REC_ALLOCATION_FAILURE 10  /* couldn't allocate record */
51      #define OPEN_MERGE_OUTPUT_FAILURE 11  /* couldn't open file */
52      #define OPEN_MERGE_INPUT_FAILURE 12  /* couldn't open file */
53      #define CLOSE_MERGE_OUTPUT_FAILURE 17 /* couldn't close file */
54
55                                    /* from smerge */
56      #define EMPTY_RUN    13       /* run had no records */
57      #define UNEXPECTED_EOF 14   /* got to EOF before run was read */
58      #define MERGE_READ_ERROR 18 /* couldn't read record */
59      #define MERGE_WRITE_ERROR 19 /* couldn't write record */
60
61      #define EOR          999     /* end of run reached */
62                                    /* (not an error condition) */
63
64                                    /* from sortmerge */
65      #define RUNS_ALLOCATION_FAILURE 15  /* couldn't allocate runs */
66
67
68
69                                    /* data structures */
70
71      typedef struct               /* data structure for runs */
72        { long start ;             /* file position where run starts */
73          long nrec ;              /* number of records in this run */
74        } RDATA ;
75
76      typedef struct               /* data for a run being merged */
77        { void *prec ;             /* pointer to record space */
78          long start ;             /* starting file position */
79          long nrec ;              /* number of records left */
80          SFILE *sf ;              /* sort file pointer */
81        } MDATA ;
82
83
84                                    /* global variables */
85      extern SIO_FUNS *sfio ;      /* ptr to I/O functions structure */
86                                    /* record compare function ptr. */
87      extern int (*sf_comp) (void * , void *) ;
88      extern size_t sf_rsize ;     /* record size (or max size) */
89
90                                    /* buffer size parameters */
91      extern size_t fi_bsize ;     /* formruns input */
92      extern size_t fo_bsize ;     /* formruns output */
93      extern size_t mi_bsize ;     /* merge input */
94      extern size_t mo_bsize ;     /* merge output */
95
96      extern size_t max_rec ;      /* no. records in a run */
97                                    /* size of array of ptrs to records */
98      extern size_t max_run;       /* no. runs to allow */
99      extern int merge_order ;     /* no. runs to merge at a time */
```

Figure 5.20   **continues**

Figure 5.20   continued

```
100
101                                      /* function prototypes */
102      int formruns(char *, char *, RDATA [], size_t *) ;
103      int readrun(void *[], size_t , size_t * , SFILE *) ;
104      int init_read(SFILE * ) ;
105      void clean_read(void *[] , size_t , int ) ;
106      int writerun(void *[] , size_t , int, SFILE *) ;
107      int domerge(char *,char *,char *,RDATA [], size_t) ;
108      int dopass(char *,char *,RDATA [], size_t , size_t *) ;
109      int smerge(MDATA [], int , long * , SFILE *) ;
110      void insertm( MDATA [] , int ) ;
111      void resortm( MDATA [] , int ) ;
```

Constants are defined for buffer sizes and other parameters. Two sets of default parameters are defined for memory models with 16- and 32-bit memory models. Global variables are declared for these parameters and for I/O and compare functions. Pointers to the SFILE data type are passed as arguments rather than the FILE pointers used in the SORTTEXT program. The SFILE type is defined in sortmerg.h. Line 3 of sortmer2.h includes this file.

sortmerg.c

The sortmerge.c function in Figure 5.21 copies pointers for the compare functions and for file I/O functions to global variables. Other global variables contain record and buffer sizes. Lines 44 to 61 select parameters to fit the memory model being used. (Lines 45 to 51 or Lines 54 to 60 may produce a warning message about unreachable code from your compiler. This message can be ignored.)

FIGURE 5.21   sortmerg.c

```
1        /* sortmerg.c - SORTMERG module */
2        #include  <stdio.h>
3        #include <stdlib.h>
4        #include "sortmer2.h"
5
6        #define SMALL_PTR 2          /* 2 byte or 16 bit pointer size */
7
8                                     /* global variables */
9        SIO_FUNS *sfio ;             /* points to I/O fun. structure */
10                                     /* record compare function ptr. */
11       int (*sf_comp) (void * , void *) ;
12       size_t sf_rsize ;            /* record size */
13                                     /* (or max allowed for lines) */
14
15                                     /* buffer size parameters */
16       size_t fi_bsize ;            /* formruns input */
17       size_t fo_bsize ;            /* formruns output */
18       size_t mi_bsize ;            /* merge input */
19       size_t mo_bsize ;            /* merge output */
20
```

Figure 5.2   continues

Figure 5.21   continued

```
21     size_t max_rec ;                 /* no. record pointers to allow */
22     size_t max_run ;                 /* number of runs to allow */
23     int merge_order ;                /* no. of runs to merge at a time */
24
25      sortmerge(infile, outfile, pio, pcomp , rec_size)
26      char infile[] ;                 /* input file name */
27      char outfile[] ;                /* output file name */
28      SIO_FUNS *pio ;                 /* points to I/O funs. structure */
29      int (*pcomp) (void * , void *) ; /* record compare function */
30      size_t rec_size ;
31      {
32          int ret ;
33          size_t nruns ;
34          char scra[] = "scra" ;
35          char scrb[] = "scrb" ;
36          RDATA *runs ;
37
38                                  /* set global variables */
39          sf_rsize = rec_size ;   /* record size */
40          sfio = pio ;            /* I/O function structure */
41          sf_comp = pcomp ;       /* compare function */
42
43                                  /* set sort merge parameters */
44          if( sizeof( char *) == SMALL_PTR )
45            { fi_bsize = SM_IN_BSIZE ; /* 16 bit pointers */
46              fo_bsize = SM_OUT_BSIZE ;
47              mi_bsize = SM_M_IN_BSIZE ;
48              mo_bsize = SM_M_OUT_BSIZE ;
49              merge_order = SM_MAX_MERGE ;
50              max_run = SM_MAX_RUNS ;
51              max_rec = SM_MAX_REC ;
52            }
53          else                        /* 32 bit pointers */
54            { fi_bsize = LG_IN_BSIZE ;
55              fo_bsize = LG_OUT_BSIZE ;
56              mi_bsize = LG_M_IN_BSIZE ;
57              mo_bsize = LG_M_OUT_BSIZE ;
58              merge_order = LG_MAX_MERGE ;
59              max_run = LG_MAX_RUNS ;
60              max_rec = LG_MAX_REC ;
61            }
62
63
64                                  /* allocate array for run data */
65          runs = (RDATA *) calloc(max_run , sizeof(RDATA) ) ;
66          if( runs == NULL )
67              return( RUNS_ALLOCATION_FAILURE ) ;
68
69                                      /* form initial runs */
70          ret = formruns(infile,scra,runs,& nruns) ;
71          if( ret != OK )
72            { remove(scra) ;
73              return( ret ) ;
74            }
75                                      /* merge runs */
76          ret = domerge(scra,scrb,outfile,runs,nruns) ;
77          return( ret ) ;
78      }
```

Line 65 allocates an array to hold information about each run formed. The `formruns` function is called to make initial runs, and then the `domerge` function is called to combine these runs into the final sorted file.

In addition to input and output files, the SORTMERG module defines names for two scratch files: `scra` and `scrb`.

formruns.c

The `formruns.c` file shown in Figure 5.22 builds initial runs from the input file. It is similar to the `dosort` function in the SORTTEXT program. In that program, failing to read the entire input file into memory was an error causing the program to exit immediately. In the SORTMERG module, it means that we must repeat the loop to form another run. Error handling and housekeeping make the `formruns` function rather long, but its basic structure is simple:

```
formruns
      open input and output files
      repeat until end of file reached
            read a run into memory
            sort with memsort
            write out sorted records
            record starting position and size of this run
      end
```

FIGURE 5.22   formruns.c

```
 1      /* formruns.c - read, sort, write initial runs */
 2      #include <stdio.h>
 3      #include <stdlib.h>
 4      #include <string.h>
 5      #include "sortmer2.h"
 6      #include "cmpfuns.h"
 7      #include "memsort.h"
 8
 9
10      int formruns(fromfile,scr,runs,pnrun)
11      char fromfile[] ;          /* input for sort */
12      char scr[] ;               /* output - scratch file */
13      RDATA runs[] ;             /* fill with data on each run */
14      size_t *pnrun ;            /* number of runs */
15      {
16          size_t nrun ;          /* number of runs made */
17          size_t   nrec ;        /* number of records in current run */
18          int ret , read_status ;
19          void  **p  ;           /* pointers to lines of text */
20          SFILE *in ;            /* input file */
21          SFILE *out ;           /* output file pointer */
22
```

Figure 5.22   continues

Figure 5.22   continued

```
23                                    /* allocate array of pointers */
24                                    /* to records */
25        p = (void **) calloc(max_rec , sizeof(void *) ) ;
26        if( p == NULL )
27            return( ALLOC_FAIL ) ;
28
29                                    /* open input file */
30         in = sfio->popen (fromfile,SF_READ,fi_bsize) ;
31        if( in == NULL )
32            return( OPEN_READ_FAIL ) ;
33        ret = init_read(in) ;  /* set up for reading runs */
34        if( ret != OK )
35          { sfio->pclose( in ) ;
36            free( p ) ;
37            return( ret ) ;
38          }
39                                    /* open output file */
40         out = sfio->popen(scr,SF_WRITE,fo_bsize) ;
41        if( out == NULL )
42          { sfio->pclose( in ) ;
43            free( p ) ;
44            return( OPEN_WRITE_FAIL ) ;
45          }
46
47        nrun = 0 ;
48        read_status = AT_EOF +1 ;
49        while( read_status != AT_EOF) /* repeat til all runs made */
50          { if( nrun >= max_run ) /* too many runs? */
51              { sfio->pclose(in) ;
52                sfio->pclose(out) ;
53                free( p ) ;
54                return( TOO_MANY_RUNS ) ;
55              }
56                                    /* read text file into RAM */
57            read_status = readrun(p,max_rec,& nrec,in) ;
58            if( (read_status != AT_EOF ) /* check for error status */
59              && (read_status != NO_SPACE )
60              && (read_status != NO_PTR) )
61              { sfio->pclose(in) ;
62                sfio->pclose(out) ;
63                free( p ) ;
64                clean_read(p,nrec,AT_EOF) ;
65                return( read_status ) ;
66              }
67            if( nrec == 0 )      /* check for no records */
68              { clean_read(p,nrec,AT_EOF) ;
69                break ;
70              }
71            memsort(p,nrec,sf_comp) ;/* sort pointers */
72                                    /* using specified compare function */
73
74                                    /* record start of run */
75            runs[nrun].start = sfio->ptell( out ) ;
76                                    /* write sorted records out */
77            ret = writerun(p,nrec,sf_rsize,out);
78            if( ret != OK )
```

Figure 5.22   continues

Figure 5.22   continued

```
79                    { sfio->pclose(in ) ;
80                      sfio->pclose(out) ;
81                      clean_read(p,nrec,AT_EOF) ;
82                      free(p) ;
83                      return( ret ) ;
84                    }
85
86                                  /* deallocate space for records */
87              clean_read(p,nrec,read_status) ;
88              runs[nrun].nrec = nrec ; /* number records in run */
89              nrun = nrun + 1 ;
90            }
91
92        free( p ) ;              /* free pointer array */
93        *pnrun = nrun ;          /* record number of runs */
94
95        if( sfio->pclose(in) != 0 )/* close input file */
96            return( CLOSE_READ_FAIL ) ;
97
98        if(sfio->pclose(out) != 0) /* close output file */
99            return( CLOSE_WRITE_FAIL ) ;
100       else return( OK ) ;
101     }
```

A call to the function init_read gets the first record from the input file and performs other initialization for the readrun function. readrun is called to read as many records as can be stored in memory. It will be called repeatedly until all records have been read.

Line 71 calls memsort to sort each run using the sf_comp pointer to the compare function. The sorted records are written to the output file. Line 75 records the file position before a run is written, and line 88 records the number of records in the run. Lines 30, 35, 40, 42, 51, 52, 61, 62, 75, 79, 80, 95, and 98 show the syntax for calling an I/O function through the SIO_FUNS data structure.

readrun.c

The readrun function in Figure 5.23 is similar to the readfile function from the SORTTEXT program. It reads records until no more space is available, the pointer array is full, or the end of the file is reached. There are two differences between the readrun function and the readfile function. First, running out of space for records or room in the pointer array is a normal condition rather than an error. Second, readrun will be called repeatedly until the entire input file has been read.

A separate function, init_read, reads the first record from the input file. It also allocates the area into which each record is read. When readrun is called, it expects a record to be waiting in the area to which rec points.

The clean_read function releases the space allocated for records. When the entire input file has been read, clean_read will also release the single record area to which rec points.

FIGURE 5.23   readrun.c

```
1    /* readrun.c - read one run from file into RAM memory */
2    #include <stdio.h>
3    #include <stdlib.h>
4    #include <string.h>
5    #include "sortmer2.h"
6
7    static int rsize ;          /* size of record found */
8    static char *rec ;          /* ptr to storage for one record */
9
10
11   int readrun(p,psize,pnrec,in)
12   void *p[] ;                 /* store pointers to records here */
13   size_t psize ;              /* size of p[] - (max. no. records) */
14   size_t *pnrec ;             /* store no. of records here */
15   SFILE *in ;                 /* input file */
16   {
17     int nrec ;                /* number of records found so far */
18     void *pnew ;              /* points to space just allocated */
19
20     nrec  = 0 ;
21
22     while( rsize > 0 )        /* stop at end-of-file */
23         {                    /* allocate space for record */
24         if( nrec >= psize ) /* room in pointer array? */
25             { *pnrec = nrec ; /*   no - error return */
26               return( NO_PTR ) ;
27             }
28
29         pnew = (void *) malloc( rsize ) ; /* allocate space */
30         if( pnew == NULL )   /* check for allocation failure */
31           { *pnrec = nrec ;
32             return( NO_SPACE ) ;
33           }
34                              /* copy record to storage area */
35         memcpy( pnew, rec,rsize) ;
36
37         p[nrec] = pnew ;      /* store pointer to record */
38         nrec = nrec + 1 ;     /* count it */
39
40                              /* get next record */
41         rsize = sfio->pget(rec,sf_rsize,in) ;
42         }
43     *pnrec = nrec ;
44     if( rsize < 0 )          /* did we stop because of an error? */
45         return( READ_ERROR) ; /*  yes - error return */
46     else return( AT_EOF ) ; /*      no normal return */
47   }
48
49
50   int init_read(in)          /* initialize for reading runs */
51   SFILE *in ;
52   {
53     rec = (char *) malloc(sf_rsize) ;
54     if( rec == NULL )
55         return( ALLOC_FAIL ) ;
56     rsize = sfio->pget(rec,sf_rsize,in) ; /* read 1st record */
57     if( rsize < 0 )
```

Figure 5.23   continues

Figure 5.23   continued

```
58                return( READ_ERROR ) ;
59           else return( OK ) ;
60      }
61
62
63      void clean_read(p,nrec,at_end) /* clean up after sorting */
64      void *p[] ;
65      size_t nrec ;
66      int at_end ;
67      {
68         while( nrec > 0 )              /* free space for records */
69            { nrec = nrec - 1 ;
70              free( p[nrec] ) ;
71            }
72         if( at_end == AT_EOF )  /* on last pass */
73             free( rec ) ;          /* free single record space */
74      }
```

writerun.c

The writerun function in Figure 5.24 is very similar to the writefile function
from SORTTEXT. It uses the sfio pointer to call the write record function.

domerge.c

The domerge function in Figure 5.25 controls the merging phase of the program. It
follows the pseudo-code described in Section 5.8. When a merge pass involves

FIGURE 5.24   writerun.c

```
1      /* writerun.c - write out sorted run */
2      #include "stdio.h"
3      #include "sortmer2.h"
4
5      int writerun(prec,nrec,rsize,out)/* write records, sorted order*/
6      void *prec[] ;                   /* array of pointers to records */
7      size_t nrec ;                    /* number of records to be output */
8      int rsize ;                      /* record size */
9      SFILE *out ;                     /* output file pointer */
10     {
11        int i , ret ;
12
13        for(i=0 ; i < nrec ; i=i+1 )     /* write in sorted order */
14           {                             /* output one record */
15              ret = sfio->pput( prec[i] ,rsize, out);
16              if( ret != 0 )        /* and check for I/O error */
17                  return( WRITE_ERROR ) ; /*  yes - error return */
18           }
19
20        return( OK ) ;
21     }
```

FIGURE 5.25   domerge.c

```
1     /* domerge.c - merge part of external sort */
2     #include <stdio.h>
3     #include "sortmer2.h"
4
5
6     int domerge(pin,pout,pfinal,runs,nruns)
7     char *pin ;                /* input file name for 1st pass */
8     char *pout;                /* output file on 1st pass */
9     char *pfinal ;             /* put final output here */
10    RDATA runs[] ;             /* data for initial runs */
11    size_t nruns ;             /* number of initial runs */
12    {
13        char *pc ;
14        int ret ;
15
16        do
17          { if( nruns <= merge_order ) /* if last pass */
18              pout = pfinal ;  /*   use output file */
19
20                              /* do a merge pass */
21            ret = dopass(pin,pout,runs,nruns, & nruns) ;
22            if( ret != OK )      /* check for errors */
23              { remove( pin) ;
24                remove( pout ) ;
25                return( ret ) ;
26              }
27            remove(pin) ;       /* delete input scratch file */
28
29            pc  = pin ;         /* swap names of scratch files */
30            pin = pout ;        /* for input and output */
31            pout = pc ;
32          } while( nruns > 1); /* stop when output has one run */
33
34        return( OK ) ;
35    }
```

MAX_MERGE or fewer input runs, there will be only one output run. domerge substitutes the name of the final output for the name of the output scratch file. This eliminates a separate step copying the final output run to the output file.

At the end of each merge pass, domerge swaps the pointer to the input and output file names. Thus the file written in one pass becomes the input for the next pass.

dopass.c

dopass (Figure 5.26) performs a single pass of the merge process. It accepts as input arguments file names for input and output files. dopass receives an array, runs, which describes the input runs. Information describing the output runs is stored in the same array.

FIGURE 5.26   dopass.c

```
1     /* dopass.c - do 1 pass of merge process */
2     #include <stdio.h>
3     #include <stdlib.h>
4     #include "sortmer2.h"
5
6
7     int dopass(inname,outname,runs,nruns_in,pnruns_out)
8     char inname[] ;
9     char outname[] ;
10    RDATA runs[] ;
11    size_t nruns_in ;
12    size_t *pnruns_out ;
13    {
14        int first ;
15        int nruns_out ;
16        int m ;              /* order of the merge */
17        int i , j , ret ;
18        MDATA md[LG_MAX_MERGE] ; /* data for runs being merged */
19        SFILE *sf ;               /* temporary file pointer */
20        SFILE *out ;              /* output file pointer */
21        char *p ;
22        long nrec_out ;
23
24                             /* allocate space for records */
25        for( i=0 ; i< min(nruns_in,merge_order) ; i=i+1)
26          { p = (char *) malloc( sf_rsize ) ;
27            if( p == NULL )
28                return( REC_ALLOCATION_FAILURE ) ;
29            md[i].prec = p ;
30          }
31
32                             /* open output file */
33        out = sfio->popen(outname,SF_WRITE,mo_bsize) ;
34        if( out == NULL )
35          { for(i=0 ; i< min(nruns_in,merge_order) ; i=i+1)
36              { free( md[i].prec ) ; }   /* free record space */
37            return( OPEN_MERGE_OUTPUT_FAILURE ) ;
38          }
39
40
41                             /* open input files  */
42                             /* check for failure to open */
43        for(i=0 ; i< min(nruns_in,merge_order) ; i=i+1)
44          { sf = sfio->popen(inname,SF_READ, mi_bsize ) ;
45            if( sf == NULL )
46              {                    /* failure - clean up and exit */
47                for( j=i-1 ; j >= 0; j=j-1) /* close input files */
48                  { sfio->pclose( md[j].sf ); }/* already opened */
49
50                sfio->pclose(out) ;/* close output file */
51                for(j=0 ; j< min(nruns_in,merge_order) ; j=j+1)
52                  { free( md[j].prec ) ; }
53                return( OPEN_MERGE_INPUT_FAILURE ) ;
54              }
55            md[i].sf = sf ;
56          }
```

Figure 5.26   continues

Figure 5.26   continued

```
57
58              nruns_out = 0 ;              /* merge merge_order runs at a time*/
59              for( first = 0; first < nruns_in; first = first+merge_order)
60                 {                          /* no. runs to merge this time */
61                 m = min( nruns_in - first , merge_order) ;
62
63                 for( i=0; i < m ; i=i+1) /* set up MDATA structures */
64                    {                          /* number of records */
65                    md[i].nrec = runs[i+first].nrec ;
66                                              /* position at start of run */
67                    ret = sfio->pseek(md[i].sf,
68                        runs[i+first].start, SEEK_SET) ;
69                    md[i].start = sfio->ptell(md[i].sf) ;
70                    }
71                 runs[nruns_out].start = sfio->ptell(out) ;
72
73                                              /* merge this set of runs */
74                 ret = smerge(  md , m , & nrec_out, out ) ;
75                 if( ret != OK )
76                    return( ret ) ;
77                 runs[nruns_out].nrec = nrec_out ; /* store no. records */
78                 nruns_out = nruns_out + 1 ;
79                 }
80
81                                              /* all runs merged - tidy up */
82              for(i=0 ; i< min(nruns_in,merge_order) ; i=i+1)
83                 { sfio->pclose( md[i].sf) ; /* close input files */
84                 free( md[i].prec ) ;   /* free record space */
85                 }
86              *pnruns_out = nruns_out ; /* store no. runs made */
87
88              if( sfio->pclose(out) != 0 ) /* close output file */
89                 return( CLOSE_MERGE_OUTPUT_FAILURE ) ;
90              else return( OK ) ;
91           }
```

dopass groups input runs into sets of runs with up to merge_order runs in a set. Each set is merged into a single output run. Lines 24 to 56 prepare for the merging process. Lines 25 to 30 allocate space for an input record from each run in a set. Lines 41 to 56 open the input file once for each run in the set.

The array md defines each run being merged. The smerge function uses this array to describe input runs. The MDATA data type in the sortmer2.h data file defines the structure used.

Lines 58 to 79 merge groups of input runs until all input runs have been merged. Line 61 sets the number of runs in the current group. Lines 63 to 70 fill out the MDATA structure for each run and position its SFILE at the start of the run. Line 74 calls the smerge function to merge this group of runs. Line 71 records the starting position of the output run, and line 77 records the number of records in the run.

smerge.c

The smerge function (Figure 5.27) performs the actual merge. Its logic is that of the pseudo-code: read the first record from each run; sort these records; output the first record and replace it with the next record from the same input run; repeat until all runs are exhausted.

FIGURE 5.27   smerge.c

```
1     /* smerge.c - do a single merge, making 1 output run */
2     #include "stdio.h"
3     #include "sortmer2.h"
4
5     int get_run( MDATA *) ;
6
7
8     int smerge(md,m,pnrec,out)
9     MDATA   md[] ;                  /* data for each run being merged */
10    int     m ;                     /* number of runs being merged */
11    long *pnrec ;                   /* put count of output records here */
12    SFILE   *out ;                  /* output file pointer */
13    {
14      int i , ret ;
15      long nrec ;
16
17      for( i=0; i< m ; i=i+1) /* get first record for each run */
18          { ret = get_run( & md[i] ) ;
19            if( ret == EOR )
20                return( EMPTY_RUN ) ;
21            else if( ret != 0 )
22                return( ret ) ;
23          }
24
25      insertm(md,m) ;               /* sort 1st records */
26                                    /* (descending order) */
27
28      nrec = 0 ;
29      while( m > 0 )                /* repeat until all runs exhausted */
30          {                         /* write record with lowest key */
31            ret = sfio->pput( md[m-1].prec ,sf_rsize, out ) ;
32            if( ret != 0)
33                return( MERGE_WRITE_ERROR ) ;
34            nrec = nrec + 1 ;
35                                       /* get next record from same run */
36            ret = get_run( & md[m-1] ) ;
37            if( ret == 0 )       /*   got record?- */
38                resortm(md, m);/*     yes - insert it */
39            else if(ret == EOR )/*     no - end of that run   */
40                m = m - 1 ;     /*         reduce merge order */
41            else                /*     error - unexpected end of file */
42                return( ret ) ; /*         or an I/O error */
43          }
44      *pnrec = nrec ;
45      return( OK ) ;
46    }
47
48
```

Figure 5.27   continues

Figure 5.27   continued

```
49      int get_run(pmd)                /* get next record for a run */
50       MDATA *pmd ;
51       {
52         int ret ;
53
54         pmd->nrec = pmd->nrec - 1 ;
55         if( pmd->nrec < 0 )  /* check for the end of the run */
56             return( EOR ) ;
57                                 /* read next record for the run */
58         ret = sfio->pget(pmd->prec,sf_rsize,pmd->sf) ;
59         if( ret < 0 )             /* EOF or error?  */
60             return( MERGE_READ_ERROR ) ;  /* error return */
61         else if( ret == 0 )
62             return( UNEXPECTED_EOF ) ;
63         else return( 0 ) ;        /* read record OK */
64       }
```

smerge uses the insertm function to sort the initial records and resortm to put each new record into its place. The md array — not the records themselves — is actually sorted. Placing the md array in descending order simplifies the merge process. The first record in sort order is pointed to by md[m-1]. This input run is the one whose record will be selected for output. When the end of a run is reached, the merge order m is decreased.

The get_run function gets the next record from a run. It first checks the number of records remaining to see if we have reached the end of the run. Since we check the number of records remaining in a run before reading the file, reaching the end of the file is an error.

insertm.c

The insertm function in Figure 5.28 is based on the inserti function in Figure 5.1. It sorts the md array into decreasing order. Note that the addresses supplied to the compare function are those of the records — not the addresses of the elements of the md array.

FIGURE 5.28   insertm.c

```
1       /* insertm.c - insert sort for merge data structures */
2       /* also resort function to insert last element */
3       /* uses pointer to sort/merge record compare function */
4       /* sorts in descending order */
5       #include <stdlib.h>
6       #include "sortmer2.h"
7
8
9       void insertm(md,m)            /* sort merge data structures */
10       MDATA md[] ;                 /* merge data array to be sorted */
11       int m  ;                     /* number to be sorted */
12       {
```

Figure 5.28   continues

Figure 5.28   continued

```
13          int i , j ;                  /* indices for loops */
14          MDATA temp ;                 /* temporary space for one element */
15
16          for( i=1 ; i < m ; i = i + 1 )
17              {                        /* insert the i-th element */
18              temp = md[i] ;           /* into the sorted array */
19              j = i - 1 ;              /* find where new element goes */
20              while( (j >= 0)
21                  && ( sf_comp(& temp.prec, & md[j].prec) > 0) )
22                  { md[j+1] = md[j] ;/*   not here - move this one up */
23                    j = j - 1 ;
24                  }
25              md[j+1] = temp ;
26              }
27          }
28
29
30      void resortm(md,m)               /* insert last merge data structure */
31        MDATA md[] ;                   /* array to be sorted */
32        int m  ;                       /* number of elements to be sorted */
33        {
34          int i , j ;                  /* indices for loops */
35          MDATA  mtemp ;               /* temporary storage for 1 element */
36
37          /* insert the last element into the sorted array */
38              i = m - 1 ;  /* last element */
39              mtemp = md[i] ;
40              j = i - 1;
41              while(    (j >= 0)
42                    && sf_comp( & mtemp.prec, & md[j].prec) > 0 )
43                  { md[j+1] = md[j] ;
44                    j = j - 1 ;
45                  }
46              md[j+1] = mtemp ;
47          }
```

The resortm function inserts the last element into the array. It uses the inner loop of the insert algorithm.

The insertm function is called once at the beginning of each output run. It sorts a small number of elements. The resortm function is called once for each record. We would not expect the speed of insertm to be important in the overall performance of SORTMERG. The speed of resortm might be important. However, the insertion algorithm is efficient for a small array as md is.

sortio2.c

The source file in Figure 5.29 defines file I/O functions for use in the SORTMERG module. The do_open, do_close, getl, and putl functions resemble those in sortio.h (Figure 5.17). Several functions have been added. The getr and putr functions read and write fixed-length records. The do_seek function sets the file position, and do_tell returns a file position.

FIGURE 5.29   sortio2.c

```
1       /* sortio2.c -  more I/O functions for SORTMERGE module */
2       /* do_open , do_close , getl , putl */
3       /* getr , putr, do_seek , do_tell */
4       #include <stdio.h>
5       #include <stdlib.h>
6       #include "sortmerg.h"
7       #include "sortio2.h"
8
9
10      #define CTRL_Z   26          /* control Z character value */
11      #define BYTE_SIZE  1         /*  fread/fwrite element size */
12
13
14      SIO_FUNS lines_of_text =    /* I/O funs. for lines of text */
15          { do_open , do_close , getl , putl , do_seek, do_tell } ;
16
17      SIO_FUNS fixed_records =    /* I/O funs. for fixed length rec. */
18          { do_open , do_close , getr , putr , do_seek, do_tell } ;
19
20      static char *iomodes [2] = { "rb" , "wb" } ;
21
22
23                                  /* open file and assign buffer */
24      SFILE *do_open(fname,fmode,bsize)
25      char fname[] ;              /* file name string */
26      int fmode ;                 /* sort file mode see header file */
27      size_t bsize ;
28      {                           /* return a SFILE pointer */
29          MYFILE *mf ;
30          FILE *fd ;
31          char *pbuf ;
32
33                                  /* allocate SFILE structure */
34          mf = (MYFILE *) malloc( sizeof(MYFILE) ) ;
35          if( mf == NULL )
36             return( NULL ) ;
37
38                                  /* open the file */
39          fd = fopen(fname,iomodes[fmode] ) ;
40          if( fd == NULL )        /* check for errors */
41            { free( mf ) ;
42              return( NULL ) ;
43            }
44          pbuf = (char *) malloc(bsize) ; /* get buffer space */
45          if( pbuf == NULL )      /* did allocation fail? */
46            { fclose(fd) ;        /*   failed - close file */
47              free( mf ) ;
48              return( NULL );     /*              error return */
49            }
50                                  /* assign buffer to the file */
51          if( setvbuf(fd,pbuf,_IOFBF,bsize) != 0 )
52            { fclose(fd) ;        /*   failed - close file */
53              free( pbuf ) ;      /*              release buffer */
54              free( mf ) ;
55              return( NULL );     /*              error return */
56            }
```

Figure 5.29   continues

Figure 5.29   continued

```
57
58              mf->fp = fd ;           /* save file pointer */
59              mf->pb = pbuf ;         /* and buffer pointer */
60
61              return( (SFILE *) mf ) ;
62          }
63
64
65      int do_close(sf)                /* close file and check for errors */
66          SFILE *sf ;                 /* file pointer */
67          {
68              MYFILE *mf ;
69              int ret ;
70
71              mf = (MYFILE *) sf ;    /*pointer to our structure */
72              ret = fclose( mf->fp ) ;
73              free( mf->pb ) ;        /* free the buffer */
74              free( mf ) ;
75              return( ret ) ;
76          }
77
78
79      int getl(rec,maxs,sf)           /* get one line from file */
80          void *rec ;                 /* put it here in string form */
81          int maxs ;                  /* maximum length permitted */
82          SFILE *sf ;                 /* file pointer for input file */
83          {                           /* getl returns no. chars used in s */
84                                      /* (or -1 if EOF reached) */
85              FILE *fd ;
86              char *s ;
87              int n , c ;
88
89              fd = ((MYFILE *) sf)->fp ;  /* file pointer */
90              s = (char *) rec ;
91              n = 0 ;
92
93              while( 1 == 1 )             /* repeat until we get a line */
94                { c = getc(fd) ;          /* get next char */
95                  if( c == EOF )          /* check for end-of-file */
96                    { if( ferror(fd) != 0 ) /* or error */
97                        { s[n] = '\0' ;
98                          return( -2 ) ;
99                        }
100                     if( n == 0 )        /* if we don't have a line yet */
101                        { s[0] = '\0';
102                          return(  0);/*  no - return 0 as length */
103                        }
104                     s[n] = '\r' ;  /*   yes - partial line, add CR   */
105                     s[n+1] = '\n' ;/*            and LF   */
106                     n = n + 2 ;    /*            adjust length */
107                     break ;        /* we have a line - normal return */
108                   }
109                 if( c == CTRL_Z )
110                   { ungetc(c,fd) ;
111                     if( n == 0 )   /* if we don't have a line yet */
112                        { s[0] = '\0';/*   no - return 0 as length */
```

Figure 5.29   continues

Figure 5.29   continued

```
113                      return( 0 ) ;
114                 }
115               s[n] = '\r' ;   /*     yes - partial line, add CR   */
116               s[n+1] = '\n' ;/*               and LF */
117               n = n + 2 ;     /*          adjust length */
118               break ;
119           }
120         s[ n ] = c ;
121         n = n + 1 ;
122         if( c == '\n' )
123             break ;
124         if( n >= (maxs-3) )/* reached maximum length? */
125            { s[n] = '\r' ;   /*    yes - add CR   */
126              s[n+1] = '\n' ;/*            and LF   */
127              n = n + 2 ;     /*          adjust length */
128              break ;         /*          and leave */
129            }
130       }
131
132     s[ n ] = '\0' ;          /* add end-of-string marker */
133     return( n+1 ) ;          /* return line length with '\0' */
134   }
135
136
137   int putl(rec,rsize,sf)      /* output one line of text */
138   void *rec ;                 /* line to output - string form */
139   int rsize ;                 /* record size (dummy for putl) */
140   SFILE *sf ;                 /* output file pointer */
141   {
142       FILE *fd ;
143       char *s ;
144
145       fd = ( (MYFILE *) sf) ->fp ;  /* file pointer */
146       s = (char *) rec ;
147       if( fputs(s,fd) == EOF)/* use fputs, check for error */
148            return( -1 ) ;      /*        yes - error return */
149       else return( 0 ) ;      /*        no  - normal return */
150   }
151
152
153
154   int getr(rec,rsize,sf)      /* read a fixed length record */
155   void *rec ;                 /* put record here */
156   int rsize ;                 /* record size */
157   SFILE *sf ;                 /* sort file pointer */
158   {
159       FILE *fd ;
160       int nr  ;               /* number of bytes read */
161
162       fd = ( (MYFILE *) sf)->fp ; /* file pointer */
163
164       nr = fread(rec,BYTE_SIZE,rsize,fd) ; /* read rsize bytes */
165       if( ferror(fd) != 0 )
166            return( -2 ) ;      /* read error */
167                               /* check for partial record */
168       if( (nr > 0 ) && (nr < rsize) )
169            return( -2 ) ;      /* partial record */
```

Figure 5.29   continues

Figure 5.29   continued

```
170
171          return( nr ) ;            /* either rsize or 0 */
172      }
173
174
175     int putr(rec,rsize,sf)        /* write a fixed length record */
176     void *rec ;                   /* record is here */
177     int rsize ;                   /* record size */
178     SFILE *sf ;                   /* sort file pointer */
179     {
180          FILE *fd ;               /* file stream pointer */
181          int nw  ;
182
183          fd = ( (MYFILE *) sf)->fp ; /* file pointer */
184
185          nw = fwrite(rec,BYTE_SIZE,rsize,fd) ;
186                                     /* check that entire record written */
187          if( nw != rsize )
188              return( -1 ) ;
189          else return( 0 ) ;
190
191      }
192
193
194
195     int do_seek(sf,new_pos,set_mode) /* set file position */
196     SFILE *sf ;                   /* file pointer */
197     long new_pos ;                /* make this the new file position */
198     int set_mode ;                /* mode for seek function */
199     {
200          FILE *fd ;
201
202          fd = ( (MYFILE *) sf)->fp ; /* file pointer */
203          return( fseek( fd  , new_pos , set_mode) ) ;
204      }
205
206
207
208     long do_tell(sf)              /* return current file position */
209     SFILE *sf ;
210     {
211          FILE *fd ;
212
213          fd = ( (MYFILE *) sf)->fp ; /* file pointer */
214          return( ftell( fd ) ) ;
215      }
```

The do_open function returns a pointer to the SFILE data type rather than a pointer to a real data type. This allows the implementation of the I/O functions to be changed without requiring that the SORTMERG module or the application program be changed or recompiled. Within the I/O functions, the SFILE pointer is converted to the MYFILE * pointer type.

All I/O functions are called through the function pointers in the SIO_FUNS data structure. Lines 14 and 15 define pointers for reading and writing lines of text. Lines 17 and 18 define pointers for reading and writing fixed-length records.

Although all these functions in `sortio2.h` are called through function pointers, Figure 5.30 defines function prototypes.

FIGURE 5.30   sortio2.h

```
 1    /* sortio2.h - internal definitions for sort I/O functions */
 2
 3    typedef struct              /* sort file structure */
 4      { FILE *fp ;              /* pointer ddor buffered I/O */
 5        char *pb ;              /* file buffer assigned to FILE */
 6      } MYFILE ;
 7
 8                                /* function prototypes */
 9    SFILE *do_open(char *, int, size_t) ;
10    int getl(void *, int , SFILE *) ;
11    int putl(void *, int , SFILE *) ;
12    int do_close(SFILE *) ;
13    int getr(void *, int , SFILE *) ;
14    int putr(void *, int , SFILE *) ;
15    int do_seek(SFILE *, long, int) ;
16    long do_tell(SFILE *) ;
```

Program Structure

It may seem simpler to use fewer functions and fewer source files than we did for the SORTMERG module. Certainly the number of keystrokes to type it could be reduced as could the number of files to compile and link. However, we kept functions and source files short and simple. Each function dealt with a single level of detail. For example, `domerge` handled the repeating of merge passes and the switching of input and output file names, `dopass` managed run numbers and file names on one merge pass, and `smerge` performed one merge operation. Combining these functions into one large file would make the logic of the program less clear and less amenable to enhancement.

5.10 Enhancements to the SORTMERG Module

Eliminating Merging for a Single Run

If the `formruns` function creates a single run, no merge pass is necessary. However, `formruns` always writes the output to the SCRB scratch file. Changing `formruns` to write directly to the final output file in this case would make the SORTMERG module faster for small files.

After `readrun` has read the first run, `formruns` can examine the `read_status` variable to see whether or not the entire file has been read. If so, it can close the scratch file, remove it, and then open the final output file instead. (It appears simpler to delay opening the output file until the first run has been read, but at that time there may not be enough memory for the file buffer and other data structures.)

▣ Faster Memory Allocation

The `readrun` function allocates space for each record read with the standard dynamic memory allocation function, `malloc`. Later, the `clean_read` function frees this space, record by record. We allocate the amount of space needed for each record, rather than the maximum amount for each record. The disadvantage is that we allocate and free space for each record read. A two-level memory allocation scheme eliminates this disadvantage.

We can call `malloc` to allocate large blocks of memory — perhaps 5,000 bytes per block. Then we can locate each record in the next available free space in a large block. After a run has been sorted, we mark all space in the large blocks as available and start on the next run. When the last run has been sorted and written to the scratch file, we would call `free` to deallocate each block.

A simpler solution is possible for fixed length records. Once fixed length record areas are allocated, they need not be freed after each run is written out. The record areas can be reused for each run.

▣ Optimal Memory Allocation

Effective use of RAM memory in the SORTMERG module is crucial to good performance. Large buffers make reading and writing records fast. Providing more memory for records makes the initial runs larger. That allows larger files to be sorted in the same number of passes. The array of pointers to records that is sorted in `formruns` is another competitor. We would like to make it large to allow for many small records, but that takes away space for storing the records themselves. Deciding how to divide memory among different uses is important, but that decision depends on the amount of memory available. The SORTMERG module should determine how much memory is available and make its own decisions on use of that memory.

Increasing the Merge Order

The merge order in SORTMERG is limited by the number of files that we can have open at a time. All the input runs are in the same disk file, but we open the input file the number of times specified by `merge_order` so that each run has its own buffer. Although we might increase the number of files MS-DOS allows to be open, there is a different and better solution: a file I/O module that provides a separate buffer for each run being merged but uses a single DOS file handle for all runs.

Making Larger Runs

Making larger initial runs is another way to sort larger files with the same number of merge passes. SORTMERG makes a run by filling memory with records, sorting the records, and writing them out. Runs are as large as the amount of memory available to the `readrun` function. The replacement selection algorithm makes runs that are twice as large on the average. The method begins by filling memory with records and partially sorting records into a heap structure. The record with the lowest key value is selected and written out. A new record is read to replace the record just written. The heap is adjusted and the lowest record remaining is selected to be written out. This process continues until the input file is exhausted. A run continues until the record to be written has a key value less than that of the previous record. Run sizes and the number of runs depend on the order of records in the original file. If the original file is in order, only one run is produced.

Replacement-selection uses the same heap data structure as the heapsort algorithm. Heapsort is a good sorting method for use with replacement selection.

Disk Space Management

For a file of n bytes, SORTMERG requires $3n$ bytes of disk space: the input file, a scratch input file and a scratch output file, or the final output file. When we sort large files on a PC, disk space limitations may be as important as execution speed. If we can delete the input file after initial runs have been made, SORTMERG only requires $2n$ bytes of disk space.

A Library of Compare Functions

The SORTMERG module would be easier to use if we also provided library functions for comparing common types of records. The compare functions in Figure 5.3 are a good starting point. An additional mechanism for specifying the offset of the key field from the start of the record will be needed.

5.11 MERGE: A Generalized External Sort Program

Our next step is a standalone program based on the SORTMERG module. We want to specify the type of data to be sorted when we execute the program. We need to specify the type of record: fixed-length data or variable-length lines of text. We also need to specify each key field to be used for the comparison: its data type, where it begins in each record, its length, and whether it is to be in ascending or descending order. To make the program more general, we will allow more than one key field to be specified. Figure 5.31 describes a standalone program based on the SORTMERG module.

FIGURE 5.31   MERGE Program Description

Name
MERGE   general sort/merge program for large data files

Usage
```
C>MERGE   input_file output_file   sort_specs
```

All sort specifications begin with a dash (-). A letter following identifies a specification. Some parameters may be expected after this letter. Specifications recognized are

Specification	Letter	Parameters
Record type		
Fixed record	r	length in bytes
Lines of text (variable length)	l	—
Sort Keys	k	data type
		sort order
		a = ascending
		d = descending
		starting offset in bytes
		field length (for char or string)
		(0=beginning)

Parameters are separated by commas. Specifications are written without spaces inside. Specifications are separated by blanks. Data types are identified by a single character: integer (i), character field (c), character string (s), long (l), and float (f). Up to 10 key fields may be specified—most significant key first.

Description
MERGE sorts an input file based on specified file, record and key field descriptions. It uses the `memsort` library function to sort initial runs, which are merged to give a final sorted output file. Default specifications are lines of text with the entire line as a key and sorted in ascending order.

Scratch files are placed on the default drive. Space must be available for two copies of the input file.

Example
```
C>MERGE test.in test.out  -r20  -ki,a,2,1  -ka,d,10,6
```

This sorts `test.in` creating `test.out`. Records are 20 bytes long. An integer at offset 2 (ascending order) and a char field 6 bytes long at offset 10 (descending order) are the sort keys.

5.12 MERGE Source Files

sortcomp.h

The header file `sortcomp.h` (Figure 5.32) defines constants and data types needed to specify key fields. The `SORTKEY` data type defines the data needed for each key field: the type of data, where the key begins in each record, its length, and whether to sort in ascending or descending order. The `keys` array allows up to 10 sort keys to be described. Symbolic constants are defined for the key type and the sort order.

FIGURE 5.32   sortcomp.h

```
1     /* sortcomp.h - definitions for compare function */
2     #define MAX_KEYS  10      /* maximum number of keys allowed */
3
4                   /* sort order constants */
5     #define ASCENDING    1
6     #define DESCENDING  -1
7
8                   /* key types */
9     #define  int16_key    0  /* 16 bit long integer */
10    #define  char_key 1  /* char field (uses klength) */
11    #define  string_key   2  /* char string ('\0' at end) */
12    #define  int32_key    3  /* 32 bit long integer */
13    #define   float_key   4  /* floating point data */
14
15
16    typedef struct          /* data to define one key field */
17      {
18        int ktype ;        /* type of field */
19        int kstart ;           /* starting offset of field */
20        int klength ;      /* field length */
21        int korder ;           /* sort order (ascending/desc.) */
22      } SORTKEY ;
23
24    extern int nkeys ;
25    extern SORTKEY keys[] ;
26
27                           /* function prototype */
28    int sortcomp (void * , void *) ;
```

sortcomp.c

The `sortcomp` function in Figure 5.33 compares two records. It loops over the key fields defined in the `keys` array. It returns as soon as a comparison shows inequality. The sort order for the key is used in the `return` statement to produce ascending or descending order.

FIGURE 5.33 **sortcomp.c**

```
1    /* sortcomp.c - data driven compare function */
2    #include "stdio.h"
3    #include <string.h>
4    #include "cminor.h"
5    #include "sortcomp.h"
6
7    int nkeys ;                   /* number of key fields to compare */
8    SORTKEY keys[MAX_KEYS] ;    /* array of sort field definitions */
9
10   /* define pointer types for data type conversion */
11   typedef int16 *PINT ;
12   typedef int32 *PLONG ;
13   typedef float *PFLOAT ;
14
15
16   int sortcomp(p1,p2)           /* compares records   */
17    void *p1 ;                   /* pointer to first data record */
18    void *p2 ;                   /* pointer to second data record */
19    {
20      int i ;
21      SORTKEY *p ;
22      char *pt1 ,
23            *pt2 ;
24      int ichar ;
25
26      p = keys ;                 /* point to first sort key desc. */
27      for( i=0 ; i < nkeys ; i = i + 1 )
28          {                      /* get starting addresses of */
29                                 /* fields in the two records */
30          pt1 = ( * (char **) p1) + p->kstart ;
31          pt2 = ( * (char **) p2) + p->kstart ;
32
33          switch( p->ktype )
34            {
35            case int16_key :
36              if( *(PINT) pt1 != *(PINT) pt2 )
37                { if( *(PINT) pt1 > *(PINT) pt2 )
38                       return( p->korder ) ;
39                  else return( - p->korder ) ;
40                }
41              break ;
42            case char_key :
43              ichar = p->klength ;
44              while( ichar > 0 )
45                { if( *pt1 != *pt2 )
46                    { if( *pt1 > *pt2 )
47                           return( p->korder ) ;
48                      else return( - p->korder ) ;
49                    }
50                  pt1 = pt1+1 ; pt2=pt2+1; ichar=ichar-1 ;
51                } ;
52              break ;
53            case string_key :
54              ichar = p->klength ;
55              while( ichar > 0 )
56                { if( *pt1 != *pt2 )
```

Figure 5.33   continues

Figure 5.33   continued

```
57                              { if( *pt1 > *pt2 )
58                                      return( p->korder ) ;
59                                else return( - p->korder ) ;
60                              }
61                        if( *pt1 == '\0' )
62                              break ;
63                        pt1 = pt1+1 ; pt2=pt2+1; ichar=ichar-1 ;
64                      } ;
65                  break ;
66              case int32_key :
67                  if( *(PLONG)pt1 != *(PLONG)pt2 )
68                    { if( *(PLONG)pt1 > *(PLONG)pt2 )
69                          return( p->korder ) ;
70                      else return( - p->korder ) ;
71                    }
72                  break ;
73              case float_key :
74                  if( *(PFLOAT)pt1 != *(PFLOAT)pt2 )
75                    {
76                      if( (*((float *) pt1)) > (*((float *) pt2)) )
77                          return( p->korder ) ;
78                      else  return( - p->korder ) ;
79                    }
80                  break ;
81              }
82            p = p + 1 ;            /* point to next sort field desc. */
83          }
84                                   /* all keys were equal */
85        return( 0 ) ;             /* return "equal to" result */
86      }
```

The following pseudo-code shows the function's logic in a compact form:

```
compare function
    repeat for each key field
        compute the starting addresses of the key fields
        select the type of data to compare
            do comparison for this data type
            if not equal
                return result (reversed if descending order)
    return equal if all keys are equal
end
```

Character string and array types are several bytes long. For these key types, the comparison is repeated for each character.

`sortcomp` contains a few optimizations. Instead of referring to the sort key specification using array notation (`key[i].ktype`, for example), a pointer p to the SORTKEY data type is used. It is initialized on line 26 to point to the first key's specification. At the end of the loop over keys, line 82 advances p to point to the next key's specification.

The comparisons for integer, long, and float data contain an assumption — namely, that alignment restrictions on integers and larger data types are not important. This is valid on computers based on the Intel 8086/8088 family of microprocessors. It would not be valid on computers using the Motorola 68000 microprocessor. In that case, the key fields should be moved to local variables of the correct data type and then compared. For example, lines 36 and 37 would be replaced by

```
memcpy(&  i1,pt1,sizeof(int16))  ;
memcpy(  &  i2,pt2,sizeof(int16))  ;
if( i1 != i2 )
  { if( i1 > i2 )
```

where i1 and i2 are declared as int16 variables. The cminor.h header file from Chapter 2 defines data types int16 and int32.

getspec.c

Figure 5.34 shows the getspec.c source file. Its job is to scan the command line looking for specifications of record type or sort keys. Each valid specification must begin with a dash followed by a letter identifying what is being specified. The getspec function's structure reflects its job: to loop over words in the command line and to call to dospec to collect and validate each specification. getspec.c is rather long; its work is spread over several functions, each focused on a single level of detail.

FIGURE 5.34   getspec.c

```
 1    /* getspec.c - get sort file spec from cmd line */
 2    #include <stdio.h>
 3    #include <stdlib.h>
 4    #include <string.h>
 5    #include "cminor.h"
 6    #include "sortcomp.h"
 7    #include "sortmerg.h"
 8
 9    #define MAX_REC_SIZE  1000    /* maximum record size allowed */
10    #define DEFAULT_REC_SIZE 500 /* default record size */
11
12
13    static char field_type[] = "icslf" ;   /* field type codes */
14
15                              /* function prototypes */
16    void dospec(char *,SIO_FUNS *,size_t *) ;
17    void getkparm(char *,size_t *) ;
18    void addkey(int, int, int, int) ;
19    void err_msg(char *) ;
20
21
22                              /* scan arguments for sort specs */
```

Figure 5.34   continues

Figure 5.34   continued

```
23      void getspec(argc,argv,psio,prsize)
24      int argc ;
25      char *argv[] ;
26      SIO_FUNS *psio ;            /* points to sort I/O structure */
27      size_t *prsize ;            /* pointer to record size variable */
28      {
29        int i ;
30        char *p ;
31        size_t rs ;
32
33
34                                  /* set up defaults */
35        *psio = lines_of_text ; /* records are lines of text */
36        *prsize = DEFAULT_REC_SIZE ; /* record size */
37        nkeys = 0 ;               /* number of sort keys */
38
39        for( i=3 ; i < argc ; i=i+1 )
40            {
41             p = argv[i] ;
42             if( *p == '-' )      /* check for dash */
43                {                 /* move past dash and get spec. */
44                  dospec(p+1, psio,prsize) ;
45                }
46              else err_msg("bad option format \n");
47            }
48
49        if( nkeys == 0 )          /* use char string as default key */
50              addkey(string_key,ASCENDING,0,*prsize) ;
51      }
52
53
54
55      void dospec(p,psio,prsize) /* classify and process one spec. */
56        char *p ;                  /* points to spec. char (and parms) */
57        SIO_FUNS *psio ;           /* points to sort I/O structure */
58        size_t *prsize ;           /* pointer to record size variable */
59      {
60        switch( *p )              /* classify the next char */
61            {
62            case 'r' :            /* fixed length records */
63              *psio = fixed_records ;
64              p = p + 1 ;         /* move past 'r' */
65                                  /* and get record size */
66                                  /* use invalid size to verify */
67              *prsize = MAX_REC_SIZE+1 ;
68              sscanf(p,"%d",prsize) ; /* sscanf reads it */
69              if( *prsize > MAX_REC_SIZE )
70                err_msg(" bad record size field \n") ;
71              break ;
72            case 'l' :            /* records are text lines */
73              *psio = lines_of_text ;
74              break ;
75            case 'k' :            /* key field spec. */
76              if( nkeys == MAX_KEYS )
77                  err_msg("too many sort keys \n");
78              p = p +1 ;          /* move past the 'k' */
79               getkparm(p,prsize);/* get and check key parms. */
```

Figure 5.34   continues

Figure 5.34   continued

```
80                 break ;
81             default :
82                err_msg("bad option \n");
83                break ;
84             }
85      }
86
87
88
89
90                                    /* collect and verify key info */
91      void getkparm(word,prsize)
92      char word[] ;               /* string with the parms */
93      size_t *prsize ;            /* pointer to record size variable */
94      {
95         int kt , ko , ks , kl , n ;
96         char tc , oc ;
97         char *p ;
98
99                                    /* get parms from cmd. line word */
100        kl = -1 ;
101         sscanf(word,"%c,%c,%d,%d",&tc, &oc, &ks, &kl);
102        if( kl == -1 )
103            err_msg("not enough info in key field\n");
104
105                                     /* convert and check field type */
106        p = strchr( field_type , tc ) ; /* find field type */
107        if( p == NULL )
108            err_msg("bad key field type \n") ;
109        else kt = p - field_type ; /* convert to number */
110
111        if( oc == 'a' )          /* convert and check sort order */
112            ko = ASCENDING ;
113        else if( oc == 'd')
114            ko = DESCENDING ;
115        else err_msg("bad key field order \n") ;
116
117                                     /* check starting offset */
118        if( (ks < 0) || (ks > *prsize) )
119            err_msg("bad key field offset \n");
120                                     /* check field length */
121        if( (kl <= 0) || ( (ks + kl) > *prsize) )
122            err_msg("bad key field length \n");
123        addkey(kt,ko,ks,kl) ;
124     }
125
126
127     void addkey(itype,iorder,ioffset,ilength)
128     int itype , iorder , ioffset , ilength ;
129     {
130        keys[nkeys].ktype   = itype ;
131        keys[nkeys].korder  = iorder ;
132        keys[nkeys].kstart  = ioffset ;
133        keys[nkeys].klength = ilength ;
134        nkeys = nkeys + 1 ;
135     }
136
```

Figure 5.34   continues

Figure 5.34   continued

```
137
138      void err_msg(s)
139      char s[] ;
140      {
141         printf("%s \n",s);
142         exit(10) ;
143      }
```

The dospec function classifies the character following the dash using a switch statement. For the r and k specifications some additional parameters are required. The pointer to the command line word is advanced past the specification character, and the sscanf function is used to get the parameters. An invalid value is placed in the last parameter before calling sscanf. If sscanf does not get all the input parameters, the validation process detects the error.

If an invalid parameter or bad format is detected, an error message is displayed and the program aborts. All the input is validated so that invalid or missing specifications do not produce mysterious behavior.

getspec has defaults for all specifications. Some are assigned at the beginning (lines 35 to 37). The default sort key field choice — a character string starting at offset zero — is applied if the command line has been scanned and no sort key field found (lines 49 and 50).

merge.c

The merge.c main function in Figure 5.35 calls the getspec function to collect specifications from the command line. Then it calls the sortmerge function to sort the input file. The sortcomp function is specified as the compare function for the sort process.

FIGURE 5.35   merge.c

```
 1      /* merge.c - generalized external sort program */
 2      /* uses SORTMERG module */
 3      #include  <stdio.h>
 4      #include "cminor.h"
 5      #include "sortcomp.h"
 6      #include  "sortmerg.h"
 7
 8      void getspec(int, char *, SIO_FUNS *, size_t *) ;
 9
10
11      main(argc,argv)
12       int argc ;                /* number of words in command line */
13       char *argv[] ;            /* pointers to each word */
14       {
15          SIO_FUNS sio ;         /* sort I/O structure */
16          size_t rec_size ;      /* record size */
```

Figure 5.34   continues

Figure 5.34   continued

```
17          int ret ;
18
19
20          if( argc < 3 )              /* file names specified? */
21            { fprintf(stderr," need file names \n");
22              fprintf(stderr,
23                " USAGE:  merge2  input-file   output-file \n");
24              exit(100);
25            }
26
27
28                                      /* get sort specifications from */
29                                      /* the command line */
30          getspec(argc,argv, & sio, & rec_size ) ;
31
32                                      /* sort the file */
33          ret = sortmerge( argv[1], argv[2],
34                & sio , sortcomp , rec_size ) ;
35
36          if( ret != 0 )              /* check return code */
37            {  fprintf(stderr,"sort failed - code = %d \n",ret) ;
38               exit(ret ) ;
39            }
40          else exit(0) ;              /* success */
41      }
```

5.13 Enhancing MERGE

The MERGE2 program is useful as it stands, but there are many potential enhancements. Here are some that we have identified.

More Sort Key Types

Although we provided several types of sort keys, even more types are possible. Character array and string types in which upper-/lowercase differences were ignored would be very useful. A key type for decimal numbers stored as ASCII characters would be useful. A character array key type with nonalphabetic characters being ignored would also be useful. (_dos_write would follow dos_read and be equivalent to dos,write.)

More Record Types

MERGE should support variable-length records whose length is specified by a binary number in front of the record. Record-length fields of 1 and 2 bytes should be supported.

A Better User Interface

The `getspec` function is rather unforgiving, and the format for specifying sort specifications is not easy to remember and use. An interactive method for collecting the sort specification could be used when the command line does not contain a specification (or an invalid one).

Handling Large Files

Sorting large data files causes extra difficulties. Finding disk space for the input, output, and scratch files may be a problem. A command line option might specify names for both scratch files (`SCRA` and `SCRB` in `sortmerg.c`). Files could be spread over several disk drives.

MERGE should check the size of the input file and compare it to the amount of disk free space available. It is much better to find out that disk space is inadequate *before* MERGE starts sorting the input file.

Better Performance for Simple Cases

The compare function in the `sortcomp.c` file is very general, but for a simple case with one key field, a simpler function would be faster. After the `getspec` function has collected command line options, we could check for simple cases. If the options specified match a simple case, we could specify a simple compare function. For example, for sorting lines of text, we could use the `pscmp` function from Figure 5.3.

5.14 Summary

We now have some tools for sorting data. The `memsort` and `insert` functions and the SORTMERG module are general-purpose library functions. SORTTEXT and MERGE2 are complete programs. In addition, this chapter should have taken the mystery out of developing your own sorting programs.

Our discussion focused on practical tools for sorting. We did not analyze the algorithms we used or present alternatives. Sorting algorithms have long been a favorite topic in computer science textbooks and research reports. Although the literature on sorting places too much emphasis on theory rather than practice, it is invaluable as a source of algorithms and ideas. The references in Appendix D provide a starting point.

6

BTREE: An Indexed File Module

The previous chapter discussed sorting data both in RAM memory and in large files. Putting whole data files in order is a common requirement in application programs. This chapter discusses another common requirement: keeping files indexed so that a single record can be retrieved based on a key value rather than its position in a file. A common complaint about C is that it lacks built-in facilities for keyed access to data files. The module we develop here provides the basic support for indexing data files.

Our module is based on the B-Tree algorithm, but our emphasis is on producing a practical tool rather than on illustrating a famous algorithm. Space limitations and the need to explain the source code have forced some simplifications. Addressing practical problems normally left as exercises for the reader led to other deviations from a pure B-Tree algorithm. Finally, since B-Trees have been discussed by a number of authors, there are differences in published descriptions of B-Trees.

The module we develop is not a complete program; it is a set of functions to be called from an application program. No amount of documentation of such a module substitutes for an example of use, so we present an application to demonstrate the BTREE module's use. The application is very simple, but it should give a feel for applying BTREE to real problems.

6.1 Developing the Concepts

Understanding the problem of keyed access to data records in disk files and the concepts behind the B-Tree algorithm is a necessary first step. Without this understanding, you will not understand the source code we present or the possible applications for it. So we will develop concepts first and then present a concrete application of those concepts.

We used the term *keyed access* already; now we will define it. DOS supports random access to data in disk files. You specify a numeric position in a file (using `lseek` or `fseek`) and then read or write at that location. But with keyed access, we supply a key value and read or write a record that corresponds to that key value. For example, in a mailing list application we might store and retrieve records based on a name. To implement keyed access, we need an index that relates keys to data records. When a key is presented, we search the index and return the location of the data record that contains that key value.

Our focus in this chapter is on searching files, but we can start by looking at the function in Figure 6.1. This function makes a linear search of an array of integers in RAM memory. How can we apply this algorithm to searching an index? Instead of an array of integers, we might search an array of index entries. Figure 6.2a shows such an index and the data file to which it points. Each index entry might have the following structure:

```
typedef struct
  { long rptr ;        /* file position of the data record */
    char key[KMAX]; /* key value for the data record */
  } index_entry ;
```

FIGURE   6.1 lsearch.c

```
1     /* lsearch.c - search an ordered array of integers for a value */
2     #include "stdio.h"
3
4     int lsearch(target,a,na,pwhere) /* search an array for a value */
5     int target ;                  /* look for this value */
6     int a[] ;                     /* the array to search */
7     int na ;                      /* size of the array */
8     int *pwhere ;                 /* store the ending subscript here */
9     {
10        int i , ret ;
11
12        for(i=0 ; i<na ; i=i+1)/* scan each element in the array */
13           { ret = a[i]-target; /* compare target to array element */
14             if( ret == 0 )      /* we're through if it matches */
15                 break ;
16           }
17        *pwhere = i ;             /* record where the search ended */
18        return( ret ) ;           /* return result of last compare */
19     }
```

This is certainly simple, but what if the index is too large to fit into RAM memory? One solution might be to place the index in a file (perhaps separate from the file containing data records) and read it sequentially each time a search is performed. Unfortunately this method is quite slow and impractical for sizable index files. We can already see, however, that storing the index in a disk file is

FIGURE 6.2   Indexing Files

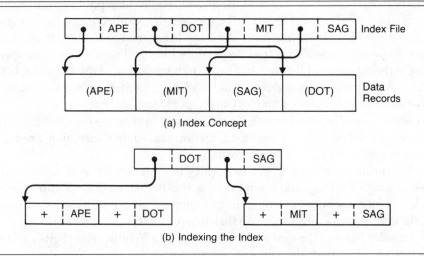

(a) Index Concept

(b) Indexing the Index

necessary and that minimizing the amount of file I/O required for a search is an important goal for a good solution.

The idea that opens the door to a solution is a simple one: Make a small index to the main index. The diagram in Figure 6.2b illustrates the idea. (The data records and pointers to them are not shown in Figure 6.2b or the diagrams that follow. Those pointers are represented by a + character in the diagrams.) We start by searching the small index. The result of that search tells us what part of the large index to search.

Each entry in the small index contains a pointer to a section of the large index and the last key in that section. We search the small index until we find a key that is greater than or equal to the search value. We extract the corresponding pointer and search the section to which it points. Searching the index in Figure 6.2b for the key value MIT would require the following steps:

Step 1. Search the small index. The second entry (whose key is SAG) is the first entry whose key is greater than or equal to MIT. Extract the corresponding pointer to the second block of the large index.

Step 2. Read this block of the large index.

Step 3. Search this block for a key with value MIT. The first entry matches this value, so the record pointer value identifies the corresponding data record.

Once we have the basic idea, we can develop it further. We can use as many levels of indices as needed. To minimize the amount of index file I/O, we can organize the indices in blocks of a fixed size. Each entry in an upper level then points to a single block on the next level of the index. The first level always contains a single block. We can structure each level in the same way and use the same functions to manage all levels.

This structure of indices is often called a *tree*. The top level of the tree (where we start a search) is called the *root*, and the lowest level (which points to data records) is called the *leaf* level. Individual blocks are sometimes called *nodes*. Index trees are usually pictured with the root level at the top in contrast to nature's trees. (Lots of things about computers appear to defy nature.) We will refer to levels as *upper* or *higher* in the direction of the root and *lower* in the direction of the leaf level. B-Trees are trees with special rules about how the blocks are maintained. The important rule is that all blocks except the root block are kept at least half full.

We have only discussed searching indices, but in practice we need to add and remove entries. These operations are more complicated than searching; the method we use is specified by the B-Tree algorithm.

In the normal case, inserting a new entry in an index file is easy. We find the position where it belongs and insert the entry into the leaf level block. But what if the leaf level block does not have room for the entry? Then we split the block, moving half the entries into a new block. We then insert an entry pointing to the new block into the index block at the next higher level. Figure 6.3 shows a tree before and after inserting an entry with the key APE. Figure 6.4 shows how the tree splits when another entry is added. Since the higher level index block is also full, it is also split. Thus an insertion may cause adjustments to several levels of index blocks. If the process causes the root block to be split, a new level is added to the tree and becomes the root level.

Deleting an entry starts with removing it from the leaf level block. If that leaves the block empty, the entry at the next level that pointed to the block is removed. If a deletion leaves a block less than half full, we try to combine it with the block to its left or right. To keep it simple, we look for neighbors in the next level block. So the leaf level block with the key DOT in Figure 6.4 has no right neighbor by this

FIGURE 6.3   Index Insertions

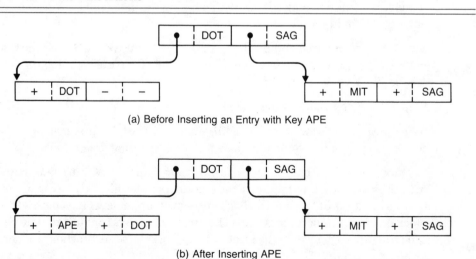

(a) Before Inserting an Entry with Key APE

(b) After Inserting APE

definition. When two blocks are combined, one is no longer needed and the entry at the next level that points to it is removed. Like insertions, deletions may affect several levels of indices. Figure 6.5 shows two deletions; the second deletion results in two blocks being combined. Deletions may leave only one entry in the root level block. In that case, the root block is no longer needed and the lower level block can become the new root block.

FIGURE 6.4   After Inserting BIG (and Splitting a Block)

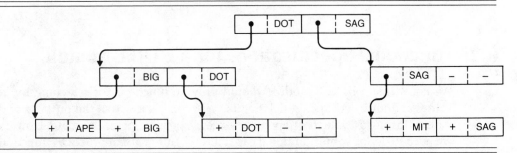

FIGURE 6.5   Index Deletions

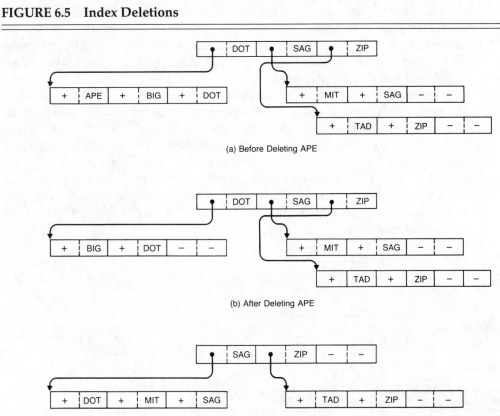

(a) Before Deleting APE

(b) After Deleting APE

(c) After Deleting BIG (and Combining Blocks)

Inserting new entries may require additional index blocks. Deleting entries may free blocks that are empty or have been combined. A scheme for allocating and freeing blocks in index files is needed to support these insertions and deletions.

Splitting and combining blocks destroy any relation between the location of a block in a file and that of its neighbors in the tree. Our original picture of a file with index entries in order from the beginning to the end of the file is not accurate anymore. The correct picture is of a tree with a pointer to the root level. From there we just follow the record pointers from one index level to another.

6.2   Functional Specifications for a BTREE Module

We know that a BTREE module should provide functions for searching for key values and for inserting and deleting keys. We also know that the purpose of the index is to return a data record pointer — the file position of a data record. However, we need to define some additional capabilities before we can produce a functional specification for our BTREE module.

Our examples have assumed that the keys are character strings. A practical module must accept any kind of data as keys. In addition, we should allow keys to vary in length from one entry to another. We will solve this problem by letting the application program that uses the BTREE module supply functions that compare entries and find the size of an entry.

The same key value may occur in more than one data record. We allow the same key value to be present in more than one entry, but we require that the combination of a key and the data record pointer in an entry be unique.

We may also want to retrieve index entries sequentially. For example, we might want to start at the first entry in an index and get each subsequent entry until the end is reached. To do this we need to keep track of our current position within the index. Then we can provide functions to move forward and backward in the index. In Figure 6.6 we have located the key BIG. The current position at each level of the index is underscored.

FIGURE 6.6   Current Position

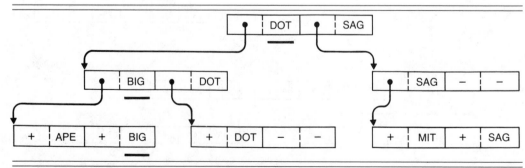

Some BTREE functions will provide a high level of function and safety. But, to make the module a flexible tool that is useful in a wide variety of applications, we will provide low-level functions such as inserting an entry at the current position in an index. It is up to the application program to ensure that using these functions does not upset the ordering of entries by key value. Our BTREE module also leaves the management of data records up to the application. BTREE just stores and retrieves record pointers that can be interpreted by the application program. Figure 6.7 documents the BTREE module to be presented in the rest of the chapter.

FIGURE 6.7   BTREE Index Module Description

Name
BTREE   A module for disk-file based indexing

Function
The BTREE module provided functions for creating and using disk files to store index entries. Each entry consists of a record location and a key value. Keys may vary in length and key values may be duplicated in different entries. The application program using the BTREE module supplies functions to compare keys and to find the size of an entry. The `btree.h` data structure supplies data structure and constant definitions for use with BTREE. Functions for searching for a specific key and for inserting and deleting entries are provided. A current position in the index is maintained and functions are provided for moving through the index sequentially. More than one index can be opened and used at a time. Most BTREE functions expect the address of an index file descriptor as an input argument to identify the index file to be used.

Use of each function in the module is described as follows:

```
char name[65] = "c:\zip.ix" ;
long ixsize = 20000 ;
IX_DESC ixd ;
ENTRY entry ;
int compare(ENTRY *, ENTRY *) ;   /* compares two entry keys */
int size(ENTRY *) ;          /* returns the size of an entry */
creatix(name, ixsize , & dummy_entry , dummy_size) ;
```

`creatix` creates an index file of the specified size. It returns 1 if the file could not be created. The calling function must supply a dummy entry whose key has the maximum possible value. This dummy key value cannot be used in other entries. The size of the dummy entry must also be supplied.

```
removeix(name)  ;
```

`removeix` deletes the index file.

Figure 6.7   continues

Figure 6.7   continued

```
openix(name, & ixd , compare , size ) ;
```

`openix` opens an existing index file. It returns –1 if unsuccessful. The addresses of functions to compare entry keys and to get the size of an entry are additional arguments.

```
closeix(& ixd ) ;
```

`closeix` closes an index file that has previously been opened.

```
go_first(& ixd ) ;
go_last(& ixd ) ;
```

`go_first` sets the current position in an index to the beginning of the file. `go_last` sets the position at the end of the index.

```
get_next( & entry , & ixd ) ;
get_prev( & entry , & ixd ) ;
get_current( & entry , & ixd ) ;
```

`get_next` advances the current position in an index file. The new current entry is copied into the address identified by the first argument. `get_previous` moves the current position backward and copies the new current entry. `get_current` copies the entry at the current position and leaves the current position unchanged.

```
find_ix( & entry , & ixd ) ;
find_exact( & entry , & ixd ) ;
```

`find_ix` locates the first entry with a key value greater than or equal to the key specified by the first argument. A return value of 0 indicates that a key equal to that specified was found. If the specified key was found, the record pointer is stored in the entry. The `find_exact` function searches for an entry in the index file with the specified key and record pointer.

```
insert_ix( & entry , & ixd ) ;
find_ins( & entry , & ixd ) ;
```

`insert_ix` adds the entry specified to the index in front of the current position in the index. After the insertion, the current position is beyond the inserted entry. A returned value of `IX_FAIL` indicates that the insertion failed. `find_ins` verifies that the entry is not in the index file already and establishes the proper position before performing the insertion. It inserts new entries following all existing entries with the same key.

```
delete_ix( & ixd ) ;
find_del( & entry , & ixd ) ;
```

`delete_ix` removes the entry at the current position in the index. After the deletion, the current position is in front of the entry following the deleted one. A

Figure 6.7   continues

Figure 6.7   continued

returned value of `IX_FAIL` indicates that the deletion failed. The `find_del` function locates the entry described by the first argument and deletes that entry if it is present.

Examples
See the `doccreat.c`, `docindex.c`, and `docscan.c` programs (Figures 6.27 through 6.33) for examples of use.

Notes
1. Up to four levels of indices are allowed with index blocks of 1,024 bytes. (These limits are set by constants in `btree.h`. The module can be recompiled if other values seem more appropriate.)

2. The maximum number of entries allowed depends on the average length of keys used (k in the following formula). Four bytes are required for the record position that accompanies each key. A rough formula for the worst case might be

records = 2 * ((1024 / 2) / (k+4)) ** 4

With keys 20 bytes long, this would be 2 * 20**4, or 160,000 records.

6.3   BTREE Pseudo-code

The following pseudo-code describes the normal cases and some exception cases. We will discuss more exceptions at the end of the section.

The find_ix function starts at the root level and moves down to the leaf level, searching an index block at each level. The search at the leaf level tells us if the key was found in the index. Searches at higher levels just direct the choice of a block on the next lower level.

```
find_ix
    start at the root block
    for each level starting at the root
        retrieve current index block
        search that block for the target key
        extract record pointer for next level
    return success or failure of the leaf level search
end
```

We have already shown a function (see Figure 6.1) to search an array of integers; searching an index block would require the same logic. New entries are inserted at the leaf level. If an index block must be split, new entries must be inserted in higher level indices. Inserting entries at higher levels requires the same logic as inserting at the leaf level, so we need describe the process only once:

```
insert entry into a specified level
        retrieve current block for this level
        if enough room for new entry
            insert entry to block
        else
            split the block into two blocks
            allocate disk space for new block
            update both blocks in index file
            insert an entry in higher index for new block
    end
```

Like inserting, deleting entries starts at the leaf level. Deletions of entries from higher level index blocks may be required if the leaf level block becomes empty or is combined with its neighbor. And like insertion, a single process applies to leaf level and higher level deletions.

```
delete current entry at specified level
        retrieve current block for this level
        remove current entry from block
        if block is empty and not the root level
            delete the block's entry on higher level
            if less than half full and not the root level
                compress with adjacent blocks
            else update the block
    end
```

Deleting entries is a messy process with lots of exception cases. Our pseudo-code shows two exceptions; others are discussed later. We want the pseudo-code to show the basic structure of the BTREE module even if some some important details must be omitted. Compressing the current block with adjacent ones is an important part of the B-Tree algorithm and requires a pseudo-code description.

```
compress adjacent blocks
        retrieve the block to the left
        if( it exists and the combined size <= 1 block )
            combine blocks into the current block
            delete higher level entry for left neighbor
            update the current block
        else
            retrieve block to the right
```

```
            if( block exists and the combined size <= 1 block )
                combine blocks into right neighbor
                delete higher level entry for current block
                update the right neighbor block
    end
```

The get_next and get_previous functions take the current position in the index and move forward or backward. They start at the leaf level and use the upper level index if they run out of the current block at the leaf level. As is the case for insertion and deletion, a single process works for all index levels:

```
    move_to_next_entry on specified level
        retrieve current leaf index block
        advance to next entry
        if( at end of block )
            move to next entry on upper level
            retrieve block pointed to by upper level
            set position at first entry in block
        return record pointer at current position
    end
```

```
    move_to_previous_entry on specified level
        retrieve current leaf index block
        move back to previous entry
        if( at beginning of block already )
            move to previous entry on upper level
            retrieve block pointed to by upper level
            set position at last entry in block
        return record pointer at current position
    end
```

The go_first and go_last functions set a new current position at the beginning or end of the index. They start at the root level and work down to the leaf level.

```
    go_first
        start with root block
        for each level from root to leaf
            retrieve this block
            make this block current for this level
            make first entry current
            save record pointer for next level
    end
```

```
go_last
    start with root block
    for each level from root to leaf
        retrieve this block
        make this block current for this level
        make last entry current
        save record pointer for next level
end
```

The openix function is analogous to the `fopen` and `open` library functions. creatix and closeix are analogous to the `open` (in create mode) and `close` library functions.

```
openix
    open index file
    set up context describing the index file
    go_first
end
```

```
closeix
    save context information
    close index file
end
```

```
creatix
    create index file
    create an initial tree structure
    allocate free blocks in file
end
```

6.4   Exceptions and Design Choices

Our pseudo-code handles some exceptions, and we can remove others with good design choices. The pseudo-code did not handle cases where an index was empty or where a search key was greater than all entries in an index. Insertions that required adding a level to the tree and deletions that required removing a level were not handled either. But simple restrictions remove these and other exception cases. We enter a dummy entry with the highest possible key value when creatix creates the index file. This dummy entry will never be deleted. This ensures that the index is never empty and that searches never go past the last key in the index. In addition, we build a tree of maximum height when the index file is created. The initial tree structure will contain one leaf level block with the dummy entry. Each higher level index will contain one entry with the dummy key and a record pointer to the lone block on the next lower level. We can avoid increasing or decreasing the height of the index tree.

The choice of a good maximum height for a B-Tree is tied to the choice of a block size. As we will see, however, trees with three or four levels can hold a large number of records for reasonable block sizes.

Several factors need to be balanced in choosing the block size. A large value minimizes the height of the tree for a given number of records. In turn, this minimizes the number of I/O operations for finding an index entry. But large block sizes require more RAM memory to store blocks being referenced. In addition, blocks larger than the units in which DOS allocates disk space to files may be fragmented, resulting in slower file I/O performance. Blocks should be a multiple of the disk sector size so that blocks are aligned on sector boundaries for faster I/O. Sector sizes are normally 512 bytes for disks formatted for DOS, and allocation units vary from 512 bytes to 4 Kbytes for different kinds of disks. As we will see later, the BTREE package requires space to hold about nine blocks in memory at one time.

The index tree becomes full when no more entries can be added without increasing the tree's height beyond the maximum we allow. At that point the root level index is full, and the lower level blocks must be at least half-full. The following formula gives the minimum capacity (worst case) of a tree with l levels:

$$\# \text{ entries when full } = (b/e) * (b/2e) ** (l\text{-}1)$$

where index entries are e bytes long on the average and blocks are b bytes long. The following table shows the worst-case index capacity for block sizes of 512 and 1,024 bytes, with an average entry size of 50 bytes.

Tree Height	Block Size 512 bytes	1,024 bytes
1	10	20
2	50	200
3	250	2,000
4	1,250	20,000

For smaller entry sizes, the capacity of an index is much larger (for 20-byte entries, a three-level index with 1,024 byte blocks holds over 31,000 entries). But, since we want the BTREE module to be a general-purpose tool, we choose conservative values of 1,024 bytes for the block size and 4 for the maximum tree height.

In addition to the index blocks, we must store some context information about the index file; the location of the root block is one such item. It is convenient to store this information at the beginning of the index file. Although only a few bytes of data are required, we must start index blocks at byte 1,024 to keep index blocks aligned on sector boundaries.

6.5   BTREE Source Files

The BTREE module is a large one with a number of source files. The files are introduced and discussed, starting with low-level functions and ending with the top-level functions that are called from application programs. The diagram of the hierarchy of function calls should provide a road map for fitting the pieces together. BTREE is not a complete program but a group of functions to be called from an applications program. For this reason, each top-level function has its own hierarchy:

```
delete_ix
    copy_current
    del_level
        retrieve_block
        del_block
            movedown
                mover
        put_free
        del_level   *
        copy_current
        first_ix
            ...
        fix_last
            copy_entry
            replace_entry
                retrieve_block
                del_block
                ins_block
                split
                    ...
                update_block
                replace_entry   *
        update_block
        compress
            neighbor
                retrieve_block
                next_entry
                prev_entry
            combine
            update_block
            last_ix
                del_level   *
```

```
insert_ix
    ins_level
        retrieve_block
        ins_block
        copy_entry
        moveup
            mover
        update_block
            chk_cache
            put_cache
            write_block
                write_if
    split
        combine
            moveup
                mover
        ins_block
            ...
        scan_blk
        next_entry
        get_block
            get_free
                read_if
        copy_entry
        update_block
        ins_level   *
        mover
        put_free
            scrub_cache
            write_free
                clr_mem
            write_block
            next_ix
                ...
    next_ix
        ...
```

```
get_next                              get_current
    next_ix                               copy_current
        retrieve_block
        next_entry
        next_ix   *
    copy_current

                                      go_first
                                          first_ix
                                              retrieve_block
                                              first_ix  *


get_previous
    last_ix
        retrieve_block
        prev_entry                    go_last
            scan_blk                      final_ix
        last_ix   *                           retrieve_block
        last_entry                            last_entry
            scan_blk                          final_ix  *
    copy_current


                                      openix
                                          open_if
                                          read_if
                                          init_bio
find_ix                                       init_cache
    call                                  go_first
    go_last
    find_level
        retrieve_block
            chk_cache
            get_cache
            put_cache
            read_block
                read_if           closeix
            find_block                write_if
                call                  close_if
                next_entry
            find_level  *
    copy_current
        retrieve_block            removeix
        copy_entry                    (no calls to other BTREE
            mover                     functions)
```

```
creatix                          find_exact
    creat_if                         copy_entry
    clr_mem                          find_ix
    mover                            get_next
    write_block
    wrt_dum
        mover
        write_block
    make_free                    find_ins
    write_free                       find_exact
closeix                              insert_ix


                                 find_del
                                     find_exact
                                     delete_ix
```

We have listed the calls made by each function just once. For example, the first time `retrieve_block` occurs in the diagram, we list every function it calls. Recursive calls are marked with an asterisk.

In reading the BTREE source files, keep in mind the relation between index blocks stored in the index file and variables of type BLOCK. Index blocks in RAM memory in such variables are mirror images of blocks stored in the file or working (scratch) copies being referenced and perhaps updated.

btree.h

The header file shown in Figure 6.8 defines constants and data types needed in application programs that use the BTREE module. (These definitions are also needed within the BTREE module.) It defines success and failure codes returned by BTREE functions. The RECPOS data type is defined for record pointers with a null value NULLREC.

FIGURE 6.8   btree.h

```
1    /* btree.h - data structures and constants for BTREE module */
2    #define EOIX        (-2)     /* return value for end-of-index */
3    #define IX_FAIL     (-1)     /* return value for failed operation*/
4    #define IX_OK        0       /* return value for success */
5
6    typedef long RECPOS ;        /* file pos. of index block */
7    #define NULLREC     (-1L)    /* special value for a RECPOS */
8
```

Figure 6.8   continues

Figure 6.8   continued

```
 9    #define MAXKEY        100      /* maximum length of a key */
10
11    typedef struct                 /* entry format in index */
12     { RECPOS rptr ;               /* points to lower level */
13       char   key[MAXKEY] ;        /* start of key value */
14                /* (actual data type unknown) */
15     } ENTRY ;
16
17    #define IXB_SIZE      1024      /* no. bytes in a block (on disk) */
18       /* IXB_SPACE = IXB_SIZE - sizeof(int)*2 - sizeof(long) */
19    #define IXB_SPACE     1016      /* no. bytes of entry space in block*/
20
21    typedef struct                 /* index block format */
22     { RECPOS brec ;               /* index file location of the block */
23                                   /* or location of next free block */
24       int bend ;                  /* first unused location in block */
25       int lvl ;                   /* records level number (-1 = free) */
26       char entries[IXB_SPACE];/* space for entries */
27     } BLOCK ;
28
29    #define MAX_LEVELS    4         /* four index levels permitted */
30
31    typedef struct                 /* disk-file index descriptor */
32     { int  nl ;                   /* number of index levels */
33       RECPOS rb ;                 /* location of root block in file */
34       RECPOS ff ;                 /* location of first free block */
35       ENTRY dume ;                /* dummy entry */
36     } IX_DISK ;
37
38    typedef struct                 /* in-memory index descriptor */
39     { int  ixfile ;               /* descriptor for open index file */
40       struct
41         { RECPOS cblock ;         /* current block number */
42           int coffset ;           /* current offset within the block */
43         } pos[ MAX_LEVELS ] ;
44       int (*pcomp) ( void *, void *) ; /* compare function ptr */
45       int (*psize) (void *) ;     /* address of entry size function*/
46       BLOCK  cache[ MAX_LEVELS] ;   /* cache for current blocks */
47       IX_DISK dx ;                /* disk resident stuff */
48     } IX_DESC ;
49
50                                   /* function prototypes */
51
52                                   /* bt_low2.c */
53    int prev_entry(BLOCK *,int) ;
54    int next_entry(BLOCK *,int) ;
55    void copy_entry(ENTRY *,ENTRY *) ;
56    int scan_blk(BLOCK *,int) ;
57    int last_entry(BLOCK *) ;
58
59                                   /* bt_file.c */
60    int creat_if( char [] ) ;
61    int read_if(RECPOS,char [],int) ;
62    int write_if(RECPOS,char [],int) ;
63    int close_if(void) ;
64    int open_if(char []) ;
65
```

Figure 6.8   continues

Figure 6.8   continued

```
66                                        /* bt_free.c */
67       void make_free(RECPOS,RECPOS) ;
68       RECPOS get_free(void) ;
69       void write_free(RECPOS,BLOCK *) ;
70
71                                        /* blockio.c */
72       void init_bio(void) ;
73        int retrieve_block(int,RECPOS,BLOCK *,int) ;
74       void update_block(BLOCK *) ;
75       int get_block(int,BLOCK *) ;
76       void put_free(BLOCK *) ;
77       int read_block(RECPOS,BLOCK *) ;
78       int write_block(RECPOS,BLOCK *) ;
79
80                                        /* bt_cache.c */
81       void init_cache(void) ;
82       int chk_cache(int,RECPOS) ;
83       int get_cache(int,RECPOS,BLOCK *) ;
84       void put_cache(int,BLOCK *) ;
85       void scrub_cache(RECPOS) ;
86
87                                        /* openix.c */
88       int openix(char [],IX_DESC *, int (*) (), int (*)() ) ;
89       void closeix(IX_DESC *) ;
90       int creatix(char [],long,ENTRY *,int ) ;
91       RECPOS wrt_dum(ENTRY *,int) ;
92       void removeix(char []) ;
93
94                                        /* bt_first.c */
95       int go_first(IX_DESC *) ;
96       void first_ix(int,RECPOS,BLOCK *) ;
97       int go_last(IX_DESC *) ;
98       void final_ix(int,RECPOS,BLOCK *) ;
99
100                                       /* bt_get.c */
101      int get_next(ENTRY *,IX_DESC *) ;
102      RECPOS next_ix(int,BLOCK *) ;
103      int get_previous(ENTRY *,IX_DESC *) ;
104      RECPOS last_ix(int,BLOCK *) ;
105      void get_current(ENTRY *,IX_DESC *) ;
106
107                                       /* bt_block.c */
108      int find_block(ENTRY *,BLOCK *,int *,int (*)() ) ;
109      void ins_block(BLOCK *,ENTRY *,int) ;
110      void del_block(BLOCK *,int) ;
111      void moveup(BLOCK *,int,int) ;
112      void movedown(BLOCK *,int,int) ;
113      void combine(BLOCK *,BLOCK *) ;
114
115                                       /* bt_find.c */
116      int find_ix(ENTRY *,IX_DESC *) ;
117      int find_level(int,ENTRY *,RECPOS) ;
118
119                                       /* bt_ins.c */
120      int insert_ix(ENTRY *,IX_DESC *) ;
121      int ins_level(int,ENTRY *,BLOCK *) ;
122      int split(int,ENTRY *,BLOCK *) ;
123
```

Figure 6.8   continues

Figure 6.8 continued

```
124                                      /* bt_del.c */
125      int delete_ix(IX_DESC *) ;
126      int del_level(int,BLOCK *) ;
127      int compress(int,BLOCK *) ;
128      int fix_last(int,RECPOS,ENTRY *) ;
129      int replace_entry(int,ENTRY *) ;
130
131                                      /* bt_low.c */
132      BLOCK *neighbor(int,int) ;
133      int copy_current(int,ENTRY *) ;
134
135                                      /* bt_top.c */
136      int find_exact(ENTRY *,IX_DESC *) ;
137      int find_ins(ENTRY *,IX_DESC *) ;
138      int find_del(ENTRY *,IX_DESC *) ;
```

The ENTRY data type is used to pass keys and record pointers to the BTREE module and to receive them back. We do not know the actual data type or key length, but we define a dummy array of 100 characters. This dummy array serves as a placeholder so that we can get the address of the start of the key field. When we declare an ENTRY variable for scratch space, the 100-byte key field provides enough space for any key.

Lines 17 to 27 in Figure 6.8 define the format of an index block. Although this structure is not used by the application, it is used in the IX_DESC descriptor structure described later. To simplify the BTREE module, we used the same structure for index blocks stored in the index file and for copies in RAM memory. Not all the members of the BLOCK structure are needed in each case, but the cost in wasted disk space is quite small.

The brec member serves two purposes. For free blocks in the file, it points to the next free block. For blocks in RAM memory, it identifies the location in the index file where the block belongs. The lvl member identifies the index level on which a block is used. Values of 0 through (MAX_LEVELS-1) correspond to leaf through root level, whereas the special value FREE_LEVEL identifies free blocks.

The entries member serves as a dummy placeholder; entries whose data type is not yet known will be stored here. The size of the member is adjusted to make the BLOCK structure exactly 1,024 bytes long. The bend member contains the number of bytes actually used in the entries field. It can also be interpreted as the offset of the first unused byte in the block.

The file also defines two data structures whose contents describe an index file. The IX_DISK structure contains permanent data that are stored in the index file between uses of the file. Its members point to the root block and the first free block; when we open an index file, we need this information to make sense of the file.

The IX_DESC structure contains the same information, with additional members needed for an index that is in use. The ixfile member contains a file descriptor for read and write calls. Addresses of compare and entry size functions are also stored here. The current position in the index is stored in the pos array of structures — a current block record pointer and an offset within the block for each index level. Space to cache recently used blocks is also provided within the structure.

The application program does not need to know about or use the fields in these descriptor data structures, but we can simplify the BTREE module by letting the application program allocate space for index descriptors. Most calls to BTREE functions will contain a pointer to a descriptor structure.

Lines 50 to 138 declare function prototypes for all BTREE functions called by the application program or by a BTREE function. (A few functions are only called from the source file in which they are defined. Their prototypes are declared in that source file.)

bt_macro.h

Figure 6.9 lists another header file whose definitions are needed only within the BTREE module. C source code that makes extensive use of pointers and dummy data types can be difficult to understand. The macros in lines 8 to 15 hide the messy details, keeping the source code looking fairly normal. Calls to the entry size function occur frequently in the BTREE module, so the ENT_SIZE macro abbreviates that expression further.

Forming the address of an entry within a block is another common requirement. The ENT_ADR macro hides the type conversions needed to add an offset to a pointer to a block. Although the expression looks complicated, most C compilers will generate a single addition instruction (with load and store instructions).

FIGURE 6.9   bt_macro.h

```
1      /* bt_macro.h - macros,constants,data types for BTREE internals*/
2
3      #define CURR  1              /* getting current block */
4      #define NOT_CURR 0           /* getting noncurrent block */
5
6
7                                   /* get address of entry in a block */
8      #define ENT_ADR(pb,off)  ((ENTRY *)( (char *)((pb)->entries)+off))
9
10                                  /* get size of an entry */
11     #define ENT_SIZE(pe)    ( (pci->psize)(pe) )
12
13                                  /* current position macros */
14     #define CB(l)    ( pci->pos[l].cblock )
15     #define CO(l)    ( pci->pos[l].coffset )
16
17     #define FREE_LEVEL (-1)      /* marks a block as free */
18
19                                  /* arguments for neighbor() */
20     #define LEFTN       (-1)     /* request left neighbor */
21     #define RIGHTN       1       /* request right neighbor */
```

The CB and CO macros provide shorthand for references to the current block and current offset. They can be used on the left or right side of assignment statements.

The variable pci occurs in several of these macros. It is explained in the next section.

Several constants that are passed as arguments between functions inside the BTREE module are also defined in the bt_macro.h file.

bt_space.c

The source file shown in Figure 6.10 defines some global variables used throughout BTREE. In a large module like BTREE, it is convenient to declare and allocate space for all global variables in a single source file that contains no functions. Then all the source files that reference these variables can declare them with the extern storage class. The global variable pci is used within BTREE to address the descriptor structure for the BTREE operation underway. This avoids the need to pass that address as an argument in all function calls within the BTREE module.

FIGURE 6.10　bt_space.c

```
 1    /* bt_space.c - declares some global variables */
 2    #include "stdio.h"
 3    #include "btree.h"
 4    #include "bt_macro.h"
 5
 6    IX_DESC *pci ;              /* refers to index descriptor */
 7                               /* for current function call */
 8
 9    BLOCK spare_block ;        /* scratch block for splits and */
10                               /* compressing */
11
12    int split_size = IXB_SPACE ; /* split a block when it contains */
13                                 /* more than this many bytes */
14
15    int comb_size = (IXB_SPACE/2); /* combine blocks with */
16                                   /* fewer than this many bytes */
```

The spare_block variable is used within BTREE whenever scratch space is needed for an extra index block.

The split_size and comb_size variables establish thresholds for splitting a full block or combining a less than half full block. In normal use, these variables are initialized to be the block size for splitting and half the block size for combining. But for testing, we can set these variables to much smaller values, allowing us to test exception conditions more easily.

The variable pci occurs in several of these macros. It is a global variable used within BTREE that contains the address of the descriptor structure for the BTREE operation underway.

bt_low2.c

The source file in Figure 6.11 provides some low-level tools for working with index entries in blocks. They hide the details of dealing with variable length entries whose data type we do not know. The next_entry function moves forward past the entry at the specified offset, whereas the prev_entry function moves backward. Both functions return the new offset or –1 if the end or beginning of the block was reached. The last_entry function finds the offset of the last function in a block.

FIGURE 6.11   bt_low2.c

```
1      /* bt_low2.c - low-level functions for BTREE module */
2      #include "stdio.h"
3      #include <string.h>
4      #include "btree.h"
5      #include "bt_macro.h"
6
7      extern IX_DESC *pci ;
8
9      int prev_entry(pb,off)        /* back up one entry */
10     BLOCK *pb ;
11     int off ;
12     {
13         if( off <= 0 )            /* at start of block ? */
14             return( -1 ) ;        /*   yes - can't back up */
15         off = scan_blk(pb,off) ; /* find previous entry */
16         return( off ) ;
17     }
18
19     int next_entry(pb,off)        /* go forward one entry */
20     BLOCK *pb ;
21     int off ;
22     {
23         if( off >= pb->bend )  /* at end of block ? */
24             return( -1 ) ;        /*   yes - can't move fwd */
25                                   /* move past this entry */
26         off = off + ENT_SIZE(ENT_ADR(pb,off)) ;
27         if( off >= pb->bend )  /* at end of block ? */
28             return( -1 ) ;        /*   yes - no entry here */
29         return( off ) ;
30     }
31
32
33     void copy_entry(to,from)      /* copy an entry */
34     ENTRY *to ;                   /* to this address */
35     ENTRY *from ;                 /* from this address */
36     {
37         int ne ;
38
39         ne = ENT_SIZE(from) ;    /* get the entry's size */
40                                   /* move that many bytes */
41         memmove((void *) to,(void *) from, ne) ;
42     }
43
44
```

Figure 6.11   continues

Figure 6.11   continued

```
45      int scan_blk(pb,n)              /* find offset of last entry */
46        BLOCK *pb ;                   /* in this block */
47        int n ;                       /* starting before this position */
48        {
49           int  i , last ;
50
51           i = 0 ; last = 0 ;
52           while( i < n )              /* repeat until position reached */
53              { last = i ;            /* save where we are now */
54                                       /* move past the entry */
55               i = i + ENT_SIZE( ENT_ADR(pb,i) );
56              }
57           return( last ) ;           /* return last offset < n */
58        }
59
60
61      int last_entry(pb)              /* find last entry in a block */
62        BLOCK *pb ;                   /* the block */
63        {
64                                       /* scan for offset of last entry */
65           return( scan_blk(pb,pb->bend) ) ; /* and return the offset */
66        }
```

Moving forward from an offset is easy. We just get the size of the entry at that offset and add it to get the new offset. Moving backward is a bit more difficult because we cannot find the size of the previous entry directly. We have to start at the beginning of the block and move forward until we reach the specified offset. The last entry found before this point is the previous entry. The scan_blk function provides this scanning.

The copy_entry function copies a single entry. It assumes that the destination area is large enough to hold an entry.

The functions in this source file remove some of the disadvantages of working with variable length entries. The cost is extra source code and some extra execution time. But it keeps the rest of the BTREE module simple and understandable.

bt_file.c

Figure 6.12 lists functions that do file I/O operations on index files. This hides our use of C library functions for unbuffered I/O from the rest of the BTREE module.

A file position is specified for each operation, and a call to lseek precedes a read or write. There is no relation between the order of reads and writes and the file position specified. Random rather than sequential I/O is required for index files.

The file mode constants and the names of the header files that define the constants are the same for Microsoft C and Turbo C but some changes might be needed for other compilers.

FIGURE 6.12   bt_file.c

```
1      /* bt_file.c - file I/O for BTREE module */
2      #include "stdio.h"
3      #include <fcntl.h>
4      #include <sys\types.h>
5      #include <sys\stat.h>
6      #include <io.h>
7      #include "cminor.h"
8      #include "btree.h"
9      #include "bt_macro.h"
10
11     #define BOF_REL 0
12     #define WR_MODE 1
13     #define RW_MODE 2
14
15     extern IX_DESC *pci ;
16
17     int creat_if(fn)        /* create a file */
18      char fn[];
19      {
20           return( open(fn,O_WRONLY| O_CREAT | O_BINARY ,
21             S_IREAD | S_IWRITE ) ) ;
22      }
23
24     int read_if(start,buf,nrd)
25      RECPOS start ;
26      char buf[] ;
27      int nrd ;
28      {
29           lseek(pci->ixfile,start,BOF_REL) ;
30           return( read(pci->ixfile,buf,nrd) ) ;
31      }
32
33     int write_if(start,buf,nwrt)
34      RECPOS start ;
35      char buf[] ;
36      int nwrt ;
37      {
38           lseek(pci->ixfile,start,BOF_REL) ;
39           return( write(pci->ixfile,buf,nwrt) ) ;
40      }
41
42     int close_if()     /* close an index file */
43      {
44           return( close(pci->ixfile) );
45      }
46
47     int open_if(fn)               /* open an index file */
48      char fn[] ;
49      {
50           return ( open(fn,O_RDWR | O_BINARY ) ) ;
51      }
```

bt_free.c

As we discussed in Section 6.3, insertions and deletions require support for allocating and freeing space in the index file. The source file in Figure 6.13 manages a list of free index blocks.

FIGURE 6.13   bt_free.c

```
1     /* bt_free.c - maintain list of free index blocks */
2     #include "stdio.h"
3     #include <string.h>
4     #include "btree.h"
5     #include "bt_macro.h"
6
7     #define FREE_LEVEL (-1)      /* marks a block as free */
8     extern IX_DESC *pci ;
9     extern BLOCK spare_block ;
10
11    void make_free(fstart,filesize) /* set up the free block chain */
12     RECPOS fstart ;              /* first free block */
13     RECPOS filesize ;            /* size of the index file */
14     {
15         BLOCK *pb ;
16         RECPOS r ;
17         pb = & spare_block ;   /* scratch block */
18         pci->dx.ff = NULLREC ;/* no blocks free to start */
19         for(r= fstart ; r < filesize ; r = r + IXB_SIZE)
20           { write_free(r,pb) ; }
21     }
22
23
24
25    RECPOS get_free()            /* grab a free block for use */
26     {
27         RECPOS r , rt ;
28
29         r = pci->dx.ff ;        /* get location of first free block */
30         if( r != NULLREC )      /* is there one ? */
31           {                     /*    yes - find where it points */
32             read_if(r, (char *) & rt,sizeof(RECPOS));
33             pci->dx.ff = rt ;   /*            and make it the 1st free */
34           }
35         return( r ) ;
36     }
37
38
39    void write_free(r,pb)        /* write out a free block */
40     RECPOS r ;                  /* record number of block to free */
41     BLOCK *pb ;                 /* use this as scratch space */
42     {
43         pb->lvl = FREE_LEVEL ; /* mark block as free */
44                                 /* zero out the block */
45         memset( (char *) & pb->entries ,0,IXB_SPACE) ;
46         pb->brec = pci->dx.ff ;/* point to current first free block*/
47         write_block(r,pb) ;    /* write the free block */
48         pci->dx.ff = r ;        /* make this block the first free */
49     }
```

The dx.ff member stores the address of the first free block. That block in the file points to the next free block. The list ends when a free block contains a pointer with the NULLREC value.

When an index file is created, the make_free function creates a list of free blocks. It receives the record position where the free list starts and the total size of the file. The file size specified may not be an exact multiple of 1,024 bytes, so make_free stops when the file's size equals or exceeds the specified size. Writing the free blocks serves two purposes. It links the free blocks into a list and it forces DOS to allocate space for the file.

The final free list links the blocks in reverse order; the last block in the file is the first on the free list. This order is easy to implement, but it might reduce disk I/O efficiency in some cases. Note also that we did not check for failure of the write operations.

The get_free function allocates the first free block. It reads that block to get the pointer to the next free block. This next block becomes the new first free block. The put_free function performs the opposite function; namely, it returns a block to the free list. Before we write the free block, we set the level member to the FREE_LEVEL value and clear the entry storage area. Clearing this area is not necessary for BTREE's function, but it makes examining an index file with the FILEDUMP program a bit easier.

blockio.c and bt_cache.c

The functions in Figures 6.14 and 6.15 provide input and output of index blocks. They implement a simple scheme of cache buffering to reduce the number of actual disk reads. The retrieve_block function gets index blocks from the cache or from the index file.

FIGURE 6.14   blockio.c

```
 1      /* blockio.c - retrieve/update index blocks */
 2      #include "stdio.h"
 3      #include "btree.h"
 4      #include "bt_macro.h"
 5
 6      extern IX_DESC *pci ;
 7      extern BLOCK spare_block ;
 8      RECPOS get_free() ;
 9
10
11      void init_bio()            /* initialize blockio */
12        {
13          init_cache() ;         /* init. cache buffers */
14        }
15
16
17                                 /* retrieve an index block */
```

Figure 6.14   continues

Figure 6.14   continued

```
18      int retrieve_block(l,r,pb,current)
19      int l ;                     /* index level for this block */
20      RECPOS r ;                  /* block's location in index file */
21      BLOCK *pb ;                 /* put it here */
22      int current ;              /* =1, put in cache */
23      {
24
25
26          if( chk_cache(l,r) != 0 ) /* look in cache first */
27              get_cache(l,r,pb) ;   /*    there - get it */
28          else
29            { read_block(r,pb);  /*    not there - read it */
30              pb->brec = r ;
31              pb->lvl  = l ;
32              if( current )         /*       current block for level l ? */
33                  put_cache(l,pb) ;/*          yes - put in the cache */
34            }
35          return( IX_OK ) ;
36      }
37
38
39      void update_block(pb)         /* update an index block in file */
40      BLOCK *pb ;                   /* address of index block */
41      {
42          if( chk_cache(pb->lvl,pb->brec) != 0 )
43              put_cache(pb->lvl,pb) ;
44          write_block(pb->brec,pb) ;
45      }
46
47
48      int get_block(l,pb)           /* allocate and set up a block */
49                                    /* retrieve an index block */
50      int l ;                       /* index level for this block */
51      BLOCK *pb ;                   /* put it here */
52      {
53          RECPOS r ;
54
55          r = get_free() ;          /* allocate disk block */
56          if( r == NULLREC )
57              return( IX_FAIL ) ;
58
59          pb->brec = r ;            /* record block's file position */
60          pb->lvl  = l ;            /* and its level */
61          return( IX_OK ) ;
62      }
63
64
65      void put_free(pb)             /* return a block to the free list */
66      BLOCK *pb ;
67      {
68          scrub_cache(pb->brec) ;/* remove from cache */
69          pb->lvl = FREE_LEVEL ; /* mark as free */
70          write_free(pb->brec,pb) ;
71      }
72
73
74      int read_block(r,pb)          /* read an index block */
```

Figure 6.14   continues

Figure 6.14   continued

```
75      RECPOS r ;                  /* block's location in index file */
76      BLOCK *pb ;                 /* store the block here */
77      {
78          int ret ;
79
80          ret = read_if(r, (char *) pb, sizeof(BLOCK) ) ;
81          return( ret ) ;
82      }
83
84
85   int write_block(r,pb)          /* write an index block */
86    RECPOS r ;                    /* block's location in index file */
87    BLOCK *pb ;                   /* the data to write */
88    {
89          int ret ;
90
91          ret = write_if(r, (char *) pb, sizeof(BLOCK) ) ;
92          return( ret ) ;
93      }
```

FIGURE 6.15   bt_cache.c

```
1      /* bt_cache.c - cache index blocks to cut disk I/O  */
2      /* this version handles only a single open index file */
3      #include "stdio.h"
4      #include <string.h>
5      #include "btree.h"
6      #include "bt_macro.h"
7
8      extern IX_DESC *pci ;
9
10     void init_cache()           /* initialize blockio cache */
11     {
12         int l ;
13
14         for(l=0 ; l < MAX_LEVELS ; l=l+1)
15            { pci->cache[l].brec = NULLREC; /* nothing in memory yet */
16            }
17     }
18
19
20     int chk_cache(l,r)          /* check cache for an index block */
21      int l ;                    /* index level for this block */
22      RECPOS r ;                 /* block's location in index file */
23      {
24          BLOCK *pb ;
25
26          if( pci->cache[l].brec != r )
27              return( 0 ) ;
28          return( 1 ) ;
29      }
30
31
32     int get_cache(l,r,to)       /* get a block from the cache */
33      int l ;                    /* index level for this block */
```

Figure 6.15   continues

Figure 6.15   continued

```
34        RECPOS r ;                    /* block's location in index file */
35        BLOCK *to ;                   /* if found, copy it here */
36        {
37            BLOCK *pb ;
38
39            if( pci->cache[l].brec != r )
40                return( 0 ) ;
41            pb = & pci->cache[l] ;
42                                /* copy it */
43            memmove((void *) to,( void *) pb, sizeof(BLOCK) ) ;
44            pb->brec = r ;
45            return( 1 ) ;
46        }
47
48
49    void put_cache(l,pb)         /* write an index block back to file*/
50    int l ;
51    BLOCK *pb ;                   /* address of index block */
52    {
53        BLOCK *to ;
54
55        to = & pci->cache[l] ;
56                            /* copy whole block */
57        memmove((void *) to,(void *) pb,sizeof(BLOCK) ) ;
58    }
59
60
61    void scrub_cache(r)          /* remove a block from the cache */
62    RECPOS r ;                   /* the block's file position */
63    {                            /*  = RECPOS scrubs all levels */
64        int l ;
65                /* search the cache */
66        for(l=0 ; l<pci->dx.nl ; l=l+1)
67          { if( (r == NULLREC)  || (r == pci->cache[l].brec) )
68              pci->cache[l].brec = NULLREC ;
69          }
70    }
```

Blocks that are in the current position are likely to be referenced again, so we cache only those blocks. Note that we rely on the calling function to tell us the level on which the block is to be used and whether it is to be a current block.

The `update_block` function puts updated copies of blocks back in the file. It immediately writes each update to the file. (This is often called a *write-through* cache strategy.) An alternate strategy would be to hold updated blocks in the cache and write them to the file only when they are replaced in the cache. Our method is simple to explain and is an effective starting point.

The information in the cache buffers must be kept consistent with the corresponding blocks in the file. When we initialize the BTREE module, we set the cache to show that no valid blocks are present. When we update blocks, we also update the cache if that block is present. When a block is freed, the `put_free` function ensures that the cache does not contain out-of-date information about the block.

read_block and write_block functions read and write index blocks directly. They bypass the cache.

The cache functions in Figure 6.15 implement the caching. The cache method is simple. We allocate space for one block at each index level and keep the current block there. Cache buffers are allocated in the descriptor, so each open index file has its own set.

Our organization is quite modular. blockio.c hides the presence of caching from the rest of the BTREE module. The details of the caching method are confined to the bt_cache.c source file. This makes it easy to enhance the caching scheme without introducing bugs in the rest of the module.

openix.c

The source file in Figure 6.16 groups the functions for opening and closing index files. The openix function opens an index file and prepares it for use. It reads the permanent descriptor data from the index file and sets up the descriptor data structure supplied by the calling function. The addresses of the compare and entry_size functions to be used for this index file are also stored in the descriptor. openix calls init_bio to clear the cache buffers and go_first to establish a valid current position.

FIGURE 6.16   openix.c

```
 1      /* openix.c - open / close an index file */
 2      #include "stdio.h"
 3      #include <string.h>
 4      #include "cminor.h"
 5      #include "btree.h"
 6      #include "bt_macro.h"
 7
 8      extern IX_DESC *pci ;
 9      RECPOS wrt_dum(ENTRY *, int) ;
10
11
12      int openix(name,pix,cfun,sfun) /* open an existing index file */
13      char name[] ;                  /* file name */
14      IX_DESC *pix ;                 /* control block for index */
15      int (*cfun) () ;               /* address of compare function */
16      int (*sfun) () ;               /* address of entry size function */
17      {
18          int ret ;
19
20          pci = pix ;
21          ret = open_if(name) ;
22          if( ret < 0 )              /* check for failure to create file */
23              return( IX_FAIL ) ;
24          pci->ixfile = ret ;
25          read_if(0L,(char *) & pix->dx, sizeof(IX_DISK) ) ;
26          pci->pcomp = cfun ;        /* record address of compare fun. */
27          pci->psize = sfun ;        /* and of entry size function. */
28          init_bio() ;               /* initialize block I/O */
```

Figure 6.16   continues

Figure 6.16   continued

```
29              go_first(pix) ;          /* position at start of file */
30              return( IX_OK ) ;
31        }
32
33
34     void closeix(pix)                 /* close an index file */
35      IX_DESC *pix ;                   /* index descriptor */
36      {
37              pci = pix ;
38              write_if(0L,(char *) & pci->dx, sizeof(IX_DISK) ) ;
39              close_if() ;             /* close the index file */
40        }
41
42
43      int creatix(name,filesize,pdum,ndum) /* create a new index file*/
44      char name[] ;                    /* name of the file */
45      long filesize ;                  /* size of the file */
46      ENTRY *pdum ;                    /* dummy entry for EOF */
47      int ndum ;                       /* size of dummy entry */
48      {
49              BLOCK b ;
50              IX_DESC ixd ;
51              int ret ;
52
53              pci = & ixd ;
54              ret = creat_if(name) ;
55              if( ret < 0 )            /* check for failure to create file */
56                      return( IX_FAIL ) ;
57              ixd.ixfile = ret ;
58              ixd.dx.nl = MAX_LEVELS ; /* all levels present */
59              memmove((void *) & ixd.dx.dume, (void *) pdum, ndum) ;
60              memset((void *) & b, 0, IXB_SIZE) ;/* make block of zeros */
61              write_block(0L,&b) ;     /* write it at BOF */
62                                       /* set up index block for each level*/
63                                       /* and record location of root block*/
64              ixd.dx.rb = wrt_dum(pdum,ndum) ;
65                                       /* set up free block list */
66                                       /* start it after dummy blocks */
67              make_free( ((RECPOS) (MAX_LEVELS+1)) * IXB_SIZE, filesize) ;
68              closeix(&ixd) ;          /* close file updating desc. info */
69              return( IX_OK ) ;        /* successful creation */
70        }
71
72
73      RECPOS wrt_dum(pdum,ndum)         /* write index block for each level */
74      ENTRY *pdum ;                    /* dummy entry */
75      int ndum ;                       /* size of dummy entry */
76      {
77              BLOCK b ;
78              int l ;
79              RECPOS r ;
80
81              pdum->rptr = NULLREC ;
82              r = 0 ;
83              for( l=0 ;l < MAX_LEVELS  ; l=l+1)
84                { r = r + IXB_SIZE ;
85                                       /* put dummy entry in block */
```

Figure 6.16   continues

Figure 6.16   continued

```
 86                    memmove((void *) & b.entries, (void *) pdum,ndum);
 87                    b.lvl = 1 ;
 88                    b.bend = ndum ;    /* block contains one entry */
 89                    write_block(r,&b) ;  /* write the block */
 90                    pdum->rptr = r ;
 91                }
 92            return( r ) ;
 93        }
 94
 95
 96
 97    void removeix(name)              /* delete an index file */
 98       char name[] ;                /* name of the file */
 99       {
100           remove(name) ;
101       }
```

closeix is called where the application finishes using an index. It updates the permanent data in the index file and then closes the file.

creatix creates a new index file. It sets up the initial structure with a single entry using the dummy key supplied by the calling function. A call to make_free allocates space for and links a list of free index blocks. It calls closeix to write the permanent descriptor data in the file and close it.

removeix deletes an index file. It just hides the way we implemented an index file from the application.

bt_first.c

The go_first and go_last functions in Figure 6.17 set the current position in an index file to the beginning or end of the file. Both functions start at the root block and work down to the leaf level. The recursive functions first_ix and final_ix set the position. This organization — a small function for interface to the application and a recursive function to do the work — is shared by other BTREE functions. Storing the address of the descriptor structure in the global variable pci is also common to many BTREE functions called from the application program.

The index file contains a dummy entry at the end. Thus go_last and final_ix set the current position in front of this dummy entry.

FIGURE 6.17   bt_first.c

```
  1    /* bt_first.c - position at start/end of index */
  2    #include "stdio.h"
  3    #include "btree.h"
  4    #include "bt_macro.h"
  5
  6    extern IX_DESC *pci ;         /* global variable for current pix */
```

Figure 6.17   continues

Figure 6.17   continued

```
7
8      int go_first(pix)            /* go to first entry in index */
9       IX_DESC *pix ;               /* points to an index descriptor */
10     {
11         BLOCK b ;
12
13         pci = pix ;
14                                    /* start at root level and */
15                                    /* position at first entry */
16          first_ix(pci->dx.nl-1,pci->dx.rb,&b) ;
17          return( IX_OK ) ;        /* success code */
18     }
19
20
21     void first_ix(l,r,pb)        /* set curr. pos. to first entry */
22      int l ;                      /* at this and lower levels */
23      RECPOS r ;                   /* curr. block for level l */
24      BLOCK *pb ;
25     {
26
27         CB(l) = r ;               /* set curr. block */
28         CO(l) = 0 ;               /* and offset */
29          retrieve_block(l,CB(l),pb,CURR); /* get the block */
30
31         if( l > 0 )               /* set lower levels too */
32             first_ix(l-1,ENT_ADR(pb,0)->rptr,pb) ;
33     }
34
35
36
37     int go_last(pix)             /* go to last index entry (dummy) */
38      IX_DESC *pix ;               /* points to an index descriptor */
39     {
40         BLOCK b ;
41
42         pci = pix ;
43          final_ix(pci->dx.nl-1,pci->dx.rb,&b) ; /* start at root */
44                                    /* position at last entry */
45          return( IX_OK ) ;        /* success return code */
46     }
47
48
49     void final_ix(l,r,pb)        /* set curr. pos. to first entry */
50      int l ;                      /* at this and lower levels */
51      RECPOS r ;                   /* curr. block for level l */
52      BLOCK *pb ;
53     {
54         int off ;
55
56         CB(l) = r ;               /* set curr. block */
57          retrieve_block(l,r,pb,CURR);/* get the block */
58         off = last_entry(pb);    /* curr. offset = last entry */
59         CO(l) = off ;
60         if( l > 0 )               /* set lower levels too */
61             final_ix(l-1,ENT_ADR(pb,off)->rptr,pb) ;
62     }
```

bt_get.c

Figure 6.18 shows the get_next and get_previous functions, which move
forward or backward in an index file. These functions use the recursive functions
next_ix and last_ix to do the work. They are similar, so we will discuss
next_ix only.

FIGURE 6.18   bt_get.c

```
1    /* bt_get.c - get_next , previous entries */
2    #include "stdio.h"
3    #include "btree.h"
4    #include "bt_macro.h"
5
6    extern IX_DESC  *pci ;        /* global variable for current pix */
7    RECPOS next_ix() ;
8    RECPOS last_ix() ;
9
10   int get_next(pe,pix)          /* get next index entry */
11    ENTRY *pe ;                  /* put the entry here */
12    IX_DESC *pix ;               /* points to an index descriptor */
13    {
14       BLOCK b ;
15
16       pci = pix ;
17                                 /* check for dummy entry */
18                                 /* at end-of-ix */
19       copy_current(0,pe) ;
20       if( pci->pcomp(pe,& pci->dx.dume) == 0 )
21           return( EOIX ) ;
22
23       if( next_ix(0,&b) != NULLREC) /* got next leaf entry ? */
24          { copy_current(0,pe); /* copy it   */
25            return( IX_OK ) ;  /* and return success */
26          }
27       else return( EOIX ) ;
28    }
29
30   RECPOS next_ix(l,pb)          /* get next entry on a level */
31    int l ;                      /* level number */
32    BLOCK *pb ;
33    {
34       int off ;
35       RECPOS newblk ;
36
37       if( l >= pci->dx.nl )   /* above top level ? */
38           return( NULLREC ) ;/*    yes - failure */
39
40        retrieve_block(l,CB(l),pb,CURR) ; /* get current block */
41        off = next_entry(pb,CO(l)); /* move to next entry in block */
42        if( off >= 0)           /* past end of the block */
43            CO(l) = off ;       /*   no - record new position */
44        else                    /*   yes - move to next index block */
45          {
46              newblk =next_ix(l+1,pb) ; /*  next block on this level */
47              if( newblk != NULLREC)/*  check for end of index */
```

Figure 6.18   continues

Figure 6.18   continued

```
48                { CB(l) = newblk ;  /*  make this the current block */
49                              /* get it into memory */
50                    retrieve_block(l,CB(l),pb,CURR) ;
51                    CO(l) = 0 ;      /*        at first entry */
52                }
53              else return( NULLREC ) ; /* at end of index - */
54            }                          /*   no next block */
55          return( ENT_ADR(pb,CO(l))->rptr ) ;/* lower level block no */
56      }
57
58
59
60      int get_previous(pe,pix)    /* get previous index entry */
61      ENTRY *pe ;                 /* put the entry here */
62      IX_DESC *pix ;              /* points to an index descriptor */
63      {
64          BLOCK b ;
65
66          pci = pix ;
67          if( last_ix(0,&b) !=NULLREC)/* got next leaf entry ? */
68            { copy_current(0,pe);/*    yes - return it */
69              return( IX_OK ) ;   /*        and success code */
70            }
71          else return( EOIX ) ;   /*    no - at BOF. return failure */
72      }
73
74      RECPOS last_ix(l,pb)         /* get previous entry for a level */
75      int l ;                      /* level number */
76      BLOCK *pb ;                  /* space for a block */
77      {
78          int off ;
79          RECPOS newblk ;
80
81          if( l >= pci->dx.nl )
82              return( NULLREC ) ;
83
84          retrieve_block(l,CB(l),pb,CURR) ; /* get current block */
85          off = prev_entry(pb,CO(l)) ;      /* back up one entry */
86          if( off >= 0 )            /* past beginning of block */
87              CO(l) = off ;         /*   no - record new offset */
88          else
89            { newblk =last_ix(l+1,pb);/*   yes - get previous block */
90              if( newblk != NULLREC )   /*    check for index begin*/
91                { CB(l) = newblk ;  /*       no - make current */
92                                    /*          get into memory */
93                    retrieve_block(l,CB(l),pb,CURR) ;
94                    CO(l)=last_entry(pb); /* offset = last entry */
95                }
96              else return( NULLREC ) ;/*       at begin. of index - */
97            }                       /*          can't back up */
98          return( ENT_ADR(pb,CO(l))->rptr ) ;/* current entry record */
99      }
100
101
102
103     void get_current(pe,pix)    /* get current index entry */
104     ENTRY *pe ;                 /* put the entry here */
```

Figure 6.18   continues

Figure 6.18   continued

```
105     IX_DESC *pix ;                    /* points to an index descriptor */
106     {
107        pci = pix ;
108        copy_current(0,pe) ;    /* copy it */
109     }
```

Unlike the `first_ix` and `final_ix` functions just discussed, `next_ix` starts at the leaf level. If there is a next entry in the leaf level block, the process is finished. If we are at the end of the block, we use `next_ix` to find the next entry at the index level above the current one. This entry contains the record pointer for the new current block, and `next_ix` returns it. `next_ix` keeps advancing the position at higher levels until we can get a next entry at some level or until we get past the root block. The `last_ix` function works in a similar way. It just looks for the previous entry instead of the next one.

Both `get_next` and `get_previous` copy the entry at the new current position to the address supplied as an input argument. Both functions must accommodate exception cases when the index file is positioned at the beginning or end of the file. Note that `get_next` avoids moving past the dummy entry at the end of the file. For `get_previous`, the beginning-of-file exception is signaled by the `last_ix` function returning a `NULLREC` value (`last_ix` is called with `l` equal to `pci->dx.nl`).

bt_block.c

We are finally in sight of the find, insert, and replace functions that are the main purpose of the BTREE module. Figure 6.19 shows functions that support those operations on a single block.

FIGURE 6.19   bt_block.c

```
 1      /* bt_block.c - block level stuff */
 2      #include "stdio.h"
 3      #include <string.h>
 4      #include "btree.h"
 5      #include "bt_macro.h"
 6
 7      extern IX_DESC *pci ;
 8
 9
10                                      /* look for a key in a block */
11      int find_block(pe,pb,poff,comp_fun)
12      ENTRY *pe ;                     /* contains the target key */
13      BLOCK *pb ;                     /* look in this block */
14      int *poff ;                     /* store offset where we stop here */
15                                      /* address of the compare function */
16      int (*comp_fun) ( void *, void *) ;
17      {                               /* returns the compare result */
18         int i ;                      /* offset */
```

Figure 6.19   continues

Figure 6.19   continued

```
19          int ret ;                  /* result of last comparison */
20          ENTRY *p ;
21
22          i = 0 ;
23          while( i < pb->bend )      /* repeat until end of block */
24            { p = ENT_ADR(pb,i);/* get entry address */
25                                      /* compare to target key */
26              ret = comp_fun( pe , p ) ;
27              if( ret <= 0 )      /* quit when the target is */
28                  break ;         /*   <= the current entry */
29              i = next_entry(pb,i) ;  /* move to next entry */
30            }
31          *poff = i ;                /* store offset where we stopped */
32          return( ret ) ;            /* result of last compare */
33        }
34
35
36
37      void ins_block(pb,pe,off)    /* add an entry to a block */
38      BLOCK *pb ;                  /* the block */
39      ENTRY *pe ;                  /* the entry to insert */
40      int off ;                    /* the offset where we insert it */
41      {
42          int ne ;
43
44          ne = ENT_SIZE(pe) ;      /* how big is the new insert ? */
45                      /* move everything to end of block */
46          moveup( pb,off,ne) ;     /* make room for new entry */
47          copy_entry(ENT_ADR(pb,off),pe) ; /* move it in  */
48          pb->bend = pb->bend + ne ;    /* adjust block size */
49        }
50
51
52      void del_block(pb,off)       /* remove an entry from a block */
53      BLOCK *pb ;                  /* the block to work on */
54      int off ;                    /* where to remove the entry */
55      {
56          int ne ;
57
58          ne = ENT_SIZE( ENT_ADR(pb,off) ) ; /* get entry size */
59          movedown(pb,off,ne) ;    /* move entries above curr. one down*/
60          pb->bend = pb->bend - ne ;    /* adjust number of bytes used*/
61        }
62
63
64      void moveup(pb,off,n)        /* move part of a block upward */
65      BLOCK *pb ;                  /* the block */
66      int off ;                    /* place to start moving  */
67      int n ;                      /* how far up to move things */
68      {
69          ENTRY *p ;
70
71                                    /* move entries */
72          memmove(  (void *) ENT_ADR(pb,off+n), /* to here */
73                  (void *) ENT_ADR(pb,off) , /* from here */
74                  pb->bend - off) ;   /* rest of the block */
75        }
```

Figure 6.19 continues

Figure 6.19   continued

```
76
77
78     void movedown(pb,off,n)      /* move part of a block downward */
79      BLOCK *pb ;                 /* the block */
80      int off ;                   /* place to start moving  */
81      int n ;                     /* how far down to move things */
82      {
83          ENTRY *p ;
84
85                                   /* move entries */
86          memmove( (void *) ENT_ADR(pb,off), /* to here */
87                  (void *) ENT_ADR(pb,off+n),  /* from here */
88                  pb->bend - (off+n)) ;  /* rest of the block */
89      }
90
91
92     void combine(pl,pr)          /* combine two blocks */
93      BLOCK *pl ;                  /* add left block */
94      BLOCK *pr ;                  /* to right block */
95      {
96          moveup(pr,0,pl->bend) ;/* make room for left block */
97                                   /* move in left block contents */
98          memmove( (void *) ENT_ADR(pr,0), (void *) ENT_ADR(pl,0),
99             pl->bend) ;
100         pr->bend = pr->bend + pl->bend ; /* adjust block size */
101     }
```

The find_block function searches a single block for a specified key value. It stops when the end of the block is reached or when an entry is found with a key greater than or equal to the search value. The result of the last compare operation is returned with the offset in the block where the search stopped.

ins_block inserts an entry into a block. It moves the entries from the insertion point to the end of the block upward to make room and copies the new entry into the block. The bend field is adjusted for the increased size of the block.

The del_block function removes an entry from a block. It moves entries downward to fill the hole and adjusts the bend field downward.

combine merges two blocks. It makes room for and copies the contents of the left block to the front of the right block. The bend field is the total of the two original sizes.

The moveup and movedown functions shuffle part of a block up to create a hole or down to fill one. They support the insertion, deletion, and combining functions just described.

bt_find.c

The find_ix function in Figure 6.20 searches an index file for a specified key value. In the process, it establishes a new current position in the index file. If the search was successful, this position is at the first entry whose key matches the search value. If the search did not find a match, the current position will be at the first entry whose key is greater than the search value. This current position can be used for subsequent insertions or deletions.

FIGURE 6.20   bt_find.c

```
1    /* bt_find.c - find function */
2    #include "stdio.h"
3    #include "btree.h"
4    #include "bt_macro.h"
5    extern IX_DESC *pci ;
6
7
8    int find_ix(pe,pix)              /* find first entry with a key */
9     ENTRY *pe ;                     /* points to key to be matched */
10                                     /* store the rec. loc. here */
11    IX_DESC *pix ;                   /* points to index descriptor */
12    {                                /* returns success=1 , failure=0 */
13        int ret ;
14        ENTRY tempe ;
15
16        pci = pix ;
17                                     /* be sure target is < dummy */
18        if( pci->pcomp(pe,&pci->dx.dume) >= 0 )
19          { go_last(pix) ;      /*     no - position at end */
20            return( 1 ) ;       /* and return not equal */
21          }
22
23        ret = find_level(pci->dx.nl-1,pe,pci->dx.rb) ;
24        if( ret == 0 )          /* if an entry was found, */
25          { copy_current(0,&tempe);   /*    store its record ptr. */
26            pe->rptr=tempe.rptr ;
27          }
28        return( ret ) ;
29    }
30
31
32    int find_level(l,pe,r)           /* find a key within a level */
33     int l ;                         /* the level */
34     ENTRY *pe ;                     /* the target entry */
35     RECPOS r ;                      /* block to look in */
36    {
37        BLOCK b ;
38        int ret , off ;
39
40        retrieve_block(l,r,&b,CURR);/* get current block */
41                                     /* look for the key there */
42        ret = find_block(pe,&b,&off,pci->pcomp) ;
43        CB(l) = r ;                  /* make this the current block */
44        CO(l) = off ;                /* and offset in the block */
45
46        if( l > 0 )                  /* now search lower levels */
47            ret = find_level(l-1,pe,ENT_ADR(&b,off)->rptr) ;
48        return( ret ) ;
49    }
```

find_ix first checks to ensure that the search key is not greater than that of the dummy entry at the end of the index. This is a simple way of ensuring that we do not leave the current position past the dummy entry. find_ix calls find_level to start at the root level. At each level find_level searches the block whose record pointer was an input argument. This establishes the current offset on this level. The record pointer from the current entry supplies the record pointer to be used in a call to find_level for the next lower level.

Note that the scratch block b is a local variable. A separate copy is allocated for each level.

bt_ins.c

Figure 6.21 lists the insert_ix function that inserts new entries and the functions that support it. insert_ix calls ins_level to insert the entry at the leaf level. If there is room in the current block, the entry is inserted and the block updated. But if there is no room to insert the entry in the block, split is called to split the block into two blocks.

split copies the current block into an oversize scratch block (allocated in line 70) and inserts the new entry. Then it finds the offset where the block must be split.

FIGURE 6.21 bt_ins.c

```
1     /* bt_ins.c - insert function */
2     #include "stdio.h"
3     #include <stdlib.h>
4     #include <string.h>
5     #include "btree.h"
6     #include "bt_macro.h"
7
8     extern IX_DESC *pci ;
9     extern int split_size ;      /* threshold for splitting a block */
10    extern BLOCK spare_block ;
11
12
13    int insert_ix(pe,pix)          /* find first entry with a key */
14      ENTRY *pe ;                  /* points to key to be matched */
15                                   /* store the rec. loc. here */
16      IX_DESC *pix ;               /* points to index descriptor */
17      {                            /* returns success=1 , failure=0 */
18         int ret ;
19         BLOCK b ;
20
21         pci = pix ;
22         ret = ins_level(0,pe,&b) ; /* insert entry at leaf level */
23
24         if( ret ==IX_OK)          /* if the insertion worked */
25            next_ix(0,&b) ;        /*    move past entry inserted */
26
27         return( ret ) ;          /* return success / failure */
```

Figure 6.21   continues

Figure 6.21   continued

```
28       }
29
30
31     int ins_level(l,pe,pb)        /* insert an entry at */
32     int l ;                       /* this level */
33     ENTRY *pe ;                   /* points to the entry */
34     BLOCK *pb ;
35     {
36        RECPOS r ;
37        int ret ;
38
39        if( l >= pci->dx.nl )  /* do we need a new level ? */
40            return( IX_FAIL ) ;/*    yes - overflow */
41
42        retrieve_block(l,CB(l),pb,CURR) ;
43                               /* does it fit into the block ? */
44        if( (pb->bend + ENT_SIZE(pe)) <= split_size )
45          { ins_block(pb,pe,CO(l)); /*   yes - put entry into block*/
46            update_block(pb) ;
47            ret = IX_OK ;
48          }
49        else ret = split(l,pe,pb);   /*   no - split the block */
50
51        return( ret ) ;
52     }
53
54
55     int split(l,pe,pb)            /* split a block into two */
56     int l ;
57     ENTRY *pe ;
58     BLOCK *pb ;
59     {
60        int half , ins_pos , last , ret ;
61        BLOCK *pbb ;
62        ENTRY e ;
63
64        ins_pos = CO(l) ;         /* remember where insert was */
65
66        if( (l+1) >= pci->dx.nl ) /* check for top level */
67            return( IX_FAIL ) ;/* (can't split top level block) */
68
69                               /* allocate a big block */
70        pbb = (BLOCK *) calloc(sizeof(BLOCK)+sizeof(ENTRY),1) ;
71        if( pbb == NULL )      /* did allocation fail ? */
72            return( IX_FAIL ) ;/*    yes - exit */
73
74                               /* do insert in big block */
75        pbb->bend = 0 ;
76        combine(pb,pbb);         /* copy contents of old buffer */
77        ins_block(pbb,pe,CO(l));  /* insert new entry */
78
79                               /* now find where to split */
80                               /* no more than 1/2 in left block */
81        last =  scan_blk(pbb, pbb->bend/2 ) ; /* start of last */
82                               /* entry in left half of big block */
83        half = next_entry(pbb,last);/* end of left half */
84
```

Figure 6.21   continues

Figure 6.21   continued

```
85                                      /* get disk space for left block */
86              if( get_block(l,pbb) == IX_FAIL )  /* check for failure */
87                { free(pbb) ;
88                  return( IX_FAIL) ;
89                }
90                                      /* make an entry for the new block */
91                                      /* on the upper level */
92              copy_entry(&e,ENT_ADR(pbb,last) ) ;
93              e.rptr = pbb->brec ;    /* point the entry to our left block*/
94
95              ret=ins_level(l+1,&e,pb); /* inserting new index entry   */
96                                      /* for left block at higher level */
97                                      /* (this makes the l+1 position */
98                                      /*  point to the left block) */
99               if( ret != IX_OK )     /* check for failure at higher level*/
100                 { free(pbb) ;       /*   yes - free big block area */
101                   put_free(pbb) ;   /*           free new index block */
102                   return( ret ) ;   /*           return failure code */
103                 }
104
105                                     /* use pb for right block */
106              memmove( (void *) ENT_ADR(pb,0),
107                       (void *) ENT_ADR(pbb,half), pbb->bend-half) ;
108              pb->bend = pbb->bend - half ;
109              pb->brec = CB(l) ;      /* restore block's location */
110              pb->lvl  = l ;          /* and its level */
111              update_block(pb) ;      /* and update it */
112
113                                     /* fix up left block */
114              pbb->bend = half ;      /* size = left half */
115                                      /* entries already in place */
116              update_block(pbb) ;     /* update left block */
117
118                                     /* adjust current position */
119              if( ins_pos >= half )   /* current entry in left or right? */
120                { CO(l) = CO(l)-half ; /*   right - adjust offset   */
121                  next_ix(l+1,pb);    /*            upper level pos. */
122                }
123              else CB(l) = e.rptr ;   /*   left - make left block current */
124              free(pbb) ;             /* free the big scratch block */
125
126              return( ret ) ;
127         }
```

A new block is allocated in the file to hold the first half of the scratch block's contents. The current block will contain the right half of the scratch block's contents.

Before we carry out the split, we call `ins_level` to insert a new entry in the higher level index pointing to the new block. If this step fails, we exit from `split` without finishing the splitting operation. This leaves the index file as it was before `insert_ix` was called. If the call to `ins_level` was successful, the right and left blocks are formed and updated.

Splitting the current block requires adjusting the current position; what to adjust depends on whether the new position is in the left or right block. Lines 119 to 122 perform this adjustment. `ins_level` and `split` leave the current position at the entry just inserted. This is what we want for higher levels, but `insert_ix` advances the final position so that it is after the entry inserted. Thus a series of insertions leaves the entries in the order of insertion.

The recursive function `find_level` (Figure 6.20) declares a local variable to store the current block each time it is called. The insertion functions use a different strategy; they use a single memory area for all levels. But since a split at one level may require further splits at higher levels, each call to `split` allocates its own oversize scratch block.

`insert_ix` is a very low-level function. It is up to the calling program to ensure that the index file is positioned where the entry belongs. The `find_ins` function discussed later searches for the right position before inserting an entry. It is safer and would normally be used.

bt_del.c

The source file in Figure 6.22 shows several functions that implement entry deletion. The application program calls `delete_ix` to delete an entry at the current position. `delete_ix` calls `del_level` to delete the current entry at the current level. If the current block is more than half full, `delete_ix` updates the block. But if the block is empty after the deletion, the block is returned to the free list and the upper level entry that points to the block is deleted (by calling `del_level`). Since the current block has been deleted, the current position at this level and below must be reestablished. The diagram in Figure 6.23 shows this situation before such a deletion and after.

If a block is not empty but less than half full, the `compress` function tries to combine it with a neighboring block on the left or right. This requires that the neighbor block exist and that the contents of both blocks fit in one block.

FIGURE 6.22   bt_del.c

```
1      /* bt_del.c - delete function */
2      #include "stdio.h"
3      #include "btree.h"
4      #include "bt_macro.h"
5      extern int split_size ;        /* threshold for spiltting blocks */
6      extern IX_DESC *pci ;
7      extern int comb_size ;         /* threshold for combining blocks */
8
9
10     int delete_ix(pix)             /* delete current entry */
11      IX_DESC *pix ;                /* points to index descriptor */
12      {                             /* returns success=1 , failure=0 */
13         ENTRY tempe ;
14         BLOCK b ;
15         int ret ;
16
17         pci = pix ;
```

Figure 6.22   continues

Figure 6.22   continued

```
18                                   /* check for dummy entry */
19                                   /* at end-of-ix */
20          copy_current(0,&tempe) ;
21          if( pci->pcomp(&tempe,& pci->dx.dume) == 0 )
22              return( IX_FAIL ) ;
23                                   /* not at end - delete it */
24          ret = del_level(0,&b) ;
25
26          return( ret ) ;
27      }
28
29
30      int del_level(l,pb)          /* delete entry within the level */
31      int l ;
32      BLOCK *pb ;
33      {
34          RECPOS r ;
35          int ret ;
36          ENTRY tempe ;
37
38          ret = IX_OK ;
39          retrieve_block(l,CB(l),pb,CURR) ; /* get current block */
40          del_block(pb,CO(l)) ;    /* delete the entry in the block */
41
42          if( pb->bend == 0 )      /* block now empty ? */
43              { put_free(pb) ;     /*    yes - free the block */
44                  ret = del_level(l+1,&tempe);/*    delete empty block entry */
45                  copy_current(l+1,&tempe) ;/*  get new curr. block ptr. */
46                                   /* reset pos. for this/lower levels */
47                  first_ix(l,tempe.rptr,pb);
48                  return( ret ) ;
49              }
50          if( CO(l) >= pb->bend )/* last entry in block deleted ? */
51              {                    /*    yes - correct upper index */
52                  fix_last(l,pb->brec,ENT_ADR(pb,last_entry(pb))) ;
53              }
54          if( pb->bend < comb_size)  /* less than half full ? */
55              ret = compress(l,pb) ; /*  yes-try combine with neigh. */
56          else update_block(pb) ;
57
58          retrieve_block(l,CB(l),pb,CURR) ; /* get our block again */
59          if( CO(l) >= pb->bend) /* is position past end of block ? */
60              first_ix(l,next_ix(l+1,pb),pb);/* y-move to next block */
61          return( ret ) ;
62      }
63
64
65      int compress(l,pb)           /* combine a block with a neighbor */
66      int l ;
67      BLOCK *pb ;                   /* the block to be combined */
68      {
69          int nb ;
70          BLOCK *pt ;
71          ENTRY tempe ;
72
73
74          if( (l+1) == pci->dx.nl )   /* is this the root level ? */
```

Figure 6.22   continues

Figure 6.22   continued

```
 75                   { update_block(pb) ; /*      yes - update the block */
 76                     return( IX_OK ) ;   /*              and return */
 77                   }
 78
 79           pt = neighbor(l,LEFTN);/* get left neighbor block */
 80           if(    (pt != NULL)
 81                  && (pt->bend +pb->bend <= IXB_SPACE) )
 82                { combine(pt,pb) ;       /* combine blocks */
 83                  update_block(pb) ; /* update right block */
 84                  put_free(pt) ;         /* free the left index block */
 85                                         /* CB(l) is OK as is */
 86                  CO(l) = CO(l) + pt->bend ; /* adjust our curr. pos. */
 87                  last_ix(l+1,pb) ;  /* point higher level to left blk. */
 88                  del_level(l+1,pb) ;/* delete ptr. to left block */
 89                  return( IX_OK ) ;
 90                }
 91
 92           pt = neighbor(l,RIGHTN) ;  /* get right neighbor block */
 93           if(    (pt != NULL)
 94                  && (pt->bend +pb->bend <= IXB_SPACE) )
 95                { combine(pb,pt) ;       /* combine blocks */
 96                  update_block(pt) ;/* update right block */
 97                  CB(l) = pt->brec ;/* right block is the curr. one now */
 98                                         /* CO(l) is ok as is */
 99                  put_free(pb);          /* free the left block */
100                  del_level(l+1,pb);/* delete ptr. to left block */
101                  return( IX_OK ) ;
102                }
103
104           update_block(pb) ;        /* can't combine - just update blk. */
105           return( IX_OK ) ;
106      }
107
108
109
110      int fix_last(l,r,pe)              /* fix higher level index */
111      int l ;                           /* level we are on */
112      RECPOS r ;                        /* rptr for higher level entry */
113      ENTRY *pe ;                       /* entry with new key */
114      {
115          ENTRY tempe ;
116                                         /* last entry in a block was */
117                                         /* deleted or replaced */
118                                         /* update higher level index */
119          copy_entry(&tempe,pe) ;/* copy key */
120          tempe.rptr = r ;              /* put in the record pointer */
121          return( replace_entry(l+1,&tempe) ) ; /* replace the entry */
122      }
123
124
125      int replace_entry(l,pe)           /* replace current index entry */
126      int l ;                           /* at this index level */
127      ENTRY *pe ;                       /* new entry */
128      {
129          BLOCK b ;
130          int ret ;
131
```

Figure 6.22   continues

Figure 6.22 continued

```
132        retrieve_block(l,CB(l),&b,CURR) ;    /* get the index block */
133        if( CO(l) == last_entry(&b))/* is this the last entry ? */
134            fix_last(l,CB(l),pe) ;   /*    yes - fix up higher lvl */
135
136        del_block(&b,CO(l)) ;   /* remove the current entry */
137                                /* room to insert the new entry? */
138        if( (b.bend + ENT_SIZE(pe)) <= split_size )
139           { ins_block(&b,pe,CO(l)) ;/*  yes - insert in the block */
140             update_block(&b) ;       /*          and update the block*/
141             ret = IX_OK ;
142           }
143        else ret = split(l,pe,&b) ; /*   no - split the block */
144        return(ret);
145    }
```

FIGURE 6.23   Deleting the Only Entry in a Block

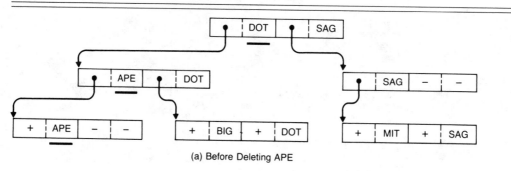

(a) Before Deleting APE

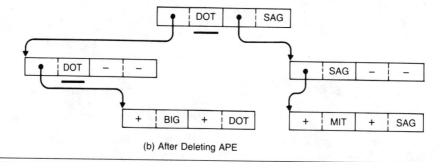

(b) After Deleting APE

Lines 79 to 90 combine the current block with its left neighbor, whereas lines 92 to 102 combine it with its right neighbor. The two cases are similar, but there are some differences. In both cases we place the combined contents into the right of the two blocks and remove the left block. The left block is freed and the higher level entry that pointed to it is deleted by calling `del_level`. The current position is adjusted after combining blocks; the adjustment needed differs for the two cases.

Deleting entries is a messy process with lots of exception cases to be handled. If the last entry in a block is deleted, the key value in the higher level entry that points to the block must be replaced by that of the new last entry. (Figure 6.24 shows an example — deleting the `DOT` entry from the tree in Figure 6.23a.) The `fix_last` and `replace_entry` functions implement this replacement. Since the new key may be different in length from the old value, the process is like a deletion followed by an insertion.

FIGURE 6.24   Deleting the Last Entry in a Block

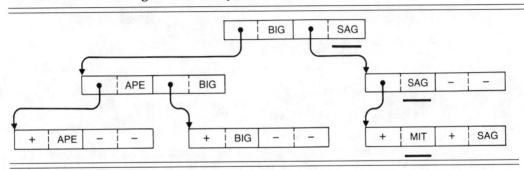

A related exception occurs when a deletion leaves the current position at the end of a block. Lines 59 and 60 check for this condition and, if it is found, reset the position to be at the first entry in the next block. The call to `next_ix` advances the higher level position and returns the record pointer to the new current block. Calling `first_ix` sets the current position to the first entry in this block and also sets the position of lower levels down to the leaf level.

Like `insert_ix`, the `delete_ix` function requires that the current position in the index file be established before it is called. The `find_del` function searches for the entry first to set the current position and then calls `delete_ix`.

bt_low.c

The `neighbor` function in Figure 6.25 looks for the left or right neighbor of the current block. It first retrieves the current block for the next higher level and checks for the presence of a neighbor block. If the requested neighbor block exists, it is retrieved and placed in the `spare_block` structure. An input argument specifies the left or right neighbor block.

The `copy_current` function gets the entry at the current position on a specified level. It first retrieves the current block and then copies the entry at the current offset.

FIGURE 6.25   bt_low.c

```
1       /* bt_low.c - low-level functions for BTREE module */
2       #include "stdio.h"
3       #include "btree.h"
4       #include "bt_macro.h"
5
6       extern IX_DESC *pci ;
7       extern BLOCK spare_block ;
8
9                                    /* get block to right of curr. one */
10      BLOCK *neighbor(l,direction)
11      int l ;                      /* level to fetch neighbor on */
12      int direction ;             /* left or right neighbor */
13      {
14          RECPOS rnext ;
15          int off ;
16          BLOCK *pb ;
17
18          pb = & spare_block ;
19          l = l + 1 ;              /* look in higher level index */
20          retrieve_block(l,CB(l),pb,CURR) ;
21                                   /* get offset on next/prev. entry */
22          if( direction == RIGHTN )
23              off = next_entry(pb,CO(l));/* get offset of next entry */
24          else
25              off = prev_entry(pb,CO(l));/* get offset of prev. entry*/
26
27          if( off < 0 )            /* at end or beginning ? */
28              return( NULL ) ;
29          rnext = ENT_ADR(pb,off)->rptr ; /* neighbor's block no. */
30                                   /* read it into memory */
31          retrieve_block(l-1,rnext,pb,NOT_CURR) ;
32          return( pb ) ;           /* return its address */
33      }
34
35
36      int copy_current(l,pe)       /* copy current index entry */
37      int l ;                      /* at this level */
38      ENTRY *pe ;                  /* to this address */
39      {
40          BLOCK *pb ;
41
42          pb = & spare_block ;
43          retrieve_block(l,CB(l),pb,CURR);/* get curr. block */
44                                   /* copy current entry */
45          copy_entry(pe,ENT_ADR(pb,CO(l) ) ) ;
46          return( IX_OK ) ;
47      }
```

bt_top.c

The functions discussed so far also provide the capabilities we need for managing index files. However, they are rather low level and dangerous. For example, the insert_ix function inserts an entry at the current position. If that position has not been set correctly by a previous call to the BTREE module, index entries may be out of order. The functions in Figure 6.26 are more convenient to use and safer.

FIGURE 6.26   bt_top.c

```
1     /* bt_top.c - find_exact, find_ins find_del functions */
2     #include "stdio.h"
3     #include "btree.h"
4     #include "bt_macro.h"
5     extern IX_DESC *pci ;
6
7     int find_exact(pe,pix)        /* find entry with same key and rptr*/
8     ENTRY *pe ;                   /* put the entry here */
9     IX_DESC *pix ;                /* points to an index descriptor */
10    {
11        int ret ;
12        ENTRY e ;
13
14        pci = pix ;
15        copy_entry(&e,pe) ;       /* make copy for find call */
16        ret = find_ix(&e,pix); /* get first entry that matches key */
17
18        while( ret == 0 )         /* keep going until keys don't match*/
19            { if( e.rptr==pe->rptr) /* compare rec. ptrs */
20                return( 0 ) ;  /* return if they match */
21                              /* ptrs. not same - continue */
22            if( get_next(&e,pix) == EOIX ) /* get next entry */
23                return( 1 ) ;  /*  at end-of-index - not found */
24            ret = pci->pcomp (&e,pe) ; /* compare keys */
25            }
26        return( ret ) ;           /* not found - nonzero code */
27    }
28
29
30    int find_ins(pe,pix)          /* find position and insert an entry*/
31    ENTRY *pe ;                   /* the entry */
32    IX_DESC *pix ;                /* points to an index descriptor */
33    {                             /* returns IX_FAIL if entry present */
34        int ret ;
35        ENTRY tempe ;
36
37        if(find_exact(pe,pix) == 0)  /* look for the entry */
38            return( IX_FAIL ) ;/*    already there - failure */
39                              /* the find set the curr. pos. */
40        return(insert_ix(pe,pix)) ;  /* do the insertion */
41    }
42
43
44    int find_del(pe,pix)          /* find position and delete an entry*/
45    ENTRY *pe ;                   /* the entry */
46    IX_DESC *pix ;                /* points to an index descriptor */
```

Figure 6.26   continues

Figure 6.26   continued

```
47      {                                    /* returns IX_FAIL if not found */
48          int ret ;
49          ENTRY tempe ;
50
51          if(find_exact(pe,pix)  !=0)    /* look for the entry */
52              return( IX_FAIL ) ;/*    not there - failure */
53                                           /* the find set the curr. pos. */
54          return(delete_ix(pix));/* delete the current entry */
55      }
```

find_exact searches for the presence of an entry in an index file. It uses find_ix to get to the first entry whose key matches the search value. Calls to get_next retrieve subsequent entries until the key field no longer matches the search value. The search may also stop when an entry is found with the same record pointer value as well as the same key value. Like find_ix, find_exact serves two purposes. It checks for the presence of an entry and it sets the current position. If the search entry was not found, find_exact sets the current position following all entries with the search key.

find_ins uses find_exact to verify that the entry to be inserted is not already present. If not, the new entry is inserted at the current position that find_exact set.

find_del checks for the presence of an entry using find_exact, and if it is found, calls delete_ix to delete it.

6.6   Analyzing BTREE

The operation of the BTREE module is complex, and it is not obvious how well it performs. This section lists some important questions about the way it uses RAM memory and the amount of disk I/O it performs. The answers are derived from analyzing the source code.

Q. How much RAM memory does BTREE require to store blocks?

Different functions allocate space for blocks differently, so the requirement is different for each function. find_ix requires 1 block per tree level or 4 Kbytes. insert_ix requires 1 Kbyte plus 1.1 Kbytes for each of the three levels split, or 4.3 Kbytes. delete_ix requires 1 Kbyte plus 1 Kbyte for replace_entry on three levels for a total of 4 Kbytes. The spare_block variable is allocated statically so it is always present. The cache buffers require 4 Kbytes per open index file. The total is 5 Kbytes plus 4 Kbytes per open index, or 9 Kbytes for a single index.

Q. What is the effect of forcing the tree to be of maximum height?

A maximum of 3 Kbytes of disk space is wasted for small index files that actually need only one level. The cost in RAM space is 1 Kbyte plus 1 Kbyte per open index file for each extra level in the tree. Since nontrivial index files would have at least two levels, the cost would be 4 Kbytes, at most, with a single index file open.

Performance is not affected much. Those tree levels that are not really needed have a single index block, which stays in the cache buffer. So there is little extra disk I/O.

Q. The functions seem to call retrieve_block a number of times. For example, calls to copy_current retrieve a block that has already been retrieved in another function. Doesn't this hurt performance?

BTREE was designed with maximum separation of its parts. So functions make minimal assumptions about what has already been retrieved. This approach relies heavily on the cache scheme to avoid actual disk I/O on the extra calls to `retrieve_block`.

Q. How many disk I/O operations are needed for common operations such as find_ix, find_ins, and find_del?

Assume that the index file has two levels with more than one index block. Then `find_ix` would require two disk reads. In the common case, an insertion or deletion does not require splitting or combining blocks. So `find_ins` or `find_del` require the same two read operations and a single write operation. (This also assumes that the key value occurs in only a few entries.) A call to `get_next`, `get_previous`, or `get_current` does not require any disk I/O in the normal case because the current block is in the cache for each level.

Q. The linear search used to find a match a key in a block is not very sophisticated. Would a fancier algorithm such as a binary search speed BTREE up much?

The important bottleneck is in disk I/O operations. The effect of a faster method of searching a block would be minimal. BTREE does make lots of function calls and that does seem to add perhaps half a second to the response time for an operation.

In practice, single insertions and deletions as well as searches seem to take a second or two even with the index file on a floppy disk.

6.7   Testing BTREE

The BTREE module is larger and more complex than the programs presented in earlier chapters. The methods we presented also apply to testing BTREE and are even more important. The complexity and size of the BTREE module makes it vital to structure BTREE in a modular way and to test each function thoroughly.

There are many exception conditions to be tested, for example, insertions that cause blocks to split and deletions that require combining a block with its neighbor. If we test the BTREE module as a whole without testing each module, it is very difficult to force the occurrence of exception conditions. Creating index files for each case can be a nightmare. When we test functions individually, we can use dummy I/O functions and force the conditions we want. Thus thorough unit tests are the first step.

Testing the module as a whole is still necessary. When we create and update real index files, we can use the FD program from Chapter 4 to examine the index file. Finding out exactly what is in the file after an update is important, not just checking to see if listing the contents seems to produce the expected result. It takes a lot of data to fit 1,024-byte index blocks, and building large test files to test exception conditions is very difficult. But we can set the `split_size` and `comp_size` variables to force exception conditions to occur for much smaller files.

Several functions in the BTREE module are recursive. It is often useful to track how many times such functions are called by inserting a `printf` statement at the beginning of the function. The following statement was used in the `ins_level` function:

```
printf(" called ins_level - l=%d  pe=%x  pb=%x \n",l,pe,pb);
```

6.8   BTREE Enhancements

Some limitations and simplifications were necessary to keep the BTREE module small enough to list and simple enough to discuss. This section discusses removing those limitations along with other enhancements.

▣   Free Space Management

BTREE manages free space for index blocks in a static way. We specify the size of the index file when it is created. A more flexible approach would be to allow BTREE to extend the index file when the free list was empty. This would reduce the space needed for small index files since they could grow later.

Changing the Tree's Height

BTREE does not allow the index tree to grow in height or shrink. This makes the index file larger than necessary for small numbers of entries. Removing this limitation requires code in `bt_ins.c` to split the root block and create a new index level. Support for shrinking the height of the index tree would be required in `bt_del.c` as well.

Making Dummy Entries

We used a dummy entry with a key value greater than any allowed for a normal entry. This might be inconvenient for some types of keys. How can we construct a dummy key if all possible key values may occur in normal index entries? The compare function must be designed to recognize the dummy entry. One way is to check the `rptr` member as well as the key itself.

Removing the need for a dummy entry is another alternative. This requires support for more exceptions like inserting an entry at the end of the index.

Better Error Handling

BTREE needs more error checking to make it really bulletproof. Disk file read and write operations may produce errors; BTREE should check for them and recover gracefully. Index files may be corrupted so that the format of index blocks is invalid. For example, the file may be missing the dummy entry; the size field `bend` may be invalid in a block; the data in the descriptor block may be invalid. The pointers in index blocks may be scrambled so that two upper level index blocks point to the same block. An index block may be pointed to by an upper level block and may also be on the free list. BTREE should validate everything it reads from an index file.

Since index files are created and used only through the BTREE module, you may wonder why we need to validate their contents. But the index file may be corrupted through misuse of DOS commands or through bugs in DOS, in the application program, or in the BTREE module. A common reason for inconsistencies is that a power failure occurred while an update was in progress (or the user turned off the computer before exiting from a program).

BTREE Utilities

Since index files may become corrupted, we need some utilities to help with the problem. A standalone program that can quickly check the integrity of an index file is good for peace of mind. A repair program that can restore a damaged index file to consistency is another worthwhile utility.

The key to checking for and restoring data integrity is redundancy in the information stored. We recorded the level number within each block, so we could interpret the use of each block without any other source of information. That redundancy could be used to restore an index using only the leaf level blocks.

Better Use of Storage

Our caching scheme is simple and adequate for one or a few indices. But if a number of indices were to be open at the same time, a common pool of buffers for caching would be more efficient in using RAM memory. Another way to reduce the amount of RAM required is to work with the cache buffers directly. We separated working space for blocks from the cache buffers to make the module easier to understand and debug. After the module works and we understand it well, optimizing it at the expense of simplicity is a reasonable next step.

Coupling BTREE with Data Record Management

Most B-Tree file management modules handle both the index and storage of the associated data records. As a result, they lack flexibility to handle the most interesting problems. Our BTREE module handles only the index and does it at a fairly low level. This makes it a flexible tool for a variety of applications. You may wish to build an indexed access module that uses BTREE to provide integrated management of the index and the data record. It should provide for storing and retrieving data records based on one or more keys. The indexed access module should also manage free space for data records as well as for the index blocks.

Key Compression

In some applications, the size of an index file may be reduced by a factor of two or more by storing key values in a compressed form. One method used with character string keys is to store the difference between a key and the one that precedes it in an index block. The part of the key that is the same is replaced by a count of characters that are equal. An example is as follows:

Keys	Stored as
Kettle	0 Kettle
Key	2 y
Kidney	1 idney
Lion	0 Lion

This compression scheme can be very effective on large files where successive keys differ little. The keys can also be truncated to the minimum needed to distinguish them from their neighbors at the expense of retrieving the data record to compare a search value to the full key.

A File Manager Application

Chapter 5 developed a sort/merge program that accepts the description of record type and sort key type when the program is run. We could develop a file manager that accepts a similar description of record and key type. This single program could be used to scan and update a number of files with different specifications. A number of file manager programs work this way. But even if you do not need to write your own program, our BTREE module should show you what is involved.

6.9   A Simple Application: Indexing Correspondence

Our discussion of the BTREE module is not complete without a concrete example of its use. We could build a simple mailing list program that indexed records by name and zip code (or some other filing application with structured records), but such applications are rather common. Instead we present a set of programs to index correspondence documents. The manual page in Figure 6.27 describes the document index programs.

FIGURE 6.27   DOCUMENT Application Description

```
Name
    DOCCREAT , DOCINDEX , DOCSCAN      programs to index documents by
name of addressee, date sent, and subject


Usage
C>doccreat   docs   15000      creates a document index named docs
                               with a 15,000 byte index file.


C>docindex docs                executes the docindex program
doc... name : abc.let
addressee : smith, fred
date sent (yy/mm/dd) : 84/08/05
subject : widget sales
doc... name :
C>


DOCINDEX prompts a document's name and its attributes. Pressing return (and
entering a null document name) ends execution.

                                                  Figure 6.7   continues
```

Figure 6.27 continued

```
C>docscan docs
which field to scan ?
a = addressee / d = date / s = subject : s
value to look for: widget

document file name: abc.let
addressed to: smith, fred
date sent: 84/08/05
subject : widget sales

document file name: weekly.rep
addressed to: jones, sam
date sent: 84/08/07
subject : widget production
...
C>
```

Function

These programs build and maintain an index of correspondence documents. The documents themselves are not stored by the programs, just their file names. DOCCREAT creates a new document index. DOCINDEX adds new documents to the index. DOCSCAN locates documents based on a search value for the addressee, date, or subject attribute. DOCSCAN lists all document references that match the specified criteria. A partial value may be specified for the search. All documents whose attributes match all of the search values are displayed.

Notes

1. Dates must be entered in the form shown: year then month then day. Each part must be two digits with slashes between them.

2. All letters should be entered as lowercase. The programs distinguish uppercase and lowercase.

3. No attempt is made to verify dates, document names, or the field type for DOCSCAN.

The programs do not store documents; they just record the document's name indexed by the addressee's name, the date sent, and the subject. Figure 6.28 shows a data structure describing a document. The document's name and its attributes are stored as character strings.

Separate programs — DOCCREAT, DOCINDEX, and DOCSCAN — create the document index files, add document references, and scan for documents on a specified subject, date, or addressee. The DOCCREAT program shown in Figure 6.29 creates two files: an index file and a data file. Since the BTREE module allocates free blocks for the index file when the file is created, DOCCREAT prompts for and accepts a file size value.

The DOCINDEX program shown in Figure 6.30 adds new document references to the index. For each document, a record is appended to the data file with the document's name, addressee, date sent, and subject. The single index file contains three entries for each document — one for each field indexed.

FIGURE 6.28   document.h

```
1     /* document.h - defines document data structure */
2
3                              /* lengths of document fields */
4     #define NAME_LEN 65
5     #define ADR_LEN  40
6     #define DATE_LEN 10
7     #define SUBJ_LEN 40
8
9     typedef struct
10      { char dname[NAME_LEN] ;  /* document file name */
11        char addressee[ADR_LEN];/* person document sent to */
12        char date[DATE_LEN] ;   /* date the document was sent */
13        char subject[SUBJ_LEN] ;/* subject of the document */
14      } DOCUMENT ;
15
16
17                             /* function prototypes */
18    int cmp_part(char *, char *) ;
19    void add_str(char *,char *, char *) ;
20    int compf( ENTRY * , ENTRY *) ;
21    int sizef( ENTRY *) ;
```

FIGURE 6.29   doccreat.c

```
1     /* doccreat.c - create a document index and data file */
2     #include <stdio.h>
3     #include <stdlib.h>
4     #include <fcntl.h>
5     #include <sys\types.h>
6     #include <sys\stat.h>
7     #include <io.h>
8     #include "btree.h"
9     #include "bt_macro.h"
10    #include "document.h"
11
12    extern ENTRY dume ;
13    extern int ndum ;
14
15
16    main(argc,argv)
17     int argc ;
18     char *argv[] ;
19     {
20       int ret ;
21       char fn[65] ;
22       RECPOS fs ;
23
24       if( argc < 3 )
25         { printf(" USAGE - doccreat doc-file-name file_size \n");
26            exit(5) ;
27          }
28
29       add_str(fn,argv[1],".idx") ;
30
31       ret = sscanf(argv[2],"%ld",&fs) ;
```

Figure 6.29   continues

Figure 6.29   continued

```
32          if( (ret == 0) || (fs < 0) )
33             {  printf(" bad file size specification \n");
34                exit(6) ;
35             }
36
37          if( creatix(fn,fs,&dume,ndum) < 0 )
38             {  printf(" can't create the index file \n");
39                exit(10) ;
40             }
41
42          add_str(fn,argv[1],".dat") ;
43          ret = open(fn,O_WRONLY | O_CREAT | O_BINARY,
44                S_IREAD | S_IWRITE ) ;
45          if( ret < 0 )
46             {  printf(" can't create the data file \n");
47                exit(12) ;
48             }
49          close(ret) ;
50       }
```

FIGURE 6.30   docindex.c

```
1       /* docindex.c - index a new document */
2       #include <stdio.h>
3       #include <stdlib.h>
4       #include <fcntl.h>
5       #include <sys\types.h>
6       #include <sys\stat.h>
7       #include <io.h>
8       #include "getstr.h"
9       #include "cminor.h"
10      #include "btree.h"
11      #include "bt_macro.h"
12      #include "document.h"
13
14      int input( DOCUMENT * ) ;
15      int indexit(DOCUMENT *, RECPOS , IX_DESC *) ;
16
17      main(argc,argv)
18       int argc ;
19       char *argv[] ;
20       {
21         int ret , datfile ;
22         char fn[65] ;
23         RECPOS fs , r ;
24         IX_DESC ixd ;
25         DOCUMENT doc ;
26
27         if( argc < 2 )
28            {  printf(" USAGE - docindex doc-file-name \n");
29               exit(5) ;
30            }
31
32         add_str(fn,argv[1],".idx") ;
```

Figure 6.30   continues

Figure 6.30   continued

```
33          if( openix(fn,&ixd,compf,sizef) < 0 )
34            {  printf(" can't open the index file \n");
35               exit(10) ;
36            }
37
38          add_str(fn,argv[1],".dat") ;
39          datfile = open(fn,O_RDWR | O_BINARY ) ;
40          if( datfile < 0 )
41            {  printf(" can't open the data file \n");
42               closeix(&ixd) ;
43               exit(12) ;
44            }
45
46          while( 1 )                /* collect and index doc. names */
47            { if( input(&doc) <= 0 ) /* get input for next doc. */
48                 break ;            /* exit if at end */
49                                    /* write doc. record at EOF */
50              r = lseek(datfile,0L,SEEK_END) ;
51              ret = write(datfile,&doc,sizeof(DOCUMENT) ) ;
52              if( indexit(&doc,r,&ixd) < 0 )   /* index the document */
53                { printf(" indexing failed \n");
54                  break ;
55                }
56            }
57
58          closeix(&ixd) ;
59          close(datfile) ;
60        }
61
62
63
64      int input(pdoc)              /* get input describing a document */
65       DOCUMENT *pdoc ;
66       {
67         int ret ;
68
69         printf("\n document name (return to quit): ");
70         ret = getstr(pdoc->dname,NAME_LEN-1) ;
71         if( ret <= 0 )
72             return( -1 ) ;
73         printf(" addressed to: ");
74         getstr(pdoc->addressee,ADR_LEN-1) ;
75         printf(" date sent (yy/mm/dd): ");
76         getstr(pdoc->date,DATE_LEN-1) ;
77         printf(" subject: ");
78         getstr(pdoc->subject,SUBJ_LEN-1) ;
79         return( 1 ) ;
80       }
81
82
83      int indexit(pdoc,r,pix)      /* index the document */
84       DOCUMENT *pdoc ;
85       RECPOS r ;
86       IX_DESC *pix ;
87       {
88         ENTRY e ;
```

Figure 6.30   continues

Figure 6.30   continued

```
 89
 90        e.rptr = r ;
 91         add_str(e.key,"A*",pdoc->addressee) ;
 92        if( find_ins(&e,pix) != IX_OK )
 93            return( -1 ) ;
 94        add_str(e.key,"D*",pdoc->date) ;
 95        if( find_ins(&e,pix) != IX_OK )
 96            return( -1 ) ;
 97        add_str(e.key,"S*",pdoc->subject) ;
 98        if( find_ins(&e,pix) != IX_OK )
 99            return( -1 ) ;
100        return( 0 ) ;
101    }
```

The loop in lines 46 to 56 collects input for each document, records it in the data file, and then adds index entries. The input function in lines 64 to 80 prompts for each field in the document record. The getstr function from Chapter 1 collects a line of console input for each field. A null string for the document name is interpreted as the signal to exit the program. Lines 50 and 51 append the document record to the end of the data file.

The indexit function in lines 83 to 101 constructs index entries and inserts them in the index file. The first two characters of the index key field distinguish the different types of entries. Since we are not inserting entries in order by key value, we use the find_ins function to first establish the position in the index.

Figure 6.31 lists the DOCSCAN program. The scan_input function in lines 71 to 86 prompts for the type of field for which we want to scan and a value for the field. It constructs a search key with the type of field — A, D, or S at the front of the key.

FIGURE 6.31 docscan.c

```
 1    /* docscan.c - scan indexed documents */
 2    #include <stdio.h>
 3    #include <fcntl.h>
 4    #include <sys\types.h>
 5    #include <sys\stat.h>
 6    #include <io.h>
 7    #include <stdlib.h>
 8    #include <string.h>
 9    #include <ctype.h>
10    #include "btree.h"
11    #include "bt_macro.h"
12    #include "document.h"
13    #include "keyio.h"
14    #include "getstr.h"
15
16    void scan_input(char *) ;
17    void display_doc(DOCUMENT *) ;
18
19
```

Figure 6.31   continues

Figure 6.31   continued

```
20      main(argc,argv)
21       int argc ;
22       char *argv[] ;
23       {
24         int ret , datfile , line ;
25         char fn[65] ;
26         RECPOS fs ;
27         IX_DESC ixd ;
28         ENTRY e , e2 ;
29         DOCUMENT doc ;
30
31         if( argc < 2 )
32           { printf(" USAGE - docscan doc-file-name \n");
33             exit(5) ;
34           }
35
36         add_str(fn,argv[1],".idx") ;
37         if( openix(fn,&ixd,compf,sizef) < 0 )
38           { printf(" can't open the file \n");
39             exit(11) ;
40           }
41
42         add_str(fn,argv[1],".dat") ;
43         datfile = open(fn,O_RDWR | O_BINARY ) ;
44         if( datfile < 0 )
45           { printf(" can't open the data file  \n");
46             closeix(&ixd) ;
47             exit(12) ;
48           }
49
50          scan_input(e.key) ;
51          ret = find_ix(&e,&ixd) ;
52          get_current(&e2,&ixd) ; /* find out where we are */
53          line = 0 ;
54          while( cmp_part(e.key,e2.key) == 0 )
55            { lseek(datfile,e2.rptr,SEEK_SET) ; /* retrieve the data */
56              read(datfile,&doc,sizeof(DOCUMENT)) ;
57              if( line >= 20 )
58                { printf("\n press a key for more \n") ;
59                  getkey() ;
60                  line = 0 ;
61                }
62              display_doc(&doc) ;
63              line = line + 5 ;
64              if( get_next(&e2,&ixd)  == EOIX )
65                  break ;
66            }
67          closeix(&ixd) ;
68       }
69
70
71      void scan_input(s)
72       char s[] ;
73       {
74          char ans[81] ;
75
```

Figure 6.31   continues

Figure 6.31   continued

```
76              printf(" which field to scan ? \n");
77              printf(" a = Addressee / d = Date / s = Subject :");
78              getstr(ans,80) ;
79              s[0] = toupper(ans[0]) ;
80              s[1] = '*' ;
81              s[2] = '\0' ;
82
83              printf(" value to look for: ");
84              getstr(ans,ADR_LEN-1) ;
85              strcat(s,ans) ;
86          }
87
88
89      void display_doc(pdoc)        /* display one document record */
90      DOCUMENT *pdoc ;
91          {
92              printf("\n document file name: %s \n",pdoc->dname);
93              printf(" addressed to: %s \n",pdoc->addressee);
94              printf(" date sent: %s \n",pdoc->date) ;
95              printf(" subject: %s \n",pdoc->subject) ;
96          }
```

The loop in lines 54 to 66 fetches consecutive entries until an entry fails to match the search key. For each entry, we read the corresponding document record and display it. The find_ix function positions the index file at the first entry less than or equal to the search key. Since find_ix does not provide the entry where the search stopped, we call current_entry to get this entry. Calls to get_next will advance our position and retrieve subsequent entries.

This loop resembles that in the find_exact function. But we use a partial compare function to determine whether to accept the entry. This is a practical requirement because we may not remember the full name of an addressee or the entire subject name of a document. This *generic key* capability of searching an index for all keys that begin with the search value is often useful. Although we did not provide it in the BTREE module itself, our design allows it to be constructed easily.

Figure 6.32 shows the partial comparison function cmp_part and the add_str function used to combine character strings. Figure 6.33 shows compare and entry size functions for character string keys.

FIGURE 6.32   doc_util.c

```
1      /* doc_util.c - utilities for document index programs */
2      #include <stdio.h>
3      #include <string.h>
4      #include <ctype.h>
5      #include "btree.h"
6      #include "document.h"
7
8
9      int cmp_part(s1,s2)            /* compare all chars in s1 to s2 */
10      char s1[] ;                    /* first string */
```

Figure 6.32   continues

Figure 6.32   continued

```
11     char s2[] ;                    /* second string */
12     {
13        int i , n , ret ;
14
15        n = strlen(s1) ;
16        for(i=0 ; i<n ;i=i+1)   /* compare no chars in s1 */
17           { ret = tolower(s1[i]) - tolower(s2[i]) ;
18             if( ret != 0 )
19                 break ;
20           }
21        return( ret ) ;
22     }
23
24
25
26     void add_str(result,s1,s2)  /* concatenate two strings */
27      char result[] ;            /* put the completed result here */
28      char s1[] ;                /* first string */
29      char s2[] ;                /* second string  */
30     {
31         strcpy(result,s1) ;
32         strcat(result,s2) ;
33     }
```

FIGURE 6.33   varsize.c

```
1      /* varsize.c - compare and size functions */
2      /* also dummy key definition */
3      #include <stdio.h>
4      #include <string.h>
5      #include "btree.h"
6      #include "bt_macro.h"
7
8      #define KEY_SIZE   16        /* max length of a key */
9
10     int ndum = 20 ;              /* length of dummy entry */
11
12     ENTRY dume =                 /* dummy entry with high key */
13        { NULLREC , { 0xff , 0xff , 0xff , 0xff ,
14                      0xff , 0xff , 0xff , 0xff ,
15                      0xff , 0xff , 0xff , 0xff ,
16                      0xff , 0xff , 0xff , 0x0 } } ;
17
18
19     int compf(p1,p2)             /* entry compare function */
20      ENTRY *p1 , *p2 ;
21     {
22         return( strcmp( p1->key , p2->key ) ) ;
23     }
24
25
26     int sizef(p1)                /* entry size function */
27      ENTRY *p1 ;
28     {
29         return( strlen(p1->key) + 1 + sizeof(RECPOS) ) ;
30     }
```

Our document index application is quite simple. We omitted features and error checking to keep it short. Better verification of input and better checking for errors would be useful improvements. Allowing dates to be entered in the natural mm/dd/yy form with single digits for month and day would make the programs easier to use as would ignoring upper-/lowercase differences in searches. A facility for deleting old document records would be necessary in a real application, but our simple application should give a helpful example of using BTREE.

Stack Space for the BTREE Module and the DOCUMENT Programs

Some BTREE functions declare index blocks as automatic variables. This requires several thousand bytes of stack space. With other stack space requirements, this is more than the default stack size for Turbo C or Microsoft C can accommodate. For Turbo C, we change the stack size by defining and initializing the _stklen global variable as shown in Figure 6.34. For Microsoft C, a command line option sets the stack size as the following command line fragment shows:

```
C>cl  /F 4000 docindex.c doc_util.c ...
```

FIGURE 6.34   docstack.c Setting Stack Size for Turbo C

```
1    /* docstack.c - set stack size for Turbo C */
2
3    unsigned _stklen = 10000 ;
```

The stack size must be set properly in any other program that uses the BTREE module. The proper size depends on the total amount of space required by the application program and by the BTREE module.

6.10 Enhancements to the DOCUMENT Programs

The DOCUMENT programs provide a simple example of using the BTREE module, but they need some improvements for serious use.

Case-Independent Generic Key Comparison

The DOCSCAN program does not convert a search key to lowercase, and the cmp_part function in Figure 6.32 is case sensitive. Thus search values must be typed in the same case that they were entered in the DOCINDEX program — an inconvenient restriction. The `strcmp` function can be replaced by another library function, `strcmpi`, which is not case sensitive.

🖫 Flexible Date Searching — Searching for Ranges

DOCSCAN should allow us to retrieve all documents dated before or after a search date. The ideas used to implement a generic key search in DOCSCAN also apply to searching for ranges of values. We use the `find_ix` function to position the index and the `get_next` function to retrieve entries that follow.

Date Entry

The DOCUMENT programs should validate date input and allow a more flexible format for dates (for example, no slashes and a single digit for month or day).

Searching with Several Index Fields

If the document index contains a number of entries, we might want to specify search values for several fields. For example, we might search for documents less than six months old written by a specific author. We could retrieve data records using a single index (author, for example), and then we could check the retrieved data records against the other search field values. Another approach would collect a list of index entries for each search field. Then we sort the lists by the record pointer field `rptr` and merge the lists of entries, keeping only those record pointer values that appear in all lists.

6.11 Summary

We have presented a usable module for building and maintaining index files. Our BTREE module provides a low level of support; it is a tool for building applications that require keyed access to data records. The low-level primitives allow you to tailor your application.

Although we had to introduce some limitations, the BTREE module does provide some powerful features. It handles duplicate keys, multiple entries that point to the same data record, multiple indices in use, variable-length keys, and sequential movement through an index. In addition, it allows keys of any data type. Since the application supplies the compare function, ascending or descending order can be arranged as can compound keys.

You should get three things out of this chapter:

1. The BTREE module should allow you to concentrate on the application and use BTREE as a tool for indexing data records.
2. The BTREE module should also provide a good base for enhancements. It is feasible to develop your own module starting from BTREE even if you would not build one from scratch.
3. Our discussion should remove the mystery from keyed file access.

7

A Low-level Toolkit of
IBM PC Specific Tools

The applications presented in earlier chapters are useful in most computer environments not just the IBM PC and MS-DOS environments. And most of the C source files presented in those chapters require no changes for other environments. But those C programs also made use of low-level, system-dependent functions. In this chapter we develop a toolkit containing some PC-specific functions that we need to produce quality applications.

Writing programs that are completely portable is a worthwhile goal. However, it is often necessary to use the features of the operating system and the computer hardware to produce good performance and smooth operation. The C language provides no special features for access to the PC's hardware or to the operating system. The standard C library does use operating system facilities to implement I/O functions, but it does not provide any services tailored to the PC's capabilities. Our toolkit supplements the standard C library with some tools that we need to make full use of the IBM PC's hardware and of the PC-DOS operating system. Once we have written a library of functions to access the PC's hardware and its operating system, we can use these functions as easily as we use C library functions.

Microsoft C, QuickC, and Turbo C all provide libraries with a number of functions for access to MS-DOS and PC features. Where those functions are appropriate, we use them as the basis for our toolkit. However, compiler library functions are often specific to one compiler, and a few library functions may contain serious bugs. Our toolkit illustrates a practical strategy for using compiler library functions. (In the rest of this chapter, references to Microsoft C apply also to QuickC, which provides the same C language features and library functions.)

The Microsoft C and Turbo C compilers support more than one *memory model*. Our toolkit functions are designed to be used with all memory models except the tiny model. Appendix C explains IBM PC memory models and the layout of C programs in RAM memory. A single toolkit function is written in assembly language. Although C is quite versatile, there are cases where assembly language functions are needed. We neither explain the 8088 instruction set nor explain assembly language, because many books discuss these subjects in detail.

The functions developed in this chapter are specific to the IBM PC family and to MS-DOS. (They also apply to PC clones.) However, an equivalent toolkit would be useful in another environment, and our methods for developing it would still apply.

This chapter focuses on some key skills for C programmers. You are not really a complete programmer until you know how to make full use of the capabilities of your computer and its operating system. You will not need all the functions presented in every program that you write, but you will need at least one in most serious programs.

We will develop a variety of tools in this chapter. We start by developing a foundation of low-level functions for basic access to PC hardware and system software. Then we develop modules for timing, printer I/O, keyboard input, and screen output.

7.1 Using Library Functions Intelligently

When C compilers were first introduced for the IBM PC/MS-DOS environment, they offered only a few standard library functions. The problem a C programmer faced was that of augmenting the meager compiler library with PC-specific functions that were needed for good performance and adequate features. Now competition has forced compiler vendors to add many useful PC-specific functions. In some cases, we may still have to write low-level functions from scratch, but we can often apply an existing library function to solve a programming problem. The Turbo C and Microsoft C libraries furnish many functions, and neither compiler's manuals explain the distinctions between alternatives adequately. The rest of this chapter illustrates how we select appropriate library functions and use them intelligently.

The PC environment provides several levels of services to accomplish the same jobs. We can call C standard library functions, which have exact equivalents in other environments but offer limited services. We can use MS-DOS services and PC BIOS services directly. When necessary, we can even read and write PC hardware devices. Turbo C and Microsoft C provide access to all those levels through library functions. Figure 7.1 shows some Microsoft C console I/O functions for each level and how they relate to each other. Note that higher level services such as the standard library make use of lower level services.

A similar hierarchy could be drawn for other services such as file I/O and memory management. This hierarchy diagram is a useful way to understand individual library functions and how they relate to alternative functions. Note that for DOS and BIOS access, the library provides functions specific to console I/O

FIGURE 7.1   Console I/O Function Hierarchy

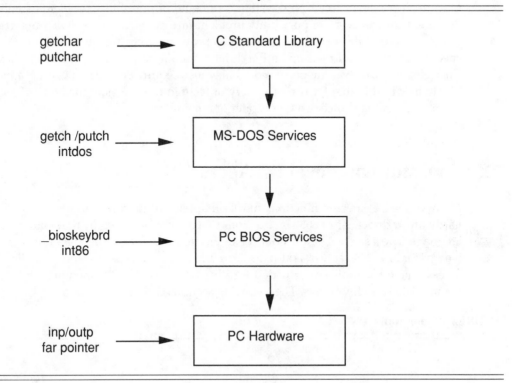

(getch, putch, and _bios_keybrd) and generic functions for access to any DOS or BIOS service (intdos and int86).

A Practical Approach to Portability

There are obvious advantages to using standard library functions rather than lower level functions. However, the standard library does not provide access to all the features of the PC architecture. For example, there are no provisions for setting cursor position or screen attributes in console output. The standard functions for console I/O illustrate another problem: inadequate performance. In most practical programs, a few PC-specific functions are needed to provide the features and performance required for success. A realistic goal is to identify where nonportable functions are needed and to minimize the problems caused by using nonportable functions. This chapter shows how we can isolate the use of nonportable functions in a library, which can be changed and retested for a different compiler, memory model, or even a different environment.

Moving a C program to a different computer environment such as the Apple Macintosh system or to a UNIX system is the kind of portability problem usually discussed. However, other portability problems are more common. Switching to a different C compiler can cause portability problems because the names of PC-specific functions and their operation differ from one compiler library to another. Changing to a different memory model may also require changes in C programs. The toolkit in this chapter uses a variety of techniques to isolate the body of a C program from the choice of a C compiler or a memory model.

7.2   Tools for Low-level PC Access

Many of the PC-specific functions in this chapter require direct access to the PC hardware or direct use of 8088 instructions that are not provided by the standard C language. The asmtools.h header file in Figure 7.2 defines some data types and macros for low-level access. It also declares function prototypes for some low-level access functions. Tools are provided for port I/O, access to PC memory, and for making DOS and BIOS calls. The following sections discuss each class of tools.

FIGURE 7.2   asmtools.h

```
1    /* asmtools.h - definitions for TOOLKIT module */
2
3    #include "cminor.h"
4
5    #define TURBOC 1              /* define this if using turbo C */
6    /* #define MSC 1 */           /* define this if using MS C */
7
8                                  /* include header file to declare */
9                                  /* port I/O functions */
10   #ifdef TURBOC
11   #include <dos.h>
12   #endif
13
14   #ifdef MSC
15   #include <conio.h>
16   #endif
17
18
19   typedef union                 /* 32 bit conversion data type */
20     { long l ;                  /* viewed as long value */
21       struct                    /* viewed as two unsigned values */
22         { unsigned low_word ;
23           unsigned high_word ;
24         } words ;
25     } long_or_words ;
26
27
28   typedef union                 /* 16 bit conversion data type */
29     { int i ;                   /* view as integer */
```

Figure 7.2   continues

Figure 7.2   continued

```
30       struct                      /* view as two bytes */
31         { unsigned char low_byte ;
32           unsigned char high_byte ;
33         } bytes ;
34     } int_or_bytes ;
35
36
37     /* flag bit definitions */
38     #define   ZF_FLAG   0x40
39     #define   AF_FLAG 0x10
40     #define   PF_FLAG 0x04
41     #define   CF_FLAG 0x01
42     #define   TF_FLAG 0x0100
43     #define   SF_FLAG 0x0080
44     #define   IF_FLAG 0x0200
45     #define   DF_FLAG 0x0400
46     #define   OF_FLAG 0x0800
47
48
49                                    /* memory access functions */
50     void lmove(word16 , word16 , word16 , word16 , int ) ;
51     unsigned getbyte(unsigned, unsigned) ;
52     void putbyte(int,unsigned, unsigned) ;
53
54
55
56                                    /* port I/O macros */
57                                    /* Turbo C version */
58     #ifdef TURBOC
59     #define inbyte(p)   ( inportb(p) )
60     #define outbyte(p,b)  ( outportb(p,b) )
61     #endif
62
63                                    /* Microsoft C / Quick C version */
64     #ifdef MSC
65     #define inbyte(p)    ( (unsigned char) inp(p) )
66     #define outbyte(p,b)  ( outp(p,b) )
67     #endif
68
69
70                                    /* macros to convert between */
71                                    /* far pointers and 8086 */
72                                    /* segment:address values */
73     #define SET_FP_OFF(p,o)   (  (*     (unsigned *) & p) = o )
74     #define SET_FP_SEG(p,s)   (  (* ( ((unsigned *) & p) + 1)) = s )
75     #define SET_FP(p,s,o)   ( SET_FP_SEG(p,s) , SET_FP_OFF(p,o) )
76     #define GET_FP_OFF(p)     (  (*  (unsigned *) & p) )
77     #define GET_FP_SEG(p)     (  (* ( ((unsigned *) & p) + 1) ) )
78
79
80                                    /* functions to convert pointers */
81                                    /* to segment and offset values */
82     void get_dads(void *, word16 * , word16 * ) ;
83     void get_fads(void (far *) () , word16 * , word16 * ) ;
84
```

Reading and Writing I/O Ports

The PC's 8088 processor provides special instructions for input and output. These instructions, IN and OUT, can address any of 64K different ports. Many of the PC's hardware capabilities are controlled through these I/O ports. Since there are no C statements to generate IN and OUT instructions and no such standard library functions for port I/O either, we need tools to perform these instructions. Both Turbo C and Microsoft C libraries provide functions for port I/O but with different names and calling sequences. Figure 7.3 describes portable macros for port I/O, which we implement for Microsoft C and Turbo C. Lines 56 to 67 define the inbyte and outbyte macros for port I/O. These macros are defined in terms of the Microsoft C functions inp and outp or the Turbo C functions inportb and outportb. To select the proper definition, we define one of the symbols, TURBOC or MSC in lines 5 and 6 on asmtools.h. (As shown, the TURBOC symbol is defined for use with Turbo C.) The function prototypes for the Microsoft functions are in the header file conio.h, whereas the Turbo C functions are declared in dos.h. Lines 10 to 16 include the appropriate file based on whether the symbols TURBOC or MSC are defined.

FIGURE 7.3   Description of Port I/O Macros

Name
```
inbyte    read in a byte from an 8088 I/O port
outbyte   write a byte to an 8088 I/O port
```

Usage
```
#include  "asmtools.h"
unsigned port_no ;       /* 8088 port number */
unsigned char b ;        /* store the byte read here */

b = inbyte(port_no) ;
outbyte(b,port_no)  ;
```

Function
inbyte performs an 8088 instruction

```
in al,dx
```

using the port number specified by the caller. The byte value read is returned in the register ax. The value returned is between 0 and 255.

outbyte performs an 8088 instruction

```
out dx,al
```

using the port number and byte value specified by the caller.

Figure 7.3 continues

Figure 7.3   continued

Examples
Using `inbyte` to read the configuration switch values on the PC system unit
board:

```
#include "asmtools.h"
int pc_switch ;
...
pc_switch = inbyte(0x62) ;   /* read PC sys. unit switches */
printf(" PC system unit switches %x \n",pc_switch) ;
```

Using `outbyte` to turn on the PC speaker:

```
unsigned char port_value ;
...
port_value = inport(0x61) ;
outport(port_value | 0x01, 0x61) ;   /* turn on PC speaker */
```

Notes
For Turbo C, `inbyte` and `outbyte` are implemented as macros that call the
library functions `inportb` and `outportb`. For Microsoft C and Quick C, `inbyte`
and `outbyte` are macros that call the library functions `inp` and `outp`.

The `asmtools.h` header file makes use of compiler specific functions. It must be
changed to support another compiler. (And lines 5 and 6 would have to be changed
to define the appropriate symbol.) However, the source files that use the `inbyte`
and `outbyte` macros need not be changed but only recompiled. Our techniques
complicate `asmtools.h`, but they make it feasible to use port I/O without making
the rest of our programs specific to one C compiler.

Accessing All of the PC's Memory

Normally, when we write a C program, we define and use variables without
concern for their location in memory. The compiler and linker take care of assigning
memory addresses to variables. This works well for referring to data defined within
our C program. When we must refer to memory areas outside our programs, we
need tools for defining fixed addresses and for reading from and writing to those
fixed addresses.

The size and capabilities of pointers in C programs depend on the memory
model used. In some memory models (the tiny, small, and medium models),
pointers to data objects are 16 bits long. They are interpreted as offsets relative to the
start of a 64 Kbyte data area within the C program. We cannot use such pointers to
refer to data areas outside a C program. In other memory models (compact, large,
and huge), pointers to data objects are 32 bits long and contain an absolute address.
We can refer to data areas outside our programs with 32-bit pointers, and one

solution is to always use a memory model with 32-bit pointers to data objects. But we can provide a solution that works for all memory models. Microsoft C and Turbo C provide a PC-specific keyword, `far`, which allows us to define 32-bit pointers in any memory model. The following code fragment shows how the `far` keyword is used in declarations of pointers:

```
char far *pc ;            /* 32 bit pointer to char data */
struct st far *pst ;  /* 32 bit pointer to struct st type */
```

These far pointers contain an 8088 address in the form of a 16-bit segment value and a 16-bit offset. The offset is stored first and the segment value is in the next 16 bits. Turbo C and Microsoft C provide functions or macros for setting and extracting segment and offset parts of far pointers. Unfortunately the names and operations of these functions are different for each compiler. Figure 7.4 describes portable macros for working with far pointer offset and segment values. Lines 70 to 77 implement these macros.

FIGURE 7.4   Description of Far Pointer Tools

Name

SET_FP_OFF	set offset address in a far pointer variable
SET_FP_SEG	set segment address in a far pointer variable
SET_FP	set offset and segment in a far pointer variable
GET_FP_OFF	get offset value from a far pointer variable
GET_FP_SEG	get segment value from a far pointer variable

Usage
```
#include "asmtools.h"
unsigned seg_adr ;  /* 8088 segment address */
unsigned off_adr ;  /* 8088 offset within a segment */
char far *p ;           /* far pointer to any data type */
SET_FP_OFF(p, off_adr) ;
SET_FP_SEG(p, seg_adr) ;
SET_FP(p, seg_adr, off_adr) ;
off_adr = GET_FP_OFF(p) ;
seg_adr = GET_FP_SEG(p) ;
```

Function

The SET_FP* macros provide a compiler-independent way to set a far pointer to a fixed address. The segment and offset values passed as input arguments may be integer or unsigned expressions (including constants). The first argument must be a pointer variable. The SET_FP macros store the segment and/or offset in the pointer variable named.

The GET_FP* macros extract a 16-bit segment or offset value from a far pointer. This value is returned as an unsigned value.

The SET_FP* and GET_FP* macros work with pointers to any data type.

Figure 7.4   continues

Figure 7.4   continued

Example
To get the first character on the PC screen (mono adapter):

```
#include  "asmtools.h"
char b ;
char far *p ;
SET_FP_OFF(p,0) ;            /* offset = 0 */  or
SET_FP_SEG(p,0xB000) ;       /* segment = B000 */
SET_FP(p,0xB000, 0) ;        /* sets segment and offset */
b = *p ;
```

The following example extracts the segment and offset from a far pointer:

```
#include  "asmtools.h"
char far *p ;
unsigned off_adr , seg_adr ;
off_adr = GET_FP_OFF(p) ;        /* get offset */
seg_adr = GET_FP_SEG(p) ;        /* get segment */
```

Although far pointers are supported by both Turbo C and Microsoft C, they are not available in other computer environments. We do not want to use them directly throughout our source files. Figure 7.5 describes functions that read and write data at locations specified by 8088 segment and offset values. The getbyte and putbyte functions read and write single bytes. The lmove function copies n bytes from one location to another. The memory.c file in Figure 7.6 implements these functions and illustrates the use of far pointers.

FIGURE 7.5   Description of Memory Access Functions

Name
getbyte   get a byte from a memory address
putbyte   store a byte at a memory address
lmove   move bytes from one memory address to another

Usage
```
#include  "asmtools.h"
unsigned seg_adr ;   /* 8088 segment address */
unsigned off_adr ;   /* 8088 offset within a segment */
char b ;                /* store the byte value here */
unsigned getbyte(seg_adr,off_adr) ;
putbyte(seg_adr,off_adr,b)   ;

unsigned from_seg ;        /* get data from here - seg. */
unsigned from_off ;        /*      "       "      - offset */
unsigned to_seg   ;        /* put data here      - seg. */
unsigned to_off   ;        /*      "       "      - offset */
int      nbytes   ;        /* number of bytes to move */

void  lmove(to_seg,to_off,from_seg,from_off,nbytes)   ;
```

Figure 7.5   continues

Figure 7.5 continued

Function

`getbyte` returns the contents of any memory location in the PC. `putbyte` stores a byte of data anywhere in memory. `lmove` moves a specified number of bytes between any two memory locations in the PC. All functions expect 8088 segmented addresses.

Example

To get the first character on the PC screen (mono adapter):

```
#include  "asmtools.h"
b = getbyte(0xb000,0) ;    /* char only */
```

To write an X as the first character on the PC screen (mono adapter):

```
#include  "asmtools.h"
putbyte('X',0xb000,0) ;      /* write char only */
```

To copy a new screenful of data from an array:

```
#include  "asmtools.h"
unsigned  screen_seg = 0xb000 ; /* mono adapter */
unsigned  seg_adr , off_adr ;
char   image[4000] ;      /* a screen image */
                    /* get segment and offset for image array */
get_dads(image, & seg_adr, & off_adr)  ;
lmove(screen_seg,0,seg_adr,off_adr,4000)  ;
```

FIGURE 7.6   memory.c

```
1      /* memory.c - access to PC RAM memory - Turbo C version */
2      #include <dos.h>
3      #include "asmtools.h"
4
5
6      unsigned getbyte(seg,off)    /* get a byte from a memory address */
7       unsigned seg ;             /* segment address */
8       unsigned off ;             /* offset address */
9       {
10        unsigned char far *pmem ;
11
12        SET_FP(pmem,seg,off) ;
13
14        return( *pmem ) ;
15      }
16
17
18     void putbyte(value,seg,off)/* store a byte at a memory address */
19      int value ;               /* value to store */
20      unsigned seg ;            /* segment address */
21      unsigned off ;            /* offset address */
```

Figure 7.6   continues

Figure 7.6   continued

```
22       {
23          unsigned char far *pmem ;
24
25          SET_FP(pmem,seg,off) ;
26          *pmem = value ;
27       }
28
29
30                                  /* move bytes from one memory */
31                                  /* address to another */
32       void lmove(to_seg,to_off,from_seg,from_off,nbytes)
33       word16 to_seg ;            /* destination segment address */
34       word16 to_off ;            /* destination offset address */
35       word16 from_seg ;          /* source segment address */
36       word16 from_off ;          /* source offset address */
37       int nbytes ;
38       {
39          unsigned char far *pto ;
40          unsigned char far *pfrom ;
41
42          SET_FP(pto,to_seg,to_off) ;
43          SET_FP(pfrom,from_seg,from_off) ;
44
45          while( nbytes > 0 )
46            { *pto = *pfrom ;
47              pto = pto + 1 ;
48              pfrom = pfrom + 1 ;
49              nbytes = nbytes - 1 ;
50            }
51       }
52
```

Converting Pointers to Segment and Offset Values

When we use DOS and BIOS services, we often need to convert a regular pointer to a data object into a segment and offset address. The get_dads function described in Figure 7.7 and implemented in Figure 7.8 performs this conversion using a far pointer. These figures also show the get_fads function, which converts a pointer to a function into segment and offset values. For pointers to data objects, this conversion may be done even if the pointer is only 16 bits long. For pointers to functions, this conversion may not be possible for all memory models. For that reason, get_fads is defined only for functions declared with the far keyword.

FIGURE 7.7   Description of Pointer Conversion Functions

Name	
get_dads	translate C data pointer into segmented address
get_fads	translate C function pointer into segmented address

Figure 7.7   continues

Figure 7.7   continued

Usage

```
#include  "asmtools.h"
char msg[] = "error 10 $" ;
void (far *fp)() ;       /* pointer to a far function */
word16 seg ;                  /* segment part of address */
word16 off ;                  /* offset part */
...
void get_dads(msg, & seg, & off) ;
void get_fads(fp, & seg, & off) ;
```

Function

get_dads translates a C pointer to data into an 8088 segmented address. This translation may be different for different memory models and compilers. get_dads hides these differences. get_dads expects three arguments: a C pointer to data of some kind and addresses where the 16-bit segment and offset values of the address will be stored.

get_fads performs a similar translation for pointers to far functions. Note that the function pointer must be declared with the far keyword. The function pointer may refer functions with any number and data types of arguments and any return type.

The word16 data type is declared in cminor.h, which is automatically included by asmtools.h.

Example

```
#include  "asmtools.h"
#include  "dos.h"
#define DISP_STRING 0x09    /* operation code */
#define SET_VECTOR  0x25    /* operation code */
                           /* set interrupt vector */
char msg[] = "error 10 $" ;
char far myfun() ;
word16 seg , off ;
union REGS sreg,dreg ;         /* defined in dos.h */
struct SREGS segreg ;          /* defined in dos.h */
                              /* put address in DS:DX */
get_dads(msg, & segreg.ds, & sreg.x.dx) ;
sreg.h.ah = DISP_STRING ;
intdos( & sreg, & dreg) ;
                              /* put function address in DS:DX */
get_fads(myfun,& segreg.ds ,& sreg.x.dx) ;
sreg.h.ah = SET_VECTOR ;
intdos( & sreg, & dreg) ;
```

Notes

1. As the example suggests, get_dads and get_fads are used to set up arguments for DOS calls.

2. The segment and offset values are defined as 16-bit words by the 8088 architecture. We define them as the word16 data type to ensure that the C compiler allocates 16-bit variables.

FIGURE 7.8   get_dads.c

```
 1     /* get_dads.c - convert C pointer to 8088 segmented address */
 2     /* relies on conversion to far pointer */
 3     /* works for any memory model */
 4     #include "asmtools.h"
 5
 6
 7     void get_dads(p,pseg,poff) /* convert data pointer to seg/off */
 8       void *p ;                   /* data pointer value */
 9       word16 *pseg ;              /* place segment value here */
10       word16 *poff ;              /* place offset value here */
11     {
12         void far *farp ;         /* far pointer variable */
13
14         farp = (void far *) p; /* convert to far pointer */
15         *pseg = GET_FP_SEG(farp) ; /* extract segment part */
16         *poff = GET_FP_OFF(farp) ; /* extract offset part */
17     }
18
19
20     void get_fads(pfun,pseg,poff) /* convert function pointer */
21       void (far *pfun) () ;       /* function pointer value */
22       word16 *pseg ;              /* place segment value here */
23       word16 *poff ;              /* place offset value here */
24     {
25
26         *pseg = GET_FP_SEG(pfun) ; /* extract segment part */
27         *poff = GET_FP_OFF(pfun) ; /* extract offset part */
```

Making DOS and BIOS Calls: Generating Software Interrupts

Using PC-DOS and BIOS services requires executing a software interrupt instruction. Neither the C language nor the standard library provides a mechanism for generating such an instruction, but both Turbo C and Microsoft C provide functions for making calls to MS-DOS and BIOS services. Using these functions requires some information and some special data structures.

When we declare a C variable, we specify a data type that reflects the meaning of the data stored in the variable and the operations we will perform on that data. Occasionally we need to interpret the same data as two different data types. Some library functions for DOS and BIOS calls return an 16-bit integer value that contains two separate 8-bit values. Lines 28 to 34 of Figure 7.2 declare a union data type, int_or_bytes, which allows us to look at a 16-bit value as a single integer or as two separate byte values. Lines 19 to 25 define a union data type, long_or_words, which allows us to view a 32-bit long value as two 16-bit unsigned values. These data types are used in toolkit functions later in this chapter.

In addition to library functions for making specific DOS and BIOS calls, Turbo C and Microsoft C provide similar generic access functions. The int86 function and its variants perform a software interrupt whose number you specify as an input argument. The `intdos` function and its variants perform a specific software interrupt (`0x21`) used for most DOS services. DOS and BIOS services receive input arguments in 8088 registers and return results in those registers. One input argument to `int86` and `intdos` specifies register values for the DOS or BIOS service. Another argument points to an area where register values are saved after the DOS or BIOS call is completed. Since `int86` and `intdos` are used for a variety of calls, they set up more registers and save more returned values than are needed for any one call. A library function that is specific for one service is often more compact and faster in execution than using `int86` or `intdos`. However, when no specific library function is available for a service, these generic functions provide a quick way to get access to the service.

Using intdos

The `int86` function is used in several functions discussed later in this chapter. The source file in Figure 7.9 illustrates use of the `intdos` and `intdosx` functions. (These functions are not intended for actual use since both Turbo C and Microsoft C libraries contain functions performing the same services.)

The `get_drive` function illustrates the basics of using `intdos`. The first argument passed to `intdos` specifies register values when the DOS call is made. The second argument specifies values in registers when the DOS call returns. The data type `union REGS` is defined in `dos.h`. The 8088 registers may be viewed as 16-bit registers or as pairs of 8-bit registers. Line 16 specifies the operation code for the DOS call in the 8-bit AL register. Specifying the operation code in the AL register is a standard convention for calls to MS-DOS functions. Line 19 gets the 16-bit AX register value returned by the DOS call and returns it as the default drive number.

The `get_cd` function gets the name of the current directory. This name is placed at the address specified by the argument `dname`. The DOS call expects a 32-bit address with the 16-bit segment part in the DS segment register and the 16-bit offset part in the SI register. The `intdos` function does not allow us to specify values for segment registers, so we use the `intdosx` function. This third argument specifies values for segment registers. The data type `struct SREGS` is defined in `dos.h`. Lines 35 to 37 check for the success or failure of the DOS call. If the call failed, the AX register indicates the cause. This DOS call indicates success or failure in the carry flag. Both `intdos` and `intdosx` store the carry flag value returned by the DOS call in the `cflag` member of the output register argument. Many DOS calls use the carry flag to indicate success or failure with an error code placed in AX.

FIGURE 7.9   usedos.c

```
 1    /* usedos.c - examples of using DOS services */
 2    #include <dos.h>
 3    #include "stdio.h"
 4    #include "asmtools.h"
 5
 6                                  /* MS-DOS operation codes */
 7    #define CURR_DISK   0x19      /* get default disk number */
 8    #define GET_DIR   0x47        /* get current directory name */
 9
10
11    int get_drive()              /* get default drive number */
12      {                          /* returns 0=A: , 1=B: , 2=C: etc */
13        union REGS s , d ;
14
15        s.h.al = CURR_DISK ;     /* operation code in AL register */
16        intdos( & s, & d ) ;
17                                 /* drive no. is in AL register */
18        return( d.x.ax & 0xff ) ;
19      }
20
21
22
23    int get_cd(dno,dname)        /* get name of current directory */
24      int dno ;                  /* for drive 0=default, 1=a: 2=b: */
25      char dname[] ;             /* put the directory name here */
26      {
27        union REGS s , d ;
28        struct SREGS sr ;        /* segment register structure */
29
30        s.x.dx = dno ;           /* drive number in DX register */
31                                 /* directory name  address in DS:SI */
32        get_dads(dname,& sr.ds,& s.x.si) ;
33        s.h.al = GET_DIR ;       /* operation code in AL */
34        intdosx(& s, & d, & sr) ;
35        if( d.x.cflag == 0 )     /* check carry flag for errors */
36          return( 0 ) ;          /*   no error - return 0 */
37        else return( d.x.ax) ; /*   error - return code in AX */
38      }
```

7.3   A TIMER Module

We often need to keep track of time differences within C programs. Many performance measurements in previous chapters were timed with an elapsed time function rather than by hand. Programs may need to pause for a specific time interval before continuing to execute. Other programs must implement a *time-out* where we wait for some input for a time interval and then perform a recovery action if that input is not received. The TIMER module presented in this section provides functions for creating delays, implementing time-outs, and measuring elapsed times.

The ANSI C standard defines a function time, which returns the number of seconds since a reference date. Although this function is easy to use, we often require a finer resolution than whole seconds. MS-DOS provides a service that returns the time of day in hours, minutes, seconds, and hundredths of seconds. Both Microsoft C and Turbo C libraries provide functions for access to the MS-DOS time service. However, although this format is convenient for displaying the current time, it is very clumsy for computing time differences. The ROM BIOS provides a more useful time-of-day service — it returns the number of ticks since the beginning of the day. Ticks occur at a rate of 18.2 per second, which is an adequate resolution for most requirements. Figure 7.10 describes our TIMER module, and the header file in Figure 7.11 provides function prototypes for the functions.

FIGURE 7.10 Description of the TIMER Module

Name

```
busy_wait        wait until time interval is up
check_wait       check for end of delay interval
elapsed_time     get elapsed time since last call
get_ticks        get time-of-day (in ticks)
```

Usage
```
#include "ct_timer.h"
long t , interval ;
long get_ticks();
long elapsed_time(t) ;
int check_delay(t,interval) ;
int busy_wait(t,interval) ;
```

Function

get_ticks returns the current time of day as a long integer value — the number of ticks since the beginning of the day. (There are about 18.2 timer ticks per second.) The ROM BIOS time-of-day service is the basis for the get_ticks function.

elapsed_time returns the difference between the current time and the time stored in the input argument. A long value is returned, representing the difference in ticks.

check_delay compares the current time to the time specified as an input argument. If that difference is less than the specified interval, check_delay returns a 0 value. If the difference is greater than or equal to the interval, a value of 1 is returned.

busy_wait accepts the same arguments as check_delay, but it does not return until the specified interval has passed. If the starting time argument is the NO_TIME value defined in the ct_timer.h file, busy_wait will get the starting time on entry.

The time-of-day value returned by the BIOS service starts over at zero at the beginning of each day. Thus a starting time may have a larger value than the current time. These functions correct for this condition by assuming that the starting time refers to the preceding day. The functions can measure time differences up to 24 hours.

Figure 7.10 continues

Figure 7.10   continued

Examples
```
#include "ct_timer.h"
long start_time , et ;
...
start_time = get_ticks() ;  /* get starting time */
for(i=0 ; i< 20000 ; i=i+1)   /* spend some time */
    { putchar('A') ; }
et = elapsed_time(start_time) ; /* get elapsed time */
printf(" %6.2f Seconds \n", ( (float) et ) / 18.2) ;

start_time = get_ticks() ;
busy_wait(start_time,182L) ;   /* wait 10 seconds */
start_time = get_ticks() ;     /* get new start time */
...
for(i=0 ; i< 20000 ; i=i+1)   /* write A */
    { putchar('A') ;           /* 20,000 times */
       if( check_delay(start_time,182L) != 0 )
            break ;            /* or for 10 seconds */
    }
printf("\n after 10 seconds, i = %d ",i) ;
```

FIGURE 7.11   ct_timer.h

```
1     /* ct_timer.h - definitions for BIOS-based timer functions */
2
3     #define TICKS_PER_DAY    0x1800B0L
4     #define NO_TIME   -1L
5
6     long get_ticks(void) ;
7     long elapsed_time(long) ;
8     int check_delay(long,long) ;
9     int busy_wait(long,long)  ;
```

Figure 7.12 shows the function get_ticks, on which the module is based. Lines 9 to 14 implement one version for Turbo C, whereas Lines 17 to 33 implement a version for Microsoft C. If the symbol TURBOC is defined in asmtools.h, the Turbo C version is compiled. If the symbol MSC is defined, the Microsoft C version is compiled. The Turbo C library provides a function biostime, which provides access to the BIOS time-of-day service. This function is the basis for the Turbo version of get_ticks. The first argument passed to the biostime function specifies which operation we requested. The second argument, a time-of-day value, is a dummy value here. If we were setting the time-of-day, the second argument would contain a real time-of-day value.

Microsoft C provides a similar function, _bios_timeofday, but in the current versions of Microsoft C (5.1 and earlier) and QuickC (version 2.0 and earlier), this function is not implemented correctly. For Microsoft C and QuickC, we use the general function int86 for access to the time-of-day service. Line 28 sets the operation code in the AH register. Line 29 specifies the software interrupt number for the time-of-day service. The BIOS service places the time-of-day value in the CX

FIGURE 7.12   ct_time1.c

```
1     /* ct_time1.c - gets BIOS time-of-day */
2     #include <bios.h>
3     #include <dos.h>
4     #include "asmtools.h"
5     #include "ct_timer.h"
6
7     #define GET_CLOCK   0           /* operation code */
8
9     #ifdef TURBOC
10                                    /* Turbo C version */
11    long get_ticks()               /* get BIOS time-of-day */
12      {
13        return( biostime(GET_CLOCK,0L) );
14      }
15
16    #else
17                                    /* Microsoft C version */
18                                    /* uses int86 library function */
19
20    #define BIOS_TOD   0x1A         /* software interrupt number */
21
22
23    long get_ticks()               /* get BIOS time-of-day */
24      {
25        union REGS s , d ;
26        long_or_words t ;
27
28        s.h.ah = GET_CLOCK ;
29        int86(BIOS_TOD, & s, & d ) ;
30        t.words.low_word = d.x.dx ;
31        t.words.high_word = d.x.cx ;
32        return( t.l ) ;
33      }
34    #endif
35
```

and DX registers. Lines 30 and 31 assemble the two 16-bit values into a 32-bit `long` value using the `long_or_words` data type.

The functions in Figure 7.13 use the `get_ticks` function to provide more useful services. The `elapsed_time` function measures the time difference between the current time and the previous time specified. If the difference is less than zero, the previous time is assumed to refer to the preceding day and the number of ticks in a day is added to the difference.

The `check_delay` function compares the current time to a starting time to see whether or not the specified interval has passed. This allows a program to check for the expiration of an interval while it is working on some other activity. The `busy_wait` function repeatedly checks for the expiration of a delay interval. It returns only when that interval has expired.

The TIMER module illustrates several points about using library functions. Both ANSI C and MS-DOS provide time services, but neither service is satisfactory for our purpose. Although the BIOS time-of-day service is satisfactory, we do not use it

FIGURE 7.13   ct_time2.c

```
 1    /* ct_time2.c - time functions based on BIOS time-of-day */
 2    /* uses get_ticks function - times are ticks - 18 per second */
 3    #include "ct_timer.h"
 4
 5
 6    long elapsed_time(start_time) /* compute elapsed time */
 7     long start_time ;           /* from this starting time */
 8     {
 9       long diff ;
10
11       diff = get_ticks() - start_time ;
12       if( diff < 0 )
13           diff = diff + TICKS_PER_DAY ;
14       return( diff ) ;
15     }
16
17
18                               /* check for end of delay period */
19    int check_delay(start_time,interval)
20     long start_time ;          /* start of delay period */
21     long interval ;            /* length of delay period */
22     {
23       long diff ;
24
25                                        /* get current time and  */
26       diff = get_ticks() - start_time ; /* compare to start_time */
27       if( diff < 0 )                   /* check for wrap-around */
28           diff = diff + TICKS_PER_DAY ; /*    yes-add 1 day's ticks*/
29       if( interval <= diff )           /* enough delay yet ? */
30           return( 1 ) ;                /*    yes - return true */
31       else return( 0 ) ;               /*    no - return false */
32     }
33
34
35    int busy_wait(start_time,interval)/* wait until interval is up */
36     long start_time ;          /* start of delay period */
37     long interval ;            /* length of delay period */
38     {
39       if( start_time == NO_TIME )    /* is start time given? */
40           start_time = get_ticks() ; /*    no - get starting time */
41
42                               /* wait until delay period is up */
43       while( check_delay(start_time,interval) == 0 )
44         { ; }
45       return(1) ;
46     }
```

directly. Both versions of the get_ticks function merely provide access to the BIOS time-of-day service. However, these source files are necessary; they provide a compiler-independent basis for timer functions, and they isolate our programs from bugs in library functions. The other functions in our TIMER module can be used with any compiler, and the programs that use our timing module are completely isolated from compiler differences and library function bugs.

7.4 Practical Printer Output Functions

The C library provides several ways to write to a printer. In the MS-DOS environment, file I/O can be used for printers that are treated as character devices. Both stream I/O and unbuffered I/O library functions may be used for output to a printer, but there are some reasons why neither is a good approach for serious programs.

First, a printer is not always ready to accept output. Its buffer may be full or it may have been turned off. If we use file I/O functions for printer output, our program may be hung up for a long time waiting to output characters. We need a way to check printer status before writing each character. Second, although printers are most commonly connected through a parallel port, printers may be connected in other ways such as through a serial port. We need a single printer interface module that applies to any printer, no matter how it is connected to the PC. Third, some printers connected via serial ports use the XON/XOFF protocol for flow control. Our printer module must support this protocol and hide the details from C programs using the module.

Figure 7.14 describes a module for printer output. The select_ptr function specifies the type of printer and a printer number. This call sets up the PTR_DATA structure for printer output operations. The structure contains addresses of driver functions for opening a printer connection, checking status, writing a character, and closing the connection. Driver functions are provided for printers connected via parallel ports, serial port printers, and for printing to a disk file.

FIGURE 7.14 Description of Printer Module

```
Name
PTRIO      generic printer module


Usage
#include "ptrio.h"
PTR_DATA pd ;
PTR_FUNS *ptype ;
int ptr_no ;
int select_ptr(& pd, ptype, ptr_no) ; /* select printer type */
            /* open printer function */
pd.funs.open_fun(& pd,options)  ;
            /* check printer status function */
pf.funs.ready_fun(& pd ) ;
            /* write char to printer function */
pf.funs.write_fun(& pd, c) ;
            /* close printer function */
pf.funs.close_fun(& pd ) ;
            /* serial port initialization */
int parms ;
int sptr_init(ptr_no, parms) ;
            /* set name for print file */
char *file_name ;   /* points to new file name string */
int dptr_setfile(file_name) ;
```

Figure 7.14 continues

Figure 7.14   continued

Function

`select_ptr` selects the type of printer to be associated with the data structure `pd`. The argument `ptype` points to a structure that defines the functions to be called to open, close, write characters, and check status for a type of printer. The `ptrio.h` header file declares `PTR_FUNS` variables for parallel printers (`parallel_ptr`), printers connected via serial ports (`serial_ptr`), and a print-to-disk pseudo-printer (`diskfile_ptr`). The printer number `ptr_no` is stored in `pd` and used in later operations. For parallel printers, 0 and 1 refer to `LPT1:` and `LPT2:`. For serial port printers, 0 and 1 refer to the `COM1:` and `COM2:` ports.

The open, ready, write, and close functions are called via function pointers. The open function should be called before any characters are written to the printer. It returns a 0 value if the operation succeeded and 1 if the operation failed. The close function should be called when output has been completed. It also returns a 0 value for success and 1 for failure.

The ready function returns 1 if the printer is ready to accept another character and 0 if the printer is not ready. The write function sends a single character to the printer. The ready function should be called before each character is written. For a parallel printer, the ready function checks the NOT BUSY bit of the printer status word. For a serial printer, the ready function checks the DATA SET READY and CLEAR TO SEND status signals and whether the serial port can accept another character (the transmit holding register bit in the serial port status word).

For serial port printers, XON/XOFF flow control may be specified when the open function is called. The `options` argument should be the constant `USE_FLOW` defined in `ptrio.h`. The open and close functions do not initialize the serial port. A separate function called `sptr_init` initializes the serial port and sets baud rate, parity, and number of stop bits. The `parms` argument specifies these settings in the packed format expected by the PC BIOS functions.

When the `diskfile_ptr` type is selected, characters output goes to a disk file. The `dos.txt` default file name may be changed by calling `dptr_setfile`. (Calling `dptr_setfile` with a `NULL` pointer restores the default file name.)

Examples

```
#include "ptrio.h"
                            /* structures for two printers */
PTR_DATA pd1 , pd2, pd3 ;
                            /* pd1 for LPT1: parallel ptr */
select_ptr(& pd1, & parallel_ptr,0) ;
                            /* pd2 for COM2: serial ptr */
select_ptr(& pd1, & serial_ptr,1) ;
                            /* pd3 for output to "myfile" */
dptr_setfile("myfile") ;
select_ptr(& pd1, & diskfile_ptr,0) ;
if( pd1.funs.open_fun(& pd1) != 0 )
    printf(" printer open failure") ;
/* wait for printer ready */
while( pd1.funs.ready_fun(& pd1) == 0 )
   { ; }
```

Figure 7.14   continues

Figure 7.14   continued

```
if( pd1.funs.write_fun(& pd1, 'X')  != 0)
    printf(" printer output failure ") ;
if( pd1.funs.close_fun(& pd1) != 0 )
    printf(" printer close failure") ;
```

Note
The PTRIO module is based on PC BIOS functions for parallel port and serial port I/O.

The header file ptrio.h in Figure 7.15 defines the PTR_DATA structure for each printer connection (lines 27 to 32) and the structure PTR_FUNS that contains driver function addresses (lines 18 to 24). Since these two structures refer to each other, line 15 makes an incomplete declaration for the printer data structure to resolve the circular references. Lines 36 to 40 declare global variables that specify functions addresses for parallel printers, serial printers, and for printing to a disk file. Lines 43 to 63 declare function prototypes for the functions in the printer module.

FIGURE 7.15   ptrio.h

```
1      /* ptrio.h - definitions for printer I/O */
2
3                                  /* option bits in flags member */
4      #define USE_XON   0x8000
5                                  /* all option bits */
6      #define OPTION_BITS ·(USE_XON)
7
8
9                                  /* state bits in flags member */
10     #define FLOW_OFF 0x0001
11
12
13                                 /* data types */
14
15     struct p_data ;             /* incomplete declaration to avoid */
16                                 /* circular forward reference */
17
18                                 /* printer function addresses */
19     typedef struct              /* (for a type of printer) */
20       { int (*open_fun) (struct p_data *, unsigned) ;
21         int (*ready_fun)(struct p_data *) ;   /* check status */
22         int (*write_fun)(struct p_data *, int ) ; /* write a char */
23         int (*close_fun)(struct p_data *) ; /* close printer */
24       } PTR_FUNS ;
25
26
27     typedef struct p_data       /* printer data structure */
28       { int pn ;                /* printer port number */
29         unsigned flags ;        /* state and options */
30         FILE *fp ;              /* file pointer - for print-to-disk */
31         PTR_FUNS funs ;         /* printer function addresses */
32       } PTR_DATA ;
```

Figure 7.15   continues

Figure 7.15 continued

```
33
34
35
36                                    /* global variables that define */
37                                    /* printer functions */
38    extern PTR_FUNS parallel_ptr ;
39    extern PTR_FUNS serial_ptr ;
40    extern PTR_FUNS diskfile_ptr ;
41
42
43                                    /* function prototypes */
44
45                                    /* generic printer select function */
46    void select_ptr(PTR_DATA *, PTR_FUNS *, int) ;
47                                    /* parallel printer functions */
48    int pptr_open(PTR_DATA *,unsigned) ;
49    int ppptr_ready(PTR_DATA *) ;
50    int pptr_write(PTR_DATA *,int) ;
51    int pptr_close(PTR_DATA *) ;
52                                    /* serial printer functions */
53    int sptr_open(PTR_DATA *,unsigned) ;
54    int sptr_ready(PTR_DATA *) ;
55    int sptr_write(PTR_DATA *,int) ;
56    int sptr_close(PTR_DATA *) ;
57    int sptr_init(int,int) ;
58                                    /* print-to-disk functions */
59    int dptr_open(PTR_DATA *,unsigned) ;
60    int dptr_ready(PTR_DATA *) ;
61    int dptr_write(PTR_DATA *,int) ;
62    int dptr_close(PTR_DATA *) ;
63    int dptr_setfile(char *) ;
```

The select_ptr function in Figure 7.16 sets up the PTR_DATA structure. Line 11 copies the PTR_FUNS structure containing driver function addresses into the PTR_DATA structure. The PC supports multiple parallel ports and serial ports, so a printer number is stored for use in subsequent operations.

Figure 7.17 contains driver functions for parallel port printers. These functions use BIOS services for printer output. The Turbo and Microsoft library functions for

FIGURE 7.16   ptrio1.c

```
1     /* ptrio1.c - generic printer select function */
2     #include <stdio.h>
3     #include "ptrio.h"
4
5     void select_ptr(pp,ptype,ptr_no) /* set up for printer output */
6     PTR_DATA *pp ;              /* address of ptr data structure */
7     PTR_FUNS *ptype ;           /* specifies ready, write functions */
8     int ptr_no ;                /* printer number */
9     {
10      pp->pn = ptr_no ;         /* store printer number */
11      pp->funs = *ptype ;       /* store function addresses */
12      pp->flags = 0 ;           /* no options, flow on */
13    }
```

BIOS printer services differ in name and in calling sequence. Lines 9 to 17 define the `callprint` macro based on the appropriate Turbo C or Microsoft C library function. (The `asmtools.h` file defines the symbol TURBOC or the symbol MSC.) Lines 76 and 77 define a PTR_FUNS structure with addresses of the parallel port driver functions.

FIGURE 7.17   ptrio2.c

```
1      /* ptrio2.c - parallel printer functions */
2      #include <stdio.h>
3      #include <bios.h>
4      #include "asmtools.h"
5      #include "ptrio.h"
6
7                                  /* define macros for BIOS call */
8                                  /* Turbo C version */
9      #ifdef TURBOC
10     #define callprint(cmd,data,port)     \
11             ( (unsigned) biosprint(cmd, data,port) )
12     #endif
13                                  /* Microsoft C version */
14     #ifdef MSC
15     #define callprint(cmd,data,port)     \
16             ( _bios_printer(cmd,port,data) )
17     #endif
18
19
20                                  /* status bits */
21     #define NOT_BUSY    0x80     /* =1, printer not busy */
22     #define TIME_OUT    0x01     /* =1, output failed */
23
24                                  /* BIOS parallel ptr command codes */
25     #define PRINT_CHAR   0       /* send a char to printer */
26     #define INIT_PTR     1       /* initialize the printer */
27     #define GET_STATUS   2       /* get printer status */
28
29
30     int pptr_open(pp,options)   /* open printer */
31     PTR_DATA *pp ;
32     unsigned options ;          /* dummy options */
33     {
34        callprint(INIT_PTR,0,pp->pn) ; /* initialize printer & port */
35        pp->flags = 0 ;          /* no options */
36        return( 0 ) ;            /* success */
37     }
38
39
40
41     int pptr_ready(pp)                /* check to see if printer is ready */
42     PTR_DATA *pp ;
43     {
44        unsigned ret ;
45
46        ret = callprint(GET_STATUS,0,pp->pn) ; /* get status */
47
48        if( (ret & NOT_BUSY) != 0 ) /* check NOT_BUSY bit */
```

Figure 7.17   **continues**

Figure 7.17   continued

```
49                  return( 1 ) ;          /*  not busy - return ready */
50            else return( 0 ) ;          /*  busy - return not ready */
51       }
52
53
54
55     int pptr_write(pp,c)               /* print a character */
56       PTR_DATA *pp ;
57       int c ;                          /* character to be printed */
58       {
59         unsigned ret ;
60                                         /* use BIOS to output the char */
61          ret = callprint(PRINT_CHAR,c,pp->pn) ;
62
63          if( (ret & TIME_OUT) != 0 )  /* check for timeout */
64                 return( 1 ) ;          /*  timeout - return failure code */
65            else return( 0 ) ;          /*  no timeout -    success code */
66       }
67
68
69     int pptr_close(pp)                 /* finished with printer */
70       PTR_DATA *pp ;
71       {
72          return( 0 ) ;                  /* return success */
73       }
74
75
76     PTR_FUNS parallel_ptr =            /* parallel ptr function addresses */
77         { pptr_open , pptr_ready , pptr_write , pptr_close } ;
```

Figure 7.18 defines functions for serial port printers. These functions are based on BIOS services for serial ports. Lines 9 to 17 define the `callserial` macro in terms of the appropriate Turbo C or Microsoft C library function. The function `sptr_open` opens the printer connection. The `options` argument may specify the use of XON / XOFF flow control. `sptr_ready` checks printer status. Lines 64 to 77 check flow control status if that option has been selected. The printer sends an XON character when it is ready to receive characters or an XOFF character when it is not able to receive characters. Lines 65 to 73 collect characters received from the printer and set the flow control state bit in the `flags` member of the `PTR_DATA` structure.

FIGURE 7.18   ptrio3.c

```
1      /* ptrio3.c - serial printer functions */
2      #include <stdio.h>
3      #include <bios.h>
4      #include "asmtools.h"
5      #include "ptrio.h"
6
7                                         /* define macros for BIOS call */
8                                         /* Turbo C version */
9      #ifdef TURBOC
```

Figure 7.18   continues

Figure 7.18   continued

```
10      #define callserial(cmd,data,port)    ( (unsigned) \
11          bioscom(cmd,data,port) )
12      #endif
13                                      /* Microsoft C version */
14      #ifdef MSC
15       #define callserial(cmd,data,port) /
16          ( _bios_serialcom(cmd,port,data) )
17      #endif
18
19
20                                      /* flow control characters */
21      #define XON_CHAR   0x11        /* starts flow */
22      #define XOFF_CHAR 0x13         /* stops flow */
23
24                                      /* BIOS comm. status bits */
25      #define XHOLD_EMPTY 0x2000 /* transmitter holding reg. empty */
26      #define DATA_READY 0x0100     /* received char waiting */
27      #define DATA_SET_READY 0x20 /* modem signal */
28      #define CLEAR_TO_SEND 0x10 /* modem signal */
29      #define TIME_OUT 0x8000       /* couldn't transmit a char */
30
31                                      /* all the following bits must be */
32                                      /* ON for the comm. port to be */
33                                      /* ready for the next char */
34       #define READY_STATUS (DATA_SET_READY| CLEAR_TO_SEND| XHOLD_EMPTY)
35
36
37                                      /* BIOS command codes */
38      #define SET_PARM      0        /* set communications parameters */
39      #define SEND_CHAR     1        /* send char to comm. port */
40      #define RCV_CHAR      2        /* get received char */
41      #define GET_STATUS    3        /* get status - xmt and rcv */
42
43
44      int sptr_open(sp,options)    /* initialize printer */
45      PTR_DATA *sp ;
46      unsigned options ;           /* flow control option value */
47      {
48         options = options & OPTION_BITS ; /* mask non-option bits */
49         sp->flags = sp->flags | options ; /* set options and state */
50         return( 0 ) ;             /* success */
51      }
52
53
54      int sptr_ready(sp)           /* check to see if printer is ready */
55      PTR_DATA *sp ;               /* printer data structure */
56      {
57         int spn ;                 /* serial printer number */
58         unsigned rc ;             /* received char */
59         unsigned ret ;            /* status */
60
61         spn = sp->pn ;
62
63         if( (sp->flags & USE_XON) != 0 ) /* using XON protocol? */
64           {                       /*   yes - check flow state */
65              while( 1 == 1 )       /* first check rcvd chars */
```

Figure 7.18   continues

Figure 7.18   continued

```
66                  { if( (callserial(GET_STATUS,0,spn) & DATA_READY) == 0)
67                      break ;
68                    rc = callserial(RCV_CHAR,0,spn) ;
69                    if( rc == XOFF_CHAR )
70                        sp->flags = sp->flags | FLOW_OFF ;
71                    else if( rc == XON_CHAR )
72                        sp->flags = sp->flags & ~ FLOW_OFF ;
73                    }
74                                    /* now check flow status */
75              if( (sp->flags & FLOW_OFF) != 0)
76                  return( 0 ) ;
77          }
78        ret = callserial(GET_STATUS,0,spn) ;   /* get port status */
79        if( (ret & READY_STATUS) != READY_STATUS )
80            return( 0 ) ;
81        else return( 1 ) ;
82      }
83
84
85    int sptr_write(sp,c)        /* write a character to the printer */
86     PTR_DATA *sp ;             /* printer data structure */
87     int c ;                    /* character to send */
88     {
89       int ret ;                /* status returned */
90
91                                 /* check flow status first */
92       if( (sp->flags & FLOW_OFF) != 0)
93           return( 0 ) ;
94
95                                 /* use BIOS to send the char */
96       ret = callserial(SEND_CHAR, c, sp->pn ) ;
97       if( (ret & TIME_OUT) != 0 ) /* check for timeout */
98           return( 1 ) ;
99       else return( 0 ) ;
100     }
101
102
103   int sptr_close(sp)           /* close printer */
104    PTR_DATA *sp ;              /* printer data structure */
105    {
106      return( 0 ) ;             /* just return success code */
107    }
108
109
110   int sptr_init(spn,comm_parms)  /* initialize serial port */
111    int spn ;                     /* serial port number */
112    int comm_parms ;              /* settings for comm. parms */
113    {
114                                  /* initialize serial port */
115         callserial(SET_PARM,comm_parms,spn) ;
116    }
117
118
119   PTR_FUNS serial_ptr =        /* serial ptr function addresses */
120    { sptr_open , sptr_ready , sptr_write , sptr_close } ;
121
```

Lines 78 to 81 check the status of the serial port. Some printers use the CLEAR_TO_SEND or DATA_SET_READY modem status lines to indicate when they are not ready to receive characters. The XHOLD_EMPTY status bit indicates whether the PC serial port is ready to accept another character.

The sptr_open function does not initialize the serial port. A separate call is provided for initializing the serial port — its baud rate and other parameters. (The Turbo C and Microsoft C compiler manuals document these parameters for the bioscom and _bios_serialcom functions.)

Figure 7.19 defines functions for output to a disk file rather than a physical printer. The dptr_open function opens the file and dptr_close closes the file. The status function dptr_ready always shows the printer to be ready. The static variable pfile_name points to the name of the file to be opened. The function dptr_setfile sets pfile_name to point to the specified file name.

FIGURE 7.19   ptrio4.c

```
 1     /* ptrio4.c - print to disk file functions */
 2     #include <stdio.h>
 3     #include <bios.h>
 4     #include "asmtools.h"
 5     #include "ptrio.h"
 6
 7                                  /* default print file name */
 8     static char default_name[] = "dos.txt" ;
 9
10                                  /* pointer to print file name */
11     static char *pfile_name = default_name ;
12
13
14     int dptr_open(pp,options)    /* open printer */
15      PTR_DATA *pp ;              /* points to printer data structure */
16      unsigned options ;         /* dummy options */
17      {
18        FILE *pfp ;               /* print file pointer */
19
20        pp->flags = 0 ;           /* no options */
21        pfp = fopen(pfile_name,"wb") ;
22        pp->fp = pfp ;
23        if( pfp == NULL )         /* check for open failure */
24            return( 1 ) ;
25        else return( 0 ) ;
26      }
27
28
29
30     int dptr_ready(pp)           /* check to see if printer is ready */
31      PTR_DATA *pp ;              /* points to printer data structure */
32      {
33        return( 1 ) ;             /* disk file is always ready */
34      }
35
36
```

Figure 7.19   continues

Figure 7.19 continued

```
37
38    int dptr_write(pp,c)          /* print a character */
39     PTR_DATA *pp ;               /* points to printer data structure */
40     int c ;                      /* character to be printed */
41     {
42       unsigned ret ;
43
44       ret = putc(c,pp->fp) ;     /* write the character */
45       if( ret == c )             /* check for failure */
46            return( 0 ) ;         /*    success */
47       else return( 1 ) ;         /*    failure */
48     }
49
50
51    int dptr_close(pp)            /* finished with printer */
52     PTR_DATA *pp ;               /* points to printer data structure */
53     {
54        return( fclose(pp->fp) ) ; /* pass fclose return code */
55     }
56
57
58    int dptr_setfile(file_name)/* set print file name */
59     char *file_name ;
60     {
61        if( file_name == NULL )
62          pfile_name = default_name ; /* no name - restore default */
63
64        else pfile_name = file_name ; /* set new print file name */
65
66        return( 0 ) ;
67     }
68
69    PTR_FUNS diskfile_ptr =     /* print to disk function addresses */
70       { dptr_open , dptr_ready , dptr_write , dptr_close } ;
71
72
```

Our printer module does not add any new low-level capabilities—it uses compiler library functions for BIOS services. But it makes those functions more useful to an application program. It provides full support for serial port printers and isolates the application program from details of communicating with each type of printer. This framework also provides a practical way to add support for new types of printers (such as printers connected via a local area network).

7.5   Keyboard Input

The C library provides several functions for keyboard input. For example, the getchar and getc(stdin) functions get a single character. However, the Microsoft C and Turbo C implementations of these functions are inappropriate for interactive programs. They collect an entire line of input before returning a single character. They also echo characters before returning. Finally, they suppress input characters corresponding to special keys such as cursor control or function keys. The solution is to build our own functions. Figure 7.20 describes our KEYIO module.

FIGURE 7.20   Description of KEYIO Module

Name

```
getkey      get one keystroke from the keyboard
keypress    check for waiting keystroke
keyflush    discard any waiting keystroke input
waitcr      discard keyboard input until CR pressed
```

Usage
```
int getkey() ;
int c , input_waiting ;
c = getkey();
input_waiting = keypress() ;
keyflush() ;
waitcr() ;
```

Function

getkey waits for the next keystroke from the keyboard. It returns an ASCII code(0–127) for keys corresponding to ASCII chars and values from 256 up for special keys such as function keys or cursor control keys. These special keystrokes are returned as (256 + extended code) using the extended code described in the *IBM PC Technical Reference Manual*.

The include file keyio.h defines symbolic constants for the values returned for many special keys.

keypress returns a 0 value if no keyboard input is waiting and a nonzero value if some input is waiting. keyflush checks for keyboard input using keypress and discards it using getkey until no more input is waiting. waitcr uses keypress and getkey to discard input until the return key is pressed.

Keyboard input is not echoed by any of these functions. Input is available as soon as a single key is pressed; it is not queued until an entire line has been typed.

Examples
```
if( getkey() == UPARROW )
   { /* start scrolling up */
     keyflush() ;
     printf(" press a key to stop scrolling\n");
     while( keypress() == 0 )
        { scroll_up() ; }
   }
...
printf(" press return to continue\n");
waitcr() ;
```

References
IBM PC DOS Technical Reference Manual.
IBM PC Technical Reference Manual — Character codes and extended codes.

The basis for the module is the `getkey` and `keypress` functions. `getkey` returns a single character without echoing it or waiting for an entire line, and `keypress` checks to see if a character is waiting. `getkey` returns an integer value; for ASCII characters this is like the value returned by `getchar` — a number between 0 and 0x7f. Some other keys produce values between 0x80 and 0xff. However, some keys such as function keys and cursor control keys do not correspond to any character value. For such keys, `getkey` returns a number greater than 0xff. The header file `keyio.h` in Figure 7.21 defines symbolic constants for some ASCII control characters and non-ASCII keys.

FIGURE 7.21   keyio.h

```
 1
 2      /* keyio.h  - definitions of values returned by getkey() */
 3
 4    /* keypress return values */
 5    #define NO_INPUT    0
 6    /* non-zero return means there is input waiting */
 7
 8                                    /* ASCII control characters */
 9    #define   ASCNUL     (256+3)
10    #define   ASCBEL       7
11    #define   ASCBS        8
12    #define   ASCTAB       9
13    #define   ASCLF      0xA
14    #define   ASCFF      0xC
15    #define   ASCCR      0xD
16    #define   ASCESC     0x1B
17    #define   ASCDEL     0x7F
18    #define   ASCSPACE   0x20
19
20                                    /* special keys for IBM PC */
21    #define   HOMEKEY    (256+71)
22    #define   BACKTAB    (256+15)
23    #define   UPARROW    (256+72)
24    #define   LEFTARROW  (256+75)
25    #define   RIGHTARROW (256+77)
26    #define   ENDKEY     (256+79)
27    #define   DOWNARROW  (256+80)
28    #define   PGUPKEY    (256+73)
29    #define   PGDNKEY    (256+81)
30    #define   INSERTKEY  (256+82)
31    #define   DELETEKEY  (256+83)
32    #define   CTLPRTSC   (256+114)
33    #define   CTLLARROW  (256+115)
34    #define   CTLRARROW  (256+116)
35    #define   CTLEND     (256+117)
36    #define   CTLPGDN    (256+118)
37    #define   CTLHOME    (256+119)
38    #define   CTLPGUP    (256+132)
39
40                                    /* function key codes */
41    #define   F1KEY      (256+59)
42    #define   F11KEY     (256+84)
43    #define   F21KEY     (256+94)
44    #define   F31KEY     (256+104)
```

Figure 7.21   continues

Figure 7.21   continued

```
45
46                                           /* alt-key + number key (top row) */
47      #define   ALT1KEY       (256+120)
48
49
50
51                                           /* function prototypes */
52      int getkey(void) ;
53      int keypress(void) ;
54      void keyflush(void) ;
55      void waitcr(void) ;
56
```

Figure 7.22 shows an implementation of getkey and keypress based on the getch and kbhit library functions. The getch function returns a single character. Function keys and other special key inputs are represented by a zero character value followed by another character whose value is the scan code for the special key. The getkey function checks for a zero character value and, if found, retrieves the scan code. One call to getkey returns one keystroke, regardless of whether it requires one or two calls to getch.

We can use getkey and keypress as the basis for additional keyboard functions. Figure 7.23 shows the waitcr and keyflush functions. waitcr calls getkey and discards keyboard input until the return key is pressed. keyflush

FIGURE 7.22   keyio1.c

```
1       /* keyio1.c - keyio module - single key input */
2       /* uses kbhit and getch library functions */
3       #include <conio.h>
4       #include "keyio.h"
5
6
7       int keypress()               /* check for keyboard input waiting */
8       {                            /* returns 0=no input, 1=input */
9         int stat ;
10
11        return( kbhit() ) ;        /* get key available status */
12      }
13
14
15
16      /* getkey - waits for and returns the next keystroke input */
17      /* keystrokes that the ROM-BIOS describes with extended codes */
18      /* are returned as integers > 255 */
19      int getkey()                 /* get the next key input   */
20      {
21        int c ;
22
23        c = getch() ;              /* get single ASCII character */
24        if(c == 0)                 /* is it a non-ASCII extended code? */
25          c = 0x100 + getch() ; /*    yes - use 256 + scan code */
26        return(c) ;
27      }
```

checks for and discards keyboard input until `keypress` indicates that no keyboard input is waiting. The following fragments show possible uses of these functions:

```
printf("press return when ready to continue \n");
waitcr() ;
```

and

```
keyflush() ;   /* flush old input */
printf("delete file? (y/n) \n");
if( getkey() == 'y' )
   { /* delete the file */
   ...
```

FIGURE 7.23   keyio2.c

```
1   /* keyio2.c - keyflush() and waitcr() functions */
2   /* system-independent part of the keyboard input module */
3   #include "stdio.h"
4   #include "keyio.h"
5
6
7   void keyflush()              /* discard waiting console input */
8     {
9                                /* repeat */
10        while( keypress() != 0)/* check for input */
11          { getkey() ; }       /* and discard if found */
12    }
13
14
15
16   void waitcr()               /* wait until a cr is typed. */
17     {
18        while(getkey() != '\r')/* discard input until CR found */
19          { ; }
20    }
```

The relation between standard library functions such as `getchar` and `scanf` and PC-specific functions such as `getch`, `bioskey`, and `_bios_keybrd` is not properly defined by the documentation supplied with Microsoft C or Turbo C. When we use both types of console input in a single program, we should experiment to ensure that the combination works as expected.

The KEYIO module hides a number of details from the programs that use it. We can choose an MS-DOS–based or BIOS-based implementation without affecting these programs. The definitions of symbolic constants for many special keys further reduces the knowledge needed to use the KEYIO module.

Experimenting With getkey

Before using the KEYIO module in your programs, you should experiment with it. Write a short program that accepts keystrokes and displays in decimal and hexadecimal form the value returned by `getkey` for each keystroke. Try all combinations of regular keys with shift, control, and Alt keys. Compare the behavior of the MS-DOS–based and BIOS-based implementations.

Although both Microsoft C and Turbo C provide the `getch` and `kbhit` functions, the two implementations are based on different MS-DOS calls. The Microsoft C version allows MS-DOS to check for control-C (program termination), control-P (echo console output to the printer), and control-S (hold screen output until another key is pressed). An MS-DOS bug causes scan codes whose values are the same as control-C, control-P, and control-S to be recognized as these characters. In the Turbo C version, MS-DOS does not check for these characters. The Turbo C version of `getch` is more suitable as a basis for `getkey` than is the Microsoft version.

A BIOS-based KEYIO Module

The `getkey` and `keypress` functions can also be implemented using BIOS services directly. The source code disks contain a replacement for Figure 7.22 using the Turbo C function `bioskey` and the Microsoft library function `_bios_keybrd`. A BIOS-based KEYIO module avoids problems with MS-DOS console input services, but it is less compatible with other software.

7.6 Video Output Functions

The VIDEO functions described in Figure 7.24 give us access to the video output services in the PC BIOS. The `video.h` header file in Figure 7.25 defines constants needed within the VIDEO module and by functions that use the module.

FIGURE 7.24   Description of VIDEO Functions

Name
VIDEO   module for access to ROM BIOS Video_IO services

Function
The functions in the VIDEO module provide access to the Video output services in the PC ROM BIOS. The header file `video.h` defines symbolic constants for video modes, screen attributes, and I/O addresses. It also declares function prototypes for the VIDEO functions. Since these functions use BIOS services, they are fairly portable but they have rather poor performance for displaying large numbers of characters.

A few assumptions are made to simplify the functions. Page 0 is selected and an 80-column-per-line width is assumed.

Figure 7.24   continues

Figure 7.24   continued

Function Descriptions

```
int new_mode ;
void vid_init(new_mode) ;
```

`vid_init` initializes BIOS Video support and the display adapter to a new mode. Modes are defined in `video.h`.

```
int ncols ;
int vid_state(& ncols) ;
```

`vid_state` returns the current video mode. The number of columns per line is stored in the integer location whose address is passed. Modes are defined in `video.h`.

```
int page ;
void vid_page(page) ;
```

`vid_page` sets the active display page position. The number of pages supported depends on the display adapter in use.

```
int row, col ;
void vid_set_cur(row,col) ;
```

`vid_set_cur` sets the cusor position on the display. (Page 0 of the display is assumed.)

```
int row, col ;
void vid_get_cur(&row,&col) ;
```

`vid_get_cur` gets the row and column numbers of the current cursor position. (Page 0 of the display is assumed.)

```
int from_row, thru_row ; /* starting and ending rows */
int from_col, thru_col ; /* starting and ending columns */
int attr ;               /* screen attribute for clearing */
void vid_clr_scn(from_row,from_col,thru_row,thru_col,attr) ;
```

`vid_clr_scn` clears the rectangular screen area defined by the row and column numbers. (Row 0, column 0 is the top left corner of the screen.)

```
int nrows ;              /* how far up to scroll the area */
int from_row, thru_row ; /* starting and ending rows */
int from_col, thru_col ; /* starting and ending columns */
int attr ;               /* screen attribute for clearing */
void vid_up(nrows,from_row,from_col,thru_row,thru_col,attr) ;
```

`vid_up` scrolls part of the screen (defined by the row and column arguments) upward by `nrows`. (Row 0, column 0 is the top left corner.)

Figure 7.24   continues

Figure 7.24   continued

```
int nrows ;                  /* how far down to scroll the area */
int from_row, thru_row ; /* starting and ending rows */
int from_col, thru_col ; /* starting and ending columns */
int attr ;                   /* screen attribute for clearing */
void  vid_down(nrows,from_row,from_col,thru_row,thru_col,attr)  ;
```

vid_down scrolls part of the screen (defined by the row and column arguments) downward by nrows. (Row 0, column 0 is the top left corner.)

```
int n ;                      /* how many blanks to write */
int attr ;                   /* screen attribute for clearing */
void vid_blank(n,attr)  ;
```

vid_blank writes n blank characters (with attribute attr) at the cursor position. Attributes are defined in video.h.

```
int c ;                      /* character to write */
int a ;                      /* screen attribute to write */
void vid_wca(c,a)  ;
```

vid_wca writes the character c with the attribute a at the cursor position. The cursor is not advanced. No special characters such as carriage return or line feed are recognized.

```
char c , a ;                 /* put char and attribute here */
int vid_gca(&c,&a)  ;
```

vid_gca gets the character and the attribute at the cursor position. Note that addresses of character variables and not integers should be passed. The cursor is not advanced. The return value contains the character read (low-order 8 bits) and the attribute (high-order 8 bits).

```
int c ;                      /* character to write */
void vid_tc(c)  ;
```

vid_tc writes the character c at the cursor position. The cursor is advanced. Special characters such as carriage return, line feed, alert, and backspace are recognized. The attribute at the cursor location is unchanged. This is the normal TTY output used by DOS for console output. (Page 0 is assumed.)

```
int disp_type ;                       /* display type */
int vid_info(& disp_type)  ;
```

vid_info returns 0 if the Video BIOS call number 0x12 is not supported, or 1 if the call is supported. This may be used to distinguish a CGA adapter (which returns 0) from an EGA or VGA adapter (which returns 1). If the call is supported, disp_type indicates whether a mono (1) or color display (0) is connected.

References

IBM PC Technical Reference Manual. Appendix A—BIOS Listing.
Programmer's Guide to PC & PS/2 Video Systems. Richard Wilton. Microsoft Press. 1987.

FIGURE 7.25   video.h

```
 1      /* video.h - define constants for Video_IO module */
 2
 3      /* screen attributes */
 4      #define   NON_DISPLAY       0x00
 5      #define   UNDERLINE         0x01
 6      #define   NORMAL_DISPLAY    0x07
 7      #define   REVERSE_VIDEO     0x70
 8      /* combine the following with the above values */
 9      #define   HI_INTENSITY      0x08
10      #define   BLINK_BIT         0x80
11
12      /* video modes (as defined by the ROM BIOS */
13      #define   BW40_MODE              0
14      #define   CO40_MODE              1
15      #define   BW80_MODE              2
16      #define   CO80_MODE              3
17      #define   CO320_MODE             4
18      #define   BW320_MODE             5
19      #define   BW640_MODE             6
20      #define   MONO_MODE              7
21
22      /* ROM BIOS function values */
23      /* (put one of these values into sreg.ah before calling */
24      /* the VIDEO_IO services in the ROM BIOS) */
25      #define   V_INIT                 0
26      #define   V_CTYPE                1
27      #define   V_SET_CUR              2
28      #define   V_GET_CUR              3
29      #define   V_SETPAGE              5
30      #define   V_SCRLUP               6
31      #define   V_SCRLDOWN             7
32      #define   V_GCA                  8
33      #define   V_WCA                  9
34      #define   V_WC                  10
35      #define   V_WTTY                14
36      #define   V_STATE               15
37
38
39                                  /* BIOS Video software interrupt */
40      #define   V_INT_NO          0x10
41
42                                  /* function prototypes */
43      void vid_init(int) ;
44      int vid_state(int *) ;
45      void vid_page(int) ;
46      void vid_get_cur(int *, int * ) ;
47      void vid_set_cur(int , int ) ;
48      void vid_clr_scn(int, int , int, int, int) ;
49      void vid_up(int, int, int, int, int, int) ;
50      void vid_down(int, int, int, int, int, int ) ;
51      void vid_blank(int, int ) ;
52      void vid_wca(int, int ) ;
53      int vid_gca(char *, char *) ;
54      void vid_tc(int) ;
55      int vid_info(int *) ;
```

Figures 7.26 through 7.29 list the VIDEO functions. Most of the functions in the module correspond directly to a BIOS service, but there are a few additions. The vid_clr_scn function clears part or all of the screen using a special-case feature of the scroll-up function. The vid_blank function blanks a number of positions that we specify along with the screen attribute to be used. The int86 library function issues the software interrupt specified by the constant V_INT_NO defined in video.h. The operation code in the AH register identifies the operation to be performed. Input arguments are placed in the data structure sreg, and returned values are removed from dreg.

FIGURE 7.26   video1.c

```
 1     /* video1.c - basic ROM BIOS calls for Video_IO   */
 2     #include <stdio.h>
 3     #include <dos.h>
 4     #include "video.h"
 5
 6
 7     void vid_init(new_mode)        /* initialize display mode */
 8      int new_mode ;                /* (See video.h for modes ) */
 9      {
10        union REGS sreg,dreg ;
11
12        sreg.h.al = new_mode ;   /* new mode number */
13        sreg.h.ah = V_INIT ;     /* operation code */
14
15        int86(V_INT_NO,& sreg,& dreg) ;
16      }
17
18
19     int vid_state(pcol)            /* get current state info */
20      int *pcol ;                   /* store number of columns here*/
21      {                             /* return the current mode value */
22        union REGS sreg , dreg ;
23
24        sreg.h.ah = V_STATE ;    /* operation code */
25
26        int86(V_INT_NO,& sreg,& dreg) ;
27
28        *pcol =  dreg.h.ah ;
29        return( dreg.h.al ) ;
30      }
31
32
33     void vid_page(new_page)        /* set display page */
34      int new_page ;                /* new page number */
35      {
36        union REGS sreg,dreg ;
37
38        sreg.h.al = new_page ;   /* page number */
39        sreg.h.ah = V_SETPAGE ; /* operation code */
40
41        int86(V_INT_NO , & sreg, & dreg) ;
```

Figure 7.26   continues

Figure 7.26   continued

```
42        }
43
44
45      void vid_set_cur(row,col)     /* set cursor position */
46       int row ;                    /* new row number */
47       int col ;                    /* new column number */
48       {
49          union REGS sreg,dreg ;
50
51          sreg.h.dh = row ;          /* row */
52          sreg.h.dl = col ;          /* column */
53          sreg.h.bh = 0 ;            /* page zero */
54          sreg.h.ah = V_SET_CUR ;    /* operation code */
55
56          int86(V_INT_NO , & sreg,& dreg) ;
57       }
58
59
60      void vid_get_cur(prow,pcol)/* get current cursor position */
61       int *prow ;                  /* store row number here */
62       int *pcol ;                  /* store column number here */
63       {
64          union REGS sreg,dreg ;
65
66          sreg.h.bh = 0 ;            /* page zero */
67          sreg.h.ah = V_GET_CUR ;    /* operation code */
68
69          int86(V_INT_NO , & sreg, & dreg) ;
70
71          *prow = dreg.h.dh ;        /* save row number */
72          *pcol = dreg.h.dl ;        /* save column number */
73       }
```

FIGURE 7.27   video2.c

```
1       /* video2.c - basic ROM BIOS calls for Video_IO   */
2       #include <stdio.h>
3       #include <dos.h>
4       #include "video.h"
5
6
7                                    /* clear part/all of screen */
8       void vid_clr_scn(from_row,from_col,thru_row,thru_col,a)
9        int from_row ;              /* top row to clear */
10       int from_col ;              /* left column to clear */
11       int thru_row ;              /* bottom row to clear */
12       int thru_col ;              /* right column to clear */
13       int a ;                     /* screen attribute */
14       {
15                                   /* use special case of scroll */
16          vid_up(0,from_row,from_col,thru_row,thru_col,a) ;
17       }
18
```

Figure 7.27   continues

Figure 7.27   continued

```
19
20                                        /* scroll part/all screen up */
21      void vid_up(nrows,from_row,from_col,thru_row,thru_col,a)
22      int nrows ;                   /* number of rows up */
23      int from_row ;                /* top row to clear */
24      int from_col ;                /* left column to clear */
25      int thru_row ;                /* bottom row to clear */
26      int thru_col ;                /* right column to clear */
27      int a ;                       /* screen attribute */
28      {
29        union REGS sreg , dreg ;
30
31        sreg.h.al = nrows ;
32        sreg.h.bh = a ;
33        sreg.h.ch = from_row ;   /* from_row */
34        sreg.h.cl = from_col ;   /* from column */
35        sreg.h.dh = thru_row ;   /* thru row */
36        sreg.h.dl = thru_col ;   /* thru column */
37        sreg.h.ah = V_SCRLUP ;   /* operation code */
38
39        int86( V_INT_NO, & sreg, & dreg) ;
40      }
41
42
43                                        /* scroll part/all screen down */
44      void vid_down(nrows,from_row,from_col,thru_row,thru_col,a)
45      int nrows ;                   /* number of rows up */
46      int from_row ;                /* top row to clear */
47      int from_col ;                /* left column to clear */
48      int thru_row ;                /* bottom row to clear */
49      int thru_col ;                /* right column to clear */
50      int a ;                       /* screen attribute */
51      {
52        union REGS sreg , dreg ;
53
54        sreg.h.al = nrows ;
55        sreg.h.bh = a ;
56        sreg.h.ch = from_row ;   /* from_row */
57        sreg.h.cl = from_col ;   /* from column */
58        sreg.h.dh = thru_row ;   /* thru row */
59        sreg.h.dl = thru_col ;   /* thru column */
60        sreg.h.ah = V_SCRLDOWN;  /* operation code */
61
62        int86( V_INT_NO, & sreg, & dreg) ;
63      }
64
65
66      void vid_blank(n,a)        /* write n blanks */
67       int n ;                   /* no. blanks to write */
68       int a ;                   /* use this attribute */
69      {
70        union REGS sreg , dreg ;
71
72        sreg.h.bl = a ;          /* attribute */
73        sreg.h.al = ' ' ;        /* blank char */
74        sreg.x.cx = n ;          /* no. chars to write */
```

Figure 7.27   continues

Figure 7.27   continued

```
75          sreg.h.ah = V_WCA ;   /* operation code */
76          int86(V_INT_NO, & sreg, & dreg) ;
77      }
```

FIGURE 7.28   video3.c

```
1       /* video3.c - char output calls for Video_IO  */
2       /* note that vid_wca() and vid_gca() do not advance the cursor */
3       #include <stdio.h>
4       #include <dos.h>
5       #include "video.h"
6
7
8       void vid_wca(c,a)              /* display char and attribute */
9        int c  ;                      /* char to display */
10       int a ;                       /* attribute */
11       {
12          union REGS sreg , dreg ;
13
14          sreg.h.bh = 0 ;            /* force display page 0 */
15          sreg.h.bl = a ;            /* attribute */
16          sreg.h.al = c ;            /* char */
17          sreg.x.cx = 1 ;            /* count of chars to display =1 */
18          sreg.h.ah = V_WCA ;        /* operation code */
19          int86(V_INT_NO , & sreg, & dreg) ;
20       }
21
22
23       int vid_gca(pc,pa)            /* get char and attribute at cursor */
24        char *pc  ;                   /* store char here */
25        char *pa ;                    /* store attribute here */
26       {
27          union REGS sreg , dreg ;
28
29          sreg.h.bh = 0 ;            /* page zero */
30          sreg.h.ah = V_GCA ;        /* operation code */
31          int86(V_INT_NO , & sreg, & dreg) ;
32          *pc = dreg.h.al ;          /* save char value */
33          *pa = dreg.h.ah ;          /* and attribute */
34          return( dreg.x.ax ) ;      /* return char and attribute */
35       }
36
37
38       void vid_tc(c)                /* output one char with TTY write */
39        int c  ;                      /* char to write */
40       {
41          union REGS sreg , dreg ;
42
43          sreg.h.bl = 0 ;            /* dummy foreground color */
44          sreg.h.al = c ;            /* character */
45          sreg.h.ah = V_WTTY ;       /* operation code */
46          int86(V_INT_NO , & sreg, & dreg) ;
47       }
```

The vid_info function in Figure 7.29 serves a special purpose. It allows us to determine the type of display adapter in use. The SCN module in the next section uses vid_info to adapt automatically to the display adapter that is present.

The BIOS functions for screen output are well standardized. All IBM PC models and PC compatibles support them. Even systems with nonstandard display adapters usually implement these BIOS calls. When it is feasible, you should use these functions for screen output. However, their performance sometimes makes them unsatisfactory. (See Chapter 4 for performance measurements.)

FIGURE 7.29   video4.c

```
 1      /* video4.c - get display info function */
 2      /* This BIOS call not supported by MDA or CGA */
 3      /* (vid_info returns 0 for MDA or CGA) */
 4      #include <dos.h>
 5      #include "video.h"
 6
 7      #define SUBSYSTEM_CONFIGURATION  0x12 /* operation code */
 8      #define GET_INFO  0x10        /* sub-code */
 9
10
11      int vid_info(pd_type)          /* get display type info */
12       int *pd_type ;                /* place active display type here */
13       {
14          union REGS sreg , dreg ;
15          int ret ;
16
17          sreg.h.bl = GET_INFO ;   /* suboperation code */
18          sreg.h.ah = SUBSYSTEM_CONFIGURATION ; /* operation code */
19          sreg.h.al = 0 ;          /* get display types */
20
21          int86(V_INT_NO , & sreg, & dreg) ;
22
23          if( dreg.h.bl == GET_INFO ) /* check return code */
24               ret = 0 ;              /* call not supported */
25          else ret = 1 ;             /* call supported - EGA or VGA */
26          *pd_type = dreg.h.bh ;   /* save display type */
27          return( ret ) ;
28       }
```

7.7 The SCN Module: Direct Screen Output

Fortunately we can bypass the BIOS video services and write characters on the screen directly. Although this is specific to the PC's hardware architecture, it provides very good performance. Since our purpose is to support interactive applications with high-speed screen output, we provide only the basic functions: writing single characters and character strings and reading back characters and attributes. Other functions control the position on the screen and the current video attribute.

Several features of the BIOS functions can be eliminated to improve perform-ance. Scrolling the screen when the cursor reaches the bottom is not required in many interactive applications. Our screen output functions will not check for the end of the screen nor will they recognize special characters such as carriage return, line feed, alert, or backspace. (Those services can be added at a higher level.) We will not update the position of the blinking cursor either, because updating the cursor position after each character is written slows output and causes distracting move-ment on the screen. To keep the module simple (and to keep performance high), we use text mode with 80 columns and force the use of page 0 of display memory.

Figure 7.30 describes the SCN module. All the functions use a structure that records where the next character will be written on the screen and the display attribute to be used. This structure keeps all the context we need to output characters. If we want to create separate output areas in different parts of the screen, we define a different structure for each area.

FIGURE 7.30   Description of the Screen I/O Module — SCN

Name
SCN   module for direct output to CRT screen

Function
The SCN module provides fast console output by writing directly to the CRT screen. The initialization function determines the display adapter type, sets the screen address, and selects the appropriate functions for reading from and writing to screen memory. For the CGA adapter, screen reads and writes are done during horizontal retrace intervals to avoid screen interference ("snow"). Functions for writing characters and strings are included with the utility functions for controlling position on the screen and the display attribute of characters written.

Some symbolic constants such as display attribute values are defined in `video.h`. The `scn.h` header file defines the data structure that contains current screen position and display attribute. It also declares function prototypes for the SCN functions.

SCN does not provide scrolling or recognize special control characters such as carriage return and line feed. Use the VIDEO module for scrolling and cursor positioning. SCN makes direct use of hardware addresses for the screen buffer memory and for other addresses. This makes SCN specific to IBM PC's and to PC compatibles.

Function Descriptions

```
#include "scn.h"
SCN_DATA sc ;
int scn_init(& sc) ;
```

`scn_init` initializes the screen data structure `sc`. The current position is set at the beginning of the screen and the display attribute to that for normal display. The

Figure 7.30 continues

Figure 7.30   continued

screen buffer address appropriate for the display adapter in use is also stored in the data structure. An 80-column text mode (with display page 0) is forced if not already selected.

```
SCN_DATA sc ;
int row, col ;           /* new screen position */
SCN_PTR scn_pos(&sc,row,col) ;
```

scn_pos sets the current position on the screen. This position is stored in sc and is also returned. (The position of the visible cursor is not affected.) The SCN_PTR data type is defined in scn.h as a far pointer. Row 0 and column 0 refers to the top left corner of the screen.

```
SCN_DATA sc ;
char attrib ;           /* screen attribute */
void scn_attrib(&sc,attrib) ;
```

scn_attrib sets the display attribute to be used when characters are written. See video.h for attribute values.

```
SCN_DATA sc ;
int c ;                 /* character to write */
void scn_wc(&sc,c) ;
```

scn_wc writes the character c at the cursor position. The cursor is advanced. Special characters such as carriage return, line feed, alert, and backspace are not recognized as special commands. The current display attribute is written with the character value at the current screen position.

```
SCN_DATA sc ;
int c ;                 /* character to write */
int a ;                 /* screen attribute to write */
void scn_wca(& sc, c, a ) ;
```

scn_wca writes the character c at the cursor position using the atttribute a. The cursor is advanced. Special characters such as carriage return, line feed, alert, and backspace are not recognized as special commands.

```
SCN_DATA sc ;
char s[10] ;            /* character string to write */
void scn_ws(& sc, s) ;
```

scn_ws writes the character string s at the cursor position. The current screen position is advanced. The current display attribute is written with each character. The null character (\0) marks the end of the string, but no other special character values are recognized.

```
SCN_DATA sc ;
char s[10] ;            /* character string to write */
```

Figure 7.30   continues

Figure 7.30   continued

```
int a ;                    /* screen attribute to write */
void scn_wsa(& sc, s, a) ;
```

`scn_wsa` writes the character string `s` at the cursor position with the attribute `a`. The current screen position is advanced. The null character (`\0`) marks the end of the string, but no other special character values are recognized.

Notes

The SCN module recognizes MDA, CGA, EGA, and VGA adapters. New adapters that do not emulate one of these adapters in text mode may require additional screen read/write functions.

Design

The characters displayed on the screen and their attributes are stored in memory locations that can be read or written by the 8088 processor, so to output characters just requires writing them to special memory locations. Some details complicate our job, however.

Several types of display adapters are used in the IBM PC: the Monochrome Display Adapter (MDA), the Color-Graphics Adapter (CGA), the Enhanced Graphics Adapter (EGA), and the Video Graphics Adapter (VGA). They differ in the address of the screen buffer and the video modes they support. Our SCN module must determine which adapter is in use and use the appropriate screen buffer address.

The layout of characters and display attributes in memory varies with the video mode in use. We will eliminate the differences by forcing the display to be in an 80-column text mode. Some adapters also support more than one display page; for simplicity we will force the use of page 0. With these limitations, the following memory layout applies to any standard adapter and any 80-column video mode. The three diagrams show the organization of lines of text in the buffer, of columns of text within a line, and of the character and attribute for each column.

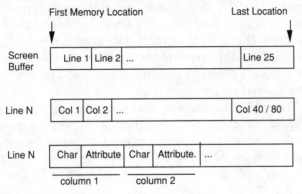

Characters and attributes each occupy one byte of memory. Characters are stored as normal ASCII values (32–126 for ASCII graphic characters). Attribute byte values are defined in the `video.h` header file.

Screen memory lies outside the data area of a C program but it can be addressed with a 32-bit pointer. The far pointers discussed in Section 7.2 provide a convenient way to read and write screen memory for any memory model. The following fragment clears the first two lines of the screen (assuming that a CGA adapter or an EGA adapter with a color display is in use).

```
typedef struct
  { char cs ;                 /* the character */
    char as ;                 /* the attribute */
  } SCN_LOC ;
SCN_LOC far *p ;
SCN_LOC sl ;
sl.cs = ' ' ;                 /* character */
sl.as = NORMAL_DISPLAY ;      /* display attribute */
SET_FP(p, 0xb800, 0) ;        /* screen address */
for(i=0 ;i< 80 ; i=i+1)
  { *p = sl ;
    p = p + 1 ;
  }
```

If we try this with an MDA, EGA, or VGA adapter, it works fine. But on a CGA adapter it produces distracting flashes on the screen. This is a hardware limitation of the color graphics adapter—if we write to the screen buffer while the CRT monitor is being updated, this flashing occurs. We can avoid the problem if we wait for *horizontal retrace* intervals when the display adapter has just finished updating a line on the CRT screen. Our functions must monitor a status port on the display adapter to detect the horizontal retrace condition.

Implementing SCN

The `scn.h` header file in Figure 7.31 defines a structure for the screen module. This structure keeps track of our current position on the screen and the display attribute being used. Each function in the SCN module uses a pointer to such a structure. The structure also contains the segment address of the screen buffer and the I/O port address of the status port. The `SCN_LOCATION` data type represents a single position on the screen. It allows us to view that position as a 16-bit unsigned data object or as two bytes containing character and attribute values. The `SCN_PTR` data type is a far pointer to a screen location.

The source file in Figure 7.32 contains several housekeeping functions. The `scn_init` function initializes the `SCN_DATA` structure. It checks the current video mode to ensure that an 80-column text mode will be used. It also forces page 0 to be the active page of display memory. A call to the `scn_type` function returns the type

FIGURE 7.31   scn.h

```
 1      /* scn.h - defines data and control values for screen module */
 2
 3
 4      #define MAX_ROWS        25   /* assume 25 rows */
 5
 6                                   /* segment addresses for screen */
 7      #define   MONO_SEG        0xb000
 8      #define   CG_SEG          0xb800
 9
10
11                                   /* screen types */
12      #define MONO_USED   0        /*    monochrome adapter */
13      #define CGA_USED    1        /*    color/graphics adapter */
14      #define EGA_USED    2        /*    EGA or VGA adapter */
15
16
17      /* definitions for display attributes are in video.h */
18
19
20
21      typedef union               /* SCREEN location data structure */
22        { unsigned ca ;           /* view as unsigned integer */
23          struct                  /* view as char and attribute */
24            { char cs ;           /*          char */
25              char as ;           /*          attribute */
26            } c_and_a ;
27        } SCN_LOCATION ;
28
29
30                                  /* pointer to screen loc. type */
31      typedef SCN_LOCATION far *SCN_PTR ;
32
33
34      typedef struct scn_data     /* screen parameters */
35        { SCN_PTR pscn ;          /* current position on the screen */
36          int nrows ;             /* number of rows on the screen */
37          int ncols ;             /* number of columns on screen */
38          int attribute ;         /* default attribute for writing */
39                                  /* function to read char and attr. */
40          unsigned (far *scn_read) ( SCN_PTR ) ;
41                                  /* function to write char and attr. */
42          void (far *scn_write) ( SCN_PTR, int , int ) ;
43        } SCN_DATA ;
44
45
46      void scn_init(SCN_DATA *) ;
47      SCN_PTR scn_pos(SCN_DATA *,int,int) ;
48      void scn_attrib(SCN_DATA *,int) ;
49      int scn_type(void) ;
50      void scn_wca(SCN_DATA *,int,int) ;
51      void scn_wc(SCN_DATA *,int) ;
52      void scn_ws(SCN_DATA *,char *) ;
53      unsigned far cga_read(SCN_PTR ) ;
54      void far cga_write( SCN_PTR ,int , int ) ;
55      unsigned far ega_read( SCN_PTR ) ;
56      void far ega_write( SCN_PTR ,int , int ) ;
```

of display adapter in use. This is used to set the screen buffer address. Addresses of functions to be called to read from and write to screen memory are also stored in the `SCN_DATA` structure. (The `ega_read` and `ega_write` functions are used for any display except for a CGA display.)

FIGURE 7.32   scn1.c

```
1    /* scn1.c - screen module - initialize for screen I/O */
2    #include <stdio.h>
3    #include <dos.h>
4    #include "asmtools.h"
5    #include "video.h"
6    #include "scn.h"
7
8                                /* screen buffer segment address */
9    unsigned scn_start[] = { 0xb000 ,   /* MDA */
10                            0xb800 ,   /* CGA */
11                            0xb800 ,   /* EGA / VGA*/
12                            0xb000    /* EGA with mono display*/
13                           } ;
14
15
16
17   void scn_init(sc)            /* initialize screen parameters */
18     SCN_DATA *sc ;             /* points to screen structure */
19     {
20        unsigned t ;
21        int stype ;             /* screen type */
22
23                                /* check video mode and reset */
24                                /* if not 80 col. text */
25       switch( vid_state(& sc->ncols) )
26         {
27         case BW80_MODE :        /* 80 column text modes */
28         case CO80_MODE :
29         case MONO_MODE :
30           break ;
31         default :               /* not an 80 column text mode */
32            vid_init(BW80_MODE) ; /* reset */
33           break ;
34         }
35      sc->nrows = MAX_ROWS ;   /* set no. rows */
36      sc->attribute = NORMAL_DISPLAY ; /* default attribute */
37      vid_page(0) ;            /* set active page = page zero */
38
39      stype = scn_type() ;     /* get screen type */
40      t = scn_start[stype] ;   /* get screen segment address */
41      SET_FP(sc->pscn,t,0) ;    /* set current screen position */
42
43      switch( stype )          /* set read/write fun. addresses */
44        {
45        case CGA_USED :          /* CGA screen - use special funs. */
46           sc->scn_read = cga_read ;
47           sc->scn_write = cga_write ;
48          break ;
49        default :               /* not CGA  - use fast funs.  */
50           sc->scn_read = ega_read ;
```

Figure 7.32   continues

Figure 7.32   continued

```
51              sc->scn_write = ega_write ;
52              break ;
53          }
54      }
55
56
57
58    SCN_PTR scn_pos(sc,row,col)    /* set current screen position */
59    SCN_DATA *sc ;
60    int row ;
61    int col ;
62    {
63        register unsigned cpos ;
64
65        cpos = row * sc->ncols + col ;
66                                 /* set position in *sc */
67        SET_FP_OFF(sc->pscn, (cpos + cpos) ) ;
68        return( sc->pscn ) ;       /* return screen position too */
69    }
70
71
72    void scn_attrib(sc,a)          /* set default attribute */
73    SCN_DATA *sc ;
74    int a ;                        /* screen attribute */
75    {
76        sc->attribute = a ;
77    }
```

The `scn_attrib` function sets the current display attribute to be used when characters are written with the screen module. `scn_pos` sets the current screen position in the same way. Note that this position is stored as an offset relative to the start of the screen buffer. This representation makes `scn_pos` slower, but it allows the functions for writing to be very fast. The assumption behind this tradeoff is that writing data will be more frequent than changing the screen position.

The `scn_type` function in Figure 7.33 determines the type of display adapter in use. The BIOS call for equipment determination in line 19 shows if the monochrome display adapter (MDA) is being used. Lines 25 to 27 call the `vid_info` function to distinguish between EGA or VGA adapters and CGA adapters.

FIGURE 7.33   scn2.c

```
1     /* scn2.c - screen module - determine screen type */
2     #include <stdio.h>
3     #include <dos.h>
4     #include "scn.h"
5     #include "video.h"
6
7
8     #define EQUIP_DET    0x11    /* software int no. for Equipment */
9                                  /* Determination */
10    #define DISP_BITS    0x30    /* mask for display type bits */
11    #define BW_DISP      0x30    /* value of bits for mono dispay */
```

Figure 7.33   continues

Figure 7.33   continued

```
12
13
14     int scn_type()          /* get type of display adapter used */
15     {
16        union REGS sreg , dreg ;
17        int stype , disp_type ;
18
19        int86(EQUIP_DET,&sreg,&dreg) ;
20        dreg.x.ax=dreg.x.ax & DISP_BITS; /* isolate display type */
21        if(dreg.x.ax == BW_DISP)/* check it */
22            stype = MONO_USED ; /*    mono type */
23        else                         /*    CGA or EGA/VGA */
24           {                         /* make a call CGA doesn't support */
25            if( vid_info(& disp_type) == 1 )
26                stype = EGA_USED ; /* call supported - EGA/VGA */
27            else stype = CGA_USED ; /* not supported  - CGA */
28           }
29        return( stype ) ;
30     }
```

Figure 7.34 lists functions for writing a single character (scn_wca and scn_wc) and writing a character string (scn_wsa and scn_ws).

FIGURE 7.34   scn3.c

```
1     /* scn3.c - screen module - write char, string functions */
2     #include "scn.h"
3
4     void scn_wca(sc,ch,at)      /* write char & attr. to screen */
5      SCN_DATA *sc ;             /* points to screen structure */
6      int ch ;                   /* character to write */
7      int at ;                   /* attribute to write */
8      {
9                                 /* write char and attribute */
10        sc->scn_write( sc->pscn, ch, at) ;
11                                 /* update current screen position */
12        sc->pscn = sc->pscn + 1 ;
13     }
14
15
16
17     void scn_wc(sc,ch)         /* write char to screen */
18      SCN_DATA *sc ;            /* points to screen structure */
19      int ch ;                  /* character to write */
20      {
21                                 /* write char and default attr. */
22        sc->scn_write( sc->pscn, ch, sc->attribute) ;
23                                 /* update current screen position */
24        sc->pscn = sc->pscn + 1 ;
25     }
26
27
28
29     void scn_ws(sc,s)          /* write string to screen */
```

Figure 7.34   continues

Figure 7.34 continued

```
30      SCN_DATA *sc ;              /* points to screen data */
31      char *s ;                   /* string to be written */
32      {
33          while( *s != '\0' )
34              {                           /* write next char */
35                                          /* with default attr. */
36                  sc->scn_write( sc->pscn, *s , sc->attribute) ;
37                                          /* update current screen position */
38                  sc->pscn = sc->pscn + 1 ;
39                  s = s + 1 ;     /* advance string pointer */
40              }
41      }
42
43
44
45      void scn_wsa(sc,s,at)        /* write string with attribute */
46        SCN_DATA *sc ;             /* points to screen structure */
47        char *s ;                  /* string to be written */
48        int at ;                   /* screen attribute */
49      {
50          while( *s != '\0' )
51              {                           /* write next char */
52                                          /* with specified attribute */
53                  sc->scn_write( sc->pscn, *s , at ) ;
54                                          /* update current screen position */
55                  sc->pscn = sc->pscn + 1 ;
56                  s = s + 1 ;     /* advance string pointer */
57              }
58      }
```

Figure 7.35 shows the functions that read from and write to screen memory. The ega_read function returns the character and attribute at the screen location to which spos points. It returns both character and attribute in a 16-bit unsigned value. The ega_write function first stores the character and attribute to be written in the temporary variable t. Then the character and attribute are copied to the screen as a single 16-bit quantity.

FIGURE 7.35 scn4.c

```
1       /* scn4.c - screen module EGA read and write functions */
2       /* also for MDA, VGA, and CGA without snow problems */
3       #include "scn.h"
4
5
6       unsigned far ega_read(spos)/* get a char and attr. from screen */
7         SCN_PTR spos ;           /* address in screen buffer */
8       {
9           return( spos->ca ) ;   /* return character and attribute */
10      }
11
12
13      void far ega_write(spos,c,a)/* put char and attr. on screen */
14        SCN_PTR spos ;           /* address in screen buffer */
```

Figure 7.35 continues

Figure 7.35   continued

```
15      int c ;                         /* char to write */
16      int a ;                         /* attribute to write */
17      {
18        SCN_LOCATION t ;
19
20        t.c_and_a.cs = c ;            /* combine char and attribute */
21        t.c_and_a.as = a ;            /* in one unsigned value */
22        spos->ca = t.ca ;
23      }
```

7.8   Writing to the CGA Screen: An Assembly Language Function

Writing to a CGA adapter requires extra care. We must detect the horizontal retrace interval and read or write to the screen immediately (within about 10 microseconds). This tight timing cannot be met by a C function that uses the `inbyte` macro to check the display adapter status port. We must write an assembly language function to meet this requirement.

Writing assembly functions for use in a C program is much easier than is writing entire programs in assembly language. Such functions are usually short and simple; we can adopt a standard format that can be copied in each source file. We can also avoid many of the complicated features of the Microsoft Macro Assembler language. The following outline shows our standard format for assembly language source files:

comments describing the contents of the file

statements defining the data area
    declarations of data variables
statements to end the data area

statements defining the code area
    1st function
        instructions for the 1st function
    2nd function
        instructions for the 2nd function
   . . .
statements to end the code area

The statements required to define data and code areas vary depending on the C compiler, the memory model, and the assembler we use. But whatever the compiler and assembler used, these defining statements can be used in every assembly source file. Most assemblers support an include statement (like the #include statement in C) that we can use to incorporate these standard statements. Figures 7.36a through 7.36d show include files appropriate for Turbo C and Microsoft C with the small memory model using version 5.0 or later of the Microsoft MASM assembler. The include files are also compatible with the Borland TASM assembler in the MASM emulation mode. The .CODE ,.DATA, and .MODEL statements are not supported by older versions of the Microsoft MASM assembler; explicit SEGMENT, GROUP, and ASSUME statements would be required. To use a different memory model, we need only change the .MODEL statement. Most of the time, we can treat the statements as "magic words"—we use whatever the compiler documentation tells us to use.

FIGURE 7.36a   begdata.ha

```
1    ;        assembler declarations before data section
2
3    ;        requires MASM 5.0 assembler or later version
4    ;        or Borland TASM assembler
5
6    ;        change this line to match the memory model in use
7            .MODEL   SMALL
8            .DATA
```

FIGURE 7.36b   enddata.ha

```
1    ;        assembler declarations after data section
2
3    ;        requires MASM 5.0 assembler or later version
4    ;        or Borland TASM assembler
5
6    ;        no statements needed here
```

FIGURE 7.36c   begcode.ha

```
1    ;        assembler declarations before code section
2
3    ;        requires MASM 5.0 assembler or later version
4    ;        or Borland TASM assembler
5            .CODE
```

FIGURE 7.36d   endcode.ha

```
1    ;        assembler declarations after code section
2
3    ;        requires MASM 5.0 assembler or later version
4    ;        or Borland TASM assembler
5
6    ;        no statements required here
```

Many of the statements in an assembly source file correspond to C statements. The following pseudo-C function shows the steps required for cga_write using a C-like syntax. One difference between C and assembly language functions should be obvious. In an assembly function, you must move data and addresses between registers and memory. In a C function, you need not worry about that level of detail. (Since the C language has no provisions for addressing ports, we fake it with the array ports.)

```
extern char ports[] ;
void cga_write(spos,c,a)      /* C analogy to cga_write */
scn_location far *spos ;      /* far pointer to screen memory */
int c ;                       /* the character */
int a ;                       /* the attribute */;
  {
    register char AL , AH ;
    register char CL , CH  ;
    register unsigned ES ;   /* put segment part of spos here */
    register unsigned DI ;   /* put segment part of spos here */

    ES = GET_FP_SEG(spos) ; /* segment part of the address */
    DI = GET_FP_OFF(spos) ; /* offset part of the address */
    CL = c ;               /* temporary home for the char */
    CH = a ;               /* temporary home for the attr. */
    while( (ports[STATUS_PORT] & 1) != 0)  /* check status */
      { ; }                                /* not retrace */
    while( (ports[STATUS_PORT] & 1) == 0)  /* check status */
      { ; }                                /* in retrace */
    AL = CL ;              /* move  char to AL */
    AH = CH ;              /* move attribute to AH */
    * (ES:DI) = AX ;       /* write char & attr. */
  }
```

Figure 7.37 shows the assembly source file containing the cga_read and cga_write functions. Lines 4, 5, 8, and 108 include the statements defining data and code areas. Lines 28 and 29 declare the function name cga_write. In C, function names are global in scope by default. In assembly language, names that are to be known by other source files must be declared as public. Note that the function is defined as _cga_write since Turbo C and Microsoft C compilers normally preface variable names with an underscore.

FIGURE 7.37　scn5.asm

```
1    ;         scn5.asm - screen module - CGA read, write functions
2
3    ;         put data here
4              include begdata.ha
5              include enddata.ha
6
7    ;         start code
8              include begcode.ha
9
```

Figure 7.37　continues

Figure 7.37   continued

```
10      CGA_STATUS_PORT equ         3DAH       ; CGA status port
11                                             ; check it for horizontal retrace
12
13      ;           cga_wrt - write char and attribute to screen
14      ;                     prevents snow with CGA adapter
15      ;
16      ;           usage:  cga_wrt(scn_pos,ca) ;
17      ;           scn_pos is a 32 bit address of the screen position
18      ;           and ca is the character and attribute to be written
19      ;
20      cga_write_args struc                ; input arguments
21              dw        0                 ; saved BP value
22              dd        0                 ; return address -32 bit far call
23      scn_pos dd        0                 ; screen position
24      schar   dw        0                 ; character to write
25      sattr   dw        0                 ; attribute to write
26      cga_write_args ends
27
28              public    _cga_write
29      _cga_write      PROC    FAR
30              push    bp
31              mov     bp,sp               ;set our arg pointer
32              push    es
33              push    di
34              les     di,dword ptr [scn_pos+bp]; get screen position
35              mov     cl,byte ptr [schar+bp]  ; get the char
36              mov     ch,byte ptr [sattr+bp]  ; and the attribute in cx
37              mov     dx,CGA_STATUS_PORT      ; load status port addr.
38              call    scn_wr1
39
40              pop     di
41              pop     es
42              pop     bp
43              ret
44      _cga_write ENDP
45
46
47      scn_wr1:               ; internal routine - writes one char
48      ;       wait for horizontal retrace, then write to screen
49              in      al,dx               ; wait until not in retrace
50              test    al,1                ; test horizontal retrace bit
51              jnz     scn_wr1
52              cli
53      scn_wr2:
54              in      al,dx               ; wait until retrace starts
55              test    al,1                ; test retrace bit
56              jz      scn_wr2
57              xchg    ax,cx               ; bring back data
58              stosw                       ; and write it to screen
59              sti                         ; now allow interrupts again
60              ret
61
62
63
64      ;       cga_read - get char and attrib from screen
65      ;                  prevents snow with CGA adapter
```

Figure 7.37   continues

Figure 7.37 continued

```
 66     ;
 67     ;          usage:  ca = cga_read(scn_pos) ;
 68     ;            scn_pos is a 32 bit address of the screen position
 69     ;          (use cga_write arg structure)
 70     ;cga_read_args struc                   ; input arguments
 71     ;       dw          0                  ; saved BP value
 72     ;       dd          0                  ; return address-32 bit far call
 73     ;scn_pos           dd         0        ; screen position address
 74     ;cga_read_args ends
 75
 76             public   _cga_read
 77     _cga_read         PROC      FAR
 78             push    bp
 79             mov     bp,sp                  ;set our arg pointer
 80             push    ds
 81             push    si
 82
 83             lds     si,dword ptr [scn_pos+bp] ; get screen address
 84             mov     dx,CGA_STATUS_PORT         ; get status port address
 85             call    scn_rd1
 86
 87             pop     si
 88             pop     ds
 89             pop     bp
 90             ret
 91     _cga_read ENDP
 92
 93
 94     scn_rd1:           ; internal routine - read one char and attribute
 95     ;       wait for horizontal retrace, then read from screen
 96             in      al,dx          ; wait until signal is low
 97             test    al,1
 98             jnz     scn_rd1
 99             cli
100     scn_rd2:
101             in      al,dx          ; wait until high
102             test    al,1
103             jz      scn_rd2
104             lodsw                  ; get char and attribute into AX
105             sti
106             ret
107
108             include endcode.ha
109             end
```

Lines 20 to 26 define the arguments to be passed to cga_write. These arguments are passed on the 8088's stack and this declaration defines their position relative to the top of the stack in cga_write. The struc statement defines a data structure much like the C struct keyword. The data declarations following the struc statement until the matching ends statement define the cga_write_args data type.

To address these arguments, lines 30 and 31 save the current value of the BP register and make BP point to the top of the stack. The same instructions will form a standard prologue at the beginning of each function. Lines 32 and 33 save other registers that are used within `cga_write`. Lines 40 to 43 form a matching epilogue restoring registers and returning to the function that called `cga_write`. This epilogue is also standard.

Line 34 loads the `far` pointer `spos` into the ES and DI registers. Lines 35 and 36 load the character and attribute into the the 8-bit registers CL and CH. (Note that input arguments are addressed with the BP register.) Line 37 loads the status port address into the DX register.

Line 38 calls the `scn_wr1` routine (lines 47 to 60) to wait for horizontal retrace and write the character. To ensure that the full retrace interval is available, lines 47 to 51 wait until horizontal retrace is not in progress. Lines 53 to 56 then wait for horizontal retrace to begin. Line 57 moves the character and attribute from CX to AX. Line 58 writes the character and attribute to the screen. The form of the `scn_wr1` routine is dictated by the short retrace time interval.

The `cga_read` function in lines 64 to 91 reads the character and attribute at the screen position. The `scn_rd1` routine in lines 94 to 106 is analogous to `scn_wr1` except that it reads the character and attribute from screen memory.

7.9   Summary

Developing toolkit functions requires understanding lots of low-level details about how the computer hardware and operating system work. Understanding the computer's instruction set and the interface between C functions and functions written in assembly language are also necessary. Testing toolkit functions is a tedious, time-consuming task. But despite the difficulty and effort involved, we had several reasons for discussing the toolkit functions.

Flexibility and the Quality of Our Applications

Without services such as single key input, fast screen output, and DOS access, most PC applications would be compromised in design or in execution speed. Our aim has been to show how to implement applications properly, and a good toolkit is essential to that goal.

Whether we implement toolkit functions from scratch or build them up from library functions, we must be able to use low-level functions when necessary. We must also be able to work around bugs and performance problems in library functions. Isolating our application programs from library functions gives control to us, not to the compiler vendor.

Portability

Some C compiler libraries implement functions similar to those in our toolkit. But if we freely used PC-specific library functions throughout an application program, it would be a substantial task to switch to a different compiler or a different environment. Our toolkit collects the functions that are dependent on the hardware, the operating system, or the C compiler. When we change compilers or environments, we know what must be changed and where to look for problems. This makes it feasible to move an application to a new compiler or a new environment.

Developing Your Skills

You may not understand all the ideas presented in this chapter yet. You may not feel at home writing or even reading assembly language functions. You may not be able to follow the descriptions in the IBM technical reference manuals either. You may even question the value of such skills since newer and better environments will replace the IBM PC and PC-DOS. But acquiring these skills is an important part of being a competent programmer. This chapter provides material that you can use to learn about how C programs interact with the operating system and the computer hardware itself.

8

A Module for Screen
Windows

The SCN functions developed in the preceding chapter provide fast screen output and full control over screen position and display attribute. However, they do not provide tools for implementing a better user interface. This chapter develops a module for defining multiple windows on the PC screen and for writing characters and strings to those windows.

Some PC environments such as Microsoft Windows and the OS/2 presentation manager provide built-in support for defining and using screen windows. But these environments are not available on every user's PC and the penalty in RAM memory and processor speed is still a significant problem. The window functions presented in this chapter do not require a special environment; they are usable on any PC or compatible. They implement a useful but somewhat limited set of functions with a corresponding small cost in RAM memory and speed.

8.1 Designing a Window Module

Many modern programs break up the PC screen into several areas or windows each devoted to a different kind of information. The basic purpose of a window interface is to simplify the writing of user interface source code for such programs. We want to direct each kind of information to its window and let the window functions confine each type of output to its area on the screen. Figure 8.1 shows the screen layout we used for the VIEW program in Chapter 3. The top area in the figure displayed information about the file being viewed. A horizontal line separated this header window from the text area. The area at the bottom of the screen displayed a list of available commands. Our implementation of the VIEW program rewrote the entire screen after each command was executed. In a more complicated program, it would be much simpler to rewrite only those parts of the screen that have changed. Defining separate windows for each type of information allows the program to remain simple and modular as more features are added and the use of the screen gets more complicated.

FIGURE 8.1   Screen Areas as Windows

```
FILE - win.h     POSITION - 0     FILE SIZE - 4366
--------------------------------------------------------------------
/* win.h - header file for window module */

                        /* need screen module definitions */
#include "scn.h"

                        /* option bits */
#define AUTO_SCROLL    0x01  /* scroll contents at end of window */
#define CLR_TO_EOL     0x02  /* clear to end-of-line when */
                             /* new line received */
#define WOPTION_MASK ( AUTO_SCROLL | CLR_TO_EOL )

                        /* presence of border lines */
#define TOP_BORDER    0x1000 /* top border line is present */
#define BOTTOM_BORDER 0x2000 /* bottom border line is present */
#define LEFT_BORDER   0x4000 /* left border line is present */
#define RIGHT_BORDER  0x8000 /* right border line is present */
--------------------------------------------------------------------


        Type one of these Input Commands
HOME  = First Page           ↑    = Previous Line   PG UP = Previous Page
END   = Last  Page           ↓    = Next Line       PG DN = Next Page

ESC   = Exit Pgm          SPACE = Move to position
```

A window module can also keep track of the location of each window on the screen. Once that location has been defined, the application program can specify positions for output relative to the window origin rather than the screen origin. These two services we have described — confining output within a window area and translating from a window relative coordinate system to the actual screen coordinate system — are the basis for a window module. To implement them, we need a data structure for each window that stores the location and size of each window:

```
typedef struct
  {
  ...
    int start_row ;    /* where window starts - row */
    int start_col ;    /* where window starts - column */
    int nrow ;         /* how many rows in the window */
    int ncol ;         /* how many columns */
  ...
  } WIN ;
```

Although this characterizes the basic purpose of a window module, more features are needed to make a useful tool. We start by looking at the real uses for windows in application programs. The windows shown in Figure 8.1 are static (they remain throughout the program's execution) and do not overlap. Figure 8.2 shows another use of a window—a help screen that appears when a help command is entered. The help window disappears when the user has read the help information and is ready to resume normal use of the program. The application program must remove the help window and restore the screen as it existed before the help command was entered. Such dynamic windows that appear and disappear without affecting the previous screen contents are often called *pop-up windows*.

FIGURE 8.2   A Help Window

```
FILE - win.h     POSITION - 0     FILE SIZE - 4366

/* win.h - header file for window module */

                          /* need screen module definitions */
#include "scn.h"
                    ┌──────────────────────────────────────┐
                    │    Type one of these Input Commands    │
                    │                                        │
#define AUTO_SCROLL │HOME  = First Page                      │  */
#define CLR_TO_EOL  │  ↑    = Previous Line                  │
                    │PG UP = Previous Page                   │
#define WOPTION_MAS │END   = Last  Page                      │
                    │  ↓   = Next Line                       │
                    │PG DN = Next Page                       │
#define TOP_BORDER  │ESC   = Exit Pgm                        │
#define BOTTOM_BORD │SPACE = Move to position                │  */
#define LEFT_BORDER │F1    = Display help screen             │
#define RIGHT_BORDE │                                        │ /
                    │press any key to return                 │
#define BORDER_BITS │                                        │
                    │                                        │
                    │                                        │
                    └──────────────────────────────────────┘
#define EOL_STATUS    0x01  /* end-of-line reached */
#define EOW_STATUS    0x02  /* end-of-window reached */
```

Figure 8.3 shows another use for pop-up windows, that is, as a window for accepting a string of characters from the keyboard. In this case, the window module must echo input, keeping the echoed characters within the window boundaries. Pop-up windows are also useful for displaying error messages and accepting input selecting a remedy. Chapter 10 illustrates using windows for handling error conditions.

FIGURE 8.3   A Pop-up Window for Collecting Input

```
       FILE - win.h     POSITION - 0     FILE SIZE - 4366
```

```
/* win.h - header file for window module */

                              /* need screen module definitions
*/
#include
        ┌─────────────────────────────────────────────┐
        │ new file position: 5000                      │
        │ file position must be <= 4366                │
#define A └─────────────────────────────────────────────┘d of
window */
#define CLR_TO_EOL   0x02   /* clear to end-of-line when */
                            /* new line received */
#define WOPTION_MASK ( AUTO_SCROLL | CLR_TO_EOL )

                            /* presence of border lines */
#define TOP_BORDER  0x1000 /* top border line is present */
#define BOTTOM_BORDER 0x2000 /* bottom border line is
present */
#define LEFT_BORDER 0x4000 /* left border line is present */
#define RIGHT_BORDER  0x8000 /* right border line is present
*/


#define BORDER_BITS 0xf000 /* mask with all boirder bits on
*/



                            /* status bits from win_wca, etc
*/
#define EOL_STATUS   0x01   /* end-of-line reached */
#define EOW_STATUS   0x02   /* end-of-window reached */
```

When windows overlap on the screen, we need some strategy for resolving conflicts. The conceptual model we will use is of opaque windows at different distances from the viewer. The front or topmost window is completely visible. Parts of other windows that lie behind the top window are not visible. Those other windows are visible where no closer window obstructs them and in turn, they obscure windows lying farther back.

In the help screen and keyboard input uses just discussed, window overlap can be handled simply. The pop-up window is in front of the other windows, and no changes to other windows are required until the pop-up window is removed. If several overlapping windows must be updated, a more complicated scheme is needed for deciding what changes appear on the screen. Some implementations of window modules ignore the problem and write all updates to the screen. Other implementations assign priorities to windows and use the priorities to decide which updates to windows are visible on the screen.

A related issue is whether the window module remembers the contents of each window. For example, when a window is removed from the screen, is the screen automatically updated to show the contents of previously obscured parts of other windows? Most window modules allow windows to be of any size up to that of the full screen. Some implementations allow windows to be larger than the size of the actual screen used.

Some windows support displaying graphics as well as text characters. Even if graphics functions are not supported, the PC display adapter can be operated in graphics mode or text mode. Although using graphics mode allows screen graphics to be integrated with text output, the penalty in RAM memory and execution speed is significant. The display adapter mode also affects the operations provided; in text mode, characters and screen attributes can be read back from the screen.

Our Design Choices

Now that we have outlined the design issues, we can describe our choices. Simplicity and good performance are favored over generality. Our module does not record priorities for windows or resolve overlap conflicts. Any output written to a window appears on the screen as though the window were in front. If updates to several overlapping windows are required, it is up to the application program to resolve conflicts and write only those updates that should be visible. Our module does not remember contents of windows. Instead, we provide functions for saving and restoring the area corresponding to a window.

For fast operation, we operate the PC display in text mode. We also rely on reading back characters and attributes from the PC screen.

More Features

A practical window module needs more features to be useful. Most windows need borders to distinguish them from the other parts of the screen. When a window extends to the edge of the screen, that edge of the border should not be used. We also provide full control of screen attributes so that fields can be highlighted and different windows can be provided contrasting attributes.

Several functions write individual characters and strings to a window. These functions maintain a current writing position, which is advanced for each character written. The module provides functions to set and get the current writing position. This writing position is separate from the position of the visible (blinking) cursor, but we provide a function for placing the cursor at a position within a window.

Clearing or scrolling a window's contents is supported as is clearing part or all of a line. Functions to write characters and strings recognize the backspace and newline characters as commands to back up a character or to advance to a new line.

In some applications, we want the window output to cause automatic scrolling when the end of the window is reached. In other cases, we do not want scrolling to occur automatically. Our module supports both choices. Another option is for clearing the rest of a line when a newline character is output.

The SCN module in Chapter 7 provides the appropriate low-level screen I/O functions for the display adapter in use. We also use that module to set screen addresses. Figure 8.4 describes the functions that make up our WINDOW module and their use.

FIGURE 8.4   Description of WINDOW Module

Name
WINDOW   module for screen output to windows

Usage
```
#include  "video.h"
#include  "win.h"
#include  "keyio.h"
WIN w1 , w2 ;
char s[21] ;
int end_keys[] = { ASCTAB , F1KEY } ;
                /* start at row 2, col 10 , 12 rows, 40 columns */
                /* AUTO_SCROLL and CLR_TO_EOL options */
                /* no border */
win_define(& w1, 2, 10, 12, 40, AUTO_SCROLL | CLR_TO_EOL, NULL ) ;
win_display(& w1) ;
win_wca(& w1, 'a' , REVERSE_VIDEO) ;
                /* start at row 0, col 20 , 5 rows, 20 columns */
                /* no options */
                /* a single line border (no top edge) */
win_define(& w2 , 0,20, 5 , 20, 0, & dline_border ) ;
win_popup(& w2) ;          /*  pop up w2 window */
win_ws( & w2, "error condition) ;
getkey() ;                 /* wait for a key to be pressed */
win_unpop(& w2) ;          /* remove pop-up window */
                           /* get string , 20 chars max */
win_gets(s,0,20,endkeys,2,& w1)  ;
```

Function
The functions in the WINDOW module create screen windows and display output in those windows. The `video.h` header file defines symbolic constants and data types needed to use the WINDOW module.

Figure 8.4   continues

Figure 8.4   continued

Window Creation and Display Function Descriptions

```
WIN * pw ;      /* points to a WIN structure you allocate */
                /* or declare - one structure per window */
int row ;       /* starting point of window- top row on screen */
int col ;       /* starting point of window - leftmost column */
int nrow ;      /* number of rows in the window */
int ncol ;      /* number of columns in the window */
BORDER *pb ;    /* specifies the type of border to use */
unsigned options ; /* specifies options for window output */
void win_define(pw, row, col, nrow, ncol, pb, options) ;
```

win_define defines window parameters in the structure to which pw points; it does not display the window or its border on the screen. The top left corner of the screen has coordinates row=0, col=0, whereas row=24, col=79 refer to the bottom right corner of the screen. The row and col coordinates defining the window starting point and the number of rows and columns (nr and nc) refer to the window area to which data will be written — the border will be written outside the area specified. The BORDER structure identified by pb defines the characters that will be written as a border around the window and the screen attribute written with the border characters. If the NULL value is specified for pb, no border will be used for this window. Global variables defining single-line borders (line_border) and double-line borders (dline_border) are defined in the WIN module and can be specified in calling win_define. The options argument specifies options for handling window output. These values are discussed along with the window output functions.

```
WIN *pw ;
unsigned options ;
void win_options(pw, options) ;
```

The win_options function changes options for a window already defined with the win_define function. The new options will be used in all subsequent output to this window.

```
WIN *pw ;
int def_attrib ;            /* new default screen attribute */
int clr_attrib ;            /* new attribute for clearing window */
void win_attrib(pw, def_attrib, clr_attrib) ;
```

The win_attrib function changes the screen attributes used for window output (def_attrib) and for clearing the window (clr_attrib). The new attributes will be used in all subsequent operations on this window.

```
WIN *pw ;
void win_display(pw) ;
```

The win_display function displays the window on the PC screen. The border specified when win_define was called is written, and the window area itself is cleared. The previous contents of the screen are not saved.

Figure 8.4   continues

Figure 8.4   continued

```
WIN *pw ;
SCN_LOCATION  *win_save_area(pw)  ;
```

The `win_save_area` function allocates space to save the screen contents to be occupied by the window and its border. The save area is allocated with the standard library function `calloc`. If allocation fails, `win_save_area` returns a `NULL` pointer value. The `SCN_LOCATION` data type is defined in the `scn.h` header file, which is included by the `win.h` header file. (You do not include `scn.h` explicitly.)

```
WIN *pw ;
SCN_LOCATION *psave ;    /* points to a save area */
void win_save_window(pw, psave) ;
```

The win_save_window function copies the screen contents corresponding to the window and its border to the area to which psave points. The SCN_LOCATION data type is defined in the scn.h header file, which is included by the win.h header file. (You do not include scn.h explicitly.)

```
WIN *pw ;
SCN_LOCATION *psave ;   /* points to a save area */
win_restore_window(pw,psave)  ;
```

The win_restore function copies previously saved screen contents back to the area corresponding to the window and its border. The SCN_LOCATION data type is defined in the scn.h header file, which is included by the win.h header file. (You do not include scn.h explicitly.)

```
WIN *pw ;
void win_popup(pw) ;
```

win_popup saves the screen contents corresponding to the window and then displays the window. The address of the save area is stored in the structure to which pw points.

```
WIN *pw ;
void win_unpop(pw) ;
```

win_unpop restores the screen contents corresponding to the window (previously saved by calling win_popup). The save area is then freed.

```
WIN *pw ;
void win_remove(pw) ;
```

win_remove is called when the window is no longer needed. The contents of the screen are not affected.

Figure 8.4   continues

Figure 8.4   continued

Window Output Function Descriptions

```
int c ;          /* character to write */
int a ;          /* screen attribute to write */
WIN *pw ;        /* points to a window structure */
unsigned win_wca(pw,c,a) ;
```

`win_wca` writes one character and attribute to the window at the current writing position. The writing position is advanced to the next screen location within the window. If the end of a line is reached, the writing position is reset to the first column of the next line. If the writing position is already on the last line of the window, the action taken depends on the setting for the `AUTO_SCROLL` option. If that option is set, the contents of the window are scrolled upward. The new writing position is set at the first column of the last row. If the `AUTO_SCROLL` option is not set, the writing position is set at the the last column of the last row.

The backspace (`\b`) and newline (`\n`) characters are treated as commands rather than as characters to be output. For the backspace character, `win_wca` moves the writing position backward and writes a space character. If the writing position is in the leftmost column of the window, no action is taken. For a newline character, the writing position is moved to the first column of the next line in the window. If the `CLR_TO_EOL` option has been set, the remaining columns of the line are cleared first. If the writing position is already on the last line of the window, action depends on the setting for the `AUTO_SCROLL` option.

The status value returned by `win_wca` shows whether the call resulted in end-of-line or end-of-window conditions. Symbolic constants for these status conditions are defined in `win.h`:

```
EOL_STATUS        — end-of-line occurred
EOW_STATUS        — end-of-window occurred
SCROLL_STATUS     — window contents were scrolled
```

```
int c ;          /* character to write */
WIN *pw ;        /* points to a window structure */
unsigned win_wc(pw,c ) ;
```

win_wc writes one character and attribute to the window at the current writing position. The default attribute previously defined by win_define or win_attrib is used. Otherwise, operation is identical to that of win_wca.

```
char *s ;        /* character string to write */
int a ;          /* screen attribute to write */
int n ;          /* maximum number of characters to write */
WIN *pw ;        /* points to a window structure */
unsigned win_wsa(pw,s,a,n) ;
```

win_wsa writes the character string s with the attribute specified to the window at the current writing position. The result is the same as though win_wca had been

Figure 8.4   continues

Figure 8.4   continued

called for each character in the string. The argument n limits the number of characters that will be written. This can be used to output an array of characters not
terminated by a null character. The symbolic constant ALL_STRING, defined in
win.h, may be used when no limit is required. The status returned is cumulative for
all characters output.

```
char *s ;        /* character string to write */
int n ;          /* maximum number of characters to write */
WIN *pw ;        /* points to a window structure */
unsigned win_ws(pw,s, n) ;
```

win_ws writes the character string s with the default attribute to the window at the
current writing position. It is otherwise identical to win_wsa.

```
int a ;          /* screen attribute to write */
int n ;          /* maximum number of locations to write */
WIN *pw ;        /* points to a window structure */
unsigned win_wa(pw, a, n) ;
```

win_wa writes the attribute a to n successive locations in the specified window,
starting at the current writing position. The writing position when win_wa returns is
after the locations changed. The status value returned reflects the same conditions
as for a call to win_wca.

```
char *pc ;       /* place characters here */
char *pa ;       /* place attributes here */
int n ;          /* maximum number of locations to read */
WIN *pw ;        /* points to a window structure */
unsigned win_gca(pw,pc, pa , n) ;
```

win_gca reads characters and attributes from n locations starting at the current
writing position. The writing position when win_gca returns is after the locations
read. The status value returned reflects the same conditions as for a call to
win_wca.

Window Output Position Function Descriptions

```
int *prow ;      /* store row position at this address */
int *pcol ;      /* store column position at this address */
WIN *pw ;        /* points to a window structure */
void win_getpos(pw, prow, pcol) ;
```

win_getpos places the row and column values of the current writing position in
the locations specified by prow and pcol. These values are relative to the origin for
the window.

```
int row ;        /* new position - row value */
int col ;        /* new position - column value */
WIN *pw ;        /* points to a window structure */
void win_setpos(pw, row, col ) ;
```

Figure 8.4   continues

Figure 8.4   continued

win_setpos sets the current writing position as specified by row and col. These values are relative to the origin for the window.

```
int row ;              /* visible cursor position - row value */
int col ;              /* visible cursor position - column value */
WIN *pw ;              /* points to a window structure */
void win_disp_cur(pw, row , col ) ;
```

win_disp_cur sets the visible cursor position as specified by row and col. These values are relative to the origin for the window. If a negative value is specified for row, the current writing position is used to set the visible cursor position.

Window Clearing Functions

```
WIN *pw ;          /* points to a window structure */
unsigned win_wbs(pw) ;
```

win_wbs performs a backspace operation as described for the win_wca function. The status value returned has the same meaning.

```
WIN *pw ;          /* points to a window structure */
unsigned win_clrline(pw ) ;
```

win_clrline writes space characters with the clearing attribute for the window to the entire line where the current writing position is located. The current writing position is not changed.

```
WIN *pw ;          /* points to a window structure */
unsigned win_clreol(pw ) ;
```

win_clreol writes space characters with the clearing attribute for the window to the rest of the line starting at the current writing position. The current writing position is not changed.

```
WIN *pw ;          /* points to a window structure */
unsigned win_clr_window(pw ) ;
```

win_clr_window writes space characters with the clearing attribute for the window to the entire window area. The current writing position is not changed.

```
WIN *pw ;          /* points to a window structure */
int n ;            /* how far to scroll */
int dir ;          /* direction to scroll */
unsigned win_scroll(pw , n , dir) ;
```

win_scroll moves the entire contents of the window up or down by n lines. The n lines vacated at the top or bottom of the window are filled with space characters with the previously defined clearing attribute. Symbolic constants for directions, SCROLL_UP and SCROLL_DOWN, are specified in win.h. The current writing position is not changed.

Figure 8.4   continues

Figure 8.4 continued

String Input Function — Echo Characters to a Window

```
char *s ;              /* place character string here */
int next ;             /* start placing characters at s[next] */
int maxs ;             /* maximum size allowed for the string */
int end_keys[] ;       /* list of keys that end string input */
int nend ;             /* number of keys in the list */
WIN *pw ;              /* echo characters to this window */
int win_gets(s, next, maxs, end_keys, nend, pw) ;
```

win_gets collects keyboard input and stores the characters in C string form at the address specified by s. ASCII graphic characters (printable characters) are stored in the string and echoed to the window specified by pw. The backspace character deletes a single character from the string and backs up one screen location. The control-X character deletes all the characters present in the string and backs up the corresponding number of locations on the screen. Neither backspace or control-X has any effect if no characters are present in the string. Carriage return and line feed characters signal the end of the string input as do any of the keys listed in the end_keys array. The ending key value is returned by win_gets. Keystrokes that do not fit any of these categories are ignored. The return value and the key values in end_keys are in the format returned by getkey. Symbolic constants for many keys are defined in keyio.h. A value of -1 is returned if the maximum length of the string is reached. The next argument indicates the number of characters already present in the string. next should normally have a value of 0 to indicate that the string is empty on entry.

8.2 WINDOW Source Files

win.h

The `win.h` file in Figure 8.5 defines constants, data types, globals, and functions prototypes for the WINDOW module. Some declarations are needed in programs that call the WINDOW functions, whereas others are needed only within the WINDOW module. The `WIN` structure in lines 53 to 70 defines the information required for each active window. The `start_row` and `start_col` members define the origin of the window (relative to 0,0 as the top left corner of the screen). The `nrow` and `ncol` members store the size of the window. `row` and `col` define the position where the next character will be written (relative to 0,0 as the origin of the window).

The member `pscn` contains the screen address corresponding to the row and column values. This screen address is set by calls to the `scn_pos` function from Chapter 7. The window origin members `start_row` and `start_col` and the size members `nrow` and `ncol` refer to the window area only; the `bstart_row` and start_col members refer to the origin of the window area and its surrounding border. bnrow and bncol refer to the size including the border. Two screen attributes are defined: a default attribute to writing characters and strings and an attribute to be used when clearing all or part of a window. The pborder member points to a BORDER structure defining the border used.

FIGURE 8.5   win.h

```
1     /* win.h - header file for window module */
2
3                                  /* need screen module definitions */
4     #include "scn.h"
5
6                                  /* option bits */
7     #define AUTO_SCROLL   0x01  /* scroll contents at end of window */
8     #define CLR_TO_EOL    0x02  /* clear to end-of-line when */
9                                  /* new line received */
10    #define WOPTION_MASK ( AUTO_SCROLL | CLR_TO_EOL )
11
12                                 /* presence of border lines */
13    #define TOP_BORDER    0x1000 /* top border line is present */
14    #define BOTTOM_BORDER 0x2000 /* bottom border line is present */
15    #define LEFT_BORDER 0x4000 /* left border line is present */
16    #define RIGHT_BORDER  0x8000 /* right border line is present */
17
18    #define BORDER_BITS 0xf000 /* mask with all border bits on */
19
20
21                                 /* status bits from win_wca, etc */
22    #define EOL_STATUS    0x01  /* end-of-line reached */
23    #define EOW_STATUS    0x02  /* end-of-window reached */
24    #define SCROLL_STATUS 0x04  /* contents were scrolled */
25
26
27                                 /* scroll directions for win_scroll */
28    #define SCROLL_UP        1  /* scroll window contents up */
29    #define SCROLL_DOWN      0  /* scroll window contents down */
30
31
32    #define ALL_STRING    2000  /* use as dummy char count in */
33                                 /* win-ws and win_wsa */
34
35                                 /* special integer values */
36    #define NO_CHAR        999  /* signals no char present */
37    #define NO_ATTRIB      999  /* signals no attribute present */
38
39
40    typedef struct               /* window border description */
41      { char top_line ;          /* char for top line of border */
42        char left_line ;         /* char for left side of border */
43        char bottom_line ;       /* char for bottom line */
44        char right_line ;        /* char for right side */
45        char top_left ;          /* char for top left corner */
46        char top_right ;         /* char for top right corner */
47        char bottom_right ;      /* char for bottom right corner */
48        char bottom_left;        /* char for bottom left corner */
49        int b_attrib ;           /* border screen attribute */
50      } BORDER ;
```

Figure 8.5   continues

Figure 8.5   continued

```
51
52
53      typedef struct               /* window data structure */
54        { int start_row ;          /* starting position - x */
55          int start_col ;          /* starting position - y */
56          int nrow ;               /* number of rows taken */
57          int ncol ;               /* number of columns taken */
58          int row ;                /* writing position - x */
59          int col ;                /* writing position - y */
60          int d_attrib ;           /* default screen attribute */
61          int c_attrib ;           /* clear line/window attribute */
62          int bstart_row ;         /* starting row with border */
63          int bstart_col ;         /* starting col with border */
64          int bnrow ;              /* number of rows with border */
65          int bncol ;              /* number of columns with border */
66          unsigned options ;       /* option bits */
67          SCN_PTR pscn ;           /* position on screen */
68          void *psave ;            /* points to a save area */
69          BORDER *pborder ;        /* points to a border description */
70        } WIN ;
71
72
73      extern SCN_DATA win_sc ;     /* screen parameters */
74      extern BORDER line_border ;  /* single line border */
75      extern BORDER dline_border;  /* double line border */
76
77                                   /* function prototypes */
78      void win_define(WIN *, int, int, int, int, BORDER *, unsigned) ;
79      void win_options(WIN *, unsigned ) ;
80      void win_attrib(WIN *, int , int ) ;
81      void win_display(WIN *) ;
82      SCN_LOCATION *win_save_area(WIN *) ;
83      void win_save_window(WIN *, SCN_LOCATION * ) ;
84      void win_restore_window(WIN *, SCN_LOCATION * ) ;
85      void win_remove(WIN *) ;
86
87      void win_getpos(WIN *, int * , int *) ;
88      void win_setpos(WIN *, int , int ) ;
89      void win_disp_cur(WIN *,int , int ) ;
90
91      unsigned win_wc(WIN *, int) ;
92      unsigned win_wca(WIN *, int , int ) ;
93      unsigned win_ws(WIN *, char *, int ) ;
94      unsigned win_wsa(WIN *, char *, int , int ) ;
95      unsigned win_wa(WIN *, int , int) ;
96      unsigned win_new_line(WIN *) ;
97      unsigned win_gca(WIN *, char *, char *, int) ;
98      void win_wbs(WIN *) ;
99      void win_clrline(WIN *) ;
100     void win_clreol(WIN *) ;
101     void win_clr_window(WIN * ) ;
102     void win_scroll(WIN *, int , int ) ;
103
104     void win_binit(WIN *) ;
105     void win_dborder(WIN *) ;
106
107     int win_popup(WIN *) ;
108     void win_unpop(WIN *) ;
109     int win_gets(char *,int,int,int [], int, WIN *) ;
```

Borders take up a single character width box around the window itself. They are drawn using PC characters. The BORDER structure in lines 40 to 50 specifies the characters used for each edge and corner of the border. Lines 74 and 75 declare global variables for single line borders and double line borders. When a window is defined, bits are set in the options member to reflect the presence of each edge of the border. Lines 13 to 16 define the symbolic constants corresponding to these bits.

The options member in line 66 also stores settings for the AUTO_SCROLL and CLR_TO_EOL options defined in lines 7 and 8 of win.h. Lines 78 to 109 define function prototypes for the functions in the WINDOW module. Since several definitions from the scn.h header file are required in win.h, line 4 includes that file.

win1.c

The win_define function shown in Figure 8.6 sets up parameters for a window. The calling function allocates space for the WIN structure. The origin and size arguments are copied to the structure. The writing position is set to the window origin and the default and clearing attributes are set to the NORMAL_DISPLAY value defined in video.h: white characters on a dark background.

A call to win_binit fills out information related to the border used. The WINDOW functions rely on the SCN functions for screen I/O, and the win_sc structure holds screen parameters. Lines 24 to 27 initialize the screen structure the first time that win_define is called.

FIGURE 8.6   win1.c

```
1      /* win1.c - window module, initialization */
2      #include <stdlib.h>
3      #include <stdio.h>
4      #include "video.h"
5      #include "win.h"
6
7      SCN_DATA win_sc ;              /* screen parameters, and ptrs to */
8                                     /* read and write functions, too */
9      static int first_call = 0;  /* allows us to detect first call */
10                                    /* to win_define. */
11
12
13                                     /* define a window */
14     void win_define(pw, rstart, cstart, nrow , ncol ,
15               pbord , woptions )
16     WIN *pw ;                      /* points to a WIN struct */
17     int rstart ;                   /* starting row value (top) */
18     int cstart ;                   /* starting col value (left) */
19     int nrow ;                     /* number of rows - without border */
20     int ncol ;                     /* number of cols - without border */
21     BORDER *pbord ;                /* points to border structure */
22     unsigned woptions ;            /* option bits */
23     {
24         if( first_call == 0 )  /* initialize screen structure */
25           { scn_init( & win_sc ) ; /* on first call */
26             first_call = 1 ;
```

Figure 8.6   continues

Figure 8.6   continued

```
27              }
28
29          pw->start_row = rstart ; /* start of window on screen */
30          pw->start_col = cstart ;
31          pw->nrow = nrow ;          /* window size */
32          pw->ncol = ncol ;
33          pw->row = 0 ;              /* current writing position */
34          pw->col = 0 ;
35          win_setpos(pw,0,0) ;      /* set screen position */
36          pw->pborder = pbord ;     /* border description */
37          pw->options = woptions &  WOPTION_MASK ;
38          pw->psave = NULL ;        /* save area address */
39                                    /* define window attributes */
40          win_attrib(pw, NORMAL_DISPLAY , NORMAL_DISPLAY ) ;
41          win_binit(pw) ;           /* set start and size with borders */
42      }
43
44
45      void win_options(pw, woptions)
46      WIN *pw ;                     /* points to a WIN struct */
47      unsigned woptions ;           /* option bits */
48      {
49          pw->options = ( pw->options & ~ WOPTION_MASK )
50                      | ( woptions & WOPTION_MASK ) ;
51      }
52
53
54      void win_attrib(pw, def_attrib , clr_attrib)
55      WIN *pw ;                     /* points to a WIN struct */
56      int def_attrib ;              /* default writing attribute */
57      int clr_attrib ;              /* attribute for clearing window */
58      {
59          pw->d_attrib = def_attrib ;
60          pw->c_attrib = clr_attrib ;
61      }
62
63
64      void win_display(pw)
65      WIN *pw ;                     /* points to a WIN struct */
66      {
67          win_dborder(pw) ;         /* display border */
68          win_clr_window(pw ) ;  /* clear contents area */
69      }
70
71
72                                    /* allocate window save area */
73      SCN_LOCATION *win_save_area(pw)
74      WIN *pw ;                     /* points to a WIN struct */
75      {
76          SCN_LOCATION *p ;
77          int nsize ;
78
79          nsize = pw->bnrow * pw->bncol ;
80          p = (SCN_LOCATION *) calloc( nsize , sizeof( SCN_LOCATION) ) ;
81          return( p ) ;
82      }
83
84
```

Figure 8.6   continues

Figure 8.6   continued

```
85
86      void win_save_window(pw,p)  /* save window area from screen */
87      WIN *pw ;                   /* points to a WIN struct */
88      SCN_LOCATION *p ;           /* points to a save area */
89      {
90        int row , nc , i , j ;
91        SCN_PTR pscn ;
92
93        if( p == NULL )
94            return ;
95
96        row = pw->bstart_row ;
97        nc = pw->bncol ;
98
99        for( i=0 ; i< pw->bnrow ; i=i+1) /* save each row */
100          { pscn = scn_pos(& win_sc,row, pw->bstart_col ) ;
101            for( j=0 ; j< nc ; j=j+1)   /* copy one row */
102              { p->ca = win_sc.scn_read(pscn) ;
103                p = p + 1 ;
104                pscn = pscn + 1 ;
105              }
106            row = row + 1 ;
107          }
108      }
109
110
111
112
113     void win_restore_window(pw,p)
114     WIN *pw ;                     /* points to a WIN struct */
115     SCN_LOCATION *p ;             /* points to a save area */
116     {
117        int row , nc , i , j ;
118        SCN_PTR pscn ;
119
120        if( p == NULL )
121            return ;
122
123        row = pw->bstart_row ;
124        nc = pw->bncol ;
125
126        for( i=0 ; i< pw->bnrow ; i=i+1)
127          { pscn = scn_pos(& win_sc,row, pw->bstart_col) ;
128            for( j=0 ; j<nc ; j=j+1)    /* copy one row */
129              { win_sc.scn_write(pscn,p->c_and_a.cs,
130                    p->c_and_a.as) ;
131                p = p + 1 ;
132                pscn = pscn + 1 ;
133              }
134            row = row + 1 ;
135          }
136      }
137
138
139
140     void win_remove(pw)           /* remove window definition */
141     WIN *pw ;                     /* points to a WIN struct */
142     {
143     }
```

The win_options function sets values for the AUTO_SCROLL and CLR_TO_EOL options. The win_attrib function sets both the default attribute for screen output and the attribute used for clearing the screen.

The win_define function fills out the WIN structure but does not display anything on the screen. The win_display function puts a window on the screen. A call to win_dborder draws the border, and a call to win_clr_window clears the window area itself.

win_save_area calculates the size of a save area large enough to hold the contents of the window and its border area. It uses the library function calloc to allocate the save area. The data type SCN_LOCATION corresponds to one position on the screen — one byte for a character and one byte for an attribute (see scn.h).

The win_save_window function copies the contents of the screen corresponding to the window and its border into the save area specified by p. It uses the screen read function whose address is stored in the SCN structure win_sc to get each character and attribute. win_restore_window copies the contents of a save area back to the screen area corresponding to a window. It uses the screen write function whose address is also in win_sc.

The win_remove function is called when the application has no further use for a window. In this application, win_remove does nothing, but if we changed the implementation, it might perform some actions.

win2.c

The win_getpos function in Figure 8.7 copies the current row and column numbers to the locations pointed to by prow and pcol. win_setpos sets the current writing position. A call to scn_pos sets the screen address for pscn. The window origin coordinates are added to the row and column values passed to scn_pos.

FIGURE 8.7   win2.c

```
1    /* win2.c - window module, get/set writing position */
2    #include "video.h"
3    #include "win.h"
4
5
6    void win_getpos(pw, prow, pcol)/* get writing position */
7    WIN *pw ;                      /* points to a WIN struct */
8    int *prow ;                    /* put row position here */
9    int *pcol ;                    /* put col position here */
10   {
11      *prow = pw->row ;
12      *pcol = pw->col ;
13   }
14
15
16   void win_setpos(pw, row , col) /* get writing position */
17   WIN *pw ;                      /* points to a WIN struct */
```

Figure 8.7   continues

Figure 8.7   continued

```
18      int row ;                        /* new row position */
19      int col ;                        /* new col position */
20      {
21         if( row >= pw->nrow )      /* check for row and col. */
22            row = pw->nrow - 1;     /* too large */
23         if( col >= pw->ncol )
24            col = pw->ncol - 1 ;
25
26         pw->row = row ;
27         pw->col = col ;
28         pw->pscn = scn_pos(& win_sc, pw->start_row + row ,
29                   pw->start_col + col ) ;
30      }
31
32
33
34      void win_disp_cur(pw, row, col)/* set visible cursor in window */
35      WIN *pw ;                        /* points to a WIN struct */
36      int row ;                        /* cursor's row position */
37      int col ;                        /* cursor's col. position */
38      {
39
40         if( row < 0 )                 /* if negative, use write position */
41            { row = pw->row ;
42              col = pw->col ;
43            }
44
45         vid_set_cur(pw->start_row + row , pw->start_col + col) ;
46      }
```

The win_disp_cur function sets the visible cursor to a position within the window specified. If the row number is less than 0, the current writing position is used as the cursor position. The vid_set_cur function is from the VIDEO module in Chapter 7.

win3.c

The win_wca function in Figure 8.8 writes the specified character and screen attribute to the window at the current writing position. It uses the screen write function whose address is stored in the win_sc structure to write the character and attribute. It advances the column number and the screen address. If the column number reaches the number of columns defined, the win_new_line function is called to handle this special case.

A backspace character is handled as a backspace command rather than as a character to be written to the window. The newline character is also handled as a command — the win_new_line function is called to move the writing position. win_wca returns a status value that indicates whether an end-of-line or end-of-window condition occurred or whether the window was scrolled.

FIGURE 8.8   win3.c

```
1     /* win3.c - window module, write chars, strings */
2     #include "video.h"
3     #include "win.h"
4
5
6     unsigned win_wca(pw,c,a)    /* write char and attrib. to window */
7     WIN *pw ;                   /* points to window data structure */
8     int c ;                     /* character to write */
9     int a ;                     /* screen attribute to write */
10    {
11
12      if( c == '\n' )
13          return( win_new_line(pw) ) ;
14      else if( c == '\b' )
15        { win_wbs(pw) ;
16          return( 0 ) ;
17        }
18
19      win_sc.scn_write(pw->pscn, c, a) ;
20      pw->pscn = pw->pscn + 1 ;
21      pw->col = pw->col + 1 ;
22
23      if( pw->col >= pw-> ncol )
24          return( win_new_line(pw) ) ;
25      else return( 0 ) ;
26    }
27
28
29    unsigned win_wc(pw,c)       /* write char to window */
30    WIN *pw ;                   /* points to window data structure */
31    int c ;                     /* character to write */
32    {
33      if( c == '\n' )
34          return( win_new_line(pw) ) ;
35      else if( c == '\b' )
36        { win_wbs(pw) ;
37          return( 0 ) ;
38        }
39
40      win_sc.scn_write(pw->pscn, c, pw->d_attrib) ;
41      pw->pscn = pw->pscn + 1 ;
42      pw->col = pw->col + 1 ;
43
44      if( pw->col >= pw-> ncol )
45          return( win_new_line(pw) ) ;
46      else return( 0 ) ;
47    }
48
49
50
51
52    unsigned win_wsa(pw,s,a,n) /* write string & attr. to window */
53    WIN *pw ;                   /* points to window data structure */
54    char *s ;                   /* character string to write */
55    int a ;                     /* screen attribute to write */
56    int n ;                     /* max. number chars to write */
57    {
```

Figure 8.8   continues

Figure 8.8   continued

```
58        unsigned status ;
59
60        status = 0 ;
61        while( (n > 0) && (*s != '\0') )
62          { if( *s == '\n' )
63              status = status | win_new_line(pw) ;
64            else if( *s == '\b' )
65              win_wbs(pw) ;
66            else
67              { win_sc.scn_write(pw->pscn, *s , a) ;
68                pw->pscn = pw->pscn + 1 ;
69                pw->col = pw->col + 1 ;
70                if( pw->col >= pw-> ncol )
71                    status = status | win_new_line(pw) ;
72              }
73            s = s + 1 ;              /* advance to next char */
74            n = n - 1 ;              /* reduce char count */
75          }
76        return( status ) ;
77      }
78
79
80
81
82
83    unsigned win_ws(pw,s,n)        /* write string to window */
84    WIN *pw ;                      /* points to window data structure */
85    char *s ;                      /* character string to write */
86    int n ;                        /* max. number chars to write */
87    {
88      int a ;
89      unsigned status ;
90
91      a = pw->d_attrib ;
92      status = 0 ;
93      while( (n > 0) && (*s != '\0') )
94        { if( *s == '\n' )
95              status = status | win_new_line(pw) ;
96          else if( *s == '\b' )
97              win_wbs(pw) ;
98          else
99            { win_sc.scn_write(pw->pscn, *s , a) ;
100               pw->pscn = pw->pscn + 1 ;
101               pw->col = pw->col + 1 ;
102               if( pw->col >= pw-> ncol )
103                   status = status | win_new_line(pw) ;
104             }
105           s = s + 1 ;              /* advance to next char */
106           n = n - 1 ;              /* reduce char count */
107         }
108       return( status ) ;
109     }
110
111
112   unsigned win_wa(pw,a,n)        /* write attribute only to window */
113   WIN *pw ;                      /* points to window data structure */
114   int a ;                        /* screen attribute to write */
```

Figure 8.8   continues

Figure 8.8   continued

```
115     int n ;                          /* no. screen positions to write */
116     {
117       SCN_LOCATION t ;
118       unsigned status ;
119
120       status = 0 ;
121       while( n > 0 )
122         { t.ca = win_sc.scn_read(pw->pscn) ; /* get char & attr */
123                          /* rewrite with new attribute */
124           win_sc.scn_write(pw->pscn, t.c_and_a.cs , a) ;
125           pw->pscn = pw->pscn + 1 ;
126           pw->col = pw->col + 1 ;
127
128           if( pw->col >= pw-> ncol )
129             { status = status | EOL_STATUS ;
130               pw->col = 0 ;
131               pw->row = pw->row + 1 ;
132               if( pw->row >= pw->nrow )
133                 { pw->row = pw->nrow - 1 ;
134                   pw->col = pw->ncol - 1 ;
135                   status = status | EOW_STATUS ;
136                 }
137               pw->pscn = scn_pos( & win_sc,
138                   pw->start_row + pw->row ,
139                   pw->start_col + pw->col ) ;
140             }
141           n = n - 1 ;
142         }
143
144       return( status ) ;
145     }
146
147
148
149     unsigned win_new_line(pw)
150     WIN *pw ;                        /* points to window data structure */
151     {
152       unsigned status ;
153       int col_save ;
154
155                              /* clear rest of line? */
156       if( (pw->options & CLR_TO_EOL) != 0 )
157           win_clreol(pw) ;     /*  yes - use win_clr_eol function */
158
159       status = EOL_STATUS ;
160       pw->col = 0 ;
161       pw->row = pw->row + 1 ;
162       if( pw->row >= pw->nrow ) /* check for bottom of window */
163         { status = status | EOW_STATUS ;
164           if( (pw->options & AUTO_SCROLL) != 0)
165             {                  /* scroll window contents up */
166               win_scroll(pw,1, SCROLL_UP) ;
167               status = status | SCROLL_STATUS ;
168               pw->row = pw->row - 1 ;
169             }
170           else                  /* not auto-scroll - set at */
171             { pw->row = pw->nrow - 1 ; /* last row */
```

Figure 8.8   continues

Figure 8.8   continued

```
172                   pw->col = pw->ncol - 1 ; /* last col */
173              }
174          }
175        pw->pscn = scn_pos(& win_sc,pw->start_row + pw->row,
176                  pw->start_col + pw->col ) ;
177        return( status ) ;
178      }
179
180
181     unsigned win_gca(pw,pc,pa,n) /* get char & attrib. from window */
182     WIN *pw ;                 /* points to window data structure */
183     char *pc ;                /* put chars here */
184     char *pa ;                /* put attributes here */
185     int n ;                   /* no. screen positions to read */
186     {
187        SCN_LOCATION t ;
188        unsigned status ;
189
190        status = 0 ;
191        while( n > 0 )
192          { t.ca = win_sc.scn_read(pw->pscn) ; /* get char & attr */
193
194            *pc = t.c_and_a.cs ;/* store char */
195            *pa = t.c_and_a.as ;/* store attribute */
196
197            pc = pc + 1 ;
198            pa = pa + 1 ;
199            pw->pscn = pw->pscn + 1 ;
200            pw->col = pw->col + 1 ;
201
202            if( pw->col >= pw-> ncol )
203              { status = status | EOL_STATUS ;
204                pw->col = 0 ;
205                pw->row = pw->row + 1 ;
206                if( pw->row >= pw->nrow )
207                  { pw->row = pw->nrow - 1 ;
208                    pw->col = pw->ncol - 1 ;
209                    status = status | EOW_STATUS ;
210                  }
211                pw->pscn = scn_pos( & win_sc,
212                    pw->start_row + pw->row ,
213                    pw->start_col + pw->col ) ;
214              }
215            n = n - 1 ;
216          }
217
218        return( status ) ;
219      }
```

The `win_wc` function uses the default attribute for the window but otherwise works as does `win_wca`.

The `win_wsa` function writes a character string to a window with a specified attribute. The last argument passed to `win_wsa` is a maximum number of characters to be written. This allows `win_wsa` to be used for C strings terminated by a null character or for character arrays where n specifies the number of characters to be written. The status value returned by `win_wsa` is the cumulative result of the status for each character written.

`win_ws` uses the default attribute for the window and is otherwise identical to `win_wsa`.

The `win_wa` function writes a specified attribute without changing the character value. The argument specifies the number of locations to be changed starting at the current writing position. The status value returned reflects the same conditions as for `win_wca`.

`win_new_line` handles moving to the next row of the window. If the `CLR_TO_EOL` option is set, the current line is cleared from the writing position to the end of the line. Then the column number is set to 0 (the leftmost column) and the row number is advanced. If the writing position was already on the bottom row, the action taken depends on the setting of the `AUTO_SCROLL` option. If set, the contents of the window is scrolled upward and the writing position is placed at the beginning of the last row. If the `AUTO_SCROLL` option is not set, the writing position is left in the last column of the last row. Once the new row and column values have been set, lines 175 and 176 use the `scn_pos` function to set the screen address.

The `win_gca` function in lines 181 to 219 reads a series of characters and attributes from the window, starting at the current writing position. Characters are stored starting at the address in `pc` and attributes are stored starting at `pa`. `win_gca` provides a low-level utility that can be used to implement more functions that move characters and attributes in a window.

win4.c

The functions in Figure 8.9 clear part or all of a window. All these functions write space characters with the clearing attribute for the window to screen locations cleared.

FIGURE 8.9   win4.c

```
 1    /* win4.c - window module, clearing, scrolling */
 2    #include "video.h"
 3    #include "win.h"
 4
 5
 6
 7    void win_wbs(pw)              /* write backspace */
 8     WIN *pw ;                    /* points to a WIN struct */
 9     {
10       if( pw->col > 0 )          /* if not at beginning of row */
11         { pw->col = pw->col - 1 ; /* back up 1 column */
12           pw->pscn = pw->pscn - 1 ;
13                                  /*     and write space */
14           win_sc.scn_write(pw->pscn,' ', pw->c_attrib) ;
15
16         }
```

Figure 8.9   continues

Figure 8.9   continued

```
17      }
18
19
20
21    void win_clrline(pw)          /* clear entire line */
22     WIN *pw ;                     /* points to a WIN struct */
23     {
24       int col ;                   /* column index */
25       SCN_PTR ps ;
26
27       ps = scn_pos(& win_sc, pw->start_row+ pw->row ,
28           pw->start_col ) ;
29
30       for( col=0 ; col < pw->ncol ; col=col+1)
31         { win_sc.scn_write(ps,' ', pw->c_attrib ) ;
32           ps = ps + 1 ;
33         }
34     }
35
36
37
38    void win_clreol(pw)           /* clear to end of line */
39     WIN *pw ;                     /* points to a WIN struct */
40     {
41       int col ;                   /* column index */
42       SCN_PTR ps ;
43
44       ps = scn_pos(& win_sc, pw->start_row+ pw->row ,
45           pw->start_col + pw->col ) ;
46
47       for( col=pw->col ; col < pw->ncol ; col=col+1)
48         { win_sc.scn_write(ps,' ', pw->c_attrib ) ;
49           ps = ps + 1 ;
50         }
51     }
52
53
54
55    void win_clr_window(pw)       /* clear entire window */
56     WIN *pw ;                     /* points to a WIN struct */
57     {
58
59       vid_clr_scn(pw->start_row,
60           pw->start_col ,
61           pw->start_row + pw->nrow -1,
62           pw->start_col + pw->ncol -1 ,
63           pw->c_attrib ) ;
64     }
65
66
67
68    void win_scroll(pw,n,dir)     /* scroll entire window */
69     WIN *pw ;                     /* points to a WIN struct */
70     int n ;                       /* number of rows to move */
71     int dir ;                     /* direction to move */
72     {
73
```

Figure 8.9   continues

Figure 8.9   continued

```
74          if( dir == SCROLL_UP )
75              vid_up( n, pw->start_row,
76                  pw->start_col ,
77                  pw->start_row + pw->nrow - 1 ,
78                  pw->start_col + pw->ncol - 1 ,
79                  pw->c_attrib ) ;
80          else
81              vid_down( n, pw->start_row,
82                  pw->start_col ,
83                  pw->start_row + pw->nrow - 1 ,
84                  pw->start_col + pw->ncol - 1 ,
85                  pw->c_attrib ) ;
86      }
```

The `win_wbs` function performs a backspace operation. It moves the writing position backward and clears that location. If the writing position was already at the leftmost column of the window, no action is taken.

`win_clrline` clears the entire line on which the writing position is located. `win_clreol` clears the line from the writing position to the end of the line. Neither function changes the writing position.

The `win_clr_window` function clears the window area (but not the border area). The `win_scroll` function scrolls the window contents up or down as specified by the `dir` argument. These functions use VIDEO functions from Chapter 7.

win5.c

The functions in Figure 8.10 handle borders for windows. `win_binit` calculates the origin and size including the border area. It also sets the border presence bits in the options member of the `WIN` structure. If a border edge would extend past the edge of the screen, that border edge will not be present. If the starting row is 0, there is no room for the top border. If the starting row added to the number of rows is equal to the screen size, there is no room for the bottom border. Similar tests are made for the left and right borders.

The `win_dborder` function draws the border for a window. The border edge presence bits are used to determine which parts of the border to draw on the screen.

Lines 23 to 33 define single line and double borders based on the PC line drawing characters. Symbolic constants for those characters are defined in lines 6 to 20.

FIGURE 8.10   win5.c

```
1       /* win5.c - window module, border functions */
2       #include <stdio.h>
3       #include "video.h"
4       #include "win.h"
5
```

Figure 8.10   continues

Figure 8.10   continued

```
6                                      /* single line border chars */
7     #define HORIZONTAL_LINE_CHAR 0xc4
8     #define VERTICAL_LINE_CHAR  0xb3
9     #define TL_ANGLE_CHAR  0xda
10    #define TR_ANGLE_CHAR  0xbf
11    #define BL_ANGLE_CHAR  0xc0
12    #define BR_ANGLE_CHAR  0xd9
13
14                                     /* double line border chars */
15    #define HORIZONTAL_DLINE_CHAR 0xcd
16    #define VERTICAL_DLINE_CHAR  0xba
17    #define TL_DANGLE_CHAR  0xc9
18    #define TR_DANGLE_CHAR  0xbb
19    #define BL_DANGLE_CHAR  0xc8
20    #define BR_DANGLE_CHAR  0xbc
21
22
23    BORDER line_border =
24        { HORIZONTAL_LINE_CHAR, VERTICAL_LINE_CHAR,
25          HORIZONTAL_LINE_CHAR, VERTICAL_LINE_CHAR,
26          TL_ANGLE_CHAR , TR_ANGLE_CHAR ,
27          BR_ANGLE_CHAR , BL_ANGLE_CHAR , NORMAL_DISPLAY } ;
28
29    BORDER dline_border =
30        { HORIZONTAL_DLINE_CHAR, VERTICAL_DLINE_CHAR,
31          HORIZONTAL_DLINE_CHAR, VERTICAL_DLINE_CHAR,
32          TL_DANGLE_CHAR , TR_DANGLE_CHAR ,
33          BR_DANGLE_CHAR , BL_DANGLE_CHAR , NORMAL_DISPLAY } ;
34
35
36
37    void win_binit(pw)            /* set border coordinates */
38    WIN *pw ;                     /* points to a WIN struct */
39    {
40
41                                  /* set row dimensions with borders */
42       pw->bstart_row = pw->start_row ;
43       pw->bnrow = pw->nrow ;
44       pw->bstart_col = pw->start_col ;
45       pw->bncol = pw->ncol ;
46                                  /* border bits = no borders */
47       pw->options = pw->options & ~ BORDER_BITS ;
48
49       if( pw->pborder == NULL)/* if no border description, */
50          return ;              /* we are through */
51
52       if( pw->start_row > 0 ) /* room for top border? */
53          { pw->bstart_row = pw->bstart_row - 1 ; /* y-adjust start */
54            pw->bnrow = pw->bnrow + 1 ; /* and number of rows */
55            pw->options = pw->options | TOP_BORDER ;
56          }
57
58                                  /* room for bottom border? */
59       if( (pw->start_row + pw->nrow) < win_sc.nrows )
60          { pw->bnrow = pw->bnrow + 1 ; /* y -adjust number of rows */
61            pw->options = pw->options | BOTTOM_BORDER ;
```

Figure 8.10   continues

Figure 8.10   continued

```
62              }
63
64          if( pw->start_col > 0 )  /* room for left border? */
65              { pw->bstart_col = pw->bstart_col - 1 ; /* y-adjust start */
66                pw->bncol = pw->bncol + 1 ; /* and number of cols. */
67                pw->options = pw->options | LEFT_BORDER ;
68              }
69
70                                  /* room for right border? */
71          if( (pw->start_col + pw->ncol) < win_sc.ncols)
72              { pw->bncol = pw->bncol + 1 ; /*  y - adjust no. cols. */
73                pw->options = pw->options | RIGHT_BORDER ;
74              }
75       }
76
77
78
79      void win_dborder(pw)            /* display border */
80      WIN *pw ;                       /* points to a WIN struct */
81      {
82          SCN_PTR ps ;                /* screen pointer */
83          int a , n , x , y ;
84
85                                  /* get border attribute */
86          a = pw->pborder->b_attrib ;
87
88                                  /* top left corner */
89          if(   ( (pw->options & TOP_BORDER)  != 0)
90              && ( (pw->options & LEFT_BORDER) != 0) )
91              { ps = scn_pos(& win_sc,pw->bstart_row,pw->bstart_col) ;
92                win_sc.scn_write(ps,pw->pborder->top_left,a) ;
93              }
94
95                                  /* top line */
96          if( (pw->options & TOP_BORDER)  != 0)
97              { n = pw->ncol ;        /* no. rows before bottom border */
98                                  /* set writing position */
99                ps = scn_pos(& win_sc,pw->bstart_row,pw->start_col) ;
100               while( n > 0 )
101                   { win_sc.scn_write(ps,pw->pborder->top_line,a) ;
102                     ps = ps + 1 ;
103                     n = n - 1 ;
104                   }
105             }
106
107
108                                 /* top right corner */
109         if(   ( (pw->options & TOP_BORDER)  != 0)
110             && ( (pw->options & RIGHT_BORDER) != 0) )
111             { ps = scn_pos(& win_sc,pw->bstart_row ,
112                   pw->bstart_col + pw->bncol - 1 ) ;
113               win_sc.scn_write(ps,pw->pborder->top_right,a) ;
114             }
115
116
117                                 /* bottom left corner */
```

Figure 8.10   continues

Figure 8.10   continued

```
118          if(    ( (pw->options & BOTTOM_BORDER)   != 0)
119            && ( (pw->options & LEFT_BORDER) != 0) )
120            { ps = scn_pos(& win_sc,pw->bstart_row + pw->bnrow - 1 ,
121                  pw->bstart_col) ;
122              win_sc.scn_write(ps,pw->pborder->bottom_left,a) ;
123            }
124
125                                /* bottom line */
126          if( (pw->options & BOTTOM_BORDER)  != 0 )
127            { n = pw->ncol  ;        /* no cols. before right border */
128              ps = scn_pos(& win_sc,pw->bstart_row + pw->bnrow - 1 ,
129                  pw->start_col) ;
130              while( n > 0 )
131                { win_sc.scn_write(ps,pw->pborder->bottom_line,a) ;
132                  ps = ps + 1 ;
133                  n = n - 1 ;
134                }
135            }
136
137                                /* bottom right corner */
138          if(    ( (pw->options & BOTTOM_BORDER)   != 0)
139            && ( (pw->options & RIGHT_BORDER) != 0) )
140            { ps = scn_pos(& win_sc,pw->bstart_row + pw->bnrow - 1 ,
141                  pw->bstart_col + pw->bncol - 1 ) ;
142              win_sc.scn_write(ps,pw->pborder->bottom_right,a) ;
143            }
144
145                                /* write left side of border */
146          if( (pw->options & LEFT_BORDER)   != 0)
147            { x = pw->start_row ; /* start past top left corner */
148              y = pw->bstart_col ;
149              n = pw->nrow ;        /* no. rows before right border */
150              while( n > 0 )
151                { ps = scn_pos(& win_sc, x, y ) ;
152                  win_sc.scn_write(ps,pw->pborder->left_line,a) ;
153                  x = x + 1 ;
154                  n = n - 1 ;
155                }
156            }
157
158                                /* write right side of border */
159          if( (pw->options & RIGHT_BORDER)   != 0)
160            { x = pw->start_row ; /* start past top right corner */
161              y = pw->bstart_col + pw->bncol - 1 ;
162              n = pw->nrow ;        /* no. rows before right border */
163              while( n > 0 )
164                { ps = scn_pos(& win_sc, x, y ) ;
165                  win_sc.scn_write(ps,pw->pborder->right_line,a) ;
166                  x = x + 1 ;
167                  n = n - 1 ;
168                }
169            }
170
171      }
```

8.3 Adding Pop-up Windows and Window Input

The functions just presented provide an adequate base for a window module. The next step is to build higher level functions on this base.

win_pop.c

The win_popup function in Figure 8.11 implements the sequence needed for a pop-up window. First a save area is allocated by calling win_save_area. Then the current screen contents corresponding to the pop-up window are saved by calling win_save_window. The save area address is stored in the psave member of the WIN structure. Finally, the pop-up window is displayed. Note that win_popup does not define a window; a preceding call to win_define is required.

The application program calls win_unpop to remove a pop-up window and restore the underlying screen contents. win_unpop releases the save area before returning.

FIGURE 8.11   win_pop.c

```
1      /* win_pop.c - display pop up window */
2      #include <stdio.h>
3      #include <stdlib.h>
4      #include "win.h"
5
6      int win_popup(pw)              /* pop up window */
7        WIN *pw ;                    /* points to window data structure */
8        {
9          SCN_LOCATION *p ;
10
11         p = win_save_area(pw) ;    /* get save area for window */
12         if( p == NULL )            /* check for allocation failure */
13             return( -1 ) ;
14
15         pw->psave = p ;            /* store save area address */
16
17         win_save_window(pw,p) ;    /* contents of window area */
18         win_display(pw) ;          /* display popup window */
19
20         win_setpos(pw,0,0) ;       /* set position at window start */
21
22         return( 0 ) ;
23       }
24
25
26     void win_unpop(pw)             /* remove popup window */
27       WIN *pw ;                    /* points to window data structure */
28       {
29                                    /* restore contents under window */
30         win_restore_window(pw, pw->psave) ;
31         free( pw->psave ) ;        /* release save area */
32       }
```

win_gets.c

The window functions we have developed have facilities for writing output to windows. We also need a function for collecting keyboard input and echoing it to a window. A single function to collect a string of characters is all that is needed for many interactive programs. The gets and fgets library functions are poorly designed for interactive input, but their shortcomings show the features our function needs:

- The handling of special key input such as function keys, arrow keys, and control characters is not defined. Some keys may be discarded and others may cause MS-DOS to trigger some action such as echoing console input to the printer.
- We need to control the echoing of characters to the screen. If we have allowed a 10-character field on the screen for a string, we must be able to stop echoing characters when the end of that field is reached.
- The gets and fgets library functions stop collecting characters and return a character string only when a carriage return character is typed. We often want to allow other characters such as the tab key, arrow keys, or function keys to terminate string input.
- No input is available to our program until a carriage return has been typed. Our program must be able to react immediately to each keystroke.

With these problems identified, we can design a genuinely useful string input function, win_gets. We use the getkey function from Chapter 7 to collect each keystroke. This provides immediate access to each keystroke, and function keys and other special keys are not discarded. getkey does not echo characters; we echo characters by calling win_wc. win_gets recognizes the backspace key as a command to back up one character and the control-X key as a command to erase the entire string. The carriage return and line feed (newline) characters signal the end of the string. A list of additional ending characters can be specified when win_gets is called. Figure 8.4 documents use of win_gets along with the other window functions.

Figure 8.12 shows our implementation of the win_gets function. It positions the visible cursor at the current writing position to indicate that input is expected. The loop in lines 33 to 70 collects input until an ending keystroke is encountered. Line 34 calls getkey to get one keystroke, and the classify_key function determines what is to be done with that keystroke. Graphic ASCII characters (space, punctuation, letters, and numbers) are added to the string. The character is echoed to the screen and the visible cursor set to the new writing position. If the maximum string length has been reached, a null character is added to the string, and win_gets returns with a special value (-1).

When a backspace character is found, the position in the string is moved backward. The win_wbs function is called to echo a backspace command and the visible cursor position is adjusted. If there are no characters in the string, the back-

FIGURE 8.12   win_gets.c

```
1     /* win_gets.c - get string input, echo to window */
2     #include <stdio.h>
3     #include <string.h>
4     #include "win.h"
5     #include "keyio.h"
6
7     #define CTRL_X    0x18        /* delete field key */
8
9                                  /* keystroke classes */
10    #define GRAPHIC_CHAR 0
11    #define BACK_SPACE   1
12    #define DEL_STRING   2
13    #define END_STRING   3
14    #define NO_ACTION    4
15
16
17    int classify_key(int, int [] , int ) ;
18
19
20                                 /* get string, echo chars to window */
21    int win_gets(s,next,maxs,end_keys,nend,pw)
22    char s[] ;                   /* put the string here */
23    int next ;                   /* put first character here */
24    int maxs ;                   /* maximum string length */
25    int end_keys[] ;             /* list of keys that end the string */
26    int nend ;                   /* no. keys in list */
27    WIN *pw ;                    /* echo chars to this window */
28    {
29      int c , cl ;
30
31      win_disp_cur(pw, -1, -1 ) ; /* show visible cursor */
32
33      while( 1 == 1 )
34        { c = getkey() ;         /* get next key */
35                                 /* classify it */
36          cl = classify_key( c,end_keys,nend ) ;
37          switch( cl )           /* handle accordingly */
38            {
39              case GRAPHIC_CHAR :  /* ASCII graphic char */
40                win_wc( pw, c) ;   /* echo the char */
41                win_disp_cur(pw, -1, -1 ) ; /* advance vis. cursor */
42                s[ next ] = c ;    /* store it */
43                next = next + 1 ;  /* advance position */
44                if( next == maxs ) /* check for max length */
45                  { s[next] = '\0';/* yes - terminate string */
46                    return( -1 ) ; /* return */
47                  }
48                break ;
49              case BACK_SPACE : /* backspace - back up 1 char */
50                if( next > 0 )  /* any chars in the string */
51                  { next = next - 1 ; /* yes - back up */
52                    win_wbs(pw) ;  /*          echo backspace */
53                    win_disp_cur(pw, -1, -1); /* reset vis. cursor */
54                  }
55                break ;
56              case DEL_STRING : /* delete entire string */
```

Figure 8.12   continues

Figure 8.12   continued

```
57                   while( next > 0 ) /* back up to start of string */
58                     { next = next - 1 ; /*   back up index */
59                       win_wbs(pw) ; /*        echo backspace */
60                       win_disp_cur(pw, -1, -1); /* reset vis. cursor */
61                     }
62                 break ;
63               case END_STRING :    /* get ending char */
64                 s[ next ] = '\0'; /* terminate string */
65                 return( c ) ;        /* return ending char */
66                 break ;
67               case NO_ACTION :    /* ignore this char */
68                 break ; •
69             }
70         }
71       return( 0 ) ;
72     }
73
74
75     int classify_key(c,end_keys,nend)
76     int c ;                        /* keystroke to classify */
77     int end_keys[] ;               /* list of ending keys */
78     int nend ;                     /* number of keys in list */
79     {
80         int i ;
81
82         if( (c >= ' ') && (c <= '~') ) /* graphic char ? */
83             return( GRAPHIC_CHAR ) ;
84         if( c == ASCBS )                /* backspace? */
85             return( BACK_SPACE ) ;
86         if( c == CTRL_X )               /* delete entire string? */
87             return( DEL_STRING ) ;
88         if( (c == '\r') || (c == '\n') ) /* carriage return or */
89             return( END_STRING ) ;    /* line feed - end key */
90
91         for(i=0 ; i < nend ; i=i+1)    /* check list of end keys */
92           { if( c == end_keys[i] )
93                 return( END_STRING ) ;
94           }
95                                   /* not an end key */
96         return( NO_ACTION ) ;   /* just ignore it */
97     }
```

space command is ignored. Entering a control-X character erases the entire string collected so far. It is equivalent to backspacing over each character of the string.

When an ending keystroke is found, a null character is added to terminate the string. The ending keystroke value is returned so that the application program can react appropriately.

The classify_key function in lines 75 to 97 decides what action is required for a keystroke. Keystrokes between the ASCII space and ~ characters are normal ASCII printable characters. Carriage return and newline characters are recognized as ending keys. The keystroke in c is also compared to the list of keys in the end_keys array.

Normally win_gets would be called with the next argument set to 0 which indicates that no characters are present in the string s. But next might be greater than 0 if s contained some input that was to be changed. Note that the calling program is always responsible for setting the writing position before calling `win_gets`.

8.4   Enhancements to the WINDOW Module

💾   Moving Windows

Sometimes we want to move a window to a new location on the screen, keep-ing its contents intact. The functions for saving and restoring a window area are the key to a `win_move_window` function as they are for implementing pop-up windows.

Setting Different Border Attributes for Each Window

The screen attribute used for a window border is taken from the border structure. All windows that use the single line border structure `line_border` have the same screen attribute. But the screen attribute helps distinguish the border from the surrounding area on the screen. A more flexible method might be to define the border attribute in the `WIN` structure. The screen attribute in the border structure would be the default value assigned by `win_define`. A new function called `win_battrib` assigns the border attribute as `win_attrib` sets the default and clearing attributes.

More Border Types

A wider variety of borders would help to distinguish screen windows from neighboring areas on the screen. Periods, hyphens, and asterisks are possible choices for border characters.

Fancier Borders

Some user interfaces label each window with a name centered on the top border. Borders that are more than one character wide might be useful for some applications. One way to implement more elaborate windows is for the application program to supply functions to replace `win_binit` and `win_dborder`.

Adaptable Screen Attributes

The choice of screen attributes for windows depends on the type of display (monochrome or color) and the adapter type (monochrome, CGA, or EGA/VGA).

Just as the low-level SCN module adapts to the type of adapter in use, we might adapt our choice of screen attributes to fit the display and adapter in use.

One solution is to specify generic screen attributes in the application program. The WINDOW module can translate those generic values into actual attributes appropriate to the display hardware in use.

Error Checking in Debugging Mode

The WINDOW module does not check row and column numbers to be sure that they are valid. The pointer to the WIN structure is not checked either. This is an appropriate choice to produce quick execution and compact size. However, it provides no help for catching programming errors. Error-checking statements can be added to the source files within #ifdef and #endif preprocessor statements. For example, calls to the win_setpos function could be checked by the statements

```
#indef DEBUG_W
    if( (row < 0) || (row > pw->nrow))
        { fprintf(stderr,"bad row number in win_setpos");
        exit(10) ;
        }
    if( (col < 0) || (col > pw->ncol))
        { fprintf(stderr,"bad column number in win_setpos");
        exit(20) ;
        }
#endif
```

These statements would be compiled only if the DEBUG_W symbol has been defined.

8.5   Revising the VIEW Program to Use Windows

To illustrate the use of the WINDOW module, we revise the VIEW program from Chapter 3. The program already divides the screen into three parts as shown in Figure 8.1. Our revision will use one window for the header information. It will start on the top line of the screen and be a full 80 columns wide. Only one line is needed for the file name, file position, and file size. We place a double line border below the header window.

Lines of text from the file being viewed start on line 3 of the screen. The first version of the VIEW program displayed 16 lines of text. A border separated the text area from the list of available commands displayed at the bottom of the screen. Our revised version of VIEW eliminates the list of commands and display 23 lines of text. The list of commands is placed on a help screen that pops up when the F1 key is pressed. That help screen is shown in Figure 8.2.

A pop-up window is also used to collect the new file position for the MOVETOPOS command. This window is two rows high, surrounded by a double line border. The window is located at row 6, column 10, and is 40 columns wide. The first line of the window has a prompting message followed by space for the file position input. Error messages describing invalid input appear on the second line of the window. Figure 8.3 shows the file position window.

8.6   Revised VIEW Source Files

These revisions to VIEW require changes to most of the `view*.c` source files. The modified files have names ending in 2 to distinguish them from the files in Chapter 3. Figure 8.13 shows the `viewcmd2.h` file that replaces `viewcmds.h`. A new help command is defined for the pop-up help feature. The `viewpar2.h` file in Figure 8.14, which replaces `viewparm.h`, defines the PAGE_SIZE as 23 lines of text rather than as 16 lines. Function prototype is added for the `init_disp` and `disp_help` functions, and the prototype for the `disp_prompt` function is removed since that function is no longer used.

The `viewfin2.c` and `viewio2.c` files are not shown since the only changes are to the `#include` statements for the `viewcmd2.h` and `viewpar2.h` files.

FIGURE 8.13   viewcmd2.h

```
 1      /* viewcmd2.h - definition of codes for input commands */
 2
 3      #define    NEXTPAGE        0
 4      #define    PREVPAGE        1
 5      #define    FIRSTPAGE       2
 6      #define    LASTPAGE        3
 7      #define    MOVETOPOS       4
 8      #define    EXITPGM         5
 9      #define    NEXTLINE        6
10      #define    PREVLINE        7
11      #define    INVALIDCMD     99
12
13      #define    HELPCMD         8
```

FIGURE 8.14   viewpar2.h

```
 1      /* viewpar2.h - parameters for view program */
 2
 3      /* number of lines in a display page */
 4      #define  PAGE_SIZE      23
 5
 6      /* number of lines of overlap between display pages */
 7      #define  LINES_OVERLAP   2
 8
 9      /* return values from get_next_char and get_previous_char */
10      /* to indicate reaching beginning or end of the file */
11      #define  EOF_MARK       -1
12      #define  BOF_MARK       -2
13
```

Figure 8.14   continues

Figure 8.14   continued

```
14      /* definition of control char marking the end of a line */
15      #define  END_LINE        10
16
17      /* define success/failure for return codes */
18      #define SUCCESS  1
19      #define FAILURE  0
20
21                                      /* function prototypes */
22      int get_cmd(void) ;             /* get a command */
23      void exec_cmd(int) ;            /* execute a command */
24      void move_forward(int) ;        /* move forward in file */
25      void move_backward(int) ;       /* move backward in file */
26      void set_top_page(void) ;       /* set top of page variable */
27      void display_page(void) ;       /* display a page of text */
28      void disp_char(int) ;           /* display one char */
29      long get_pos(long) ;            /* get file position input */
30      void get_filename(char *) ;/* get file name input */
31      int open_file(char *) ;         /* open the file */
32      void set_filesize(void) ;       /* find file size */
33      void check_ctrl_z(void) ;       /* adjust file size for control Z */
34      void move_to(long) ;            /* change file position */
35      long where_now(void) ;          /* return file position */
36      int get_next_char(void) ;       /* get a character - forward */
37      int get_previous_char(void) ;   /* get a character - backward */
38      void close_file(void) ;         /* close the file */
39
40      void init_disp(void) ;          /* set up display (windows) */
41      void disp_help(void) ;          /* display help screen */
```

view2.c

The main function in Figure 8.15 calls the new function init_disp to the header and text windows. The disp_prompt function is no longer called to display the list of commands. Before the main function finishes executing, it clears the screen and sets the position of the visible cursor so that the screen will be readable when VIEW2 exits to MS-DOS.

viewget2.c and viewexe2.c

The get_cmd function in Figure 8.16 now recognizes the F1 key as the help command (HELPCMD). The exec_cmd function in Figure 8.17 executes the help command by calling the disp_help function .

viewgtf2.c

The get_filename function in Figure 8.18 is unchanged. This function is called before the windows are defined and displayed. get_pos is changed extensively to use a pop-up window. Lines 47 to 51 define this window the first time get_pos is

FIGURE 8.15   view2.c

```
1       /* view2.c -  VIEW program - main function */
2       #include <stdio.h>
3       #include <string.h>
4       #include "viewcmd2.h"
5       #include "viewpar2.h"
6       #include "video.h"
7
8       char filename[65] = "" ;
9
10
11      main(argc,argv)
12       int argc ;
13       char *argv[] ;
14       {
15          int cmd ;                /* holds current cmd      */
16
17          if( argc >= 2 )          /* get file name from command line */
18             strcpy(filename,argv[1]) ;  /* (if present) */
19
20          get_filename(filename);/* get file name and open file */
21          set_filesize();          /* set up file size variable */
22          check_ctrl_z() ;         /* adjust file size for control Z */
23          init_disp() ;            /* set up display windows */
24
25          cmd = FIRSTPAGE ;        /* force display of 1st page */
26
27          while( cmd != EXITPGM )/* repeat until told to exit */
28            { exec_cmd(cmd);       /* execute the current command */
29              cmd = get_cmd();     /* get the next command */
30            }
31
32          close_file() ;
33                                   /* clear entire screen */
34          vid_clr_scn(0,0,24,79,NORMAL_DISPLAY) ;
35          vid_set_cur(0,0) ;       /* set visible cursor */
36       }
```

FIGURE 8.16   viewget2.c

```
1       /* viewget2.c - get_cmd function - get an input command   */
2       #include <stdio.h>
3       #include "viewcmd2.h"
4       #include "viewpar2.h"
5       #include "keyio.h"
6
7
8       int get_cmd()            /* get next input command from keyboard */
9       {                        /* returns the command type entered */
10         int key ;             /* the keyboard input value */
11                               /* ( see keyio.h ) for values */
12         int cmd ;             /* the command type value */
13
14         cmd = INVALIDCMD;     /* get next keyboard input */
15         while( cmd == INVALIDCMD )
16           { key = getkey() ;/* get next keyboard input */
```

Figure 8.16   continues

Figure 8.16   continued

```
17              switch( key )    /* classify the key pressed */
18              {
19              case PGDNKEY : cmd = NEXTPAGE       ;break;
20              case PGUPKEY : cmd = PREVPAGE       ;break;
21              case ASCESC  : cmd = EXITPGM        ;break;
22              case ' '     : cmd = MOVETOPOS      ;break;
23              case HOMEKEY : cmd = FIRSTPAGE      ;break;
24              case ENDKEY  : cmd = LASTPAGE       ;break;
25              case UPARROW : cmd = PREVLINE       ;break;
26              case DOWNARROW : cmd = NEXTLINE     ;break;
27              case F1KEY   : cmd = HELPCMD        ;break;
28              default      : cmd = INVALIDCMD     ;
29              }  /* end of switch stmt */
30          }
31      return(cmd) ;
32  }
```

FIGURE 8.17   viewexe2.c

```
1   /* viewexe2.c file - executes one input command   */
2   #include <stdio.h>
3   #include "viewcmd2.h"
4   #include "viewpar2.h"
5   extern long filesize ;     /* position of effective eof */
6
7   void exec_cmd(cmd)           /* execute input command */
8    int cmd ;                   /* command to execute */
9   {
10      long new_pos ;
11
12      switch( cmd )  {
13      case PREVPAGE  :    /* move backward to last page */
14          move_backward(PAGE_SIZE - LINES_OVERLAP) ;
15          display_page() ;
16          break;
17      case NEXTPAGE  :    /* move forward to next page */
18          move_forward(PAGE_SIZE - LINES_OVERLAP);
19          display_page() ;
20          break;
21      case EXITPGM :
22          break;
23      case MOVETOPOS :
24          new_pos = get_pos(filesize) ; /* get file position */
25          move_to(new_pos) ;  /* move to specified position */
26          set_top_page() ;    /* make it top_of_page for now */
27          move_backward(0);   /* move to start of this line */
28          display_page() ;
29          break;
30      case FIRSTPAGE  :
31          move_to(0L);        /* move to beginning of file */
32          set_top_page() ;    /* make it the top of the page */
33          display_page() ;
34          break;
35      case LASTPAGE  :
36          move_to(filesize) ; /* move to end of file */
37          set_top_page() ;    /* make it the top of the page */
38          move_backward(PAGE_SIZE);/* back up to put end of */
```

Figure 8.17   continues

Figure 8.17   continued

```
39                      display_page() ;     /* file at bottom of screen */
40                      break;
41          case   PREVLINE :
42                   move_backward(1) ;  /* move back one line */
43                   display_page() ;
44                   break;
45          case   NEXTLINE :
46                   move_forward(1);    /* move forward one line */
47                   display_page() ;
48                   break;
49          case   HELPCMD :
50                   disp_help() ;
51          }
52      }
```

called. Providing a separate initialization function would be a cleaner solution, but this method allows us to confine the details of the file position window to the viewgtf2.c source file and does not require an additional initialization function.

Line 53 displays the pop-up window and saves the underlying screen contents. Line 88 restores the screen contents before exiting from the function. Before accepting the new file position, line 57 displays the prompt message. Line 58 saves the writing position row and column values at the end of the prompt message.

The loop in lines 63 to 87 collects a file position from the keyboard and validates it. The win_gets function collects a string from the keyboard. The sscanf function retrieves the numeric file position from this string. Lines 69 to 77 validate the file position value and specify the appropriate error message if the file position is not valid. If the file position passes the validation tests, line 78 escapes from the loop. For an invalid value, line 84 produces an audible beep and lines 85 and 86 display an error message on line 2 of the file position window. The invalid input remains displayed, and the invalid string is passed to win_gets for correction.

FIGURE 8.18   viewgtf2.c

```
 1      /* viewgtf2.c -  get file name and position input */
 2      /* uses pop-up window in get_pos() */
 3      #include <stdio.h>
 4      #include <string.h>
 5      #include "viewpar2.h"
 6      #include "win.h"
 7
 8      #define START_ROW      6    /* starting row for window */
 9      #define START_COL     10    /* starting column for winodw */
10      #define NO_ROWS        2    /* number of rows in window */
11      #define NO_COLS       40    /* number of columns in window */
12
13      #define MAXS   15           /* string length for input */
14
15      static int first_time = 0; /* used to detect 1st call to */
16                                 /* get_pos */
```

Figure 8.18   continues

Figure 8.18   continued

```
17     static WIN posw ;              /* position window structure */
18
19
20     void get_filename(fn)          /* get name of file and open it */
21      char *fn ;                    /* file name string */
22      {                             /* (filled out by caller) */
23         if( strlen(fn) == 0 )
24            { printf("file name:") ;
25               scanf("%s",fn) ;
26            }
27                                     /* open the file (verify name) */
28         while( open_file(fn) == FAILURE )
29            { printf("\n file - %s can not be opened\n",fn);
30               printf("file name:") ;      /* try again */
31               scanf("%s",fn) ;
32            }
33      }
34
35
36
37     long get_pos(filesize)         /* get file position input */
38      long filesize ;               /* use to validate new position */
39      {                             /* return the new position */
40         long pos ;
41         int row , col , next ;
42         char s[ MAXS ] ;
43         char m2[40] ;
44         char *msg ;
45
46
47         if( first_time == 0 )   /* define window on first call */
48            { win_define(& posw, START_ROW, START_COL,
49                 NO_ROWS, NO_COLS, & dline_border,CLR_TO_EOL);
50               first_time = 1 ;
51            }
52
53         win_popup(& posw) ;      /* save screen contenst */
54                                   /* and display position window */
55
56         win_setpos(& posw, 0 , 0 ) ;
57         win_ws(& posw, " new file position: ", ALL_STRING );
58         win_getpos(& posw, & row , & col ) ;
59
60         /* get a new position from the keyboard and validate it */
61         /* if it is not valid, repeat the process */
62         next = 0 ;
63         while( 1 == 1 )
64            { win_setpos(& posw, row, col) ; /* set writing position */
65                                   /* get string from keyboard */
66               win_gets(s, next, MAXS-1 , NULL, 0, & posw) ;
67
68                                   /* now get number and validate */
69               if( sscanf(s,"%ld",&pos) == 0 )
70                  msg = " file position must be numeric" ;
71               else if( pos < 0L )/* got a number - check its range */
72                  msg = " file position must be >= zero" ;
73               else if( pos > filesize )
74                  { sprintf(m2," file position must be <= %ld",
```

Figure 8.18   continues

Figure 8.18   continued

```
75                      filesize) ;
76                 msg = m2 ;
77              }
78           else break ;          /* valid file position - return it */
79
80                                 /* some error occurred */
81           win_getpos(& posw, & row,& col) ; /* remember position */
82           next = strlen(s) ; /*    and end of string */
83
84           putchar('\a') ;      /*    beep and display error msg */
85           win_setpos(& posw, 1, 0 ) ;
86           win_ws(& posw, msg , ALL_STRING) ;
87        }
88     win_unpop(& posw) ;
89     return( pos ) ;
90    }
```

viewdis2.c

The new function init_disp in lines 128 to 143 of Figure 8.19 defines and displays the header window and the text window. The help window is defined but not displayed. The disp_help function in lines 104 to 125 displays the pop-up window and writes the list of commands in that window. Line 123 waits until a key is pressed before restoring the screen and returning.

In the display_page (lines 36 to 66) and disp_char (lines 70 to 100) functions, calls to putchar have been replaced by calls to win_wc. Calls to printf that simply output a character string have been replaced by calls to win_ws. Lines 43 to 45 use sprintf to format the file name, file size, and file position in a string before calling win_ws. The CLR_TO_EOL option is used for the header and text windows to ensure that the previous contents of each line is erased. This is an alternative to clearing the windows before rewriting them.

FIGURE 8.19   viewdis2.c

```
1     /* viewdis2.c file - display current page of file */
2     #include <stdio.h>
3     #include "viewpar2.h"
4     #include "win.h"
5     #include "keyio.h"
6
7     #define TAB_WIDTH      8
8     #define PAGE_WIDTH    80
9
10    #define HEAD_R  0              /* heading window - start row */
11    #define HEAD_C  0              /* heading window - start col */
12    #define HEAD_NR 1              /* heading window - no. rows */
13    #define HEAD_NC 80             /* heading window - no. cols */
14
15    #define TEXT_R  2              /* text window - start row */
16    #define TEXT_C  0              /* text window - start col */
```

                                                          Figure 8.19   continues

Figure 8.19   continued

```
17      #define TEXT_NR 23          /* text window - no. rows */
18      #define TEXT_NC 80          /* text window - no. cols */
19
20      #define HELP_R  6           /* help window - start row */
21      #define HELP_C  20          /* help window - start col */
22      #define HELP_NR 16          /* help window - no. rows */
23      #define HELP_NC 40          /* help window - no. cols */
24
25      extern char    filename[] ;
26      extern long    filesize ;    /* size of file in bytes */
27      extern long    top_of_page;  /* file position of top of page */
28      int   row ;                  /* current line of page */
29      int   col ;                  /* current column of page */
30      static WIN hw ;              /* header window structure */
31      static WIN tw ;              /* text window structure */
32      static WIN hpw ;             /* help window structure */
33      static char s[81] ;          /* format header line here */
34
35
36      void display_page()          /* display a page on screen */
37        {
38          int c ;                  /* hold the character here */
39          int i ;                  /* counter for loop */
40
41          move_to(top_of_page);   /* start at top of the page */
42                                   /* write a header line */
43          sprintf(s,
44             " FILE - %s    POSITION - %ld    FILE SIZE - %ld \n",
45               filename,top_of_page,filesize);
46          win_setpos(& hw ,0,0) ;
47          win_ws(& hw , s, ALL_STRING) ;
48
49
50          /* get chars from file until we've written (PAGE_SIZE) */
51          /* lines or we have reached the end of the file */
52          row = 1 ;                /* starting row & column values */
53          col = 1 ;
54          win_setpos(& tw , 0 , 0 ) ; /* set writing position */
55          c = get_next_char() ;
56          while( c != EOF_MARK ) /* quit at end of file */
57            { disp_char(c) ;       /* display current character */
58              if(row > PAGE_SIZE)/* quit at end of page */
59                break ;
60              c = get_next_char();/* get next char */
61            }
62
63          while( row <= PAGE_SIZE )  /* pad out page if eof reached */
64            { win_wc(& tw , '\n'); row = row + 1 ; }
65
66        }
67
68
69
70      void disp_char(c)            /* display one char */
71                                   /* and update row and column */
72        int c ;                    /* char to write */
73        {
74          /* classify the character and handle accordingly */
```

Figure 8.19   continues

Figure 8.19   continued

```
75
76          if( (c >= ' ') && (c <= '~') )
77            { win_wc(& tw, c);       /* ASCII graphic char - display it */
78              col = col + 1 ;        /* advance column number */
79              if( col > PAGE_WIDTH ) /* check for wrap-around */
80                { row = row + 1 ;/*       yes - advance row no and */
81                  col = 1 ;       /*              set to first column */
82                }
83            }
84          else if( c == END_LINE )
85            { win_wc(& tw,'\n') ;/* end_line char - force a new line */
86              row = row + 1 ;      /* advance row no. */
87              col = 1 ;            /* set column back to first col */
88            }
89          else if( c == '\t' )
90            {
91              do                            /* tab - expand it */
92                { win_wc(& tw,' ');  /* print spaces        */
93                  col = col + 1 ;      /* and advance column no. */
94                  if( col > PAGE_WIDTH)   /* checking for wrap-around */
95                    { row = row + 1 ;
96                      col = 1 ;
97                    }
98                } while( (col % TAB_WIDTH) != 1) ; /* until tab stop */
99            }
100        }
101
102
103
104    void disp_help()             /* display help screen for commands */
105      {
106        win_popup( & hpw) ;      /* save contents under help window */
107                                 /* and display help window */
108
109
110        win_ws(& hpw,
111          "   Type one of these Input Commands\n", ALL_STRING);
112        win_ws(& hpw, "\n HOME  = First Page       ", ALL_STRING);
113        win_ws(& hpw, "\n  \x18    = Previous Line    ",ALL_STRING);
114        win_ws(& hpw, "\n PG UP = Previous Page ",ALL_STRING);
115        win_ws(& hpw, "\n END   = Last  Page       ", ALL_STRING);
116        win_ws(& hpw, "\n  \x19    = Next Line        ",ALL_STRING);
117        win_ws(& hpw, "\n PG DN = Next Page ", ALL_STRING);
118        win_ws(& hpw, "\n ESC   = Exit Pgm        ", ALL_STRING );
119        win_ws(& hpw, "\n SPACE = Move to position ", ALL_STRING);
120        win_ws(& hpw, "\n F1    = Display help screen", ALL_STRING) ;
121
122        win_ws(& hpw, "\n\n press any key to return", ALL_STRING );
123        getkey() ;               /* wait until a key is pressed */
124        win_unpop( & hpw ) ;   /* restore previous screen contents */
125      }
126
127
128    void init_disp()
129      {
130                                 /* header window */
131        win_define( & hw , HEAD_R, HEAD_C, HEAD_NR, HEAD_NC,
132          & dline_border,CLR_TO_EOL) ;
```

Figure 8.19   continues

Figure 8.19   continued

```
133          win_display( & hw ) ;
134          win_disp_cur( & hw, 0 , 0 ) ;
135                                        /* text window */
136          win_define( & tw , TEXT_R, TEXT_C, TEXT_NR, TEXT_NC,
137             NULL,CLR_TO_EOL) ;
138          win_display( & tw ) ;
139
140                                        /* help window - pop up */
141          win_define( & hpw , HELP_R, HELP_C, HELP_NR, HELP_NC,
142             & dline_border,0) ;
143       }
```

8.7   Further Enhancements to VIEW

The WINDOW functions provide a good basis for further revisions to VIEW. Without a powerful tool for organizing screen output, adding even a small feature to a program can cause major changes to the source code responsible for screen output.

Using a Window for File Name Input

The get_filename function that collects a file name from the keyboard still uses the printf and scanf library functions. Using a pop-up window and the win_gets function would make this part of the user interface consistent with the rest of the program.

The VIEW program requires users to know the name of the file they want to examine. A better approach might be to present a directory listing on the screen if the file name is not typed correctly on the first try. The list of file names might be too long to fit on the screen, so a mechanism should be provided for scrolling through the directory listing. Both Microsoft C and Turbo C provide functions for searching a file directory.

Some further improvements should be incorporated. The list of file names should be sorted into alphabetical order. The user should be allowed to select a file name from the list rather than typing it in. The cursor control keys could be used to highlight a file name. When the right name has been highlighted, pressing the return key would select a file to be opened.

Better Validation of New File Position Input

The get_pos function does not validate the new file position input completely. The sscanf function does not provide an error indication if a nonnumeric character follows valid numeric characters. The atoi library function also scans a character string for a number, but like sscanf, it does not report the presence of a nonnumeric character in the string. A replacement for atoi that provides a clear error return is easy to implement.

⬚ An Abort Command Exit

The MOVETOPOS command calls get_pos to collect a new file position. We should allow the user to cancel the command by typing a special character (the ESC character for example). The end_key array passed to the win_gets function should include the key chosen to abort the command.

Specifying Forward and Backward Searches

Section 3.7 suggested a command to search for a character string. A pop-up window and the win_gets function are good tools for implementing this enhancement. However, we would like to specify forward or backward searches. One way is to use the up and down arrow keys as ending keys when collecting the search string. Pressing the return key or the down arrow key to end the string might specify a forward search; pressing the down arrow key might specify a backward search.

Allocating Window Save Areas Before Use

The calls to win_popup in get_pos and in disp_help can fail because memory cannot be allocated for a save area. Adding error-checking code to those functions is possible, but a better solution might be to allocate the save area before starting to view the file. Dynamic allocation of memory is a powerful tool, but it can also create more error conditions that must be checked. A good compromise is to perform all dynamic allocation during program initialization. This keeps most checking for memory allocation problems confined to a few initialization functions.

8.8 Summary

The WINDOW module presented here combines good performance from direct screen output with the functionality we need for writing good user interfaces. Although this module is less elaborate than the functions provided by the Microsoft Windows or OS/2 environments, it provides a practical, low-overhead tool usable on any PC. Even in these environments, our WINDOW module defines an portable interface we can use with MS-DOS or with OS/2.

9

A Terminal Emulation Program

The subject of this chapter is terminal emulation programs. These programs allow you to use an IBM PC as a dumb ASCII terminal to talk to another computer via an RS-232 cable or a modem and a phone line. We start with a very bare-bones program that illustrates the basic requirements of the problem and then introduce improvements. (We name these terminal emulation programs with the acronym TTY. TTY stands for teletype, the first widely used terminal.)

Like program editors, terminal emulator programs are widely available. However, no product may fit your needs completely. The programs developed here can serve as the basis for your own custom-tailored program.

A terminal emulator program is an example of a *real-time* program — one that communicates with the outside world and must meet absolute deadlines for handling input or producing some output. Our programs will illustrate techniques such as polling, priority driven scheduling, interrupts, and input buffering commonly used in real-time programs.

As in Chapter 7, there are lots of low-level details. It is necessary to use the PC hardware directly to produce satisfactory results. The programs we present will have lots of references to I/O port addresses and control and status bit assignments. We will explain what we are doing but not why the PC hardware works as it does. If the details of the PC's hardware and of asynchronous communications are a mystery, read this chapter along with the references listed in Appendix D. A number of books discuss how the IBM PC's hardware works; our purpose is to show how to use that information to do something useful.

9.1   What Terminal Emulation Programs Do

The basic functions of a terminal emulation program are simple. When we type a character, the program transmits it to the other computer. When we receive a character from the other computer, the program displays the character on the PC's screen. To be genuinely useful, a TTY program needs to do more than this, but we will start with a program that does only these functions.

Our TTY program uses *asynchronous communications*, or *async*, to send and receive characters. A PC can communicate with the outside world in many ways, but the terminals we emulate talk async, so that is what we must use.

We will not describe the historical and technical reasons why asynchronous communication is used or explain how it works; the references in Appendix D contain good discussions. We list here some terms needed to discuss the TTY program and their definitions.

Asynchronous Communications: The asynchronous communication method sends characters one bit at a time (serially) rather than all at one time in parallel. A single wire is used to transmit data; low and high voltage levels correspond to 0 and 1 bits. The line is kept at a high voltage level when no character is being transmitted. A transition to a low voltage level, the *start bit*, signals the start of transmission of a character. Each bit in the character is transmitted and then a *stop bit* follows to allow a return to the high voltage or idle level. The interval between bits is fixed by the *baud rate* used, but the interval between characters is not fixed. The term "asynchronous" refers to the lack of a fixed time interval between characters.

Synchronous communications: In this communication method, a number of characters are transmitted without an interval between them. A fixed bit pattern marks the start of a message, and the characters follow without added start and stop bits. Both methods have advantages and applications in which they are appropriate. The choice is usually made on a practical basis; one method is supported by the other computer for the application you want to do.

Communication methods are like human languages because both parties in the conversation must speak the same language to get anything done. Such agreements are called *protocols*, whether they specify the way a single character is transmitted or the way to interpret those characters as whole messages.

Asynchronous communication is more widely used on PCs than synchronous communication. Our TTY program emulates an async terminal, so we will be concerned exclusively with asynchronous communication.

Async Adapter: The hardware needed in an IBM PC for async communication is an Asynchronous Communications Adapter. IBM supplies plug-in boards that perform this single function; multifunction boards from other vendors may perform additional functions. Some PC compatible models include the functions of one or more async adapters in the PC unit. The function of these boards and the I/O addresses they use and commands they accept are well standardized.

8250 UART Chip: The heart of the async adapter is a single LSI chip — an INS8250 asynchronous communications element or its equivalent. Chips that transmit and receive characters serially for async communications are called UARTs (Universal Asynchronous Receiver-Transmitters). The 8250 is only one of many UART chips, but it is the standard for async communications in IBM PCs. Just remember the number 8250 and the acronym UART as names for the chip that transmits and receives characters in async protocol.

RS-232: The async adapter connects to the outside world through an RS-232 connector. RS-232 is the name of a standard for async and synchronous communications. It covers the size and shape of connectors, the number of pins in those connectors and their use, and the voltage levels used for signaling. Two voltage levels, high and low, are used to encode information.

Two devices communicating with async protocol may be connected directly through an RS-232 cable or via phone lines. *Modems* translate the RS-232 voltage levels into tones that the phone lines can transmit successfully. Some of the pins in an RS-232 connector allow a device to sense a modem's status and to control the modem. We refer to the cable or modems (and phone line) that connect two computers as an *RS-232 line*.

Break Signals: In addition to transmitting characters, we can transmit a special signal called *break*. Think of it like whistling; if you wanted to get the attention of a crowd, a loud whistle is an alternative to talking. Like the whistle, it does not convey much information. The RS-232 standard defines a break signal as being a low voltage level held for at least 200 milliseconds.

Baud Rate: Baud rate describes the speed at which data is transmitted. A rate of 300 baud is 30 characters per second, whereas 1,200 baud and 9,600 baud correspond to 120 and 960 characters per second. (The baud rate is the number of bits sent; two overhead bits are sent with each 8-bit character — a start bit and a stop bit. At 110 baud, two stop bits are normally used, making a rate of 10 characters per second.)

9.2 A Basic Terminal Emulation Program

Figure 9.1 shows a very simple terminal emulation. It has no options or extra features, but it illustrates the nature of terminal emulators. The loop in lines 24 to 35 is the heart of the program. It repeatedly checks for either keyboard input or a character received from the communication line. When a character is received from the RS-232 line, it is displayed. When keyboard input is available, it is transmitted on the RS-232 line (if it is an ASCII character).

FIGURE 9.1 tty1.c

```
1    /* tty1.c - bare-bones tty emulation program */
2    #include <stdio.h>
3    #include <stdlib.h>
4    #include "cminor.h"
5    #include "keyio.h"
6    #include "async.h"
7    #include "video.h"
8
9    #define  CARD  COM2         /* which RS-232 port to use */
10   #define  THRU_KEY  F1KEY    /* define key for exiting pgm */
11
12   main()
13     {
14         int c ;
15         int ret ;
16
17         ret = comm_init(CARD) ;/* set up for RS-232 use */
18         if( ret != 0 )          /* check for error */
19           { printf(" unrecognizable RS232 address - %x \n", ret) ;
20             exit(10) ;
21           }
22
23         c = ' ' ;                 /* force execution the first time */
24         while( c != THRU_KEY )
25           {
26             if( chk_rcv() != 0)/* check for rcvd data */
27               { c = rcv_char();/*   yes - get it */
28                 vid_tc(c) ;    /*          and display it */
29               }
30             else if(keypress() != 0)/* check for keybd. input */
31               { c = getkey() ; /*    yes - get it */
32                 if( c < 0x80 ) /*          and transmit if ASCII */
33                     send_char(c) ;
34               }
35           }
36     }
```

TTY1 uses the KEYIO and VIDEO modules from Chapter 7 for console input and output. The RS-232 functions comm_init, chk_rcv, rcv_char, chk_xmt, and xmt_char are in the async1.c module to be discussed in the next section.

Async I/O Support

The TTY1 program requires some support for serial I/O to the async hardware on the IBM PC. It needs functions to receive and transmit characters and to check receive and transmit status. The PC BIOS does provide these services but with poor performance and no flexibility. We will implement an ASYNC module that bypasses the BIOS and uses the PC 's async I/O hardware directly.

Figure 9.2 shows the source file for this module. The module performs port input and output operations to control the async hardware. The async.h header file in

Figure 9.3 lists port addresses and control and status bit values for those ports. Two async ports, COM1: and COM2:, are supported by the PC BIOS and by MS-DOS. For each async port there is a range of I/O ports for control, status checking, and receiving and transmitting data. The async.h file defines this range of addresses. The comm_init function in lines 21 to 38 of Figure 9.2 determines which set of port addresses is to be used.

FIGURE 9.2 async1.c

```
1      /* async1.c - basic async I/O module */
2      #include <stdio.h>
3      #include "asmtools.h"
4      #include "async.h"
5
6      typedef struct
7        { int base_port ;             /* 1st I/O port for this async card */
8          int int_no ;                /* associated interrupt level */
9        } ASY_ADRS ;
10
11     #define BIOS_DATA   0x40        /* segment address of BIOS data area*/
12     int  rs232card ;               /* save card number here */
13     int iobase ;                   /* 1st port address of async card */
14     int iasync ;                   /* index into aadr table */
15
16     ASY_ADRS aadr[2] =
17       { PRIMARY , PRI_INT ,         /* primary async adapter (COM1:) */
18         SECONDARY , SEC_INT         /* secondary adapter (COM2:) */
19       } ;
20
21     int comm_init(card)
22      int card ;                     /* card number for RS232 I/O */
23      {
24          rs232card = card ;         /* save card number */
25                                     /* get the corresponding port */
26                                     /* address from the BIOS data seg. */
27          iobase = getbyte(BIOS_DATA,card*2) |
28              ( getbyte(BIOS_DATA,card*2+1) << 8 ) ;
29          switch( iobase )           /* check for valid I/O address */
30            {
31             case PRIMARY   : iasync = 0 ; break ;
32             case SECONDARY : iasync = 1 ; break ;
33             default :
34                return( iobase ) ;   /* not a valid I/O address */
35                break ;
36            }
37          return( 0 ) ;
38      }
39
40
41     int chk_rcv()                   /* check for received char */
42      {
43          int s ;
44
45          s = inbyte(iobase + LINE_STATUS) ; /* get line status */
46          return( s & DTA_RDY ) ;
47      }
```

Figure 9.2   continues

Figure 9.2 continued

```
48
49
50    int rcv_char()              /* get a received char */
51      {
52        int s , c ;
53                                /* check status for errors */
54        s = inbyte(iobase + LINE_STATUS) & RCV_ERRS ;
55        c = inbyte(iobase + RCV_DATA) ; /* get the char itself */
56        if( s == 0 )
57              return(tochar(c));/* no errors return char */
58        else return( -1 ) ;     /* error - return (-1)    */
59      }
60
61    int chk_xmt()               /* check to see if ready */
62      {                         /* to transmit next char */
63        int s ;
64
65        s = inbyte(iobase + LINE_STATUS) ; /* get line status */
66        return( s & XMT_RDY ) ;
67      }
68
69
70    void xmt_char(c)            /* transmit a char */
71      int c ;                   /* char to be transmitted */
72      {
73        outbyte( iobase + XMT_DATA, c) ;
74      }
75
76
77    void send_char(c)           /* check Xmt status and then */
78      int c ;                   /* transmit this char */
79      {
80        while( chk_xmt() == 0 )  /* wait until ok to xmt char */
81          { ; }
82        xmt_char(c) ;           /* transmit the char */
83      }
```

FIGURE 9.3 async.h

```
1     /* async.h - defines constants for async I/O */
2
3     /* async port names */
4     #define COM1    0
5     #define COM2    1
6
7     /* software interrupt number for ROM BIOS async support */
8     #define  RS232_IO   0x14
9
10    /* service codes for rom BIOS calls (put in AX) */
11    #define  RS_INIT      0x0000
12    #define  RS_XMT       0x0100
13    #define  RS_RCV       0x0200
14    #define  RS_STATUS    0x0300
15
16    /* bit definitions for BIOS status returns */
```

Figure 9.3 continues

Figure 9.3   continued

```
17      #define   TIM_OUT_BIT       0x8000
18      #define   XMT_RDY_BIT       0x2000
19      #define   BRK_DET_BIT       0x1000
20      #define   FRM_ERR_BIT       0x0800
21      #define   PAR_ERR_BIT       0x0400
22      #define   OVR_RUN_BIT       0x0200
23      #define   DTA_RDY_BIT       0x0100
24      #define   CAR_DET_BIT       0x0080
25      #define   RNG_IND_BIT       0x0040
26      #define   DSR_BIT           0x0020
27      #define   CTS_BIT           0x0010
28
29      /* mask for receive error conditions */
30      /*  (TIM_OUT_BIT|FRM_ERR_BIT |PAR_ERR_BIT |OVR_RUN_BIT) */
31      #define  RCV_ERR_BIT  0x8E00
32
33
34      /* the following are parms for the RS232_init service */
35      /* choose one from each group and combine (+ or |) */
36      /* and put into REGS.AX (with service code) */
37
38      /* baud rates  */
39      #define   BAUD_110          0x00
40      #define   BAUD_300          0x40
41      #define   BAUD_1200         0x80
42      #define   BAUD_4800         0xc0
43
44      /* parity settings  */
45      #define   PAR_NONE          0x00
46      #define   PAR_ODD           0x08
47      #define   PAR_EVEN          0x18
48
49      /* number of stopbit settings */
50      #define   STOP_1            0x00
51      #define   STOP_2            0x04
52
53      /* data word length settings */
54      #define   DATA_7            0x02
55      #define   DATA_8            0x03
56
57      /* I/O port offsets for async card */
58      /* (add the base address for the card being used) */
59      #define RCV_DATA          0
60      #define XMT_DATA          0
61      #define INT_ENABLE        1
62      #define INT_ID            2
63      #define LINE_CTRL         3
64      #define MODEM_CTRL        4
65      #define LINE_STATUS       5
66      #define MODEM_STATUS      6
67
68      /* Line Status Register Bits */
69      #define   XMT_RDY     0x20    /* 1 = ok to transmit */
70      #define   BRK_DET     0x10    /* 1 = break rcvd */
71      #define   FRM_ERR     0x08    /* 1 = framing error detected */
72      #define   PAR_ERR     0x04    /* 1 = parity error detected */
```

Figure 9.3   continues

Figure 9.3   continued

```
73        #define   OVR_RUN      0x02    /* 1 = rcv overrun   */
74        #define   DTA_RDY      0x01    /* 1 = rcvd data ready */
75        #define   RCV_ERRS     0x1E    /* all rcv error bits above */
76
77        /* Modem Status Register bits */
78        #define   CAR_DET      0x80
79        #define   RNG_IND      0x40
80        #define   DSR          0x20
81        #define   CTS          0x10
82
83
84
85        /* various control register bits */
86        #define SET_BRK_BIT        0x40
87        #define INT_PENDING        0x01
88        #define ENABLE_RCV_INT     0x01
89        #define OUT2               0x08 /* in MCR. = 1 to allow ints. */
90
91        /* 1st I/O port addresses for com1: and com2: */
92        #define PRIMARY            0x3f8
93        #define SECONDARY          0x2f8
94
95        /* corresponding interrupt numbers */
96        #define PRI_INT            4
97        #define SEC_INT            3
98
99                                     /* function prototypes */
100       int  comm_init(int) ;
101       int  chk_rcv(void) ;
102       int  rcv_char(void) ;
103       int  chk_xmt(void ) ;
104       void xmt_char(int) ;
105       void send_char(int) ;
```

The PC BIOS maintains a table relating the COM1: and COM2: ports to I/O ports. comm_init uses the card number supplied as an index into this table. The result is checked to see that it corresponds to one of the async ports supported by the PC.

The chk_rcv function in lines 41 to 47 checks a status port to determine whether a received character is available. The rcv_char function in lines 50 to 59 collects that character for the receive data port. Several types of errors may occur; for example, the character may have overwritten a previously received character, the received character may have a parity error (one or more bits in error), or a break signal may have been received. The rcv_char function reads a status port to check for these conditions. If an error has occurred, a –1 error value will be returned. Otherwise, the received character (a value between 0 and 0xff) will be returned.

The xmt_char function in lines 70 to 74 writes a character to the transmit data port. The corresponding status function, chk_xmt, tests the status port to see that the hardware is ready to accept another character. The final function, send_char, combines chk_xmt and xmt_char to wait until the async hardware is ready before transmitting a character.

9.3 How TTY1 Performs

Although TTY1 is too simple to be very useful, we can learn something from measuring its performance. Figure 9.4 shows a program that transmits a continuous stream of characters at the full baud rate. The stream is a series of lines of ASCII characters with each line being one character longer than the previous one. (Part A of Figure 9.5 shows a sample of the sawtooth pattern.) To run the test, we need two IBM PCs connected by an RS-232 cable. If we execute the PERFTTY1 program in one PC and run TTY1 in the other, we should see the pattern shown in the figure. If the TTY1 program loses any characters, the change in the pattern should be apparent.

FIGURE 9.4 perftty1.c

```
 1    /* perftty1.c - generate a character stream for TTY pgm */
 2    #include <stdio.h>
 3    #include "cminor.h"
 4    #include "keyio.h"
 5    #include "async.h"
 6
 7
 8    main()
 9     {
10        int i , j , imax , ret ;
11
12        ret = comm_init(1) ;    /* set up for RS-232 use */
13        if( ret != 0 )          /* check for error */
14          { printf(" unrecognizable RS232 address - %x \n", ret) ;
15            exit(10) ;
16          }
17
18        printf("max line length: \n");
19        scanf("%d",&imax) ;
20        printf("press a key to quit \n");
21        while( keypress() == 0 )
22          {
23            for(i= 0 ; i < imax ; i=i+1)
24              {
25                for(j=0 ; j<i ; j=j+1)
26                  { send_char('0'+j) ; }
27                send_char('\r');
28                send_char('\n');
29              }
30          }
31     }
```

FIGURE 9.5 Performance of TTY1

```
1
2    A) Display from TTY1 at 300 Baud
3
4    ...
5    012345
6    0123456
```

Figure 9.5   continues

Figure 9.5   continued

```
 7    01234567
 8    012345678
 9
10    0
11    01
12    012
13    0123
14    01234
15    012345
16    0123456
17    01234567
18    012345678
19
20    0
21    01
22    ...
23
24
25
26    B) Display from TTY1 at 1200 Baud
27
28    ...
29    12345
30    123456
31    1234567
32    12345678
33
34
35    1
36    12
37    123
38    1234
39    12345
40    123456
41    1234567
42    12345678
43
44
45    1
46    12
47    ...
48
49    C) Display from TTY1 at 9600 Baud
50
51    ...
52    0134
53
54    0134
55
56    0134
57
58     0234
59
60    0145
61
62    01345
63    ...
```

At 300 baud (Figure 9.5a), the sawtooth pattern is displayed correctly — no characters are lost. Figures 9.5b and 9.5c show the results at 1,200 baud and 9,600 baud, respectively. At 1,200 baud, the TTY1 program receives most of the characters correctly, but it drops the character immediately after a line feed control character. At 9,600 baud, TTY1 loses so many characters that the pattern is completely altered. Although TTY1's performance at 9,600 baud is obviously unsatisfactory, the loss of even a few characters at 1,200 baud makes it useless at that speed, too. The results in Figure 9.5 were collected using a PC XT, but similar results would be obtained with faster PCs.

When TTY1 receives a line feed character, the entire screen is scrolled upward. This requires so much time that the next character received is overwritten before we finish scrolling the screen. Although TTY1 may handle received characters at an average rate of more than 1,200 baud, it fails to meet the worst-case test of handling every character in 1/120 second or less.

We can also test to see how well TTY1 handles keyboard input while receiving data at the full baud rate. We can run the test and hold down a key; this produces keyboard input at the rate of 10 to 15 characters a second. If TTY1 fails to collect keyboard input fast enough, the BIOS keyboard support software sounds a warning beep to indicate that input has been lost. The result of this test is that data received from the async line are far more likely to be lost than is keyboard input.

We can already see in TTY1 some characteristics of real-time programs in general. The following sections discuss these characteristics.

Polling

The *polling loop* in `tty1.c` is a common structure in real-time programs. We cannot predict which type of input will be received next and wait for it. Instead, we check the *status* for each input until something is received.

There are two problems with waiting for a single type of input. First, the PC provides a limited amount of storage for keyboard and RS-232 inputs. If we wait for the next keyboard input and 10 characters arrive over the RS-232 port, some of those characters will be lost. But even if the PC could buffer all 10 characters, we would not see them displayed until we typed a character. So whatever provisions our computer and operating system make for buffering input, we need to accept and process any inputs promptly.

Priority-Driven Scheduling

The program also illustrates the concept of *priority-driven scheduling*. Checking for and handling input on the RS-232 line has priority over handling keyboard input. Keyboard input arrives at a slow rate (about 10 to 15 keystrokes per second at most), and the BIOS support provides a buffer for several keystrokes (16 in some PC models). The async hardware provides a two-character buffer and at 1,200 baud the RS-232 input rate may be a maximum of 120 characters per second. So giving higher priority to RS-232 input is a good design decision.

Analyzing the Problem

Our example illustrates another characteristic of real-time problems, which is that good analysis of the input rates and the processing deadlines is vital to producing good real-time programs.

Performance

Our program works correctly at 300 baud (30 characters per second). When we use it at 1,200 baud, it loses a few received characters. This illustrates another characteristic of real-time programs: If the program is not fast enough, input is lost (or some equivalent misfortune occurs). Poor performance might make programs presented in Chapters 1 through 8 less pleasant to use, but it makes TTY work incorrectly. Although good *average* performance is satisfactory for ordinary programs, real-time programs must have good *worst-case* performance.

9.4   Improving TTY1's Performance: Interrupts

The IBM PC hardware and the PC BIOS keyboard support provide buffering, or *queueing*, of keyboard input. When a key is pressed, a hardware interrupt occurs, and software in the PC BIOS is executed. This interrupt-handling code collects the keyboard input and places it into a buffer. Keystroke data are removed from this buffer on demand in the order entered. The interrupt handler must still act promptly to collect each keystroke, but the application program (such as TTY1) may fall behind occasionally.

Without interrupts and buffering, an application program must handle each keystroke before the next one arrives. But with these aids, the program need only keep the buffer from overflowing. For a buffer of sixteen keystrokes, this requires handling sixteen keystrokes in any interval in which sixteen keystrokes arrive. A similar strategy using hardware interrupts and a buffer can improve the performance of TTY1. We develop these techniques in the following sections.

Interrupts are a foreign concept to many programmers. The following analogy may help show the purpose of interrupts and how we can use them.

The TTY1 program is like a phone-order business run by one person with a one-track mind. When he receives a call, he writes up the order. Then he finishes filling the order. If a phone call comes in while he is filling the order, he ignores it. Unless our clerk works at superhuman speed, he will lose some orders. A more flexible clerk would stop to answer the phone immediately. After the order has been taken, the clerk goes back to what he was doing. Phone calls may preempt the other work, but the clerk remembers where he left off. Since the clerk may receive several orders before the current order has been processed, he must store a list of orders not yet filled.

Applying these ideas to the TTY program requires several new elements:

1. We need to make the async hardware preempt our current activity when a character arrives. The IBM PC provides hardware interrupts that we can use; we just have to initialize the async adapter to generate interrupts and initialize the PC hardware to accept them. Part of that initialization is to specify the address of an interrupt handler to be executed when the interrupt occurs.

2. When the interrupt occurs and our interrupt handler begins execution, its first job is to preserve register values and anything else that we will need to return to the activity interrupted. The last thing the interrupt handler does is to restore this context information and return control to the activity interrupted.

3. The interrupt handler must collect the received character from the async adapter and store it in a queue.

4. The interrupt handler must tell the async adapter and the PC hardware that the interrupt has been handled. (In the case of our phone-order analogy, answering the phone makes it stop ringing.)

5. The TTY program must regularly check the queue for characters that have been received. It must remove characters at the same average rate that they are added by the interrupt handler. The queue allows the program to fall behind temporarily without losing characters. The larger the queue, the farther we can fall behind. If we have a 100-character buffer, the performance constraint is that we must remove 100 characters for every interval in which 100 characters are added to the buffer.

The ideas involved apply to many real-time programming problems. To get better performance, we split a task into a small part accomplished by an interrupt handler and a larger part that involves a less stringent time constraint. A storage buffer provides communication between the two parts. This programming solution does not improve the average performance of the program, but it improves the worst-case performance by relaxing the time constraint for most of the work.

9.5 Specifying the TTY Program

Now that we understand the lessons of the TTY1 program, we can specify what the next TTY program is to do. First, TTY1 had a few omissions in the emulation of a dumb terminal. The keyboard input did not allow us to send an ASCII null character or to send a break signal. In addition, we want commands to record received data to a disk file or to replay (send) an existing disk file. Figure 9.6 describes our next TTY program.

It is a good practice to initialize the async adapter hardware completely before use. Setting baud rate, parity, and other communications parameters are a part of

FIGURE 9.6   Description of TTY program

Name
TTY   terminal emulation program

Usage

```
C>tty 1200 n 8
```

specifies 1200 baud, no parity, and 8 data bits.

```
C>tty 300 e 7
```

specifies 300 baud, even parity, and 7 data bits.

Function
TTY emulates a dumb async terminal (a teletype or tty terminal). It can be used to communicate with another computer over an async RS-232 line. This connection may be via async modems or an RS-232 cable.

ASCII characters typed on the keyboard are sent out on the RS-232 line, and characters received are displayed on the screen. The carriage return, line feed, backspace, and bel control characters are interpreted as display commands. (The line feed character (newline) moves the cursor to the start of a new line. The contents of the display are scrolled up if the cursor was already on the last line of the screen. The carriage return character does not affect the display.) Other control characters are displayed as ^c, where c is a printable ASCII character whose value is 0x40 plus the value of the control character.

TTY can record received data in a disk file or transmit data from an existing data file. Baud rate, parity, and number of data bits are specified on the command line when TTY is executed.

Keyboard Input
Keyboard input is interpreted as ASCII characters or as input commands. Control characters are input with the control key and an alphanumeric key. (To send control-A, press the control and A keys.) Control-@ is interpreted as the ASCII null character. The following input commands are recognized:

Figure 9.6   continues

Figure 9.6   continued

F1 key	Exit to DOS.
F10 key	Start/stop recording received data.
	(TTY will prompt for a file name.)
Shift F10 key	Start/stop replaying an existing file.
	The contents will be sent on the RS-232 line.
	(TTY will prompt for a file name.)
Alt-B	Send a Break sequence on the RS-232 line.

Notes

1. TTY has limited features; it is a basis for expansion by the reader.

2. TTY operates correctly at 300 to 9,600 baud. It may lose some data if more than 10,000 characters are transmitted without a pause.

3. Baud rate and other parameters are as described for the DOS MODE command.

4. The TTY batch file executes the `tty2.exe` program. If the `tty2.exe` program has been compiled with Microsoft C, some control characters typed on the keyboard will be interpreted as commands. The control-Break, control-C, and control-@ keystrokes cause the program to abort.

---

the initialization process. To keep TTY small and easy to discuss, we will use the MS-DOS MODE command to initialize the async adapter and to set the communications parameters. The batch file in Figure 9.7 packages the MODE command with the TTY2 program. This TTY2 program does the rest of the TTY function; its implementation is discussed in the next section.

FIGURE 9.7   tty.bat batch file

```
1     mode com%1:%2,%3,%4
2     tty2
```

9.6   TTY2 Source Files

The following sections discuss source files that make up the TTY2 program. In addition, the `async.h` and `async1.c` files are also part of the TTY2 program.

The structure of function calls in the TTY2 program is shown here. Note that the interrupt handler `rcv_int` is executed as a result of a hardware interrupt rather than by being called from another function. To keep the diagram to a manageable size, we have omitted the names of toolkit functions such as `keypress`, `getkey`, `inbyte`, and `outbyte`.

```
main
    comm_init
    init_disp
    start_rcv
        initq
        dis_asy
            dis_8259
            install
        clr_int
        rcv_char
        en_asy
            install
            en8259
    chk_asy
        intsoff
        chkq
        intson
    get_asy
        intsoff
        getq
        intson
    disp_char
    rec_char
    get_kbd
    exec_cmd
        send_char
            chk_xmt
            xmt_char
        record
            get_file
            disp_msg
            end_record
                disp_msg
        replay
            get_file
            disp_msg
            end_replay
                disp_msg
            send_brk
                xmt_brk
                end_brk
    chk_xmt
    rep_char
        end_record
            disp_msg
    xmt_char
```

```
        stop_rcv
            dis_asy
                install
        end_record
                disp_msg
        end_replay
                disp_msg



    (hardware interrupt occurs)
        rcv_int
            rcv_char
            putq
            clr_int
```

Header Files for TTY2

Figures 9.8 and 9.9 show two header files for the TTY2 program. `tty2cmds.h` defines the keyboard input commands recognized by TTY2. `tty2parm.h` contains other definitions needed by TTY2 source files. Lines 3 to 5 define status bits for a global state variable. Lines 8 to 12 specify the dimensions for the window in which received characters are displayed. Lines 30 to 59 declare function prototypes for the functions in the TTY2 program.

FIGURE 9.8   tty2cmds.h

```
 1
 2      /* tty2cmds.h - define keyboard input commands */
 3
 4      #define   NOCMD          0
 5      #define   ASCIICMD       1
 6      #define   EXITCMD        2
 7      #define   RECCMD         3
 8      #define   REPCMD         4
 9      #define   BRKCMD         5
10
11      /* return codes for exec_cmd */
12      #define   NOT_THRU       0
13      #define   THRU           1
```

FIGURE 9.9   tty2parm.h

```
 1      /* tty2parm.h - definitions for TTY2 program */
 2
 3      /* bit definitions for state variable */
 4      #define REC_BIT   0x0001   /* on if we are recording rcvd data */
```

Figure 9.9   continues

Figure 9.9   continued

```
5       #define REP_BIT    0x0002    /* on if we are replaying  a file */
6
7
8                                    /* origin, size of output window */
9       #define OUT_ROW 0
10      #define OUT_COL 0
11      #define OUT_NROW 25
12      #define OUT_NCOL 80
13
14
15                                    /* define interrupt function type */
16                                    /* and pointer to it */
17                                    /* TURBO C version */
18      #ifdef TURBOC
19      #define IFUN void interrupt
20      typedef void interrupt (*PIFUN) () ;
21      #endif
22                                    /* Microsoft C version */
23      #ifdef MSC
24      #define IFUN void interrupt far
25      typedef void (interrupt far *PIFUN) () ;
26      #endif
27
28      extern unsigned state ;
29
30                                    /* function prototypes */
31      int get_kbd(int *) ;
32      int exec_cmd(int, int) ;
33      void init_disp(void) ;
34      void disp_char(int) ;
35      void disp_msg(char *) ;
36      int record(void) ;
37      void end_record(void) ;
38      void rec_char(int) ;
39      int replay(void) ;
40      void end_replay(void) ;
41      int rep_char(void) ;
42      FILE *get_file(char *, char *, char *) ;
43      void send_brk(void) ;
44      void start_rcv(void) ;
45      void stop_rcv(void) ;
46      IFUN rcv_int() ;              /* interrupt handler function */
47      int chk_asy(void) ;
48      int get_asy(void) ;
49      void install(int, PIFUN , PIFUN *) ;
50
51      void xmt_brk(void) ;
52      void end_brk(void) ;
53      void en_asy( PIFUN ) ;        /* enables serial port interrupt */
54      void dis_asy(void) ;
55      void en8259(int) ;
56      void dis8259(int) ;
57      void clr_int(void) ;
58      void intsoff( void ) ;
59      void intson( void ) ;
60
```

The rcv_int function declared on line 46 handles hardware interrupts. Both Turbo C and Microsoft C provide the interrupt keyword for defining a C function as an interrupt handler. Unfortunately the syntax is not the same for the two compilers. Lines 15 to 26 define a macro, IFUN, and a data type, PIFUN, which hide the compiler differences. The symbols TURBOC and MSC in the asmtools.h header file from Chapter 7 are used to select the appropriate definitions. The PIFUN data type is also an argument to the functions en_asy and install.

tty2.c

The main function for the TTY2 program is shown in Figure 9.10. Lines 19 to 27 initialize parts of the program, and lines 48 to 52 clean up before returning to DOS. The polling loop in lines 29 to 47 is similar to that in the TTY1 program, but since the program is much larger, calls to functions keep the main function small and uncluttered. The loop enforces the same priority as did TTY1: Received data has priority over keyboard input.

FIGURE 9.10 tty2.c

```
1     /* tty2.c - second tty emulation program */
2     #include <stdio.h>
3     #include <stdlib.h>
4     #include "asmtools.h"
5     #include "keyio.h"
6     #include "async.h"
7     #include "video.h"
8     #include "tty2parm.h"
9
10    extern int nrerr , nrqo ;   /* receive error counters */
11    int adapter   = COM2 ;      /* which async adapter to use */
12    unsigned state ;            /* record/replay state */
13                                /* bits defined in ttyparm.h */
14
15    main()
16      {
17        int c , cmd , thru , ret ;
18
19        ret = comm_init(adapter); /* set up for using comm. port */
20        if( ret != 0 )
21          { printf(" unrecognizable RS232 address - %x \n", ret) ;
22            exit(10) ;
23          }
24        init_disp() ;            /* set up display */
25        start_rcv() ;
26        thru = 0 ;
27        state = 0 ;              /* not recording or replaying now */
28
29        while( thru  == 0 )      /* scan for input until thru */
30          {
31            if( chk_asy() != 0 )     /* check for rcvd. data */
32              { c = get_asy() ;      /*    data waiting - get it */
```

Figure 9.10   continues

Figure 9.10   continued

```
33                  disp_char(c) ;
34                  if((state & REC_BIT) != 0)/* are we capturing data?*/
35                      rec_char(c) ;     /*   yes - put char into file*/
36              }
37          else if(keypress() !=0)  /* check for keybd. input */
38              { c = get_kbd(&cmd);   /*   data waiting - get it */
39                thru=exec_cmd(cmd,c) ;
40              }
41          else if( ((state & REP_BIT) != 0) /* sending a file ? */
42                 && (chk_xmt() !=0)) /* if so and XMT ready */
43              { c = rep_char() ;      /* get next char from file */
44                if( c != EOF )
45                    xmt_char(c) ;      /*   send next char from file */
46              }
47          }
48      stop_rcv() ;             /* shut down async rcv */
49      end_record() ;           /* stop recording */
50      end_replay() ;           /* stop replaying */
51      vid_clr_scn(0,0,24,79,NORMAL_DISPLAY) ; /* clear screen */
52      vid_set_cur(0,0) ;       /* put blinking cursor at top left */
53      printf(" %d receive errors \n %d buffer overflows \n",
54        nrerr , nrqo ) ;
55  }
```

Support for recording data has been added to the handling of received characters in lines 34 and 35. Lines 41 to 46 provide similar support for replaying data from an existing file. Note that this activity is lowest in priority, and that transmit status is checked before transmitting a character so that the program never waits for the transmit hardware to be available.

tty2get.c

The get_kbd function in Figure 9.11 collects the next keystroke and translates it into a command. Keystrokes corresponding to ASCII characters are classified as ASCII commands, including the control-@ keystroke. Some non-ASCII keys are identified as valid commands; a keystroke that is not recognized is classified as the null command NOCMD.

get_kbd stores the command type where the pcmd argument specifies. It also returns the character value (or its replacement in the case of control-@).

get_kbd is only called when keyboard input is available. So getkey always returns immediately with a keystroke. As suggested in Section 7.5, the getkey function behaves somewhat differently for Turbo C and Microsoft C. For Microsoft C, some control characters are handled by DOS as commands rather than as input characters. For example, typing control-C or control-@ causes the TTY2 program to abort if the program has been compiled with Microsoft C. A BIOS-based version of getkey as suggested in Section 7.5 would solve this problem.

FIGURE 9.11   tty2get.c

```
1     /* tty2get.c - get keyboard input */
2     #include "stdio.h"
3     #include "keyio.h"
4     #include "tty2cmds.h"
5
6                                 /* define special keys */
7     #define   ALT_B   (256+48)  /* 48 is scan code for Alt-B */
8     #define   CTRL_AT (256+3)   /*  3 is scan code for Ctrl-@ */
9     #define   F10KEY  (F1KEY+9) /* F10 */
10    #define   F20KEY (F11KEY+9) /* Shift-F10 */
11
12    int get_kbd(pcmd)
13     int *pcmd ;                /* store the command type here */
14     {
15        int c ;
16
17        c = getkey() ;
18        if( c == F1KEY )        /* F1 = Exit */
19            *pcmd = EXITCMD ;
20        else if( c == (ALT_B) )/* ALT B = Send Break */
21            *pcmd = BRKCMD ;
22        else if( c == F10KEY )  /* F10 = Record input */
23            *pcmd = RECCMD ;
24        else if( c == F20KEY )  /* Shift-F10 = Replay a File */
25            *pcmd = REPCMD ;
26        else if( c == CTRL_AT )/* Ctrl-@ = ASCII Null char */
27          { c = 0 ;             /* convert to null char */
28            *pcmd = ASCIICMD ;
29          }
30        else if( c <= 127 )     /* ASCII char */
31            *pcmd = ASCIICMD ;
32        else                    /* not a recognized key  */
33            *pcmd = NOCMD ;
34        return( c ) ;
35    }
```

tty2exec.c

Figure 9.12 lists the exec_cmd function that executes input commands. A switch statement provides an action for each command, including the null command NOCMD. The value returned by exec_cmd determines whether the program continues or exits (when the EXITCMD is typed).

tty2disp.c

The functions in Figure 9.13 use the WINDOW module from Chapter 8 for displaying single characters and strings. The init_disp function defines the output window based on the dimensions in tty2parm.h.

FIGURE 9.12   tty2exec.c

```
1      /* tty2exec.c - execute a keyboard command */
2      #include "stdio.h"
3      #include "asmtools.h"
4      #include "async.h"
5      #include "tty2cmds.h"
6      #include "tty2parm.h"
7
8      int exec_cmd(cmd,c)
9       int cmd ;                    /* type of command */
10      int c ;                      /* char input (if asciicmd) */
11      {
12         int ret ;
13
14         ret = NOT_THRU ;
15         switch( cmd)
16           {
17           case NOCMD :                      break ;
18            case ASCIICMD : send_char(c);    break ;
19           case RECCMD : record() ;          break ;
20           case REPCMD : replay() ;          break ;
21           case BRKCMD : send_brk() ;        break ;
22           case EXITCMD : ret = THRU ;       break ;
23           }
24        return( ret ) ;
25      }
```

FIGURE 9.13   tty2disp.c

```
1      /* tty2disp.c - display chars */
2      /* uses VIDEO module functions (BIOS I/O funs.) */
3      #include "stdio.h"
4      #include "asmtools.h"
5      #include "keyio.h"
6      #include "video.h"
7      #include "win.h"
8      #include "tty2parm.h"
9
10     static WIN out_win ;
11
12     void init_disp()
13     {
14                                  /* no border, scroll contents */
15        win_define(& out_win, OUT_ROW, OUT_COL,
16            OUT_NROW, OUT_NCOL , NULL , AUTO_SCROLL ) ;
17        win_display( & out_win ) ;
18        win_disp_cur(& out_win, -1 , -1 ) ; /* set visible cursor */
19     }
20
21
22     void disp_char(c)               /* display one character */
23      int c ;                        /* the character */
24      {
```

Figure 9.13   continues

Figure 9.13 continued

```
25          c = toascii(c) ;
26          if( ( (c >= ' ') && (c <= '~') )  /* printable char ? */
27              || ( c==ASCLF) || ( c==ASCBS) )  /* or  LF , BS */
28                  win_wc(& out_win, c) ;
29          else if( c == ASCCR )
30              { ; }                      /* Carriage return - ignore it */
31          else if( c == 0x7f )
32              {  win_wc(& out_win, '^') ;
33                 win_wc(& out_win, 'r') ;
34              }
35          else if( c == ASCBEL )
36              {  vid_tc(c) ;             /* BEL char - sound it */
37                 win_wc(& out_win, '^') ;
38                 win_wc(& out_win, 'b') ;
39              }
40          else                           /* other control char */
41              {  win_wc(& out_win, '^') ; /* display as */
42                 win_wc(& out_win, c+'@');/* ^printable char */
43              }
44          win_disp_cur(& out_win, -1, -1) ; /* update visible cursor */
45      }
46
47
48      void disp_msg(s)                   /* display a message */
49        char s[] ;                       /* message char string */
50        {
51            win_ws(& out_win, s, ALL_STRING ) ;
52            win_disp_cur(& out_win, -1, -1) ; /* update visible cursor */
53        }
```

The disp_char function displays each character received on the RS-232 line. It treats some ASCII control characters as display commands — carriage return, line feed, backspace, and bel. The line feed (newline) character is passed to win_wc; it causes output to start in the first column of a new line. The carriage return character is just ignored. For the bel character, a call to vid_tc produces an audible beep, and ^b is displayed. Other control characters are displayed in the form ^c, where c is a printable character with a value 0x40 higher than the control character. For example, the control character 0x03 is displayed as ^C. (C has the value 0x43.) The rubout control character (0x7f) is displayed as ^r.

Line 10 sets the high-order bit in the character to 0 before displaying it; characters with values from 0x80 through 0xff are displayed as normal ASCII characters with values 0x00 through 0x7f.

The disp_msg function displays messages originated by the TTY2 program. Both disp_char and disp_msg update the cursor position to match the writing position maintained by the WINDOW module. This provides a cue to the user about the position where the next character will be displayed.

tty2rec.c

The source file in Figure 9.14 implements functions to record received data in a disk file and to transmit the contents of an existing file.

FIGURE 9.14   tty2rec.c

```
1     /* tty2rec.c - disk file record/replay functions   */
2     #include "stdio.h"
3     #include "asmtools.h"
4     #include "tty2parm.h"
5
6     static char rec_name[130] ;/* store name of record file here */
7     static char rep_name[130] ;/* store name of replay file here */
8     static FILE *rec_file ;     /* record file pointer */
9     static FILE *rep_file ;     /* replay file name */
10
11    #define RECBUF_SIZE 4096    /* record file buffer size */
12    #define REPBUF_SIZE 4096    /* replay file buffer size */
13    static char recbuf[ RECBUF_SIZE ] ; /* record file buffer */
14    static char repbuf[ RECBUF_SIZE ] ; /* replay buffer */
15
16
17    int record()                  /* start/stop recording */
18    { if( (state & REC_BIT) == 0) /* are we already recording ? */
19        {                         /* no - open capture file */
20           rec_file = get_file("record",rec_name,"ab") ;
21           if(rec_file == NULL)/* check for abort */
22               return( -1 ) ;  /*  yes - return failure */
23                               /* assign buffer to file */
24           if( setvbuf(rec_file,recbuf,_IOFBF,RECBUF_SIZE) != 0)
25             { disp_msg("\n can't assign file buffer \n") ;
26               return( -1 ) ;
27             }
28           state = state | REC_BIT ;
29           disp_msg("\n ** Starting File recording ** \n ") ;
30        }
31      else end_record() ;       /* already recording. So stop */
32      return( 0 ) ;             /* success return code */
33    }
34
35
36    void end_record()           /* stop recording and close file */
37    { if( (state & REC_BIT) != 0 )
38        { fclose(rec_file) ;  /*    yes - close it */
39          disp_msg("\n ** File recording completed ** \n ") ;
40          vid_tc('\a') ;
41        }
42      state = state & ( ~REC_BIT);/* turn off record flag */
43    }
44
45
46    void rec_char(c)            /* record a char */
47     int c;
48     {
49        fputc(c,rec_file) ;      /* put char into the file */
```

Figure 9.14   continues

Figure 9.14   continued

```
50       }
51
52
53    int replay()                  /* start replaying a file */
54      { if( (state & REP_BIT) == 0) /* are we already replaying ? */
55          {                        /*    no - open replay file */
56            rep_file = get_file("replay",rep_name,"rb") ;
57            if(rep_file == NULL)/* check for abort */
58                return( -1 ) ;   /*  yes - return failure */
59                                  /* assign buffer to file */
60            if( setvbuf(rep_file,repbuf,_IOFBF,REPBUF_SIZE) != 0)
61              { disp_msg("\n can't assign file buffer \n") ;
62                return( -1 ) ;
63              }
64            state = state | REP_BIT ;
65            disp_msg("\n ** Starting File Replay ** \n ") ;
66          }
67        else end_replay() ;        /*   yes - file open. close it */
68        return( 0 ) ;              /* success return code */
69      }
70
71
72    void end_replay()              /* stop replay and close file */
73      { if( (state & REP_BIT) != 0) /* is the replay file open ? */
74          { fclose(rep_file) ;     /*    yes - close it */
75            disp_msg("\n ** File replay completed ** \n ") ;
76            vid_tc('\a') ;
77          }
78        state = state & ( ~REP_BIT);/* turn off the flag */
79      }
80
81
82    int rep_char()                 /* get next char from replay file */
83      {
84        int c ;
85
86        c = fgetc(rep_file) ;       /* get next char */
87        if( c == EOF )              /* check for end-of-file */
88            end_replay() ;
89        return( c ) ;               /* return char or EOF */
90      }
```

The record function is called when a record command is typed. It checks to see whether the TTY2 program is already recording data. If not, it prompts for a file name and opens the file. If recording is already underway, record ends recording and closes the file. A bit in the global variable state records whether or not we are currently recording received data.

The rec_char function is called to record each character received. end_record, called by record and by the main function before it exits to DOS, closes the recording file if it is open and turns off the record status bit in the variable state.

The replay, rep_char, and end_replay functions perform corresponding roles for replaying an existing file. A replay status bit in the variable state tracks the current status of replaying a file.

Recording characters may involve delays of 50 to 1,000 milliseconds to perform disk reads and writes. During this time, additional characters may be received. If interrupts were not used to handle these characters, characters could be overwritten in the async hardware and lost. The interrupt function will continue to collect these characters and to place them into the queue for received data. So this queue must be able to store all the data received for a 50 to 1,000 millisecond period. Prompting for a file name and opening a file may take much longer; TTY2 provides about 80 seconds of buffering at 1,200 baud, but the program's user may wait even longer to type a file name.

Even with interrupts and buffering of received characters, recording must keep up with receiving characters over some time interval. Calls to the setvbuf library function in lines 24 to 27 and 60 to 63 assign 4,096 byte buffers to record and replay files.

These record and replay functions hide the details of file I/O from the rest of the TTY2 program. Our implementation used C library functions for buffered I/O; we could change it to use other functions without disturbing the rest of TTY2.

tty2getf.c

The get_file function in Figure 9.15 collects the name of a record or replay file. It validates that name by trying to open the file. If the file cannot be opened, an error message is displayed, and the user may correct the file name or type a replacement. The escape key (ESC) may be typed to abort the operation. get_file uses a pop-up window for the prompt, the input file name, and any error messages. The structure of the get_file is similar to that of the get_pos function in Chapter 8.

FIGURE 9.15   tty2getf.c

```
 1      /* tty2getf.c -  get record / replay file name */
 2      /* uses pop-up window */
 3      #include <stdio.h>
 4      #include <string.h>
 5      #include "asmtools.h"
 6      #include "keyio.h"
 7      #include "video.h"
 8      #include "win.h"
 9      #include "tty2parm.h"
10
11      #define START_ROW        6    /* starting row for window */
12      #define START_COL       10    /* starting column for winodw */
13      #define NO_ROWS          2    /* number of rows in window */
14      #define NO_COLS         40    /* number of columns in window */
15
16      #define MAXS   129            /* string length for input */
17
18      static int first_time = 0;  /* used to detect 1st call to */
19                                  /* get_file */
```

Figure 9.15   continues

Figure 9.15   continued

```
20
21      static WIN fnw ;               /* file name window structure */
22      static int end_keys[] = { ASCESC } ;
23      #define NEND 1                 /* number of keys in end_keys */
24
25
26                                     /* get name of file and open it */
27      FILE *get_file(prompt,name,fmode)
28       char prompt[] ;               /* display this prompt */
29       char name[] ;                 /* store file name here */
30       char fmode[] ;                /* file open mode */
31      {
32          int row , col , next , ret ;
33          int cur_row , cur_col ;
34          FILE *rfile ;
35
36          if( first_time == 0 )  /* define window on first call */
37            { win_define(& fnw, START_ROW, START_COL,
38                NO_ROWS, NO_COLS, & dline_border,CLR_TO_EOL);
39              first_time = 1 ;
40            }
41
42                                     /* save cursor position */
43          vid_get_cur(& cur_row, & cur_col ) ;
44          win_popup(& fnw) ;       /* save screen contents */
45                                     /* and display file name window */
46                                     /* write prompt string */
47          win_setpos(& fnw, 0 , 0 ) ;
48          win_ws(& fnw, prompt, ALL_STRING) ;
49          win_ws(& fnw, " file name: ", ALL_STRING );
50          win_getpos(& fnw, & row , & col ) ;
51
52          next = 0 ;
53          while( 1 == 1 )
54            { win_setpos(& fnw, row, col) ; /* set writing position */
55                                     /* get string from keyboard */
56              ret = win_gets(name,next, MAXS-1, end_keys,NEND, & fnw) ;
57              if( ret == ASCESC )/* check for abort key */
58                { rfile = NULL ;
59                  break ;
60                }
61
62              rfile = fopen(name,fmode) ; /* open the file */
63              if( rfile != NULL) /* check for failure */
64                  break ;        /*  OK - exit from loop */
65                                     /*  failed - try again */
66              win_getpos(& fnw, & row,& col) ; /* remember position */
67              next = strlen(name); /*    and end of string */
68
69              vid_tc('\a') ;       /*    beep */
70              win_setpos(& fnw, 1, 0 ) ;
71              win_ws( & fnw,      /*    and display error msg */
72                  " can't open the file. Try again", ALL_STRING );
73            }
74          win_unpop(& fnw) ;
75          vid_set_cur( cur_row,cur_col ) ; /* restore cursor pos. */
76          return( rfile ) ;
77      }
78
```

tty2brk.c

The `send_brk` function in Figure 9.16 transmits a break signal — a low voltage level on the RS-232 line lasting for approximately 200 milliseconds. `send_brk` implements the 200-millisecond timing. It calls the `xmt_brk` function to start transmitting the RS-232 low voltage level. `send_brk` calls the `busy_wait` function from Chapter 7 to delay for about 200 milliseconds. During this delay, buffering the received data prevents losing characters. Sending a break signal would be more difficult to implement without interrupts and buffering of received data. When the `busy_wait` function returns, a call to `end_brk` ends transmission of the low voltage signal.

FIGURE 9.16   tty2brk.c

```
 1     /* tty2brk.c - send a break on the async line */
 2     #include "stdio.h"
 3     #include "ct_timer.h"
 4     #include "asmtools.h"
 5     #include "tty2parm.h"
 6
 7     #define brk_length   4L      /* break length in timer ticks */
 8
 9
10     void send_brk()              /* start transmitting break */
11       {
12         int t ;
13
14         xmt_brk() ;              /* start sending break */
15
16                                  /* wait (brk_length ticks) */
17         busy_wait(NO_TIME,brk_length) ;
18
19         end_brk() ;             /* stop sending break */
20       }
21
```

`xmt_brk` and `end_brk` manipulate the PC's async hardware and are specific to that hardware. `send_brk` is not specific to the hardware but implements the 200-millisecond timing of the break signal in a particular way. If we wanted to adapt TTY2 for different hardware, we would change the `async1.c` and `async2.c` modules that interface to the async hardware. If we wanted to change the implementation of the 200-millisecond timing so that the program did not wait in a delay loop, we would change the `tty2brk.c` source file.

tty2rcv.c

The `tty2rcv.c` source file in Figure 9.17 handles the details of receiving data. The `start_rcv` function, called by `main` during initialization, sets up the receive queue and calls `en_asy` to enable interrupts for received characters. An special interrupt handler function, `rcv_int`, is installed to handle async interrupts.

FIGURE 9.17   tty2rcv.c

```
 1      /* tty2rcv.c - handle rcving chars */
 2      #include "stdio.h"
 3      #include "asmtools.h"
 4      #include "queue.h"
 5      #include "async.h"
 6      #include "tty2parm.h"
 7
 8      int nrerr ;                      /* count of rcv. errors */
 9      int nrqo ;                       /* count of rcv Q overflows */
10      QUEUE rq ;                       /* queue for rcving chars */
11      #define RQS   10000              /* size of rcv queue */
12      char rd[ RQS ] ;                 /* store rcvd chars here */
13
14
15      void start_rcv()                 /* setup async rcv */
16        {
17          nrerr = 0 ; nrqo = 0 ;  /* zero error counters */
18          initq(&rq,rd,RQS) ;          /* setup queue for rcvd data */
19
20          dis_asy() ;                  /* disable int. on async board */
21          clr_int() ;                  /* clear interrupt in 8259 */
22          rcv_char() ;                 /* clear any waiting char */
23          en_asy(rcv_int) ;            /* enable int. on async board */
24        }
25
26
27      void stop_rcv()                  /* shut down async rcv */
28        {
29          dis_asy() ;                  /* disable int. on async board */
30        }
31
32
33      IFUN rcv_int()                   /* called by gotint when a rcv. */
34        {                              /* data interrupt occurs */
35          int c ;
36
37          c = rcv_char() ;             /* get the char */
38          if( c == (-1) )              /* check for rcv error */
39              nrerr = nrerr + 1 ;/*     error - bump counter */
40          else
41            { if(putq(c,&rq) == Q_FAIL) /* no error - put char into Q*/
42               nrqo = nrqo + 1; /*    Q overflow - bump counter */
43            }
44          clr_int() ;                  /* clear interrupt in the 8259 */
45        }
46
47
48      int chk_asy()                    /* check for a received char */
49        {
50          int ret ;
51
52          intsoff() ;                  /* turn off ints while we   */
53          ret = chkq(&rq) ;            /* look at rcv Q - empty ? */
54          intson() ;                   /* now turn ints back on    */
55          return( ret ) ;
56        }
57
```

Figure 9.17   continues

Figure 9.17 continued

```
58
59     int get_asy()                  /* get next char from rcv Q */
60     {
61         int ret ;
62
63         intsoff() ;                /* turn ints. off while we  */
64         ret = getq(&rq) ;          /* get next char from rcv Q */
65         intson() ;                 /* now turn ints. back on   */
66         return( ret ) ;
67     }
```

When a character is received, the `rcv_int` function in lines 33 to 45 is executed. It calls `rcv_char` (in Figure 9.2) to collect the character and then places that character in the receive queue. (Queues are explained in the next section.) If a receive error is detected or if the queue is full, an error counter is incremented and nothing is added to the queue.

The `interrupt` keyword tells the compiler to create special instructions so that `rcv_int` function can be used to handle interrupts. The `IFUN` macro defined in `tty2parm.h`, hides syntax differences between Turbo C and Microsoft C.

The `chk_asy` and `get_asy` functions are used by the main polling loop to check for and collect received characters (from the queue). Although we could call `chkq` and `getq` directly, our approach isolates the rest of TTY2 from the details of buffering received data.

queue.c

Buffers that keep data in a first-come, first-served order are often called *FIFO queues*, for first-in, first-out. These queues are useful building blocks in many programming problems. In the TTY2 program, we need one queue for a specific purpose— buffering received characters. However, it is easy and sensible to design a tool for more general use—a QUEUE module. Before we show the QUEUE module implementation, we will discuss how queues work and how they can be implemented. The following drawing shows how we might think of a FIFO queue—a long, elastic tube with data going in at the left and out at the right. Inside the tube, the data stay in order so that the first item entered is the first removed.

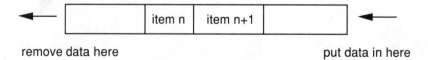

This picture works fine for expressing the concept of a FIFO queue, but it does not tell us how to implement one. We can come closer to that goal with a picture of a queue as a ring. Two pointers — a *head pointer* and a *tail pointer* — keep track of where we should remove or add the next item. When the head and tail point to the same place, the queue is empty. As we add and remove data, the head pointer chases the tail pointer around the ring as shown in Figure 9.18.

FIGURE 9.18   FIFO Queue as a Ring

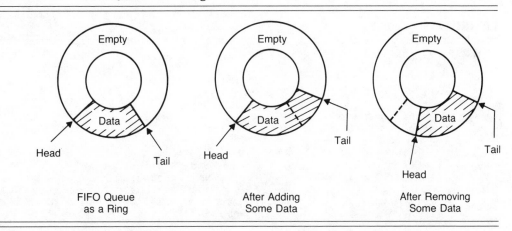

| FIFO Queue
as a Ring | After Adding
Some Data | After Removing
Some Data |

One change gives us a model that we can implement. We cut the circle so that it is a linear area of fixed size. When one of the pointers reaches the end of the area, we reset it to point to the beginning of the area.

FIFO queue as linear array

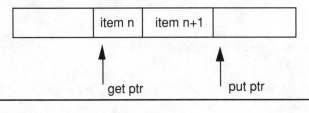

FIFO queue after adding an item

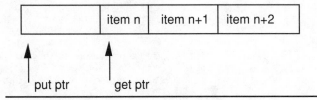

FIFO queue after removing an item

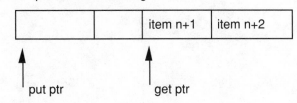

The header file in Figure 9.19 defines the QUEUE data structure, which keeps track of the state of a queue. The actual data storage area is outside the QUEUE structure; the structure contains pointers to the beginning and end of the data area and the current head and tail locations. Figure 9.20 lists the functions that make up the QUEUE module.

FIGURE 9.19 queue.h

```
 1    /* queue.h - header file for queue module */
 2
 3                                /* return codes */
 4    #define  Q_SUCCESS    0
 5    #define  Q_FAIL      (-1)
 6    #define  Q_EMPTY      0
 7    #define  Q_FULL       1
 8
 9
10    typedef struct            /* queue data structure */
11      { char *head ;          /* get next char from here */
12        char *tail ;          /* put next char here */
13        char *bbuf ;          /* beginning of data area */
14        char *ebuf ;          /* end of data area */
15      } QUEUE ;
16
17                                /* function prototypes */
18    void initq(QUEUE *, char [], int ) ;
19    int getq(QUEUE * ) ;
20    int putq(int , QUEUE * ) ;
21    int chkq(QUEUE * ) ;
22
```

FIGURE 9.20 queue.c

```
 1    /* queue.c - general-purpose FIFO queue module */
 2    #include "stdio.h"
 3    #include "cminor.h"
 4    #include "queue.h"
 5
 6    void initq(pq,buf,nbuf)       /* initialize a queue */
 7      QUEUE *pq ;                 /* address of a Q structure */
 8      char buf[] ;                /* store characters here */
 9      int nbuf ;                  /* size of the buffer */
10      {
11        pq->head = buf ;          /* point head and tail to start */
12        pq->tail = buf ;          /* of buffer. (Q empty) */
13        pq->bbuf = buf ;          /* store starting & end addresses */
14        pq->ebuf = buf + nbuf ;
15      }
16
17
18    int getq(pq)                  /* get a char from a Q */
19      QUEUE *pq ;                 /* address of a Q structure */
20      {                           /* returns first char in Q or -1 */
21        register char *p ;
```

Figure 9.20   continues

Figure 9.20   continued

```
22          char c ;
23
24          p = pq->head ;
25          if( p != pq->tail )     /* is the Q empty ? */
26             { c = *p ;           /*    no - get first char */
27              p = p + 1 ;         /*       advance head ptr */
28              if( p == pq->ebuf )/*        check for end of buffer */
29                  p = pq->bbuf ;  /*          yes - set to buf. start*/
30              pq->head = p ;      /*          store updated head ptr */
31              return(tochar(c)); /*          return the char */
32             }
33          else return( Q_FAIL ); /*    yes -Q empty, return fail code */
34       }
35
36    int putq(c,pq)               /* put a char into a Q */
37     int c ;                     /* char to store */
38     QUEUE *pq ;                 /* address of a Q structure */
39     {
40        register char *p ;
41
42        p = pq->tail ;
43        *p = c ;                  /* store the char */
44        p = p + 1 ;               /* advance the tail ptr */
45        if( p == pq->ebuf )       /* check for end of buffer */
46            p = pq->bbuf ;        /*    yes - set to buf. start */
47        if( p != pq->head )       /* check for Q overflow */
48           { pq->tail = p ;       /*    no - store updated tail ptr */
49            return( Q_SUCCESS );/*        and return success code */
50           }
51        else return( Q_FAIL ) ; /*    yes - don't update tail ptr */
52     }                           /*              and return failure code */
53
54
55    int chkq(pq)                 /* check for data in a Q */
56     QUEUE *pq ;                 /* address of a Q structure */
57     {
58        if( pq->tail == pq->head)/* compare head and tail pointers */
59            return( Q_EMPTY ) ; /*    equal - Q empty */
60        else return( Q_FULL ) ; /*    not equal - Q not empty */
61     }
```

The initialization function, initq, is called before a queue is used. The area where characters are stored is separate from the queue structure; the address of this area and its size are supplied as arguments to initq. This allows the data area to be allocated statically or dynamically, as appropriate for the program as a whole. Since the QUEUE module expects the address of the queue structure as an input argument, it can be used for a single queue or for a number of queues.

The putq function stores one character in a queue. After it stores the character, it updates the queue's tail pointer, checking for the end of the data area and for overflow (the tail pointer overtaking the head pointer). This points up a small tradeoff: To keep things simple, we interpret a queue with the pointers at the same position as being empty. So we can only put (N-1) characters into a queue with an N byte buffer.

The getq function removes one character from a queue and updates the queue's head pointer, checking for the end of the data area. getq also checks for an empty queue, returning a special value in that case. The chkq function checks for data in the queue without removing the character.

We can think of a queue as connecting two independent parts of a program: a producer who puts data in the queue and a consumer who removes it. The producer calls putq advancing the tail pointer and examining but not changing the head pointer. The consumer calls getq and chkq advancing the head pointer and examining but not changing the tail pointer. This separation of function in the QUEUE module prevents subtle time-dependent bugs in interrupt handlers and makes debugging much easier.

async2.c

The async1.c source file presented earlier (Figure 9.2) provided basic support for sending and receiving characters. The async2.c file in Figure 9.21 adds functions for transmitting a break signal and for setting up interrupts for received data.

FIGURE 9.21   **async2.c**

```
 1    /* async2.c - async I/O rcv interrupts and xmt break */
 2    #include "stdio.h"
 3    #include "async.h"
 4    #include "asmtools.h"
 5    #include "tty2parm.h"
 6
 7    typedef struct
 8      { int base_port ;            /* 1st I/O port for this async card */
 9        int int_no ;               /* associated interrupt level */
10      } ASY_ADRS ;
11
12    #define BIOS_DATA    0x40      /* BIOS data segment address */
13    extern int   rs232card ;       /* save card number here */
14    extern int iobase ;            /* 1st async io port to be used */
15    extern ASY_ADRS aadr[]   ;
16    extern int iasync ;            /* index into aadr table */
17
18    #define VECSTART    8          /* interrupt no. of 1st H/W int. */
19    PIFUN save_ifun = NULL ;       /* save address of old handler here */
20
21
22    void xmt_brk()                 /* start transmitting break */
23      {
24        int ctl ;
25
26        ctl = inbyte(iobase+LINE_CTRL) | SET_BRK_BIT ;
27        outbyte( iobase+LINE_CTRL , ctl );
28      }
29
30
31    void end_brk()                 /* stop transmitting break */
```

Figure 9.21   **continues**

Figure 9.21   continued

```
32        {
33            int ctl ;
34
35            ctl = inbyte(iobase+LINE_CTRL) & ( ~ SET_BRK_BIT ) ;
36            outbyte( iobase + LINE_CTRL , ctl );
37        }
38
39
40      void en_asy(pfun)              /* setup async rcv int */
41       PIFUN pfun ;                  /* address of int. handler */
42        {
43            int int_no , t ;
44
45            int_no = aadr[iasync].int_no; /* get int. level no. */
46                                    /* install our int. handler */
47            install(int_no + VECSTART, pfun, & save_ifun ) ;
48            en8259(int_no) ;         /* enable int. in 8259 */
49                                     /* turn on 8250 enable */
50             outbyte(iobase+INT_ENABLE,ENABLE_RCV_INT);/* rcvd data only*/
51                                     /* turn on async board enable */
52            t = inbyte(iobase+MODEM_CTRL) | OUT2 ;
53            outbyte(iobase+MODEM_CTRL,t) ;
54        }
55
56
57      void dis_asy()                 /* turn off async rcv int */
58        {
59            int t , int_no ;
60
61            int_no = aadr[iasync].int_no; /* get int. level no. */
62            dis8259(int_no) ;        /* disable int. in 8259 */
63                                     /* turn off async board enable */
64            t = inbyte(iobase + MODEM_CTRL) & (~ OUT2) ;
65            outbyte(iobase + MODEM_CTRL,t) ;
66                                     /* turn off 8250 enable */
67            outbyte(iobase+INT_ENABLE,0) ; /* all 8250 ints off */
68            dis8259(int_no) ;        /* disable int. in 8259 */
69                                     /* restore old int. handler */
70            install(int_no+ VECSTART, save_ifun, NULL ) ;
71        }
72
73
74      /*   functions for manipulating the 8259 interrupt controller */
75
76      #define MASK_PORT    0x21      /* interrupt enable register */
77      #define EOI_PORT     0x20      /* clear int. here */
78      #define EOI_CMD      0x20      /* write this value to clear int. */
79
80      void en8259(int_no)            /* enable an interrupt in the 8259 */
81       int int_no ;                  /* interrupt number to enable */
82        {
83            unsigned t ;
84
85            t = inbyte(MASK_PORT) ; 86            t = t & ~ (1 << int_no) ;
87            outbyte(MASK_PORT,t) ;
88        }
89
```

Figure 9.21   continues

Figure 9.21   continued

```
90      void dis8259(int_no)            /* disable an interrupt in the 8259 */
91       int int_no ;                   /* interrupt number to disable */
92       {
93           unsigned t ;
94
95           t = inbyte(MASK_PORT) ;
96           t = t | (1 << int_no) ;
97           outbyte(MASK_PORT,t) ;
98       }
99
100     void clr_int()                   /* clear an interrupt from the 8259*/
101      {
102          intsoff() ;
103          outbyte(EOI_PORT,EOI_CMD) ;
104      }
```

The `xmt_brk` function in lines 22 to 28 sets a bit in a control port to start transmitting the break signal. The `end_brk` function clears that bit to stop transmitting the break signal.

The `en_asy` function sets up the PC hardware for received data interrupts. The function address passed as an input argument is installed as the interrupt vector for the interrupt. This address must refer to a function defined with the `interrupt` keyword. The `PIFUN` data type in `tty2parm.h` defines the right syntax for Turbo C or Microsoft C. Then the interrupt is enabled at several levels: in the 8250 UART chip, on the async adapter, and in the PC's 8259 interrupt controller. Note that the interrupt vector is installed first so that an interrupt occurring immediately will be handled correctly.

When the TTY2 program finishes execution, interrupts from received data must be disabled. Leaving this interrupt enabled would produce a dramatic crash as the interrupt handler function is overwritten by part of the next program being executed. Thus the `dis_asy` function reverses the actions of `en_asy`, disabling received data interrupts at all levels. The original interrupt vector for this interrupt is replaced as the last action in the function.

Two functions, `en8259` and `dis8259`, enable and disable a single interrupt in the PC's 8259 interrupt controller. To avoid disturbing settings for other interrupt levels, the functions read the current value of the interrupt mask and alter the bit for the specified interrupt level.

The interrupt level to be used is related to the communications port addresses. The primary async port at I/O port `0x3f8` uses level 4, whereas the secondary async port uses level 3. The `aadr` table shows this relationship, and the `iasync` index set by `com_init` selects the values we should use. Hardware interrupt levels 0 through 7 correspond to PC interrupt vectors 8 through 15, so we add the `VECSTART` constant in specifying the interrupt vector we are installing.

install.c

The `install` function in Figure 9.22 sets up a specified interrupt vector. It first gets and saves the current interrupt vector so that it can be replaced later. Then it installs the new interrupt vector address. If the new interrupt vector is NULL, no action is taken. If the address of the save area for the old vector is NULL, the old vector is not saved.

The original vector address is stored where the calling function specifies. Later `install` can be called again to reinstall this original address.

FIGURE 9.22 install.c

```
1       /* install.c - install/remove interrupt vectors */
2       #include <stdio.h>
3       #include <dos.h>
4       #include "asmtools.h"
5       #include "tty2parm.h"
6
7       #ifdef TURBOC
8       #define _getvector(ino)  getvect(ino)
9       #define _setvector(ino, ifun) setvect(ino,ifun)
10      #endif
11
12      #ifdef MSC
13      #define _getvector(ino)  _dos_getvect(ino)
14      #define _setvector(ino, ifun) _dos_setvect(ino,ifun)
15      #endif
16
17                              /* install interrupt vector */
18      void install(vecno,new_ifun,pold_ifun)
19      int vecno ;             /* number of interrupt vector */
20      PIFUN new_ifun ;        /* install this function address */
21      PIFUN *pold_ifun ;      /* install this function address */
22      {
23          if( new_ifun != NULL ) /* is there a valid new address? */
24          { if( pold_ifun != NULL ) /*  yes - check for save area */
25              *pold_ifun = _getvector(vecno) ; /* yes-get old vec.*/
26            _setvector(vecno,new_ifun) ; /* install new one */
27          }
28      }
```

tty2int.asm

When the TTY2 program is receiving characters, the main function is continually calling chk_asy, which calls chkq to check for received characters. The interrupt handler function, rcv_int, is placing received characters into that queue. During a call to chkq, a received character may trigger an interrupt, causing a call to putq while chkq is checking the queue. We cannot control the timing of interrupts, but we can inhibit the processor's response to interrupts. The tty2int.asm assembler source file in Figure 9.23 enables and disables response to interrupts. After we call intsoff, interrupts will not be handled until we call the intson function to enable interrupts.

The include files from Chapter 7 provide the directives appropriate for the compiler and the memory model we are using.

FIGURE 9.23 tty2int.asm

```
 1      ;          tty2int.asm - enable / disable processor interrupts
 2
 3      ;          data section
 4                 include begdata.ha
 5                 include enddata.ha
 6
 7      ;          code section
 8                 include begcode.ha
 9
10      ;          intson - enable 8088 interrupts
11      ;
12      ;          USAGE -  intson() ;
13      ;
14                 public _intson
15      _intson PROC
16                 sti
17                 ret
18      _intson ENDP
19
20      ;          intsoff - disable 8088 interrupts
21      ;
22      ;          USAGE -  intsoff() ;
23      ;
24                 public _intsoff
25      _intsoff PROC
26                 cli
27                 ret
28      _intsoff ENDP
29
30                 include endcode.ha
31                 end
```

9.7 Compiling, Testing, and Measuring TTY2

Some of the C functions in TTY2 are executed from an interrupt handler (in the tty2rcv.c, async1.c, queue.c, and async2.c source files). The stack-checking option should be disabled when these source files are compiled. Otherwise, the stack-checking code may produce an error message and halt execution when an interrupt occurs.

Testing TTY2 presents several problems. Real-time programs are sensitive to the volume of input and to the exact timing of events. Bugs may be very subtle and hard to duplicate. The first defense against the problem is to design out time-dependent bugs. The modular construction and unit testing we have stressed throughout the book are more important than ever here. Even functions executed inside an interrupt handler such as `rcv_int`, `rcv_char`, and `putq` can be thoroughly tested in a normal environment.

The `QUEUE` data structure that connects the interrupt handler with the rest of TTY2 is designed to eliminate bugs. The interrupt handler examines the head pointer and modifies the tail pointer. The `chkq` and `getq` functions called from the polling loop examine the tail pointer and modify the head pointer. This is much safer than a structure where both interrupt handler and the polling loop modify the same variable.

Another problem is that we need a terminal or another computer to fully test the TTY2 program. There is no way around this — you need something to transmit characters to TTY2 and to display what TTY2 transmits. Once TTY2 as a whole has been tested, small modifications can often be tested without another computer. But if you work with communications programs, a second computer is just a cost of doing business.

Section 9.3 discussed measuring the performance of TTY1. The same program, `perftty1.c`, listed in Figure 9.4 is also useful for measuring TTY2. That program illustrates two requirements for testing real-time programs: a way to generate a worst-case load and a mechanism for spotting incorrect behavior. When we measure TTY2, we find some improvement relative to TTY1. The TTY2 program is not much faster than TTY1 on the average. But the 10,000-character buffer allows operation at even 9,600 baud without lost characters in normal operations. Even a pathological case such as a stream of line feed characters does not cause lost data; the program just lags behind in displaying characters.

If considerably more than 10,000 characters were sent to TTY2 without a pause, data might eventually lost. Where such large numbers of characters were to be transmitted, a protocol is needed to prevent loss of data. For interactive applications, only one or two screens of data are sent before a pause occurs.

TTY2 makes direct use of the async hardware and of the interrupt system of the PC. This does limit its use to computers that are fully compatible with the PC hardware architecture. This is a necessary condition for a useful async communications program.

9.8   Small Enhancements

We have concentrated on performance issues rather than on features. The techniques we developed for using buffering and interrupts make it straightforward to add features without disrupting the TTY program. Our TTY program has a useful basic structure, but it lacks many features that make a terminal emulation program truly useful. This section lists some additions that require a small amount of coding.

Usage Parameters

Although the async protocol is supported by a wide variety of computers, the details vary widely. Some computers echo input, whereas others expect the terminal to echo typed characters. Some expect a carriage return character to end each line of input. Others expect a newline or line feed character. Lines sent to the terminal may be ended by a carriage return, a newline (line feed), or by a carriage return followed by a line feed. To match a variety of computers, the TTY2 program should provide usage parameters for specifying local echo and translating end-of-line conventions. This requires a convenient way of setting usage parameters and a way to save a set of parameters.

Other options might be stripping unwanted control characters such as control-Z or the ASCII bel character and displaying 8-bit characters (not forcing the high-order bit to be zero).

Setting Communications Parameters

Our program relies on the DOS MODE command for setting the baud rate, the parity setting, and the number of data bits in a word. It would be much more convenient to be able to set these from within TTY2. TTY2 should also allow the user to specify whether COM1: or COM2: is to be used.

Using Modem Signals

The RS-232 interface defines several signals that can be used to signal that a terminal is ready or to sense the state of a modem. A terminal uses the Data Terminal Ready (DTR) and Ready to Send (RTS) lines to signal the modem that it is ready to send and receive data. The Data Set Ready (DSR) and Clear to Send (CTS) lines are used by a modem to signal the terminal that it is ready to send and receive data. In addition, if we connect our computer directly to another computer through a modem eliminator cable, the other computer may expect our program to set the DTR and RTS lines before starting data transfers.

Handling Break Signals and Bel Characters Without Waiting

TTY2 is inactive while a break signal is being sent. We can use the `check_delay` function from Chapter 7 to send a break signal without waiting. We can define a `SENDING_BREAK` bit in the state variable. The polling loop can test that bit, and if a break signal is being sent, it can check for the end of the break interval by calling `check_delay`.

The `disp_char` function calls the PC BIOS to create an audible beep for a bel character. The BIOS service does not return until the beep is terminated. The polling technique just discussed can be applied to creating sounds without waiting inactive for the duration of the sound. (It does require turning the PC speaker on and off.)

Better Reporting of Errors

TTY2 provides no indication that receive errors are occurring. One alternative is to place a special marker value in the receive queue when a receive error has occurred. When the marker is removed by the polling loop, a distinctive pattern might be displayed on the screen. (Perhaps it could be a character with the reverse video attribute.)

We do not want error markers to slow down the program, so we should use a single error marker to represent a string of errors. We also have to define an escape sequence to distinguish the marker from a genuine character with the same value.

A Status Line for Messages

TTY2 displays messages in the same window with received characters. We could define a separate window for messages.

Making an ASYNC Library

Many programs require some use of async communications. The components of the TTY2 program can be made into a library for use in other programs. To start, you should define the services that the library should offer. Then you should define the interfaces.

9.9 Larger Enhancements

The enhancements in this section require more programming. Some require more knowledge about data communications and about specific protocols. However, they do add greatly to the utility of the TTY2 program.

Using Interrupts for Transmitting Data

Interrupts can be used to transmit characters as well as to send them. The UART chip generates an interrupt when there is room for the next character. This allows output to proceed even while disk I/O is in progress. A single interrupt vector is used for both receive and transmit interrupts, so the handler must check a status register to see which event has occurred.

🖫 Supporting XON/XOFF Flow Control Protocol

When large amounts of data must be transferred, some means of flow control helps to prevent loss of data. The XON/XOFF protocol is a simple and widely used method for flow control.

Error-Checking Protocols — XMODEM

TTY2 can send and receive data files, but we do not have any protection against losing or garbling characters. A protocol for ensuring correct transmission and reception of files is an important feature for a terminal emulation program. The elements of such a protocol are as follows:

1. The file is transmitted in packets (perhaps 50 to 1,000 bytes) with an accompanying *checksum* that verifies correct reception.
2. Correct reception of packets is acknowledged. (In some protocols, packets received incorrectly are negatively acknowledged.)
3. Timeout intervals allow recovery when a packet or acknowledgement is lost.
4. Packets that are not acknowledged (or negatively acknowledged) are retransmitted.

The XMODEM protocol and its variants are a standard in the PC world. They are not well designed and are poorly documented, but they are widely supported. The source code disks provide an implementation of the basic XMODEM protocol.

🖫 Dialing Phone Numbers — The Hayes Modem Protocol

A session with TTY usually starts with dialing the phone number of the computer with which we will talk. Most modems used with PCs can dial a phone number. The dialing protocol originated by D. C. Hayes modems is a standard for PC modems. An escape sequence, usually +++, signals the start of a command string. Commands are prefaced by another sequence, normally AT. The modem replies with an ASCII string. Implementing this feature requires adding modes to TTY. When it is in the dialing mode, it handles input differently from its actions in the data transfer state. The source code disks contain support for the basic Hayes dialing commands.

Emulating Specific CRT Terminals

Many applications of terminal emulation require that the program emulate a specific model CRT terminal. For example, if we want to talk to a DEC VAX system, we would emulate a DEC VT-52 or VT-100 terminal. Talking to a Hewlett-Packard minicomputer might require emulating some Hewlett-Packard terminal.

Most CRT terminals support special commands for moving the cursor position, for inserting or deleting characters, and for performing other functions. Unfortunately the commands that control these features vary from one terminal model to another.

Bulletin Board Systems

Our program emulates a terminal and lets us talk to a mini- or mainframe computer. A bulletin board system emulates a computer so that people with terminals or personal computers can call up and get messages or files from our system.

Bulletin board systems are passive. They wait for someone to call and then respond to commands from the caller. In a sense, such systems are the complement of terminal emulation programs. A really complete program might combine both roles.

More Speed

TTY2 is usable even at 9,600 baud, but it does fall behind when receiving a long stream of characters at high baud rates. Rewriting the `rcv_int`, `rcv_char`, and `putq` functions is one possibility. Still another approach is to combine functions to reduce the number of function calls (`rcv_int` and `rcv_char`, for example). A careful analysis of TTY2's current performance to identify the real bottlenecks is a good first step.

9.10 Summary

We have presented a terminal emulation program as an example of a real-time program. We introduced techniques for buffering input and for using interrupts. The TTY2 program is short on features but has good performance and provides a good basis for enhancement. In addition, its components can be used for related programs such as bulletin board systems.

The chapter should also prepare you to understand other real-time problems. The same theme —polling, worst-case performance, buffering, and using interrupts—will be useful in attacking many real-time problems.

The TTY2 program is filled with I/O port addresses and definitions of bits in control and status ports. Those details may seem difficult and foreign to you. The references listed in Appendix D should help somewhat. One lesson you should absorb from this chapter is that the low-level programming we have done here is not really harder than more system-independent programming. The main difficulty is finding out how the hardware really works.

10
Optimization and
Error Handling

The C source files in Chapters 1 through 9 did not use many of the unique features in C. We review some programming techniques for using these features and examine the benefits and costs of using them. Then we discuss optimizing C programs in a broader sense. Handling errors was another topic often neglected in previous chapters; we will present interrupt handlers that give control of control-Break and critical error conditions.

10.1 Using the Rest of C: Optimization

The programs in this book were written in a subset of C. Many of the features that are unique to C were not used at all, and other features were used in a restricted way. Producing clear, readable programs was stressed over execution speed, but we paid a penalty for this choice. This section looks at some advanced features in C and measures their effect on performance.

Many of the features that we did not use have something in common. They allow you to give hints to the compiler about what you really mean. For example, instead of the line

```
i = i + 1 ;
```

we can use the *increment operator* (++)

```
i ++ ;    or      ++ i ;
```

This means the same thing, but it tells the compiler that we are putting the result back where we got it. We can also use the increment operator inside expressions. In an expression, ++ does two things: It increments the value in a variable and it has a value that is used in the rest of the expression. Placed in front of a variable, ++ increments the variable and then gets its value. Placed after a variable, ++ gets the value of a variable and then increments the variable. The following examples show each use:

```
i = i + 1 ;              or     sum = sum + a[ ++i ] ;
sum = sum + a[i] ;

tot = tot + a[i] ;       or     tot = tot + a[ i++ ] ;
i = i + 1 ;
```

The *decrement operator* (--) is analogous: it subtracts rather than adds. C also provides *assignment operators* for more general cases. Instead of

```
a = a + b ;
```

we can write

```
a += b ;
```

This tells us and the compiler that we are adding the value of b to that of a and storing the result back in a. Other operators such as minus (-), multiply (*), divide (/), BitOr (|), and BitAnd (&) can be combined with the assignment operator.

Assignments can be placed inside expressions. The following example condenses a loop for reading characters from a file:

```
c = getchar() ;
while( c != EOF )
    { n = n + 1 ;
      c = getchar() ;
    }
```

or

```
while( (c=getchar()) != EOF )
    { n = n + 1 ; }
```

Pointers can often be used instead of array subscripts. This is most appropriate when the program steps through the array one element at a time. The following example shows how the technique works:

```
sum = 0 ;
for(i=0 ; i< n ; i=i+1)
    { sum = sum + a[i] ; }
```

or

```
sum = 0 ;
pa = a ;
for(i=0; i<n ; i=i+1)
   { sum = sum + *pa++ ; }
```

Register variables provide another way for us to give hints to the compiler. The `register` keyword in a declaration of a C variable defines its storage class as do the `static` and `extern` keywords. The effect is to suggest to the compiler that the variable should be kept in a computer register rather than in RAM memory. The compiler may obey or ignore the suggestion. If the compiler ignores the suggestion, the declaration has the same effect as if the `register` keyword had not been included. The number of registers, their size, and their use depend on the computer architecture being used. For a register variable declaration to be effective, the variable must be of a size and type compatible with the computer's actual registers. (In the MS-DOS/IBM PC environment, registers are 16 bits long, and only two are available for register variables.) Since register variables may not have a RAM memory location and a corresponding address, taking the address of a register variable is not allowed. The following declarations show register variable declarations for `i` and `pa` in the preceding code fragments:

```
register int i ;
register int *pa ;
```

It is possible to combine these techniques to produce very compact source files. Such source files look as though the program should run much faster; this is rarely true. Unfortunately such programs also are harder to read, enhance, and maintain. In the next section we examine the effect of using the shortcuts we have described.

10.2 Applying C Shortcut Optimizations

Several of these optimization techniques were used in modifying the integer quicksort function from Chapter 5. The original function was shown in Figure 5.2 and the modified version is shown in Figure 10.1. Line 12 declares pointer variables `pi` and `pj` that replace the array indices `i` and `j` in Figure 5.2. Replacement of `j` by `pj` is simple:

```
j = na ;             becomes      pj = & a[na] ;
j = j - 1 ;          becomes      --pj ;
a[j] > part          becomes      *pj > part ;
do { j=j-1 ; }       becomes      do { --pj ; }
   while( a[j] > part) ;             while( *pj > part ) ;
```

FIGURE 10.1   qsorti2.c

```
1    /* qsorti2.c - optimized quicksort on an array of integers */
2
3
4    void qsorti(a,na)
5     int a[] ;                  /* array of integers to be sorted */
6     int na ;                   /* number of elements to be sorted */
7     {
8        int i , j ;             /* indices for loops */
9        int temp ;              /* temporary storage for an element */
10       int nr ;                /* number in right partition */
11       int part ;              /* element used as partition value */
12       register int *pi, *pj ; /* pointer style indices */
13
14       if( na < 2  )
15           return ;
16
17       part = a[na/2] ;        /* use middle element to partition */
18
19       pi =  a ;               /* left - point to 1st element */
20       pj = & a[na] ;          /* right - point past last element */
21
22       while( 1 == 1 )
23          {                    /* find first element to move right */
24             while( *pi < part )
25                { pi ++ ; }
26
27                               /* find first element to move left */
28             while( * --pj > part ) { ; }
29
30             if( pi >= pj )     /* have the boundaries met ? */
31                 break ;        /*     yes - through partitioning */
32
33                               /* swap elements at pi and pj */
34             temp = *pi ;  *pi = *pj ; *pj = temp ;
35             pi ++ ;            /* advance left pointer */
36          }
37
38       i = pi - & a[0] ;       /* number in left partition */
39       nr = na - i ;
40                               /* now deal with each partition */
41       qsorti( a , i ) ;       /* sort left side  */
42       qsorti( pi ,nr);        /* sort right side */
43
44    }
```

Then line 28 can be condensed further by placing the decrement operation inside the comparison:

```
while(  * --pj > part )   { ; }
```

Line 20 initializes pj to point just after the last element in a. The ANSI standard for C allows a pointer to point past the last element of an array. But setting a pointer to an address before the beginning of an array may not be legal. So we cannot replace i = -1 ; by pj = a - 1 ;. Instead, we initialize pi to point to the first element in a. The loop in lines 24 and 25 increments pi after the comparison to the partition value part. Line 35 increments pi to point to the next element after each swap is made.

As this example suggests, algorithms are often simpler and easier to debug when array indices are used instead of pointers. It is a good practice to create a simple version first and then apply optimization techniques only if a performance bottleneck is found.

Optimization Results for qsorti

Using Turbo C (version 2.00), the modified version of qsorti is 20 to 30% faster than the original version depending on the ordering of data in the array. For Microsoft C (version 5.1), the modified version is 12 to 40% faster.

Compilation options also make a significant difference in the performance of the qsorti function. For Turbo C, selecting optimization for speed, register optimization on, and jump optimization on produces a 5 to 30% improvement. For Microsoft C, the /Ox option produces a similar improvement.

Applying the same techniques to the memsort function in Chapter 5 produces little improvement. The calls to the compare function are the performance bottleneck here, so optimizing the loops in the memsort function is irrelevant.

10.3 Putting C Shortcuts into Perspective

Although using C shortcuts produced a measurable performance improvement, the improvement is minor compared to the difference between the quicksort and insertion sort algorithms (23 times as fast).

It might seem that our hints or shortcuts should save more time. However, good compilers are fairly effective at analyzing expressions and generating effective programs. A compiler that does little or no optimization and generates poor code might benefit greatly from our hints. But if your compiler is reasonably efficient, it makes more sense to write straightforward programs that can be enhanced with better algorithms. Rewriting local bottlenecks to make full use of C's features is a valid optimization technique, but the payoff will be a small one.

Writing compact source files that make full use of C's shortcut operators has been a test of manhood for many C programmers. Many C hackers and even some authors of C books will tell you that you have to use all of C's features and write compact but unreadable source files. It just is not true. Writing obscure, tricky programs is good for a hacker's ego but unnecessary and dangerous in serious programming projects.

The previous chapters have suggested an alternate approach to producing fast, effective C programs. First, we create a good specification that defines what the program should do. We should also define the level of performance expected and how much effort we are willing to invest to achieve this performance. Next, we design the structure of the program, and the data structures and algorithms to be used. We create a well-structured, clearly written program with the basic features needed. Then we measure this program's performance and locate the bottlenecks. We eliminate the bottlenecks using the appropriate techniques. In the previous chapters, better algorithms were far more important than making full use of C shortcuts.

10.4 Handling Control-Break Conditions

MS-DOS interprets the control-C and control-Break keystrokes in a special way. (In this section we will refer to control-Break conditions although they may be triggered by control-C keystrokes as well.) Many DOS calls for console I/O, printer output, and even file I/O check to see if these keys have been pressed. If so, DOS outputs the characters ^ and C followed by carriage return and line feed characters and then issues a software interrupt to execute an exception handler. DOS provides a simple default handler that aborts the program that was executing. Files may not be closed properly, and the disk directory and file allocation tables may be left in an inconsistent state. In addition, the application program is not able to tidy up its files or to disable hardware interrupts.

Since this default action is not satisfactory for most applications, we need to avoid it. There is no single, clean remedy for the problem, but the following approaches together solve our problem:

1. Turn Off Checking —MS-DOS provides a call to turn off control-Break checking for some operations (file I/O).
2. Avoid DOS Calls That Check — Most DOS console I/O and printer I/O calls always check for control-Break. The standard I/O functions in the C library use these DOS calls and should be avoided. The toolkit functions in Chapter 7 provide an alternative. (The Microsoft C version of the `getch` function does check for control-Break. To avoid control-Break checking, an implementation of `getkey` for Microsoft C should be based on the BIOS function `_bios_keybrd`.)
3. Handle the Exception in a Harmless Way — We can install our own handler for control-Break exceptions. This handler does not terminate the program; it sets a flag indicating that the exception occurred and returns to its caller.

Figure 10.2 describes functions to implement our strategy. The function `set_break_handler` installs our control-Break handler. When we have finished using our handler, `rm_break_handler` replaces the previous handler. The function `chk_break_handler` is called from a program to check for the occurrence of a control-Break exception. The `set_cbreak` function turns off Break checking in file I/O calls. The `break_save_scn` and `break_restore_scn` functions save and restore the part of the screen that DOS overwrites with the ^C characters.

FIGURE 10.2   Description of Break Handling Functions

Name

`set_break_handler`	installs control-Break handler
`rm_break_handler`	removes control-Break handler
`chk_break_flag`	check to see if Break occurred
`set_cbreak`	sets MS-DOS Break state
`break_save_scn`	save part of screen before possible Break
`break_restore_scn`	restore part of screen after Break occurs

Usage

```
int  set_break_handler() ;
void rm_break_handler() ;
int  chk_break_handler() ;
int  state ;                    /* new DOS break state */
int  set_cbreak(state) ;
int  save_type ;                /* dummy argument */
int  break_save_scn( save_type) ;
```

Function

These functions modify the default action when the control-Break or control-C keys are pressed. Calling the `set_break_handler` function installs a handler for the control-Break exception. This handler sets a flag to record the occurrence of the exception and then returns. (The default handler aborts the program.) `chk_break_flag` returns 0 if a control-Break exception has not occurred and 1 if an exception has occurred. `chk_break_flag` resets the flag to 0 so that future exceptions can be recognized. The `rm_break_handler` function restores the handler that was in place when `set_break_handler` was called. `set_break_handler` returns a nonzero value if the handler could not be installed. (This would indicate a programming problem in `set_break_handler`.)

The `set_cbreak` function sets the DOS Ctrl-Break state. When this state is set to 0, DOS calls involving file I/O do not check for control-Break exceptions. When the state is set to 1, DOS calls involving file I/O check for control-Break exceptions. DOS calls involving console I/O or printer I/O always check for control-Break exceptions, whatever the setting of this state. `set_cbreak` returns the existing state value so that it may be restored in a later call to `set_cbreak`.

The `break_save_scn` function saves the position of the blinking cursor and the next two characters and attributes starting at that position. These screen locations may be overwritten by the two characters ^C, which MS-DOS displays when a Break exception occurs. The `break_restore_scn` function restores the cursor position and the two screen locations to the values previously saved by

Figure 10.2   continues

Figure 10.2   continued

break_save_scn. The break_save_scn function returns a nonzero value if the cursor is on the last line of the screen because it cannot prevent the MS-DOS message from scrolling the screen upward.

Examples
```
#include "handbrk.h"
#include "breakscn.h"
int old_state ;
...
set_break_handler() ;                /* install our handler */
old_state = set_cbreak(0) ;          /* turn off break checking */
                                     /* in file I/O calls */
break_save_scn(0) ;                  /* save part of screen */
   /* actions that  might  trigger a break exception */
   if( chk_break_flag() != 0)
     { break_restore_scn() ;
       printf(" break occurred") ;
     }
       set_cbreak(old_state) ;       /* restore break state */
       rm_break_handler() ;          /* restore break handler */
```

Figure 10.3 defines function prototypes for the Break functions, and the source file in Figure 10.4 lists the functions. The signal function defined in the ANSI C standard allows us to install a normal C normal function to handle control-C exceptions. (The SIGINT interrupt signal corresponds to the DOS control-Break exception.) The set_break_handler function calls signal, specifying that our function signal_handler handle SIGINT signals. The address of the old handler is saved so that we can restore it later. The special return value SIG_ERR indicates that the call to signal failed. The rm_break_handler function restores the old handler.

FIGURE 10.3   handbrk.h

```
1      /* handbrk.h - definitions for control-Break handling */
2
3                              /* function prototypes */
4      int set_break_handler(void) ;
5      void rm_break_handler(void) ;
6      int chk_break_flag(void) ;
7      int set_cbreak(int) ;
```

FIGURE 10.4   handbrk.c

```
1      /* handbrk.c - handles control-Break, control-C */
2      #include <stdio.h>
3      #include <signal.h>
4      #include <dos.h>
5      #include "asmtools.h"
```

Figure 10.4   continues

Figure 10.4   continued

```
 6     #include "handbrk.h"
 7
 8     #define CTRL_BRK_CHK 0x33   /* DOS operation code */
 9
10     static int break_flag ;      /* 1=break has occurred */
11     static void (*old_handler) () ; /* address of old handler */
12
13
14     void signal_handler(sig)     /* handles control-break signals */
15      int sig ;                   /* identifies which signal */
16     {
17        break_flag = 1 ;          /* set our indicator */
18         signal(SIGINT,signal_handler) ;
19     }
20
21
22     int set_break_handler()      /* install our ctrl-break handler */
23      { old_handler = signal(SIGINT,signal_handler) ;
24        if( old_handler == SIG_ERR )
25             return( -1 ) ;
26        else return( 0 ) ;
27     }
28
29
30     void rm_break_handler()      /* remove our break handler */
31      {
32        signal(SIGINT, old_handler ) ;
33     }
34
35
36     int chk_break_flag()         /* returns break flag */
37      {
38        int ret ;
39
40        ret = break_flag ;
41        break_flag = 0 ;
42        return( ret) ;
43     }
44
45
46     int set_cbreak(new_state)    /* sets DOS ctrl-break handling  */
47      int new_state ;             /* 1=check during all DOS calls */
48      {                           /* 0=don't check all calls */
49        int old_state ;           /* old ctrl-brk value returned */
50
51     #ifdef TURBOC
52        old_state = getcbrk() ; /* Turbo version - uses */
53        setcbrk(new_state) ;     /* library function */
54     #endif
55
56     #ifdef MSC
57        union REGS s, r ;
58                                  /* Microsoft version - uses intdos */
59        s.h.ah = CTRL_BRK_CHK ;/* DOS operation ocde */
60        s.h.al = 0 ;             /* get break state */
61        intdos(& s, & r) ;       /* do DOS call */
62        old_state = r.h.dl ;     /* old break state */
```

Figure 10.4   continues

Figure 10.4   continued

```
63
64          s.h.ah = CTRL_BRK_CHK ;/* DOS operation ocde */
65          s.h.al = 1 ;             /* set break state */
66          s.h.dl = new_state ;     /* new break state */
67          intdos(& s, & r) ;       /* do DOS call */
68      #endif
69
70        return( old_state ) ;
71      }
```

The function `signal_handler` is called when the interrupt signal occurs. It sets the `break_flag` variable and returns. The program may call `chk_break_flag` to determine whether control-Break has been pressed. These two functions allow us to handle the exception within the context of the C program.

The `set_cbreak` function makes a DOS call to set the Ctrl-Break State variable. It first saves the old state value so that it may be restored later. The Turbo C library contains functions for checking and setting the Ctrl-Break state. For Microsoft C, we use the `intdos` function for getting and setting the state value. The symbols `TURBOC` and `MSC` defined in `asmtools.h` select the appropriate version.

The program in Figure 10.5 illustrates the use of the Break functions. Lines 12 and 13 prepare for handling control-Break exceptions. Lines 49 and 54 restore the old Break handler and the old Break state. Lines 17 to 19 and lines 42 and 43 check for the occurrence of an exception but do not halt execution. Lines 24 to 27 end execution if an exception occurred. Running this program is a good way to understand how control-Break exceptions interact with library functions.

FIGURE 10.5 testbrk.c

```
1      /* testbrk.c - test control-Break handling */
2      #include <stdio.h>
3      #include <stdlib.h>
4      #include "handbrk.h"
5
6      main()
7        {
8          int n , i , c ;
9          unsigned char s[512] ;
10         int old_state ;
11
12         old_state = set_cbreak(0) ; /* break testing OFF */
13         set_break_handler() ;   /* install our break handler */
14
15         printf(" enter a number: \n");
16         scanf("%d",&i) ;
17         if( chk_break_flag() != 0 )
18           { printf(" BREAK typed - continuing \n") ;
19           }
20         printf(" the number entered was %d \n",i) ;
21
```

Figure 10.5   continues

Figure 10.5   continued

```
22              printf(" enter a another number: \n");
23              scanf("%d",&i) ;
24              if( chk_break_flag() != 0 )
25                 { printf(" BREAK typed - exiting \n") ;
26                   exit(10) ;
27                 }
28              printf(" the number entered was %d \n",i) ;
29
30              c = getchar() ;       /* flush rest of input line */
31              while( (c != '\n') && (c != '\r') )
32                 { c = getchar() ; }
33
34              printf(" enter a line of text: \n");
35              c = getchar() ;
36              n= 0 ;
37              while( (c != '\n') && (c != '\r') )
38                 { s[n] = c ;
39                   n = n + 1 ;
40                   c = getchar() ;
41                 }
42              if( chk_break_flag() != 0 )
43                 printf(" BREAK typed - continuing \n") ;
44              printf(" the characters typed were <") ;
45              for(i=0 ; i<n ; i=i+1)
46                 { printf(" %02x", s[i] ) ; }
47              printf(">\n");
48
49              rm_break_handler() ; /* restore default handler */
50              printf("\n default handler restored \n") ;
51              printf(" enter a another number: \n");
52              scanf("%d",&i) ;
53              printf(" the number entered was %d \n",i) ;
54              set_cbreak(old_state) ; /* restore break state */
55          }
```

Although our Break handler allows the program to continue execution, DOS has already sent the characters ^, C, carriage return, and line feed to the display. If it is important to preserve the contents of the display, we can save and restore part of the display screen. Figure 10.6 defines prototypes for these functions, and Figure 10.7 lists the functions themselves. break_save_scn saves the position of the blinking cursor and the two screen locations, which would be overwritten by the ^C characters written by DOS. break_restore_scn restores the cursor position and the two screen locations as they were when saved. There are limitations to this procedure. If the cursor was located on the last line of the screen, the line feed character written by DOS causes the screen contents to be scrolled upward. If the operation being performed moves the cursor itself or displays characters, break_restore_scn cannot restore the display correctly. Although these functions may be changed to save and restore the entire screen, operations that move the cursor and display characters are not consistent with saving and restoring the screen.

FIGURE 10.6   breakscn.h

```
1       /* breakscn.h - definitions for breakscn.c */
2
3                                /* function prototypes */
4       int break_save_scn(int) ;
5       void break_restore_scn(void) ;
6
```

FIGURE 10.7   breakscn.c

```
1       /* breakscn.c - screen save / restore for control-Break */
2       #include <stdio.h>
3       #include "video.h"
4       #include "win.h"
5       #include "breakscn.h"
6
7       static WIN ws ;                /* save window structure */
8       static int first_time = 0 ;
9       static char save_c[2] ;        /* save 2 chars here */
10      static char save_a[2] ;        /* save 2 attributes here */
11      static int row , col ;         /* save blinking cursor position */
12
13
14      int break_save_scn(save_flag) /* save part screen before break */
15       int save_flag ;
16       {
17         if( first_time == 0 )    /* 1st call, define window */
18           { win_define(& ws, 0,0,25,80,NULL,0) ; /* full screen */
19             first_time = 1 ;
20           }
21
22         vid_get_cur(& row,& col); /* get cursor position */
23         if( row == 24 )          /* can't save if cursor */
24           return( -1 ) ;         /* is on last line */
25
26         win_setpos(& ws, row,col) ;  /* set position in window */
27                                /* save 2 screen locations */
28         win_gca(& ws, save_c, save_a, 2) ;
29         return( 0 ) ;            /* normal return - screen saved */
30       }
31
32
33      void break_restore_scn()    /* restore screen after break */
34       {
35         vid_set_cur(row,col) ;   /* restore cursor position */
36         win_setpos(& ws, row,col) ; /* set window position */
37                                /* restore screen locations */
38         win_wca(& ws, save_c[0], save_a[0] ) ; /* 1st char & attr. */
39         win_wca(& ws, save_c[1], save_a[1] ) ; /* 2nd char & attr. */
40       }
```

10.5 Handling Critical Errors

Handling data errors is an unpleasant fact of life in real-world programs. The diskette on which we want to write a file may be unformatted or write-protected; we may find a bad sector in reading a file. DOS reports some errors to the application via an error return code. For example, if a write operation fails because the disk runs out of free space, an error return notifies the program. A different method is used for other error conditions such as a time-out when writing to a printer or writing to a floppy disk drive that does not contain a floppy disk. In these cases, DOS executes a software interrupt (INT 24H). The default error handler that DOS provides for this interrupt displays the message

```
Abort, Retry or Ignore
```

and offers a chance to abort the program, to retry the operation, or to ignore the error. The ignore alternative gives the program no indication that the operation failed; this option is both dangerous and useless. The retry option repeats the operation, which may be effective for errors that can be corrected by the user's own action. The abort alternative ends execution without allowing the program to close files or disable interrupts. This is rarely a satisfactory solution for an application program. Programs that are used for important work must respond to such error conditions in a way that makes sense for the application. The combination of techniques we used for control-Break exceptions apply here. We avoid printer time-outs by using the printer functions in Chapter 7. We install a critical error handler so that errors can be handled by the program in context.

Figures 10.8 describes functions for handling critical errors. Figure 10.9 defines function prototypes. Figure 10.10 lists the source file containing the functions.

FIGURE 10.8   Description of Critical Error Functions

Name
```
set_cerror_handler    installs critical error handler
rm_cerror_handler     removes critical error handler
chk_cerror_flag       check to see if critical error occurred
```

Usage
```
int  set_cerror_handler() ;
void rm_cerror_handler() ;
int  chk_cerror_handler() ;
```

Function
These functions modify the default action when a critical error occurs. The
set_cerror_handler function installs a handler for critical errors. This handler

Figure 10.8   continues

Figure 10.8 continued

sets a flag to record the occurrence of the critical error exception and then returns. (The default handler aborts the program.) `chk_cerror_flag` returns 1 if a critical error has occurred or 0 if no error has occurred since the flag was reset. `chk_cerror_flag` resets the flag to 0 so that future exceptions can be recognized. The `rm_cerror_handler` function replaces the handler that was in place when `set_cerror_handler` was called.

Examples

```
#include "handerr.h"
...
set_cerror_handler() ;                    /* install our handler */
    /* actions that  might  trigger a critical error */
    if( chk_cerror_flag() != 0)
      printf(" critical error occurred") ;
...
    rm_cerror_handler() ;    /* restore critical error handler */
```

FIGURE 10.9   handerr.h

```
1    /* handerr.h - definitions for critical error handling */
2
3
4                            /* function prototypes */
5    void set_cerror_handler( void ) ;
6    void rm_cerror_handler( void ) ;
7    int chk_cerror_flag( void ) ;
```

The `set_cerror_handler` function installs our handler `cerror_handler`. Although both Turbo C and Microsoft C provide functions for building a critical error handler, function names and some syntax differ. We use the TURBOC and MSC symbols in the `asmtools.h` file from Chapter 7 to select the right version. Lines 46 to 67 implement a Turbo C version, and lines 71 to 92 implement a Microsoft C version. The error handler function `cerror_handler` saves register values that describe the reason for the critical error and the device on which the error occurred. Then it sets the variable `cerror_flag` and calls `hardretn` or `_hardretn` to return directly to the application. These functions simulate an error return so that the operation appears to have failed.

The `chk_cerror_flag` function checks the `cerror_flag` to see whether an error occurred. It also issues a DOS call to return DOS to a consistent state. The `rm_cerror_handler` function restores the old error handler. Lines 9 to 19 define macros for making the get interrupt vector and set vector DOS calls in terms of Turbo C or Microsoft C library functions.

Figure 10.11 uses our functions to handle file I/O errors. Lines 34 to 50 attempt to open the file. If the file cannot be opened because of a regular error or because of a

FIGURE 10.10   handerr.c

```
1     /* handerr.c - handles critical errors */
2     #include <stdio.h>
3     #include <signal.h>
4     #include <dos.h>
5     #include "asmtools.h"
6     #include "handerr.h"
7
8                                    /* macros for Turbo/MS differences */
9     #ifdef TURBOC
10    #define _getvector(ino) getvect(ino)
11    #define _setvector(ino, ifun) setvect(ino,ifun)
12    typedef void interrupt (*PIFUN) () ;
13    #endif
14
15    #ifdef MSC
16    #define _getvector(ino) _dos_getvect(ino)
17    #define _setvector(ino, ifun) _dos_setvect(ino,ifun)
18    typedef void (interrupt far *PIFUN) () ;
19    #endif
20
21
22    #define GET_VERIFY  0x54   /* DOS get verify flag op. code */
23    #define CRIT_ERR_INT 0x24  /* interrupt number */
24
25                               /* bit define for attributes member */
26    #define CHAR_DEVICE 0x8000 /* if 1, character device */
27
28    typedef struct dh          /* device header structure */
29      { struct dh far *next_dev;/* points to next device header */
30        unsigned attributes ;    /* tells block or char device */
31        unsigned strategy_offset ; /* offset of strategy routine */
32        unsigned interrupt_offset ; /* offset of interrupt routine */
33        char dev_name[8] ;       /* gives name if a char device */
34      } DEVHDR ;
35
36
37    static int cerror_flag ;   /* 1=critical error has occurred */
38    static PIFUN old_vector ;  /* address of old error handler */
39
40    unsigned ce_ax ;           /* critical error AX value */
41    unsigned ce_di ;           /* critical error AX value */
42    DEVHDR far *ce_dhdr;       /* pointer to device header */
43
44
45                               /* Turbo C versions of functions */
46    #ifdef TURBOC
47                               /* handles critical errors */
48     int cerror_handler(errval,deverror,dhdr_seg,dhdr_off)
49     int errval ;              /* error code from DI register */
50     int deverror ;            /* device error code (AX value) */
51     unsigned dhdr_seg ;       /* dev. header addr. - segment (BP) */
52     unsigned dhdr_off ;       /*                         offset (SI) */
53     {
54        cerror_flag = 1 ;      /* set critical error flag */
55        ce_ax = deverror ;     /* save ax value */
```

Figure 10.10   continues

Figure 10.10   continued

```
56          ce_di = errval ;         /* save di value */
57          SET_FP(ce_dhdr,dhdr_seg,dhdr_off) ; /* device hdr. addr. */
58          hardretn( -1 ) ;          /* return directly to appln. */
59      }
60
61
62     void set_cerror_handler()     /* install our crit. error handler*/
63      {
64          old_vector = _getvector(CRIT_ERR_INT) ;
65          harderr( cerror_handler ) ;
66      }
67     #endif
68
69
70                                    /* MS C versions of functions */
71     #ifdef MSC
72                                    /* handles critical errors */
73     void far cerror_handler(deverror,errcode,dhdr_addr)
74     unsigned deverror ;          /* device error code (AX value) */
75     unsigned errcode ;           /* error code from DI register */
76     unsigned far *dhdr_addr ;    /* device header address (BP:SI) */
77      {
78          cerror_flag = 1 ;        /* set critical error flag */
79          ce_ax = deverror ;       /* save ax value */
80          ce_di = errcode ;        /* save di value */
81                                   /* save pointer to device header */
82          ce_dhdr = (DEVHDR far *) dhdr_addr ;
83          _hardretn( -1 ) ;        /* return directly to appln. */
84      }
85
86
87     void set_cerror_handler()     /* install our crit. error handler*/
88      {
89          old_vector = _getvector(CRIT_ERR_INT) ;
90          _harderr( cerror_handler ) ;
91      }
92     #endif
93
94
95     void rm_cerror_handler()      /* remove our error handler */
96      {
97          _setvector(CRIT_ERR_INT,old_vector) ;/* install old handler */
98      }
99
100
101    int chk_cerror_flag()        /* returns critical error flag */
102     {
103       int ret ;
104
105       if( cerror_flag != 0  )  /* has an error occurred? */
106         { bdos(GET_VERIFY,0,0); /*  yes - stabilize DOS */
107         }
108       ret = cerror_flag ;
109       cerror_flag = 0 ;
110       return( ret ) ;            /* return flag */
111     }
```

critical error, lines 39 to 42 prompt for a new name, or for another try with the previous file name. Entering q aborts the program. Although this somewhat parallels the abort, retry, and ignore options offered by the default error handler, we can control the options and how each option is implemented.

The correct response to an error depends on the type of error as well as the action in progress. A disk write that fails requires a different reaction than does a failed attempt to open a file. Lines 60 to 65 check for and handle an error in writing data to a file. If an error occurred, the file is closed and the program aborts.

You can use the program in Figure 10.11 to experiment with error handling with your compiler's library functions. The easiest way to cause a critical error is to open the door of a floppy disk drive before the program performs an I/O operation.

FIGURE 10.11   makefile.c

```
 1    /* makefile.c - illustrates Critical Error handling functions */
 2    /*    using the open and write I/O functions */
 3    #include "stdio.h"
 4    #include <stdlib.h>
 5    #include <string.h>
 6    #include "keyio.h"
 7    #include "handerr.h"
 8    #include "getstr.h"
 9
10    #define NWRITE 1024
11    char buffer[ NWRITE ]   ;
12
13    #define MAXNAME 129
14    char fname[ MAXNAME ] ;
15    char s[ MAXNAME ] ;
16
17
18    main(argc,argv)
19     int argc ;
20     char *argv[] ;
21     {
22        int i , ret ;
23        FILE *out ;
24
25        set_cerror_handler() ; /* install our handler */
26
27        for(i=0;i< NWRITE ; i=i+1)    /* fill data buffer */
28          { buffer[i] = ' ' + (i % 96) ; }
29
30        if( argc > 1 )              /* get file name from command line */
31           strcpy(fname,argv[1]) ;
32        else fname[0] = '\0' ;
33
34        while( 1 == 1 )            /* open file */
35          { out = fopen(fname, "w") ;
36           if( out != NULL )
37                break ;
38           chk_cerror_flag() ;    /* clear error */
39           printf(" can't create file \n");
```

Figure 10.11   continues

Figure 10.11   continued

```
40              printf("type new file name (or q to quit) \n") ;
41              printf("just press return to try with previous name \n");
42              getstr(s,MAXNAME-1) ;
43
44              if( strcmp(s,"q") == 0 ) /* check for quitting */
45                 { printf(" *** aborting program *** \n") ;
46                   exit(10) ;
47                 }
48              if( s[0] != '\0')  /* use old name? */
49                    strcpy(fname,s) ; /* no - use new name */
50           }
51
52       if( out < 0 )
53           exit(6) ;
54
55       printf(" press a key to write records \n");
56       getkey() ;
57
58       for(i=0 ; i< 10 ; i=i+1 )
59          { ret = fwrite(buffer, 1, NWRITE, out ) ;
60            if( ret != NWRITE )
61               { ret = chk_cerror_flag() ;
62                 printf(" write error (%d) quitting \n",ret );
63                 fclose(out) ;
64                 exit(20) ;
65               }
66          }
67
68       if( fclose(out) != 0 )
69          printf(" error in closing file \n");
70
71       rm_cerror_handler() ;   /* restore default handler */
72    }
```

10.6 Summary: Final Thoughts

Our objective in this book has been to open some doors for you. Chapters 3 through 9 discuss important algorithms and techniques in a realistic context. The information we discuss has genuine usefulness, and we provide practical tools to allow immediate use of the information.

Developing good tools once and then using them many times in a variety of programs is our main theme. Programming is hard unproductive work when you do everything from scratch. The programs and toolkit functions in the book can give you a head start; they are large enough and complicated enough to do something interesting. You can make useful modifications to them and get quick results for a minimum of effort.

We have also described the process of creating programs. The main message is to break problems up into small parts and work through them in bite-sized chunks. If you do not understand the problem completely, explore it with small experiments. Do simple prototype programs before you add all the bells and whistles the final solution requires. Organize programs into a number of small modules — each with a single clear function. Test all the modules before you put the entire program together. Look for good tools that can be applied to other problems.

You may find parts of the book hard to understand at first. That is natural since we picked topics that are not trivial and tried to cover them in useful depth. In choosing material for the book, we had to balance simplicity and clarity against depth and content. We opted for more depth and tougher topics than most authors choose. Our chief fear was that the book would not contain enough meat to make it worth reading, so if there is enough meat for a second reading, think of it as added value.

Programmers often learn by reading each others work. Most working programmers have benefitted greatly from their contact with their colleagues. This book attempts to give you another shoulder to look over; another set of program listings to explore. We tried to make the view over that shoulder unique.

Appendix A

Instructions for Compiling, Linking, and Executing the C Programs in This Book

Building the programs and tools listed in this book is a straightforward process, but the instructions in this appendix will help you avoid problems due to missing files. The first section lists the steps you should follow to compile and link C Toolbox programs successfully. The second section lists the files that must be compiled and linked for each program. (Building the programs will be much easier if you use libraries rather than object files for the toolkit functions.) The third section discusses compiling C Toolbox files on a PC without a hard disk.

Appendix B illustrates how compiler options are specified for Turbo C, Microsoft C, and QuickC.

Steps for Building C Toolbox Programs

Follow these steps and then use the list of files for the program you wish to build.

Step 1. Create the following subdirectories:

```
\ctb
\ctb\chap1     \ctb\chap2     \ctb\chap3     \ctb\chap4
\ctb\chap5     \ctb\chap6     \ctb\chap7     \ctb\chap8
\ctb\chap9     \ctb\chap10    \ctb\include   \ctb\lib
```

Step 2. Place all the source files (.c, .h, .asm, .ha, and .bat extensions) from each chapter in the corresponding subdirectory. Move the following header files to the directory, \ctb\include.

```
(from Chapter 1)    getstr.h
(from Chapter 2)    cminor.h
```

```
(from Chapter 3)    viewcmds.h
(from Chapter 5)    sortmerg.h
(from Chapter 7)    asmtools.h   keyio.h   ct_timer.h
                    ptrio.h  video.h   scn.h
(from Chapter 8)    win.h
```

Step 3.   Edit the `asmtools.h` header file in `\ctb\chap7` and in `\ctb\include` to #define the symbol TURBOC or the symbol MSC. Define the memory model to be used in `\ctb\chap7\begdata.ha`.

Step 4.   Set the PATH= environment variable so that MS-DOS can locate and execute your compiler. Set the compiler option for searching for header files to include the directory where the compiler's standard header files are located. Set the compiler option for locating libraries to include the directory where the compiler's standard libraries are located. (The compiler installation process may do part or all of this.)

Step 5.   Set the compiler option for header file and library directories. Add the `\ctb\include` directory to the list of directories to be searched for header files. Add `\ctb\lib` to the list of directories for libraries. (See Appendix B for instructions for each compiler.)

Step 6.   Build the following library files in the `\ctb\lib` directory:

```
sortmerg.lib   btree.lib   toolkit.lib   win.lib
```

Step 7.   Set the default drive and current directory. The source files you want to compile should be in the current directory on the default drive. For example, to compile the VIEW program from Chapter 3 (which might be in `\ctb\chap3`), you would type the following MS-DOS commands:

```
A>C:
C>cd \ctb\chap3
```

Step 8.   Compile and link the program you want.

Lists of Source Files Making Up Each Program

The following sections list the source files that must be compiled and linked together to build each C Toolbox program. The components of each library file are also listed. The name of the program or library to be built is followed by a colon (:). On subsequent lines, the source files to be compiled and linked are listed, indented from the program name. When a file from a different chapter is required, the complete path name is given. For some programs, two lists are given — one list uses `.lib` files and the other list uses all source files directly.

Chapter 1

```
hello.exe:
    hello.c
sumsq.exe:
    sumsq.c
weather.exe:
    weather.c
sortnum.exe:
    sortnum.c
sentence.exe:
    sentence.c
reverse.exe:
    reverse.c    getstr.c
curve.exe:
    curve.c
notabs.exe:
    notabs.c
```

Chapter 2

```
copya.exe:
    copya.c
copyb.exe:
    copyb.c
copyc.exe:
    copyc.c
copyd.exe:
    copyd.c
clean.exe:
    clean.c
notabs2.exe:
    notabs2.c    do_it.c
tail.exe:
    tail.c
```

Chapter 3

Some VIEW source files are used in the FD program in Chapter 4, and Chapter 8 enhances the VIEW program.

```
expread.exe:
    expread.c
expback.exe:
    expback.c
view.exe:
    view.c    viewget.c    viewexec.c    viewgetf.c
    viewfind.c    viewdisp.c    viewio.c
    \ctb\chap7\keyio1.c
testmain.exe:
    testmain.c    view.c
testget.exe:
    testget.c    view.c    viewget.c
    \ctb\chap7\keyio1.c
```

```
testexec.exe:
    testexec.c    view.c    viewget.c    viewexec.c
    \ctb\chap7\keyio1.c
testgetf.exe:
    testgetf.c    viewget.c
testfind.exe:
    testfind.c    viewfind.c    \ctb\chap7\keyio1.c
testdisp.exe:
    testdisp.c    viewdisp.c    \ctb\chap7\keyio1.c
testio.exe:
    testio.c    viewio.c
perfdisp.exe:
    perfdisp.c    viewdisp.c

viewturb.exe:            (Enhancement for Turbo C)
    view.c    viewget.c    viewexec.c    viewgetf.c
    viewdisp.c    viewio.c    viewback.c
    viewfin2.c            (replaces viewfind.c)
    \ctb\chap7\keyio1.c
```

Chapter 4

```
fd.exe:
    fd.c    fdfind.c    fddisp.c    fdio.c
    \ctb\chap3\viewget.c    \ctb\chap3\viewgetf.c
    fdexec.c            (use viewexec.c, change #include
                        "viewparm.h to "fdparm.h")
    \ctb\chap7\keyio1.c

gendata.exe:
    gendata.c
gendata2.exe:
    gendata2.c
expio.exe:
    expio.c
fd2.exe:            (1st enhancement)
    fd.c    fdfind.c    fdio.c
    fddisp2.c        (enhanced to use BIOS VIDEO funs.)
    \ctb\chap3\viewget.c    \ctb\chap3\viewgetf.c
    fdexec.c            (use viewexec.c, change #include
                        "viewparm.h to "fdparm.h")
    \ctb\chap7\video1.c    \ctb\chap7\video2.c
    \ctb\chap7\keyio1.c
```

or

```
fd2.exe:
    fd.c    fdfind.c    fdio.c
    fddisp2.c        (enhanced to use BIOS VIDEO funs.)
    \ctb\chap3\viewget.c    \ctb\chap3\viewgetf.c
    fdexec.c            (use viewexec.c, change #include
                        "viewparm.h to "fdparm.h")
    \ctb\lib\toolkit.lib

fd3.exe:            (2nd enhancement)
    fd3.c            (enhanced)
    fdfind.c        fdio.c
```

```
        fddisp3.c         (enhanced to use screen I/O funs.)
        \ctb\chap3\viewget.c     \ctb\chap3\viewgetf.c
        fdexec.c          (use viewexec.c, change #include
                              "viewparm.h to "fdparm.h")
        \ctb\chap7\video1.c     \ctb\chap7\video2.c
        \ctb\chap7\video4.c
        \ctb\chap7\scn1.c     \ctb\chap7\scn2.c
        \ctb\chap7\scn3.c     \ctb\chap7\scn4.c
        \ctb\chap7\scn5.asm
        \ctb\chap7\keyio1.c
```

or

```
    fd3.exe:            (using libraries)
        fd3.c          (enhanced)
        fdfind.c       fdio.c
        fddisp3.c         (enhanced to use screen I/O funs.)
        \ctb\chap3\viewget.c     \ctb\chap3\viewgetf.c
        fdexec.c          (use viewexec.c, change #include
                              "viewparm.h to "fdparm.h")
        \ctb\lib\toolkit.lib
```

Chapter 5

The `config.sys` file should include the line `FILES=20`.

```
    sorttext.exe:
        sorttext.c   dosort.c    readfile.c    writefil.c
        sortio.c   cmpfuns.c   memsort.c   insert.c

    \ctb\lib\sortmerg.lib:
        cmpfuns.c memsort.c   insert.c    sortio2.c
        sortmerg.c    formruns.c    readrun.c    writerun.c
        domerge.c   dopass.c   smerge.c   insertm.c

    merge.exe:         (using SORTMERG files directly)
        merge2.c   getspec.c   sortcomp.c
        cmpfuns.c memsort.c   insert.c    sortio2.c
        sortmerg.c    formruns.c    readrun.c    writerun.c
        domerge.c   dopass.c   smerge.c   insertm.c
```

or

```
    merge.exe:          (using the sortmerg library)
        merge2.c   getspec.c   sortcomp.c
        \ctb\lib\sortmerg.lib
```

Chapter 6

The BTREE functions require more stack space than the default amount provided by Turbo C or by Microsoft C — at least 7 Kbytes. The application program that calls

BTREE functions may require additional stack space. (See Appendix B for instructions for setting stack size.)

```
\ctb\lib\btree.lib:
    bt_space.c    bt_low2.c    bt_file.c    bt_free.c
    blockio.c     bt_cache.c   openix.c     bt_first.c
    bt_get.c      bt_block.c   bt_find.c    bt_ins.c
    bt_del.c      bt_low.c     bt_top.c
doccreat.exe:
    doccreat.c    doc_util.c   varsize.c
    docstack.c       (needed only for Turbo c)
    bt_space.c    bt_low2.c    bt_file.c    bt_free.c
    blockio.c     bt_cache.c   openix.c     bt_first.c
    bt_get.c      bt_block.c   bt_find.c    bt_ins.c
    bt_del.c      bt_low.c     bt_top.c
docindex.exe:
    docindex.c    doc_util.c   varsize.c
    docstack.c       (needed only for Turbo c)
    bt_space.c    bt_low2.c    bt_file.c    bt_free.c
    blockio.c     bt_cache.c   openix.c     bt_first.c
    bt_get.c      bt_block.c   bt_find.c    bt_ins.c
    bt_del.c      bt_low.c     bt_top.c
    \ctb\chap1\getstr.c

docscan.exe:
    docscan.c     doc_util.c   varsize.c
    docstack.c       (needed only for Turbo c)
    bt_space.c    bt_low2.c    bt_file.c    bt_free.c
    blockio.c     bt_cache.c   openix.c     bt_first.c
    bt_get.c      bt_block.c   bt_find.c    bt_ins.c
    bt_del.c      bt_low.c     bt_top.c
    \ctb\chap1\getstr.c     \ctb\chap7\keyio1.c
```

or

```
doccreat.exe:        (using libraries)
    doccreat.c    doc_util.c   varsize.c
    docstack.c       (needed only for Turbo c)
    \ctb\lib\btree.lib

docindex.exe:        (using libraries)
    docindex.c    doc_util.c   varsize.c
    docstack.c       (needed only for Turbo c)
    \ctb\lib\btree.lib     \ctb\chap1\getstr.c

docscan.exe:         (using libraries)
    docscan.c     doc_util.c   varsize.c
    docstack.c       (needed only for Turbo c)
    \ctb\lib\btree.lib     \ctb\lib\toolkit.lib
    \ctb\chap1\getstr.c
```

Chapter 7

The `usedos.c` source file is not included in the toolkit library since it is not intended for actual use.

```
toolkit.lib:
    memory.c    get_dads.c   ct_time1.c   ct_time2.c
    ptrio1.c    ptrio2.c     ptrio3.c     ptrio4.c
    keyio1.c    keyio2.c
    video1.c    video2.c     video3.c     video4.c
    scn1.c    scn2.c    scn3.c    scn4.c    scn5.asm
```

Chapter 8

```
\ctb\lib\win.lib:
    win1.c    win2.c    win3.c    win4.c    win5.c
    win_pop.c    win_gets.c

view2.exe:
    view2.c    viewget2.c    viewexe2.c    viewgtf2.c
    viewdis2.c
    viewio2.c           (use viewio.c, change #include
                          "viewparm.h" to "viewpar2.h")
    viewfin2.c          (use viewfind.c, change #include
                          "viewparm.h" to "viewpar2.h")
    win1.c    win2.c    win3.c    win4.c    win5.c
    win_pop.c    win_gets.c
    (from \ctb\chap7)
    video1.c    video2.c    video4.c    keyio1.c
    scn1.c    scn2.c    scn3.c    scn4.c    scn5.asm
```

or

```
view2.exe:          (using libraries)
    view2.c    viewget2.c    viewexe2.c    viewgtf2.c
    viewdis2.c
    viewio2.c           (use viewio.c, change #include
                          "viewparm.h" to "viewpar2.h")
    viewfin2.c          (use viewfind.c, change #include
                          "viewparm.h" to "viewpar2.h")
    \ctb\lib\toolkit.lib    \ctb\lib\win.lib

viewt2.exe:          (Turbo enhancement using libraries)
    view2.c    viewget2.c    viewexe2.c    viewgtf2.c
    viewdis2.c
    viewio2.c           (use viewio.c, change #include
                          "viewparm.h" to "viewpar2.h")
    viewfi2t.c          (use viewfin2.c, change #include
                          "viewparm.h" to "viewpar2.h")
    \ctb\chap3\viewback.c
    \ctb\lib\toolkit.lib    \ctb\lib\win.lib
```

Chapter 9

The stack overflow checking option should be disabled when the following files are compiled: `tty2rcv.c`, `async1.c`, `queue.c`, `async2.c`.

```
tty1.exe:
    tty1.c    async1.c    \ctb\chap7\memory.c
    \ctb\chap7\keyio1.c    \ctb\video3.c
perftty1.exe:
    perftty1.c    async1.c    \ctb\chap7\memory.c
    \ctb\chap7\keyio1.c

tty2.exe:    (using libraries)
    tty2.c    async1.c    tty2get.c    tty2exec.c
    tty2disp.c    tty2rec.c    tty2getf.c  tty2brk.c
    tty2rcv.c    queue.c    async2.c    install.c
    tty2int.asm
    \ctb\lib\toolkit.lib    \ctb\lib\win.lib
```

or

```
tty2.exe:    (using object files)
    tty2.c    async1.c    tty2get.c    tty2exec.c
    tty2disp.c    tty2rec.c    tty2getf.c  tty2brk.c
    tty2rcv.c    queue.c    async2.c    install.c
    tty2int.asm
    (from  \ctb\chap7)
    memory.c    keyio1.c    ct_time1.c    ct_time2.c
    video1.c    video2.c    video3.c    video4.c
    scn1.c    scn2.c    scn3.c    scn4.c    scn5.asm
    (from  \ctb\chap8)
    win1.c    win2.c    win3.c    win4.c win5.c
    win_pop.c    win_gets.c
```

Chapter 10

The screen save functions in `breakscn.c` use functions from Chapters 7 and 8.

```
testbrk.exe:
    testbrk.c    handbrk.c
makefile.exe:
    makefile.c    handerr.c
    \ctb\chap7\keyio1.c    \ctb\chap1\getstr.c
```

Using a System With Two Floppy Drives and No Hard Disk

If you do not have a hard disk on your computer, you will not be able to keep all C Toolbox files on a single floppy disk. Instead, you should format one disk for each chapter. On each disk, create the directories \ctb, \ctb\include, and \ctb\lib. Each disk should also have a directory for the files from one chapter. (The Chapter 3 disk would have the directory \ctb\chap3.) Place the header files listed in Step 2 on each disk. As you create each .lib file, copy it to each chapter's disk in the \ctb\lib directory.

Appendix B
Information on Using Specific C Compilers

The Turbo C, Microsoft C, and QuickC compilers provide similar facilities for compiling, linking, and building libraries. Program names differ and details of use vary, but the same techniques are used. We describe these common techniques first.

Batch Files and MAKE Programs

A batch file is a convenient way to compile and link a small program. For example, to compile and link the REVERSE program from Chapter 1 with Microsoft C, we could use the following batch file:

```
cl -c reverse.c
cl -c getstr.c
cl reverse.obj getstr.obj
```

With a batch file, we can compile and link a program with a single short command. We can also be sure that every `.obj` file is up to date. There is no danger that we have failed to recompile a modified source file. For a larger program, this security is even more important, but we do not want to waste time recompiling unmodified files. MAKE programs combine the security of a batch file with the speed of selective recompilation. We supply a list of target file with the source files on which they depend. A target file is recompiled only if one or more of the source files has been modified since the target file was last changed. For each target file, we also supply a command to be executed to recreate the file. Using the Microsoft MAKE program, the make file (`reverse.mak`) for the REVERSE program would be

```
reverse.obj:   reverse.c
    cl -c reverse.c
getstr.obj:  getstr.c  getstr.h
    cl -c getstr.c
```

```
reverse.exe:   reverse.obj   getstr.obj
     cl reverse.obj getstr.obj
```

The target file, `reverse.obj`, is recompiled only if the `reverse.c` file or the `getstr.h` file has a later date. In that case, the command `cl -c reverse.c` will be executed to re-create `reverse.obj`. Similar checks are made to see whether the `getstr.obj` and `reverse.exe` files must be rebuilt. Note that header files may appear in the list of source files on which a target file is dependent. The make file can be created with any text editor. The syntax required for each compiler's MAKE program is discussed below.

Automatic Response Files

Command lines are limited to approximately 128 characters. Linking a large program may require a list of file names that exceeds this limit. An automatic response file may be specified instead. This is a text file containing file names and other command line information. For the REVERSE program, we could link the program with the command,

```
link   reverse, @reverse.arf ;
```

and the response file

```
reverse.obj +
getstr.obj
```

Borland's Turbo C

Turbo C is an excellent C compiler for most uses. The compiler combines very fast compilation with very good error detection. The integrated environment version (`TC.EXE`) makes entering, compiling, and testing C source files quick and easy. The command line version (`TCC.EXE`) is also quick and reliable.

Setting Stack Size

For versions 1.x and 2.0 of Turbo C, the default stack size is 4 Kbytes. To set a larger stack size, you must initialize the global variable `_stklen` to a new value.

```
/* stack20.c - sets stack size to 20 K bytes */
unsigned _stklen = 20480 ; /* outside any function */
```

(The stack size is set before the C program starts execution. The value must be set by initialization in the declaration rather than by an assignment statement.)

Checking for Stack Overflow

In the integrated environment, stack checking is turned on or off with the *Options/ Compiler/Code generation/Test stack overflow* menu option. With TCC, the -N option places stack checking logic in compiled files.

Specifying Directories for Include Files and Libraries

In the integrated environment, the *Options/Directories/Include directories:* menu option specifies the list of directories to be searched for header files. Directory names are separated by semicolons; the directory containing the compiler's own header files should be first in the list. The *Options/Directories/Library Directories:* option specifies directories to be searched for library files. With TCC, the -I*directory-name* option specifies an additional search directory for header files. The -L*directory-name* option specifies directories to be searched for libraries. The library's file name must also be listed on the command line.

Project Files

In the integrated environment, the *Project/Project name* menu option specifies a project file. The project file (*.prj) is a plain text file with a list of .c files to be compiled and linked to form the complete program. If .asm files are a part of the program, they are first assembled separately. The resulting .obj file is added to the list in the project file. Library files may also be listed with the .lib extension.

The MAKE Program

For the REVERSE program, we would execute the Turbo C MAKE program with the command

```
make -freverse.mak reverse.obj getstr.obj reverse.exe
```

Note that the command line specifies each target file to be checked. The make file reverse.mak would contain

```
reverse.obj:   reverse.c  getstr.h
    tcc -c reverse.c
getstr.obj:  getstr.c  getstr.h
    tcc -c getstr.c
reverse.exe:   reverse.obj  getstr.obj
    tcc -c reverse.obj  getstr.obj
```

Building a Library

The TLIB librarian program builds a `.LIB` library file from `.OBJ` object files. The following example adds the object files `keyio1.obj` and `keyio2.obj` to the `toolkit.lib` library file.

```
C>tlib \ctb\lib\toolkit.lib +keyio1.obj +keyio2.obj
```

Microsoft C

Version 5.1 of Microsoft C, used in preparing the second edition of the book, does not provide an integrated environment. Earlier versions of Microsoft C may not support the interrupt keyword or provide the `_dos*` and `_bios*` library functions. The operation of the `setvbuf` functions may also be different when a `NULL` buffer address is supplied.

Setting Stack Size

The command line option `/F hex-number` specifies the stack size for a program compiled with the `CL` command. The following example specifies a stack size of `0x4000` bytes (16,384 bytes in decimal notation).

```
C>cl /F4000 hello.c
```

Enabling Stack Checking

The CL command includes stack overflow checking code as the default choice. The command line option `/Gs` disables stack overflow checking.

Specifying Include and Library Directories

The `/I directory` option specifies an additional directory to be searched for include files. The `/link link-info` option may specify additional directories to be searched for library files. The following example specifies `\ctb\include` to be searched for include files and `\ctb\lib` to be searched for libraries.

```
C>cl /I\ctb\include  hello.c /link \ctb\lib
```

Search directories for include files may also be specified by adding them to the `INCLUDE=` environment string. Library directories can be specified in the `LIB=` environment string. The following DOS commands specify the `\ctb\include` and `\ctb\lib` directories (assuming that Microsoft C has been installed in the `\ms` directory):

```
C>set  INCLUDE=\ms\include;\ctb\include
C>set  LIB=\ms\lib;\ctb\lib
```

The MAKE Program

To rebuild the REVERSE program using the Microsoft MAKE program and the MAKE program supplied with the compiler, we would use the `reverse.mak` file described in the first section and type the command

```
C>make  reverse.mak
```

Building a Library

The librarian program LIB builds a `.lib` library file from `.obj` object files. The following example adds the `keyio1.obj` and `keyio2.obj` object files to the `\ctb\lib\toolkit.lib` library :

```
C>lib \ctb\lib\win.lib +keyio1 +keyio2 ;
```

QuickC

QuickC offers the same library and the same C language extensions as does Microsoft C. References to Microsoft C throughout the book apply also to QuickC. Most compiler options are also common to CL and QCL, the command line version of QuickC. We only mention differences in options below. Methods for setting options in the interactive environment QC are discussed in full.

Enabling Stack Checking

The QCL command includes stack overflow checking code as the default. The `/Gs` command line option disables stack overflow checking.

Specifying Include and Library Directories

The *Options/Environment* menu has fields for specifying include and library file source directories.

Program Lists in the Integrated Environment

The *Make/Set Program list* menu specifies the name of a program list file (with the .mak file extension). This program list file lists the source files, .obj files, and library files that make up the program to be built. Names of these files are added to the program list via the *Make/Edit Program List* menu option. The *Make/ Build Program* option recompiles only those files in the program list that have been changed since they were last compiled.

The NMAKE Program

The following command rebuilds the REVERSE program using the NMAKE program supplied with QuickC:

```
C>nmake reverse.mak reverse.obj getstr.obj reverse.obj
```

with the reverse.mak make file containing

```
reverse.obj:   reverse.c
    qcl -c reverse.c
getstr.obj:   getstr.c   getstr.h
    qcl -c getstr.c
reverse.exe:   reverse.obj   getstr.obj
    qcl reverse.obj getstr.obj
```

Building a Library

The Microsoft librarian program LIB is included with QuickC.

Other C Compilers

Chapters 7, 9, and 10 use library functions specific to Microsoft C, QuickC, and Turbo C. To use a different compiler such as Lattice C or MIX Power C, you must identify equivalent library functions and alter the source files in these chapters.

The Microsoft MASM Assembler

You must specify the /MX option when assembling .ASM files. This preserves upper- /lowercase differences in public names. For example, to assemble the scn5.asm file in Chapter 7, you would type the command

```
C>cd \ctb\chap7
C>masm   scn5 /MX ;
```

You must also ensure that DOS can locate the `masm.exe` program file to execute it. For example, if you place `masm.exe` in the `\masm` directory , the `PATH` command should include `\masm`.

TASM: The Borland Assembler

The Borland macro assembler `tasm.exe` may be used to assemble `.ASM` files in this book. The `/MX` option should be used to preserve upper-/lowercase differences in public names. To assemble the `scn5.asm` file from Chapter 7, type the following command:

```
C>cd \ctb\chap7
C>tasm /MX scn5.asm
```

You must also ensure that DOS can locate the `tasm.exe` program file to execute it. For example, if you place `tasm.exe` in the `\tasm` directory, the `PATH` command should include `\tasm`.

Appendix C
The IBM PC Architecture and
C Memory Models

The 8086 family of processors used in the IBM PC computers can address up to 1 Mbyte of memory. (The 80286 and 80386 processors used in some PC models can address even more memory in the protected mode. Under MS-DOS, these processors operate in real address mode and are limited to 1 Mbyte.) Since registers and address fields in instructions are only 16 bits long (and thus can specify only 64 Kbytes directly), some trickery is required to address the whole 1 Mbyte range. In addition to its general-purpose registers, the processor has four segment registers: code (CS), data (DS), stack (SS), and extra segment (ES) registers. When an instruction references memory, it specifies a 16-bit effective address — either directly or through a register value and an offset. This 16-bit value is combined with one of the four segment register values as follows:

    full address = effective_address + 16 * segment_value

The four segment registers allow a program to reference four different 64 Kbyte areas. Segment register values can be changed by a program, but there is a penalty in terms of program size and execution speed. There are several different strategies (called *memory models*) for using segment registers in a program:

Tiny Model: All four segment registers are set to point to the same 64 Kbyte area when the program begins execution and are left unchanged. This model is simple and has no overhead for changing segment registers but is limited to a total of 64 Kbytes.

Small Model: The code segment register points to an area containing the program's instructions, and the other segment registers point to a separate area for data. The segment registers are not changed during execution. Code and data areas may be up to 64 Kbytes each with no overhead for changing segment registers.

Medium Model: The code segment register is changed when function calls are made. The other segment registers point to a data area and are not changed. This allows up to 1 Mbyte for code and a separate 64 Kbyte area for data. The penalty in code size and execution speed is modest.

Large Model: The code segment register is changed during function calls. In addition, the data and extra segment registers are changed as needed to address up to 1Mbyte of data. The cost in extra execution time may be 25% or more. Programs may also require more RAM memory.

Compact Model: The code segment register is not changed by function calls. This limits code size to 64 Kbytes. Data and extra segment registers are changed as required to address up to 1M byte of data. The penalty in speed and program size is almost as great as for the large model.

Huge Model: This model is similar to the large model. However, arrays are allowed to be larger than 64 Kbytes. This requires that subscript and pointer calculations produce both a segment value and an offset. The extra cost in execution time may be substantial.

Memory Layout of C Programs

Figure C.1 shows the memory layout for a C program compiled with Microsoft C or QuickC in the small memory model. The program's code is placed in RAM memory just above the area DOS occupies. All the functions that make up the program are grouped together. The data area is made up of several parts. The static data area contains variables declared with the `static` keyword or declared outside a function. The *heap* area contains objects allocated with dynamic allocation functions (`malloc` and `calloc`). The heap grows upward when more memory is needed to satisfy allocation requests. The *stack* area contains return addresses, saved register values, function arguments, and automatic variables. This stack grows downward and shrinks upward as the program enters and leaves functions. The shaded area below the stack is reserved for stack growth.

FIGURE C.1   Memory Layout for Microsoft C — Small Model

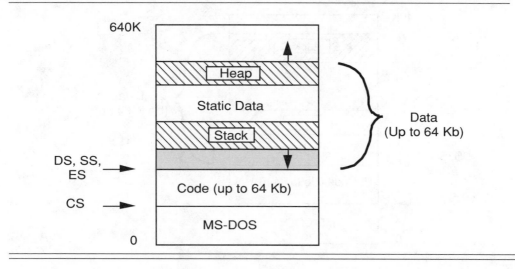

Memory Layout and Stack Size

The code and static data areas have a fixed size determined when the program is built with the linker. But the sizes of the heap and stack areas vary during program execution. In some computers, memory management hardware can be used to adjust these sizes during execution. However, in the IBM PC/MS-DOS environment, the position of the stack and the heap are fixed when program execution begins. In Figure C.1, if the program uses more stack space than the shaded area provides, the program may overwrite other data areas or the stack itself may be corrupted. The PC hardware does not provide automatic checking for stack overflow; the C compiler can include stack checking code in the program, which catches many stack overflow problems. With Microsoft C and QuickC, you must specify a stack size that is adequate for the program.

Turbo C uses a different memory layout in the small memory model as shown in Figure C.2. Here the stack is placed at the top of the 64 Kbyte data area. Stack overflow will not occur until the stack and heap grow together. So when you use Turbo C in the small memory model, you may not need to worry about a stack size.

Figure C.3 shows the memory layout used by Microsoft C and by Turbo C for large model programs. You must specify an appropriate stack size.

FIGURE C.2   Memory Layout for Turbo C — Small Model

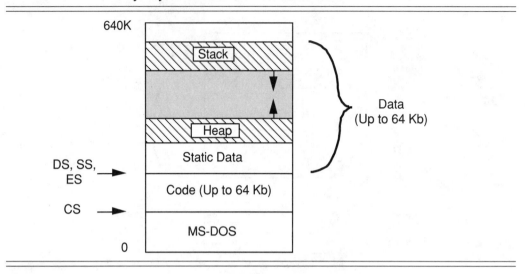

FIGURE C.3   Memory Layout for Large Model Programs

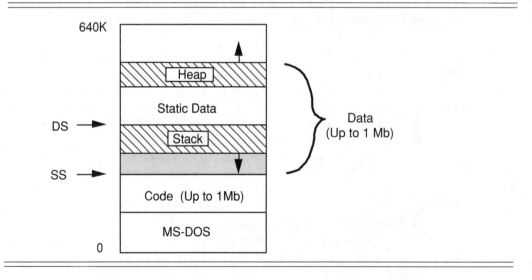

Memory Models and Far Pointers

In memory models that are limited to a maximum of 64 Kbytes of data, pointers to data are offsets relative to the DS segment register value. Thus data pointers may not reference memory locations outside the program such as display adapter memory. However, both Microsoft C and Turbo C provide the far keyword, which specifies a 32-bit address — segment plus offset values. A far pointer may refer to memory locations outside the program in any memory model.

The far keyword may also be applied to a function. Here it specifies that a function will be called with a 32-bit address (and will return using a 32-bit address). This is useful for interrupt handler functions that are called through hardware or software interrupts.

Gluing the Program Together: Segment and Group Directives

A C compiler translates source files into computer instructions. But this produces only part of a complete program. The linker combines one or more .obj files from the compiler with other object code stored in libraries. Each .obj file may contain both code and data areas. Figure C.4 shows how the linker might combine these areas from two .obj files to get a memory layout like that in Figures C.1 through C.3. When the linker glues object files together to form a program, it needs some guidance in grouping instructions, static data, and the stack to produce the memory

FIGURE C.4   Linking .obj Files Together

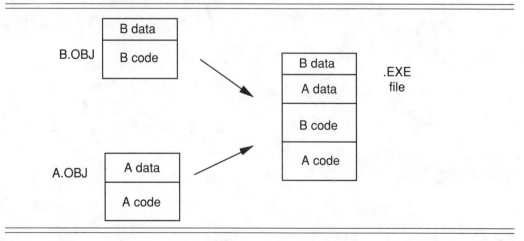

layout shown in the preceding figures. The C compiler normally supplies this information, but we have to provide it for assembler source files.

Two levels of grouping are recognized by the linker: segments and groups. All data and variables in the same segment are contiguous in the program. All segments in the same group are contiguous as well. Each C compiler uses different segment and group names; our assembler files must specify segment and group names that match those of the compiler we use. That is the reason for the `*.ha` include files discussed in Chapter 7. The `.CODE`, `.DATA`, and `.MODEL` directives supported by TASM and by recent versions of MASM hide the details, but you should understand the purpose of the directives.

Appendix D
Reference Materials

Chapters 1 and 2: Introductory Books on C

Programming in ANSI C, Stephen G. Kochan. Hayden Books. 1988. This is a serviceable but plodding introduction to the elements of the C language — one chapter on variables, then a chapter on loops and so on. However, it is competently done, and many beginners liked the predecessor book, *Programming in C*.

The C Primer, Second Edition, L. Hancock and M. Krieger. McGraw-Hill Byte Books. 1986. This is the best-written primer available, but it does not cover topics like file I/O adequately.

The C Programming Language, Second Edition, Brian Kernighan and Dennis Ritchie. Prentice-Hall. 1988. For years the first edition was the de facto standard for the C language. Now the ANSI draft standard defines the modern C language, but K&R still offers concise and elegant examples and explanations. Beginners may find that this book moves too fast and assumes the reader to possess too much knowledge about computer and programming. However, unlike most primers, it does show the reader what to do with the elements of C.

Standard C, P. J. Plauger and Jim Brodie. Microsoft Press. 1989. This small, inexpensive reference covers the ANSI standard and is somewhat easier to read than the ANSI standard document itself.

Chapters 5 and 6: Sorting and Searching

Quicksort, *Computer Journal* vol. 5, 1 (1962): pp 10–15. C. A. R. Hoare. This article presents the quicksort algorithm, perhaps the most elegant and useful sorting algorithm ever invented.

The Art of Computer Programming, Volume 3 — Sorting and Searching, Donald Knuth. Addison-Wesley. 1973. Sorting and searching algorithms used to be popular topics for computer science research. This book is the standard work on the subject. Thorough mathematical analysis of running times is the unique feature of this book. Examples are hard to read since they use unstructured pseudo-code and the assembler language for the hypothetical MIX computer.

Algorithms, Second Edition, Robert Sedgewick. Addison-Wesley. 1988. The author discusses refinements to the quicksort algorithm in great detail. Sorting, searching, graph algorithms, and many more algorithms are covered in this textbook on algorithms and data structures.

Data Structures and Program Design, Second Edition, Robert L. Krause. Prentice-Hall. 1987. Textbooks on data structures and algorithms are plentiful, but this one has a more practical flavor than most.

Algorithms + Data Structures = Programs, Niklaus Wirth. Prentice-Hall. 1976. Algorithms are presented in Pascal with less analysis than in Knuth's book.

Software Tools in Pascal. B. W. Kernighan and P. J. Plauger. A chapter on sorting presents a sort/merge program. The tools presented in this book are all old-style noninteractive programs, but the programming style and the explanations are excellent.

Chapter 7: PC Specific Toolkit

IBM Disk Operating System Technical Reference Manual. IBM Corporation. 1984. Versions are issued for each new release of PC-DOS. This documents DOS function calls and the format of directory information.

IBM PC Technical Reference Manual. IBM Corporation. New versions of the manual are issued for new IBM PC models. Add-on devices are now documented in a separate manual as well. This is the definitive guide to IBM hardware and to the ROM BIOS. Early versions of these manuals contain listings of BIOS code, which are very useful in understanding how to use the PC hardware.

The MS-DOS Encyclopedia, Second Edition, Ray Duncan, Editor. Microsoft Press. 1988. This 1570-page book should be the best reference on using MS-DOS services and it is. The discussion of DOS calls, interrupts, device drivers, and Terminate-and- Stay-Resident programs is the most thorough in print.

Programmer's Guide to PC and PS/2 Video Systems, Richard Wilton. Microsoft Press. 1987. This book documents the operation of display adapters commonly used with IBM PC and PS/2 computers. BIOS calls and data areas are described, and there are good discussions of programming for text and graphic modes.

Chapter 8: Window Modules

Advanced C Programming for Displays, Marc J. Rochkind. Prentice-Hall. 1988. The author discusses single keyboard input and multiwindow screen output for UNIX and IBM PC systems. The author's perspective is more appropriate for UNIX than for the IBM PC environment, and the source code is not very readable. However, the book does show how the ASCII terminal-oriented UNIX world relates to the PC environment with its memory mapped display.

Chapter 9: Terminal Emulation Programs

Technical Aspects of Data Communication, Second Edition, John McNamara. Digital Equipment Corporation. This book discusses data communications at the hardware level thoroughly.

Interrupts and the IBM PC, Parts 1 and 2, *PC Tech Journal* Vol. 1, 3-4 (November 1983–January 1984). All the steps needed to use interrupts on the IBM PC are discussed with the asynchronous communications adapter as an example. Part 2 gives concrete examples with I/O port numbers and bit definitions detailed. I strongly recommend this as the best material on async interrupts on the IBM PC.

C Programmer's Guide to Serial Communications, Joe Campbell. Howard W. Sams. 1988. This book covers data communications programming for the IBM PC with information on PC interrupt programming, the Xmodem protocol, and CRC calculations.

Chapter 10: Optimization

Efficient C, Thomas Plum and Jim Brodie. Plum Hall. 1985. The authors discuss writing C programs to be efficient in execution time and memory required. Tables of execution times for C statements are a useful feature, but they are based on a long obsolete compiler version. The authors provide no information about problems specific to the PC environment.

The MS-DOS Encyclopedia discusses control-Break and critical error exceptions.

The DOS Technical Reference Manual documents register contents for INT 23H and INT 24H interrupt handlers for these exceptions.

Index to Programs and Illustrations

This index lists all figures in this book with a source file name and a brief description.

Chapter 1

Chapter 2

Chapter 3

Chapter 6

Chapter 7

Chapter 8

Chapter 9

Chapter 10

Appendix C

Index

Throughout this index, figures are cited as F1.1, F1.2, and so on. Page numbers are not included for references to figures.

Order Form for Source Disks

All the C and assembly language source code from *The C Toolbox, Second Edition* are available on floppy disks ready for use. The disks also contain source code for many of the enhancements to *C Toolbox* programs. (Those enhancements are marked with the disk symbol (⌸).Changes needed for new compiler versions are described as are fixes for any bugs in *C Toolbox* source files.

You may order the source disks by mail from the following address. Orders are normally filled within 24 hours of receipt. Source disks are shipped by first class mail and should arrive in one to three days for most U.S. destinations. (Orders to destinations outside the United State sare shipped by air mail.)

William James Hunt
C Toolbox Disk, 2nd Edition
P.O. Box 30784
Walnut Creek, CA 94598

To order, fill out the following form and send it with a check or money order for $ 30.00 payable to William James Hunt. ($ 35.00 for orders outside the U.S.A.) Checks must be in U.S. funds and be payable through a bank in the U.S.A. *All orders must be accompanied by payment. No phone orders and no credit card charges will be accepted.* The price includes all shipping, handling, and sales tax.

Your name and address:

_____

_____

_____

_____

_____

Which C Compiler do you use? _____

Please specify your IBM PC Floppy Disk Format:
        5 1/4 inch disks 360 Kbyte format ❏
        3 1/2 inch disk 720 Kbyte format ❏

(You need not use this order form if you supply the same information.)